Grimm's Trailer
Full of Secrets

Grimm's Trailer Full of Secrets

Character and Gender in the Television Series

RHONDA V. WILCOX

McFarland & Company, Inc., Publishers
Jefferson, North Carolina

This book has undergone peer review.

ALSO EDITED BY RHONDA V. WILCOX—AND SUE TURNBULL

Investigating Veronica Mars: *Essays on the Teen Detective Series* (McFarland, 2011)

ISBN (print) 978-1-4766-8350-8
ISBN (ebook) 978-1-4766-4568-1

LIBRARY OF CONGRESS AND BRITISH LIBRARY
CATALOGUING DATA ARE AVAILABLE

Library of Congress Control Number 2021062274

© 2022 Rhonda V. Wilcox. All rights reserved

No part of this book may be reproduced or transmitted in any form or by any means, electronic or mechanical, including photocopying or recording, or by any information storage and retrieval system, without permission in writing from the publisher.

Front cover images © 2022 Shutterstock

Printed in the United States of America

*McFarland & Company, Inc., Publishers
Box 611, Jefferson, North Carolina 28640
www.mcfarlandpub.com*

To Richard,
who still reads everything first

Acknowledgments

First of all, thanks go to the writers, actors, producers, and crew of *Grimm* (many of whom are named in these pages). You made me want to write this book. Enormous thanks to Mary Alice Money for encouraging me to watch. Thanks to the folks at McFarland for their consistent helpfulness. Thanks to fellow conferees at the Popular Culture Association in the South, the national Popular Culture Association, and the *Slayage* conference for thoughtful questions and comments. Thanks to Tanya R. Cochran, Stephanie Graves, Julie Hawk, Ananya Mukherjea, Heather Porter, Shauntae White, and Kandace L. Harris for research advice. Thanks especially to Ananya, Heather, and Kristopher Karl Woofter for reading chapters (the remaining problems are my own). Thanks to Jeff Gess and all my family for unfailing support. Above all, thanks to Richard Gess for reading all the chapters in all their forms, and for watching *Grimm* with me. And thanks to you for reading this book.

Table of Contents

Acknowledgments   vi

Introduction: Characters Full of Secrets   1

One. "The dark does have its bright side": Monroe and the Liminal Hero-Sidekick Tradition of Spock, Spike, and Illya Kuryakin   19

Two. "I don't have a problem with it": Killing, Sex, and the African American Cop—Hank   40

Three. "I'm in control": Sergeant Wu, Wit, and Sexual Ambiguity   56

Four. "I never choose sides": Prince-Father-Captain Sean Renard and the Gothic Hero-Villain of Patriarchy   75

Five. "You know, Nick—he's a sensitive Grimm": Nick Burkhardt, Emotional Engagement, and Male Melodrama   94

Six. "Women become aware sooner than men": Marie Kessler, Kelly Burkhardt, and the Crones of Portland   121

Seven. "Smoking that hat": The Shape of Power for Fred/Illyria in *Angel* and Juliette/Eve in *Grimm*   137

Eight. "I've seen this before": Rosalee Calvert and Practical Magic   152

Nine—"I just drank my mother": The Abjection of Adalind Schade   169

Ten. "I really didn't expect to live this long": Trubel and the Combative Female   192

Eleven. "You haven't named her yet?": Diana as Demon Child   205

Conclusion: Character and Auteurism	217
Appendix: Grimm Episode List	221
Chapter Notes	227
Works Cited	237
Index	247

Introduction

Characters Full of Secrets

Almost every night for the last two years, my husband and I have watched—or, rather, re-watched—an episode of *Grimm*. We wanted to see Nick and Monroe do that wonderfully funny, awkward little dance as Nick takes Monroe's coat before their first dinner at Nick and Juliette's, while they try to convince Juliette that theirs is a normal working relationship instead of a secret partnership to kill monsters. We wanted to listen as Rosalee makes that inimitable (I've tried) high-pitched noise of joy when she shares her plans to take Monroe away for a birthday weekend. We wanted to see Hank raise his eyebrows and pause in silent disbelief (to be followed by eloquent disapprobation) as he hears one more barbaric tale of Nick's Wesen-killing ancestors. We wanted to watch the captain stop, shrug his shoulders, and eat a cookie as he realizes that his little daughter could wipe the floor (literally) with the man who has kidnapped her. We wanted to hear Adalind complain, with the edge of a rising shriek, "I can't have another baby! I don't even know where the first one is!" We wanted to watch Sergeant Wu tap his pretend microphone and emit another sarcasm, or to view with enjoyable loathing as he morphs into Neander-Wu, grunting, "Killed him. Felt good." We wanted to hear the new, witchy Juliette whoop with glee as she magically forces Nick to shoot at Monroe. We wanted to experience Monroe riding through one more marvelously verbose, historically loaded peroration, and Nick pulling him back to the here and now with another "Anyway..."[1] We wanted to be with these people, to visit these characters.

At least as early as Horace Newcomb in 1974, scholars have talked about the importance of character in television.[2] In 1985, Ien Ang made the case for the significance of viewers' involvement with television characters (29–34). By 1996, Robert Thompson identified Quality TV and its characters as having memory (108). More recently, Jason Mittell has offered

Introduction: Characters Full of Secrets

in-depth discussion of character as "the focal point" of television creativity (118), drawing on the work of authors such as Murray Smith (*Engaging Characters*), Roberta Pearson (*Reading "Lost"*), and Jens Eder et al. (*Characters in Fictional Worlds*).[3] Academic books on television, however, are not normally organized around character. A few writers, such as Lorna Jowett and Eve Bennett, have arranged discussions by *categories* of characters, using separate in-depth illustrations of the dramatis personae. Online discussions by series fans often do center around fictional personalities; so, too, ancillary publications about popular series. Scholars, though, are more likely to foreground themes, cultural implications, symbols, narrative—or (less often) language, music, camera work. *Grimm* (2011–2017) is a television series that deserves more academic attention in part because of its highly meaningful set of characters.[4] The co-creators and showrunners of *Grimm* were David Greenwalt and Jim Kouf,[5] both of whom had worked with Joss Whedon and his associates on critically acclaimed television series; in fact, Greenwalt had helped Whedon to start *Buffy the Vampire Slayer* (1997–2003) and was co-creator and showrunner for its spin-off *Angel* (1999–2004). Greenwalt acknowledges Whedon's influence (Fahy 86–88), and *Grimm* has much in common with series by Whedon and company: It is symbolic fantasy television that is based in consistent long-term narrative presented through linguistically lively interactions among memorable, developing characters. All of these elements interweave. Sometimes, however, good television series display a tension between the symbolic implications of the larger narrative and the resonance of an individual character or characters.[6] Because such tensions can be seen in much of *Grimm*, the series makes a particularly good choice to explore the nature and power of television character. The purpose of this introduction is in part to introduce the narrative symbology that the characters resist; the book as a whole will explore that resistance, through separate analysis of the characters and their multiple vectors of meaning. The intersections of age, race and ethnicity, status, gender, and sexuality, among other matters, help to create these characters. In particular, while the characters only partially succeed in resisting problematic racial implications, these same characters much more successfully complicate gender (and to a lesser degree, sexuality). This meaning-making owes a great deal to the effective long-term serial development of character.

The premise of *Grimm* is a narratively fruitful one. Detective Nicholas Burkhardt, of the Portland, Oregon, police department, comes into unexpected powers as a Grimm. His Aunt Marie, who raised him from the time he was twelve, explains that these powers are inherited by some members of their family, dating back at least to the German Brothers Grimm. She is herself a Grimm who has waited to explain Nick's legacy until his emerging abilities and her impending death from cancer have made it necessary. Some people, called Wesen (the German word for *creature* or *being*), have, hidden within them, a bestial nature—wolf-like, lion-like, fox-like and so forth—a nature that gives them animalistic powers—a nature that Nick can see even if they wish to keep it hidden. This perception, this special sight, is the most important trait of the Grimms, though they have others, such as apparently greater strength and, interestingly, more acute hearing. Aunt Marie tells Nick that it is his duty to "hunt down the bad ones" (1.2). Greenwalt and Kouf and their writing team then proceeded to create plots based on Grimms' fairy tales, starting with Red Riding Hood and the Big Bad Wolf. However, as the co-creators explain in a DVD extra ("*Grimm*: Myths"), they soon began to expand past the Brothers Grimm and into tales and myths from cultures around the world, ranging from the Mexican Chupacabra to the Filipino Aswang, the central European Krampus, the Haitian Baron Samedi, and more. Thus the hero and his ensemble have an almost infinite variety of antagonists, whom Greenwalt, Kouf, and company frame in new adventures.

Trailer Full of Secrets and the Secret-Keepers

One of the most interesting elements of *Grimm* is its use of written lore, most notably found in Aunt Marie's Airstream trailer, which she bequeaths to Nick. The trailer contains more than books: It holds bottles of potions, esoteric substances that can cure or kill, and a wooden cabinet full of fascinating weapons. The opening of the double doors to this cabinet, along with the reaction shot whenever a character looks in for the first time, represents entry into the world of magic—the crossing of the threshold for character after character who is close to Nick (with odd echoes of *The Lion, the Witch, and the Wardrobe*). Despite the importance of this visually iconic scene, however, the most important cargo of the trailer is its trove of handwritten books, full of hard-won knowledge recorded by Grimms of the past. Angela Tenga argues that Nick's "entry into the past is [...] figured visually in his regular visits" to this space (35). Aunt Marie's trailer, which she purchased with Nick's mother Kelly, is a place of lore passed down by women (on which, more to come). Nick and his friends consult these books again and again; furthermore, he begins to record his own experiences, sometimes with input from those friends. The trailer is full of secrets, full of knowledge beyond the reach of most ordinary humans. There are other troves of knowledge in the series, most notably the books in the apothecary shop owned by Nick's Wesen friend Rosalee Calvert; and there are his Wesen friend Monroe's family books, the trunk full of Grimm books from Josef Nebojsa provided by Monroe's Uncle Felix, the trunk of Grimm materials from Josh and Rolek Porter, and even the young Grimm Theresa Rubel's private notebook. But the story begins and ends with the trailer: Even though it is at one point burned, it is nonetheless replaced, phoenix-like, for the last episode. All the important characters (with one exception) enter the trailer and become one with its secrets: Nick, Monroe, Renard, Hank, Juliette, Trubel, Wu, Diana—and the sisters Marie and Kelly, earliest of all. No others are allowed to enter. And the series' last scene, set twenty years later, is of Nick's two children in the trailer,[7] one writing and the other closing the book on the tale.

Narrative Symbolism of Ethnicity and Race versus Character Complexity

The trailer's books focus on Wesen—what their powers and characteristics are and how to kill them. While the frequent searches in ancient tomes belonging to erstwhile librarian Marie Kessler may bring joy to the heart of book-lovers in the audience, the content of these Wesen encyclopedias introduces one of the main problems of the pervasive symbolism of *Grimm*. Each Wesen species is described as having not only specific physical characteristics, but also predictable moral and psychological qualities. Thus the Blutbaden (wolf-like) are violent and bad-tempered (1.1); the Fuchsbaue (fox-like) are clever but deceptive (1.18); the Klaustreichs (cat-like) are sadistic (1.16); the Genio Innocuo are, as their name would indicate, harmless (though, as Nick's partner Hank Griffin sardonically points out to him, ancient Grimms would kill them anyway, 2.8). As scholars such as Jeannette Covington point out, the idea that particular kinds (or races, or ethnicities) of people have inborn moral or psychological qualities is an illogical foundation of essentialist prejudice (157). It is part of the larger social construction of race, the history of which has been traced by Cheryl L. Harris, Kimberlé Crenshaw, Richard Delgado and Jean Stefancic, among many others. *Grimm*'s problematic symbolism did not go unnoticed by fans. In a post titled "Is it just me or is the TV show 'Grimm' kind of racist?" one viewer says, "I like the show," but adds that because of the "personality characteristics" being identified by type of Wesen, "the message sort of becomes 'your personality and potential are determined by your race'" (Byshop).[8] The problem is exacerbated by the fact that the Wesen as a whole are represented as an oppressed minority: There is repeated reference to "play[ing] the Wesen card" instead of "playing the race card," for instance (e.g., 3.11). Monroe and Rosalee are targeted for the sin of intermarriage, or miscegenation, and on their lawn is placed what the African American Hank calls a "burning cross" (4.6).

A related serious problem in the narrative symbolism of *Grimm* is the pattern of Nick's response. Consider first that Wesen represent racial minorities. Then consider that Nick, as a policeman who is also a Grimm, is confident that he can see their true natures and know whether or not he is justified in shooting them down. Furthermore, this police officer knows that ordinary people would not understand his justification. He and his partner therefore feel it is right to keep secret their extralegal kills. The narrative symbolism could hardly be more troubling in terms of its real-world equivalence regarding the killing of minorities by police.

However, the effect of the text is drastically changed because of the impact of major characters. Starting with the pilot, the idea of essentialist, racist nature is undermined by the character of the Blutbad Wesen Monroe. As played by Silas Weir Mitchell, Monroe is the first character to come to David Greenwalt's mind in an interview, and Greenwalt describes him as a "standout" (Fahy 84). The term for the memorable Monroe's Wesen type, Blutbad, means *bloodbath*; he is one version of the Big Bad Wolf. Yet Monroe has chosen to be a vegetarian, plays the cello, and went to Brown for graduate school; his charmingly erudite, rambling language makes a gentle humor inherent to the character. He is himself first wrongly accused by Nick. But because of Monroe's extraordinary willingness to see outside norms and Nick's open-mindedness, they become friends. Their reaching across cultural differences appears throughout the series. Soon Rosalee Calvert appears on the scene, another Wesen of a different type, a Fuchsbau. As a result of her brother's murder and Nick's investigation, she too learns that Nick is not the typical Grimm—or the typical cop?—and she becomes his second close Wesen friend. Although Fuchsbaue (to use the plural) are called deceptive and untrustworthy (e.g., 1.18), Rosalee is the most emphatically loyal of friends. The racist symbolism is also undermined by characters who are not just symbolically persons of color. Casting of the series, like that of many progressive modern series, includes bit parts for diverse actors and cross-ethnic or ethnic-blind casting: For example, a character named Dan is played by Pritesh Shah (3.4); a character named Jenna is played by Camille Chen (2.16). More notably, at the start of the series, a third of the regulars were persons of color: African American Detective Hank Griffin and Filipino Chinese American Sergeant Drew Wu. The stalwart, intelligent, all-American normality of Hank and the quizzical wit and sharp efficiency of Wu are brought to emotional life by Russell Hornsby and Reggie Lee. The presentation of all these characters works against the racially problematic narrative symbolism of the cop who knows just whom to kill.

The ethnic or racial symbolism is also complicated by long-term narrative arcs involving two secret Wesen groups, one of which could be described as right-wing terrorists and the other as left-wing revolutionaries: the Wesenrein (Season Four) and Black Claw (Seasons Five and Six). The Wesenrein, or Secundum Naturae Ordinem Wesen, is described as an ancient Wesen organization whose beliefs are no longer officially supported by the Wesen government—the Wesen Council—though there are still some Council members with the same beliefs. Wesenrein are the ones who are against intermarriage among different kinds of Wesen because of their desire for so-called blood purity; these are also the ones who burn the "cross"—actually a Wesen symbol called a Wolfsangle—in Monroe and Rosalee's yard when they marry (4.5 and 4.6). The burning cross connects the Wesenrein with the Ku Klux Klan as a racist organization, and, like Klansmen, members wear hoods that conceal their identity and call their leader Grand Master (4.10). Thus racial prejudice is shown not just against but among Wesen. The symbolism in this context detaches (to a degree) the prejudice from biological categories in the story-world and switches the prejudice to whatever kind of person holds the attitude. In contrast, various kinds, including Blutbad, Eisbieber (beaver-like Wesen), Zauberbiest (warlock-like), and normal humans, or Kehrseite, fight against the Wesenrein.

The Wesenrein invoke not only the KKK but also the Nazis. The Grimms, coming from German roots, often use German language in their terminology, and the Wesen themselves do as well. Not all Germanic matters connect with Nazis, of course, and there is much use of German in the series that has nothing to do with Nazis. (Angela Tenga makes a strong case for seeing the immigrant experience as represented in *Grimm*.) However, the series suggests other Nazi connections beyond language. Fairly early in the series, Nick discovers that Hitler was Wesen (1.13). The Wesenrein trial features hangings of red and black that echo Nazi insignia (4.10). The trial, in which Monroe is condemned to death for his lack of purity, connects religious and state imagery (as Nazis sought to subsume religion). Nick and his friends succeed in their fight against the Wesenrein, and the friends celebrate by sending Monroe and Rosalee off on a long-delayed honeymoon—a very human-sized triumph at the level of character.

But the next group, Black Claw (or Schwarz Kralle) presents a different problem in narrative symbology. Wesen who join Black Claw wish to overthrow non–Wesen control of society in order to, in the words of their motto, "free the hidden"—"Occultatem libere" (e.g., 5.2). They do not wish to pursue ancient ways but revolution—they are not conservative, but radical. They, too, however, are connected with Nazis. Members of Black Claw destroy shops and break windows in an episode titled "Wesen Nacht," a clear reference to the Nazis' Kristallnacht. (The epigraph for the episode is "Awake, arise, or be forever fallen"—seemingly a ringing call to arms, but also a quote from Satan exhorting the fallen angels in Milton's *Paradise Lost*, and thus a condemnation of the revolutionaries as demons [Book I, line 330].) Whereas the Nazis wore brown shirts, members of Black Claw wear black shirts.[9] Recalling Nick's earlier discovery that Hitler was Wesen, one of those fighting against Black Claw observes that, like Hitler, they are planning a Wesen takeover of the world (5.8). Like Jews (such as Anne Frank and her family) hiding from Nazis, some characters hide from Black Claw in secret passages within homes. Wesen who do not join the revolution will be killed. Grimms and Kehrseite are targets, too.

In the latter seasons of the series, Black Claw also serves to bring to the fore the issue of Nick's (and other police officers') extrajudicial killings. The character of the police captain, Renard, who is both a bastard prince and a half-Wesen (half-Zauberbiest), helps to explicate the allure of the Black Claw group. Wesen, after all, do have serious complaints about the structure of society, and the captain for a time joins Black Claw. A network television series is unlikely to support violent revolution, and of course Black Claw is itself a thoroughly racist organization, allowing no non–Wesen members—so they hardly call for support. But the series' showrunners use the arc to confront the main protagonists with the implications of those police/Grimm killings. The captain, thoughtfully portrayed by Sasha Roiz, struggling with the desire for power and the draw of family connections, helps to complicate the issues while still clarifying the dangers of Black Claw. Crenshaw warns against ultimate legitimation of such institutions as white-dominated police ("Race, Reform"), but *Grimm* at least raises doubts.

Even more importantly, Nick himself as a character resists racist reading, in spite of the symbolic structure of his role as a Grimm. Notably, his parents are dead (as far as he knows) and so have not raised him in traditionally Grimm ways. His aunt has apparently decided not to try to explain Wesen until he can see them. When Aunt Marie recognizes that he is coming into his powers, she is close to death and dies without being able to give him more than the briefest of indoctrinations. Thus it is the Blutbad Monroe who, at first reluctantly, teaches Nick about the magic world. In the first episode of the fifth season, Monroe's comments to Nick draw a parallel between the birth of Nick's child in this episode and Nick's birth into being a Grimm. A Grimm instructed by a Wesen (raised by wolves!) is something new in the world—and the character of Nick Burkhardt is central to both the overall optimism of the series and the complex recognition of ethnic/racial issues. Nick knows Wesen in a way his mother never has (not to mention other Grimms). The humor-laden, kindly chemistry between Silas Weir Mitchell as Monroe and David Giuntoli as Nick is crucial to purveying that hope for humane connection. The narrative symbology of ethnicity/race in *Grimm* is often troubling, but the characters ameliorate that effect.

Narrative Symbolism of Gender and Sexuality versus Character Complexity

A seeming sexism in the narrative structure of the series is also in tension with characters that oppose a sexist reading and complicate gender roles (as well as, to some degree, sexuality). In terms of work, of labor, there is an emphatic gendering in *Grimm*, just as there has been in society for centuries. It is no surprise that a scholar such as Nancy Taber, writing early in the series' broadcast run, should say that "*Grimm* is a prime example of a story that privileges masculinity" (16). It should be noted preliminarily that there are occasional nods to a spectrum of variety in gender and sexuality (see, e.g., Alicia's symbolic "coming out," 3.10[10]; Monroe's concern about "forcing someone to be one sex," 4.15; Amos's resistance, as a gay man, to being in a "Maiden Quest," 5.4; or Rosalee's curiosity about Juliette/Eve's gender-swapping sexual experience, 5.17), but the series mainly presents two genders and two sexual orientations. All the male regulars in the series—Nick Burkhardt, Hank Griffin, Drew Wu, Sean Renard—work for the police department except for Monroe, who is sometimes described as a police informant (1.22; see Taber 16). Thus all the males are directly connected to institutional, patriarchal authority. *Grimm* is, among other things, a police procedural, so the presence of a plethora of cops is no surprise; however, none of the police character regulars are female. All the main female characters work separately for most of the series: Juliette Silverton (Bitsie Tulloch) is a veterinarian; Rosalee Calvert (Bree Turner) is an apothecary; Adalind Schade (Claire Coffee), as well as employing skills as a Hexenbiest (or witch), is a lawyer (sometimes with and sometimes outside a law firm). Her young daughter is a powerful recurring character, Diana Schade Renard (Hannah R. Loyd), who is not yet part of any labor group and, in any case, an unpredictable force until we see her in the series' last scene, twenty years later, pursuing a Grimm-like path. The recurring character Theresa Rubel, aka Trubel (Jacqueline Toboni), is a Grimm; later in the series, she joins the secret organization Hadrian's Wall, which opposes Black Claw. When Juliette transforms to the coldblooded, extraordinarily powerful Hexenbiest Eve, she too becomes part of Hadrian's Wall; these two women for a time take on elements of what Eve Bennett investigates as Weaponized Females, and as such might be seen as tools of a patriarchal fighting group, led by former resistance fighter Martin Meisner—an organization that Monroe, Rosalee, Hank, and Wu are reluctant to join.

In spite of the superficial gender and sex segregation, the long-term characters resist simple categorization. Monroe in particular presents an uninhibited combination of qualities ascribed to different genders. Wu varies from the typical presentation of a cop with his sexual ambiguity. The unequivocally traditionally masculine Hank is also unequivocally comfortable working with women such as the perceptive medical examiner Harper (Sharon Sachs). Nick's male melodrama complicates his gendering (not to mention his participation in childcare duties). The most distinctly patriarchal male is also the character most often connected with villainy, Sean Renard.

As for the female characters, each is powerful in her own way—but no cardboard cut-out superhero. They are lively and various. As Elizabeth Rambo (among others) has pointed out, in the Whedon- and Greenwalt-run *Angel*, female characters have a notable habit of getting dead. At the end of the fourth season of the Greenwalt- and Kouf-run *Grimm*, it seemed this series might have a similar problem: Three powerful women characters are killed within the space of three episodes (4.20–4.22). The death, dearth, or diminishment of female characters is much less of a problem, however, in *Grimm*.[11] Two of the three dead return, in one fashion or another. The showrunners thus use the dark fairy tale milieu to advantage in this series. There are women aplenty in *Grimm*—enough to provide moral and psychological variety among the characters with complicated gender and sexual identities that ground this fantasy in reality.

While the male characters of *Grimm* do not seem to reflect any unifying mythic imagery, there are connections among the females through ideas and images of the Crone. Crone theory is based in part on Julia Kristeva's ideas about abjection and Barbara Creed's further expansion of the subject, but it is also based in the study of historically prevalent archetypes. Diane Purkiss, Justyna Sempruch, and Ronald Hutton, in very different ways, warn against the mythologizing of the figure of the Crone in its multiple aspects, but *Grimm*, as a creation of popular culture, is based in such culturally absorbed mythologizing. Barbara Walker, D.J. Conway, Jane Caputi and others, exploring the three connected female archetypes of the Maiden, the Mother, the Crone, remind us that the Crone herself has multiple facets. The form which, of the three stages of female life, represents the aged woman was omitted when modern patriarchal religions absorbed the Virgin Maiden and the Mother. Instead, the old wise woman became the reject, the Witch—clearly relevant in the dark fairy tale world of *Grimm*. When witches show their secret faces in *Grimm*, they are the faces of misshapen ancient hags—of Crones.

However, the Crone is not only the Witch but also much more: She is a figure of wisdom, the Healer; she is a figure of death, the Huntress.

Most of the major female characters (both regular and recurring) connect to one or more of these figures of power. It is worth noting that the female characters of *Grimm* are for the most part grown women, not teenagers or early twenty-somethings. Recurring characters include women in their forties, fifties, and older.[12] Some of the recurring female characters are problematic in racial and ethnic terms (as will be discussed in Ch. 6). But the overall variety of morality, personality, and performance mitigates against traditional restrictions of gender. The older tradition of the Crone, visible behind the more recent scrim of the Witch, helps to deepen these characters.[13]

Each of these characters is incarnated by a talented actor. Tom Cantrell and Christopher Hogg ask that we distinguish between acting and performance, saying, "We have used 'acting' to refer specifically to the actor's portrayal of a character within a dramatic context . […] [W]e identified that 'performance' extends to the inflection of an actor's work by other performative elements beyond the contributions of the actor themselves, such as costume, lighting, framing and editing, for example" (4). Thus acting is within the performance. I would add that performance is within the character, with the character being created in a long televisual narrative (or perhaps one might argue that they overlay each other simultaneously). While acting, performance, and character are not identical, I will interweave discussions of acting and performance within studies of characters. I will sometimes discuss actors' placement in the mise-en-scène, as George Toles does for Jon Hamm's Don Draper in *Mad Men* (2007–2015) (163); I will sometimes comment on actors' voices, as Elliott Logan does of Claire Danes' Carrie Mathison in *Homeland* (2011–2020) (30–31); I will sometimes write about actors' bodies, as Steven Peacock does comparing Henry Fonda's Wyatt Earp in *My Darling Clementine* (1946) with Timothy Olyphant's Seth Bullock in *Deadwood* (2004–2006) (97, 105–106). I will quote extensively, since characters also live in words. Scholars such as Roberta Pearson (in "The Multiple Determinants of Television Acting") and Richard Hewett (in "Performing Sherlock") focus on the creative process of actors; this book attends mainly to the text. Attention to acting as part of the television text has been, until late, limited, as many scholars have noted—probably in part because of the difficulty of conveying analysis of acting through the written word.[14] As Sue Turnbull explains (following Stern and Kouvaris), *ekphrasis* is the attempt to put into (a thousand?) words the picture—and sound—we receive from the text showing acting. Complicated and imperfect as such an attempt may be, it ought to be made, for actors are too important to characters for scholars to disregard them—especially in television creation. Recall the fact that Claire Coffee's Adalind had two lines in the pilot but became central to the show: Over time, the combination of successful acting, the chemistry of inter-acting, and elements of Adalind's written nature created more and more narrative opportunities for the writers, opportunities to be memorably performed—using *performance* in Cantrell and Hogg's sense. Actors, writers, directors, costumers, directors of photography—all made Adalind. And Adalind, in turn, helped make the story. Every character has weighted and shifted the narrative; every character has shaped the series as a whole.

There is an element of playfulness that runs throughout the series and that cannot be conveyed by describing the narrative alone. It resides most clearly in the depiction of the characters. It is a relative to jouissance. Even as we immerse ourselves, even as we suspend our disbelief, we know that we are playing: We live in a world of heightened emotion, of heightened language, of quicker laughter. As Huizinga says, it is "a representation of something [...] different, something more beautiful, or more sublime, or more dangerous" than our reality (14). There is a delicate balance between concern and escape. Certain television series can accomplish this cocoon of safe but serious play with the long-term friends who are the characters.[15] *Grimm* is one such series. The characters of *Grimm* play well together. In my descriptions of them, I hope to convey not only their more serious implications but also some of that joyful play.

A quarter of a century ago, David Lavery gave his seminal collection on the television art of *Twin Peaks* the title *Full of Secrets*. This book is a more humble enterprise (as the word *Trailer* in the name may hint), but its title is meant in part to pay homage to Lavery's legacy of academic exploration. The phrase "full of secrets" in the context of *Twin Peaks* refers to the mystery of character, a mystery that this book explores. As Horace Newcomb said long ago, "there are numerous characters who develop their personalities into the themes of series" (102). Character, narrative, and theme are all connected. Story, language, acting, and visuals work together. But the negative symbolic implications of some of the long-term narrative arcs and structures of *Grimm* are pervasively counter-balanced by the weight of characters of human complexity and thematic richness.[16] Problems of race/ethnicity are moderated to some degree; issues of gender/sexuality are, overall, more successfully addressed. This introduction can only suggest some of the characters' complexity; the following chapters will introduce the men and women of *Grimm* more fully. Each character can open a different door to understanding the series. The perspectives on the characters are different as well; they do not fit within a single theoretical frame (and several different ones will be employed, from Crone theory to conventions of male melodrama to subtypes of the demon child). *Grimm* deserves much more attention, and television characters certainly do as well. Meaning is embedded in narrative, but—for television—it is embodied in character.

This book, then, offers a glimpse of the vision we can gain through the angle of a well-created television character.

The first chapter is devoted to the most popular character of *Grimm*: Monroe. Monroe's popularity derives not only from Silas Weir Mitchell's acting and the character's performance (per Cantrell and Hogg), but also, I argue, from his character type: the liminal hero-sidekick, highly popular characters who have qualities of both hero and sidekick. This type should be recognizable to many viewers, though it has heretofore been unnamed and uncategorized. Monroe belongs to the lineage of Spock, Spike, and Illya Kuryakin (as analyzed by Cranny-Francis, Amy-Chinn, and Worland, among many others). Such characters have five traits in common: each in some way is a hybrid and/or Other; each is culturally knowledgeable and eloquent; each has unexpected physical strength; each has strong feelings, often hidden; each is gender-liminal. The fact that Monroe is both popular and gender-liminal emphasizes the work of gender complication effected by the series. This chapter also serves to introduce arguably the most important relationship in the series, the friendship between Nick and Monroe, who occupy different spots on the spectrum of gendered behavior, with a connection that crosses many lines, including those of symbolic race/ethnic difference. Focusing on their relationship, the chapter thus introduces analysis of the title character as well as Monroe. Overall, the chapter, using extensive textual evidence, is meant to introduce the multiplicity of techniques, the many fine brush strokes the creators use to paint the character: narrative context, acting, the body of the actor (do we call that acting?), costume, lighting, parallel movements, mise-en-scène, visual composition, music, and more. These are all elements the creators use to build a television character such as the weirdly, wonderfully compelling Monroe.

The second chapter covers the character whose actor gets second billing: Hank, played by Russell Hornsby—who, after *Grimm*, was given his own television series. Like Monroe, Hank expands past the bounds of the role of sidekick—and more specifically, resists the role of the African American buddy. Unlike the typical sidekick/buddy described by such as Zimmerly and Buchanan, Hank is consistently shown as intelligently, expertly contributing to the solution of the crimes. The cisgendered Hank is also a physically powerful presence, fighting and sometimes killing villains. Intersectional concerns complicate Hank's representation as a Black male. Polarized stereotypes are repudiated: Hank is neither Uncle Tom nor savage, neither oversexed nor sexless. But his powerful participation in the violence of police- and Grimm-work also involves him (along with Nick's other friends) in extrajudicial killings (among other extrajudicial categories of actions). One might apply Derrick Bell's term of interest convergence: While it is true that the African American Hank is accepted in the force, it is also true that the white-dominated power structure finds his support useful, sometimes to questionable ends, particularly extralegal ones. Although usually Hank "[doesn't] have a problem with it," the series sometimes has this character and others question these patterns, both for situations of symbolic and literal racial problems. Hank's straight male gendering is also complicated in relation to his sexuality in contrast against a history of stereotypical depictions of African American males. Having had multiple marriages, Hank is far from sexless; neither is he sexually aggressive. His on-screen sexual relationships suggest him to be, instead, a strong, tender person who is a failed romantic—and thus, he stretches traditional gender and sexual representations of males in a way that would be less noticeable if the intersection of race were disregarded. Russell Hornsby's convincing portrayal of a complex character makes the difficulties resonate, makes the issues matter more.

Just as for Hank, the intersection of race with gender and sexuality is significant in the depiction of Wu; in fact, sexual orientation is a notable part of the character equation, too, as Chapter Three explains. Reggie Lee literally made a place for the Asian American (and, as he notes, stereotype-breaking) Wu: The role was created for him. For a cop who seems lower in status and is smaller in size, Lee enlarges the part through body language. The wit of Wu's dialogue and Lee's delivery also make the role more substantial, and as the seasons proceed, story arcs develop the character more fully. One of those stories shows his involvement with fellow Filipino American Dana Tomas; it is at the heart of Wu's intriguing sexual ambiguity. Stereotypes of Asian men as asexual might make an asexual Wu problematic (per Hamamoto, Shimizu, and others), but the series leaves uncertain whether he is asexual, heterosexual, or homosexual. Through the years, Wu—masculine in gender—comments from a position of seeming satisfaction on the benefits of a non-normative sexual orientation. These remarks are from the perspective of a character we come to see as not only witty but brave, and ultimately a part of the beloved community. Wu's struggle with his mental health (a struggle shared by several *Grimm* characters) is founded in the insanity of a world that symbolically refuses to recognize its social problems—that does not see Wesen. By the series end, Wu has become part of the preternatural world, and he controls his power, just as Reggie Lee controls his character.

Power is central to the character treated in Chapter Four: Sean Renard. Renard is multiply marked as a figure of the patriarchal power structure: police captain, secret prince, even mayor-elect, and of course a father—at the essence of patriarchy. His impressive physique represents that power: Sasha Roiz is the tallest of the cast and maintains a sharply defined, muscular body, frequently on display. But the body also demonstrates his liminality: Renard has a hidden, abject face, the face of a half-Zauberbiest. This liminal character can be understood as an example of the Gothic hero-villain—darkly mysterious, wealthy, aristocratic, attractive, and dangerous—both patriarchal and yet illegitimate, Other (as recognized by Moers, Gilbert and Gubar, and many more). Renard is traditionally, markedly masculine and heterosexual, yet in *Grimm*, this pairing of gender and sexuality are shown to be ultimately unsuccessful: He ends up romantically unloved and alone. In this and other ways he is shown to be a foil of the hero. His training in the lack of trust, his maneuvers and manipulations, reveal the dangers of the desire for patriarchal power. This morally grayest of *Grimm* characters has a chance at partial redemption only after Gothic battering, through emotional connection to his daughter and a comrade-in-arms whom he himself has killed. Sasha Roiz conveys both patriarchal, masculine violence and secret uncertainty in the memorable Renard.

The culminating chapter on male characters covers the Grimm himself, Nicholas Burkhardt. Nick is superficially traditional; he is given many normative masculine traits, symbolized by his superpower of sight—an indicator of both clear judgment and power. He even, on some occasions, exhibits horrific violence. But these traits are moderated and complicated, especially in the way he functions as a hero of male melodrama. Nick does not fit the standard pattern of the killer Grimm. With blocking and body language, David Giuntoli represents Nick's vulnerability. Both kindness and paternalistic dominance impel male protectiveness; however, the series calls attention to Nick's repeated failures of protection, suggesting the illusoriness of patriarchal safeguards. Nick's relatively unusual superpower of acute hearing connects with his emotional engagement, which in turn connects with male melodrama. Linda Williams argues that pathos and action combined constitute the crux of melodrama; these are at the heart of *Grimm* overall and Nick's depiction in particular. What Williams calls "sensation scenes" both center the hero's emotions and help free him of traditional male gender restrictions. Touches of abjection (sometimes voluntary) further distance Nick from the image of the hypermasculine superhero. Giuntoli is especially successful with the humor that humanizes Nick, both through language and body. The series even makes a multi-episode running gag of a gender-mocking phallic symbol closely identified with the hero—a strategy at once comic and meaning-laden. The slowly accruing details of character presentation are perhaps most important in evaluating the nature and effect of the main protagonist—a protagonist who is much more complex than a smoothly handsome superhero cop might seem.

Chapter Six, the first of the chapters on female characters, discusses an array of supporting characters as well as (more briefly) major ones, all of whom connect to some aspect of the Crone, whether as Witch, Huntress, or Wise Woman. Perhaps most notable of the secondary characters are the Kessler sisters. We first see Marie, unidentified, as a fearsome creature, in appearance a Witch. Owner of the trailer, she is the keeper of lore. When attacked, she fights fiercely: She is the Warrior Huntress, too. She occupies fully the role of the Crone—yet she has also mothered Nick, so she touches another side of the Maiden/Mother/Crone archetype as well. Her sister Kelly also first appears unidentified, even as to gender. She is seen fighting more efficiently than Nick himself and is clearly the Huntress—though she is also his mother. Nick's two lovers, Juliette and Adalind, are Witches, Wise Women, and Warriors. Both beautiful, they show the Crone face when they enact power. Their ultimate choices of gender roles are very different. The apothecary Wise Woman Rosalee mixes her remedies sometimes in the glass flask of a scientist, sometimes in the cauldron of a Witch. The young Grimm Trubel calls herself a Hunter (3.20). She is marked, even to her clothing, as following in the path of Nick's Hunter Mother, and not marked in terms of traditional female gender attributes. Adalind's daughter Diana is unnervingly Witchlike from birth and later hunts as well. Not only the major figures but also almost a dozen significant female recurring characters can be illuminated by facets of the Crone, demonstrating both strength and variety. They include a group of especially elder Crones (such as Elizabeth Lascelles and Henrietta) and those connected to the law (such as M.E. Harper and Agent Chavez). Three recurring Crones present problematic stereotypes. But overall, the Crones display intersections of age, race/ethnicity, body type, and more in a spectrum of female difference that stretches traditional gender expectations.

Chapter Seven analyzes the sole female of the original six regulars—a character who changes through four different versions of herself and, over the years, turns from the customary gendered path repeatedly offered to her. Juliette's qualities can be illuminated by comparison with another transformed female figure in another Greenwalt-created series: Fred/Illyria of *Angel*. Both Juliette/Eve and Fred/Illyria notably change in terms of bodily presentation and psyche. Each starts as a scientist who has heterosexual relationships; each becomes an affectless, detached, super-powered being. Both can be examined in terms of the trope of the damsel in distress and in terms of heterosexual romance. Fred/Illyria is forced to become a new self and in the end can be seen as acting because of the love of a good man, whereas Juliette/Eve initiates her own transformation and rejects traditional romance, acting out of her own determination to fulfill a greater purpose. Fred/Illyria fights in the body and costume of a female comic book superhero, but Juliette/Eve moves past the cat-suit as she continues the fight. Recurring ring symbolism implies that traditional marriage should not be elevated as the automatic, default preference. As the veterinarian and hero's girlfriend; as the angry witch; as the cold soldier Eve; and as the reborn combination of Juliette and Eve, she slowly grows into her own morally complex, purposeful self. Freighted with the responsibility for wrongdoing and humanized by humor (especially accentuated by Elizabeth Tulloch), this woman is not an either/or, Virgin/Whore. In the end, this non-traditional character is welcomed as part of the family of *Grimm* fighters and friends.

Rosalee Calvert, the Wesen apothecary, is the focus of Chapter Eight. In some ways seemingly unobtrusively norm-embracing, in others she is authoritative and transgressive. Her careful introduction to the series shows her to be much more than just a romantic interest for Monroe. Attractive but unglamorous, she has a history of drug addiction and family estrangement. Nonetheless, she long ago learned medical skills from her parents, and she conducts research in books inherited from her brother (just as Nick, in a gender flip, inherits books from his aunt). Again and again, Rosalee's characterization operates against gender stereotypes that are still too current. Not just a Wise Woman of traditional lore, she is also a woman of science; not just a hard worker, she is a business owner; not just a friendly neighbor, she is a community leader, politically connected. The stereotype of jealous enmity in female friendships is undone as well by the connections she establishes with the other main women characters. And while Rosalee is highly moral, she is pragmatic: She avoids the self-abnegation scholars such as Julie O'Reilly warn against for heroic females, even though she repeatedly displays physical bravery. Her bravery also shows in the transgressiveness of her relationships with Nick, someone she might have seen as an enemy, and Monroe, someone she might not have seen as a mate. Both her limitations and her strengths make the Wesen Rosalee a very human character, and Bree Turner's irregular vocalizations and assertive body language create a believable specificity of personhood. Rosalee is magic, but Rosalee is real.

Chapter Nine addresses the complexity of the third major female, the last to be given status as a regular: Claire Coffee's Adalind Schade. Through Adalind, the series conveys the idea that sexuality and motherhood do not need to mean submission but can be connected to power. The structure of Adalind's relationship with Nick follows, from the beginning, patterns of classic romantic comedy and even screwball comedy (as defined by Wes Gehring), a genre linked to issues of gender. Parallels between Nick and Adalind suggest a parity of power. There is a kind of character chiasmus for Juliette and Adalind that also implies parallel power. The motif of the doomed engagement ring for a forced marriage between Adalind and

Renard continues the ring imagery begun with Juliette, suggesting the failure of traditional, patriarchy-based marriage. Adalind's multiple relationships with powerful men show her as sometimes the dupe, sometimes the manipulator of patriarchy—and more and more aware of its nature, especially as embodied by Renard. Her first pregnancy (with Renard) coincides with her intense pursuit of the grueling process to regain the Hexenbiest powers taken from her by Nick. Both her humorous abjection through that process and her growing empathy for her child help rehabilitate the character. Her furious determination to recover her soon-stolen child parallels her determination to recover her powers. Her second pregnancy occurs through a sexual encounter in which she takes Nick's powers away, suggesting *her* power. The arrival of her second child is placed in the context of a sequence of episodes with other characters illustrating that motherhood (like marriage) should not be a default. Again a mother, one who has embraced motherhood, Adalind is temporarily isolated, confined to her home like a nineteenth-century Angel (or Hexenbiest?) in the House. But she emerges once more. Once in love with a prince, Adalind in the fifth season is asked to become a princess, but she repudiates that choice. Adalind's deep knowledge (as a lawyer and a witch), her extraordinary rhetorical skill, and her hard-earned magical power are part of the strength that defines her in the end. Claire Coffee's performance makes it easy to credit the peculiar, engaging growth of the hilarious, hateful, loving Adalind Schade.

Chapter Ten turns to Trubel, the other Grimm who appears most often besides Nick. Trubel fits into the "Combative Female" category described by Ewan Kirkland, yet she does not experience the "snap," the retraction from power Sara Crosby notes as prevalent for female characters. Trubel is introduced as a homeless young woman struggling against rape, something she does repeatedly. When she realizes the truth of her power, she is more than ready to fight. A person of strong physicality, she resists gender patterns in her enthusiastic consumption of food. Her clothing suggests at first poverty and later a disregard for appearance (a rather second-wave feminist attitude). She resembles Nick—someone with a normal body rather than super-muscularity or size; she even more closely resembles Nick's mother, whose shoes (and clothes) she in some senses fills, even while she is almost a daughter to Nick. She becomes part of the larger family of friends surrounding Nick, yet she individuates, following her own path to serve Hadrian's Wall—another group of comrades. Trubel, raised in the foster care system, spent many years being told she was mentally ill because of her visions of Wesen, and there is a darker side to her responses to Wesen that shows in some dismaying tactics of Hadrian's Wall. She is appropriately imperfect. But she is also, after her time with Nick and Juliette, open in her affections and astute in her emotional perception. In the end, like Juliette, she chooses a purpose outside the family while still being connected to it. With a switch of traditional gender positions regarding emotion and rationality, she is strong enough to successfully rebuke and guide her mentor Nick as they fight to save the world. From start to finish, Toboni's emotionally emphatic physicality fully embodies the character of Trubel.

The eleventh and last chapter considers the significance of Diana, a character who both fits into and emerges from the archetype of the demon child. As Karen J. Renner, in her multiple studies on the subject, explains, the demon child has traditionally been considered irredeemable. But *Grimm* reverses that pattern. Even before birth, Diana is associated with skulls, spiders, and death. As a young child, she is surrounded by portents, and her power is frightening. The child of not only Adalind but also Renard, she is a magic princess, pushed to be part of (and later rescued from) patriarchy. In this way, as in others, she displays Gothic doubling with her witch mother, even as to their names. Her eerie, potentially evil naiveté is effectively conveyed by the innocent-faced Hannah R. Loyd. Yet over the course of years in the series, repeated exposure to models of loving care helps Diana to grow into a champion for good, as the last scene of the series shows. She is (as her words in that scene make clear) part of a loving community, a family. The growth of this character depicts a central theme: Whether we will come to know the fearsome Other as demonic or powerfully good depends on our interaction. And for its conclusion, this series chooses to embody powerful goodness in the shape of a young woman.

The book ends with a brief essay adverting to a resurgence in the study of character in literature and contemplating character as a window to see beyond auteurism in the study of television.

ONE

"The dark does have its bright side"

Monroe and the Liminal Hero-Sidekick Tradition of Spock, Spike, and Illya Kuryakin

At the 2012 DragonCon on Labor Day weekend in Atlanta, exhibitors sold artistic renderings of Monroe—and no other character from the TV series *Grimm*, so far as I could see.[1] *Grimm* had premiered a year before, on October 28, 2011, and the werewolf-like character of Monroe, played by Silas Weir Mitchell, had rapidly become what the popular press called a "breakout" star (Turnquist). At the *Grimm* series website store, T-shirts of Monroe are the only ones to be sold with the image of a single character. David Greenwalt further asserts, "If ever an actor and a character were designed for one another, I think this is it" ("The World of Grimm"). Monroe fits into a tradition of highly popular characters that I will call the liminal hero-sidekick.[2] These include Illya Kuryakin of *The Man from U.N.C.L.E.*, *Star Trek*'s Mr. Spock, and the vampire Spike, from *Buffy the Vampire Slayer*. The term "liminal" refers at its root to limning, to the line: the liminal is near the borderline, crossing between worlds or states.[3] Among other things, these characters are on the border between sidekick and hero. Nick Burkhardt's detective partner Hank Griffin is more than just a sidekick (see Ch. 2), and in that regard Hank and Nick's unofficial partner Monroe are alike; however, Monroe has liminal qualities that everyman Hank does not. The liminal hero-sidekicks share five significant traits. First, each character in some ways represents the Other and/or a hybrid nature; second, each character is culturally aware and/or intellectual, with notable verbal skills; third, each is deceptively strong physically; fourth, each has emotional depths; and fifth, each is gender-liminal. The characters share these traits to greater or lesser degrees. They vary from the typical patriarchal, cisgendered hero yet approach or supersede the hero's stature in terms of audience response. I will discuss each of my four exemplars in chronological order, focusing at greatest length on the most recent case: Monroe.

Illya Kuryakin of The Man from U.N.C.L.E.

The Man from U.N.C.L.E., a spy drama/spoof modeled on the popular James Bond films, debuted in the fall of 1964, during the Cold War between the U.S. and Russia. The Russian agent Illya Kuryakin was therefore very much Other for audiences of the time. Played by Scottish actor David McCallum, the character—like *Grimm*'s Adalind—was given only two lines in the pilot, which was dominated by the more traditionally masculine and Bond-like character of Napoleon Solo, played by Robert Vaughn. But Napoleon Solo's partner rapidly became popular; Robert Vaughn notes in a DVD featurette interview that there was "quite a lot of fan mail coming in for the mysterious Illya Kuryakin" and adds that "they had no intention to make Illya Kuryakin a co-starring role [...] it just came from audience response" ("Cloak & Swagger"). Writer Dean Hargrove adds that "David became a huge star in relation to the show" ("Cloak"). While Russianness was unquestionably Other for the audience, McCallum's British accent in some way hybridized the character: For an American audience, the British can be seen as both Other and not-Other. Rick Worland, in "The Cold War Mannerists: *The Man from U.N.C.L.E.* and TV Espionage" argues that "McCallum/Illya's popularity may have siphoned some of the energy of Beatlemania" (157–158). In terms of intellect, culture, and notable language, Kuryakin has a Ph.D. in quantum mechanics ("The Her Master's Voice Affair"). He plays multiple instruments and easily references significant cultural figures in sophisticated terms. For instance, when the recurring guest character of Marian Raven, played by McCallum's then-spouse Jill Ireland, says, "Someone once said where there's music there can be no mischief," Illya responds, "Cervantes. But he was wrong. There's mischief all around us" ("The Quadripartite Affair"). McCallum delivers his lines with understated expressiveness of face and voice. When section chief Mr. Waverly (Leo G. Carroll) mentions the name of an abductee, Illya immediately recognizes it as that of a pianist who "plays Bach with impeccable style" ("The Shark Affair"). In terms of his deceptive strength, the show's co-creator Norman Felton commented on his "slim" build in comparison to other male stars of the time, especially in Westerns ("Cloak"), but Illya fights and shoots quite effectively. In contrast to his promiscuous partner Napoleon, the "brooding and cryptic" (Worland 158) Illya is less frequently engaged sexually, but the lack of promiscuity may suggest more of an emotional connection. In "The Quadripartite Affair," he says to Marian Raven,

"Please—I must think" and asks her to pretend he is "part of the walls," but she responds, "All right [...] pretend you're part of the walls [...] or a rock. But just for once [...] couldn't you pretend you're a human being?" By the end of the episode, they steal away together. Extratextual elements probably added to the character's emotional depth. As Worland notes, fans recognized the series' textual playfulness, and many would have known that Ireland and McCallum were married (156–157). Illya might look weak, but he is really strong; he might act cold, but he is really emotional. The emotion fits in with the transgression of strict gender role requirements. Though it is hard to envision today, Illya's hair style was gender-transgressive because of its relative length, and in fact, NBC executives at first wanted to cut the character specifically because of his hair (Hargrove, "Cloak"). In a video interview, leading man Robert Vaughn, coyly touching McCallum, also says, "I thought he was beautiful on screen," adding, "I mean, it wasn't anything terribly intense, but I had an optical thing" ("Cloak"). We might also note that Illya's signature black turtleneck is a garment Anne Hollander describes as the traditional clothing of the female intellectual; and for men, she sees it as indicating "a kind of freedom" (387)—a cross-gender intellectual garment. In sum, Illya's liminal hero-sidekick qualities established him as more compelling than the more gender-traditional, dominant leading man.

Spock of Star Trek

Worland compares Illya Kuryakin to *Star Trek*'s Spock, our next exemplar, as "originally a secondary character who unexpectedly seized the imagination of viewers and soon became the major icon of the program" (155). Spock, first explored in the 1966–69 version of *Star Trek*, has become so well known to popular culture scholars and fans that a comparatively brief treatment should suffice to establish his connection to the liminal hero-sidekick pattern. As a member of an alien race, Spock is unquestionably Other; he is also by definition hybrid, since he has an alien father but a human mother. One scholar notes that "Spock, as Vulcan, serves as the racial 'Other' companion to Kirk; the blending of Leonard Nimoy's real-life Jewish identity with the invented Vulcan culture furthermore reiterated the racial or ethnic distinctions between Kirk and Spock (even as, in fact, both Nimoy and Shatner were Jewish)" (Kies 419). The power of Spock's intellect is widely known, as is his devotion to logic. We would do well, however, to remember that he is culturally knowledgeable too—able to identify lines of *Hamlet* by their act and scene (*Star Trek IV*), and able to quote Byron off the cuff ("Is There in Truth No Beauty?"). Like Illya Kuryakin, he is a skilled musician, playing the Vulcan lyre. He expresses himself verbally with precision and cool wit. When a crew member defends raising his voice because of having "a human thing called an adrenalin gland," Spock responds, "That does sound inconvenient, however. Have you considered having it removed?" And Sulu soon comments, "Try and cross brains with Spock, he'll cut you to pieces every time" ("The Corbomite Maneuver"). Mr. Spock is also capable of physically cutting others to pieces, though he normally shows marked restraint. Taller than Captain Kirk, he is less muscular, and, as a Vulcan, is a pacifist. However, we gradually learn that he is not only able to incapacitate others with a special Vulcan neck grip but is also enormously stronger than his human shipmates. His physical power is shown, for instance, in the episode "Amok Time," during which he must respond to the Vulcan urges of *pon farr* and physically fight for his mate. This episode (among others) also demonstrates that the supposedly emotionless Vulcan has volcanic depths of feeling, less in terms of his response to his forgettable mate than in his response to Captain Kirk: Spock believes that, under the influence of *pon farr*, he has killed the captain, and his joy at discovering Kirk to be alive is undeniable. Actor Leonard Nimoy's body language as he physically reaches out to Kirk, and the utterly unexpected smile on Spock's face, make the moment striking—though Nimoy's ability to indicate subtle inflections of emotion is the more important part of his performance of Spock over the decades. The relationship to Kirk in general and this episode in particular connect to the idea of gender liminality. Many scholars—such as Constance Penley, Karin Blair, April Selley, Patricia Frazer Lamb and Diana L. Veith—have commented on what Anne Cranny-Francis calls the "ambiguity" of Spock's gendering (276). As Bridget Kies says in a recent discussion, "Original Spock is [...] a mix of the masculine and feminine, and this is particularly reinforced through his Vulcan physiology [...]. Its seven-year cycle parallels *pon farr* to sexual processes like ovulation" (425). The complex history of K/S (Kirk/Spock) slash fan fiction, in which the two share a romantic and/or sexual relationship, plays with this ambiguity (Lamb and Veith). Spock is perhaps the most powerful or at least the most famous example of the attraction of the liminal hero-sidekick.

Spike of Buffy the Vampire Slayer

Buffy the Vampire Slayer's vampire Spike appeared in the late nineties and has moved into the early twenty-first century. At first a dangerous adversary, Spike later, to his dismay, realizes he is in love with Buffy and becomes her ally. Spike's popularity as a character has bled into scholar fandom: An entire issue of *The European Journal of Cultural Studies*, for example, was devoted to the character (Amy-Chinn and Williamson). As a vampire, Spike is automatically both Other and hybrid, monster yet human, neither alive nor dead but undead. He is even more markedly hybrid because he is, like only one other vampire in the storyworld, possessed of a soul by the last season of the series, like the humans he works among. Spike does not have the educational background of an Illya Kuryakin or a Mr. Spock, but he was, in his original human existence, a poet—though an exceptionally bad one. As he has lived through the centuries, his cultural taste seems to have improved, though he rejects high culture in favor of popular culture; he is, for instance, a fan of the Sex Pistols. That cultural knowledge comes through in the wit of his language, perhaps never more memorably than on a visit to the *Buffy* spinoff series *Angel*, in which, unseen on a nearby rooftop, he mocks the eponymous character after the rescue of Rachel, a young woman beset by vampires. Spike, in a voice he imagines to be like Rachel's, says, "How can I thank you, you mysterious black-clad hunk of the night thing? [...]" and, in a parody of Angel's voice, he replies to himself, "Say no more. Evil's still afoot. And I'm almost out of that nancy-boy hair gel I like so much. Quickly, to the Angel-mobile, away" ("In the Dark"). Actor James Marsters' facial expressions and vocal tones, not to mention the camera angles and placement of Spike on the building from which he literally looks down on Angel, make the moment vivid. Spike also shows his perceptiveness time and again in his understanding of others' emotional issues, such as Willow's desperate sadness after Oz leaves her, or Buffy and Angel's inability to be friends instead of lovers. Spike's physical strength is something that comes as a result of being a vampire, but that is, once again, a deceptive strength: Spike is smaller than any of the other male regular characters; in particular, he is notably shorter than Angel. Yet Buffy identifies him in the seventh season as one of their strongest fighters: He holds nothing back. His strength arises from the depths of his emotion. While Spike arrives in town seeming to be a cold and ferocious killer, it is not long before he is shown to have strong emotional ties, even as a vampire, to his beloved Drusilla—and later to Buffy—a set of feelings seemingly rooted in his earlier self ("Fool for Love"). He also displays non-romantic emotion to other characters, such as Buffy's sister Dawn and his rival Angel (though that relationship may have elements of the romantic too). Numerous scholars have also commented on Spike's gender liminality; Arwen Spicer has made it the focus of an article. Stacey Abbott notes that Spike's appearance is important to him ("From," 336). Like Kuryakin and Spock, Spike has notable hair. Dee Amy-Chinn points out that his bleached blond locks cross stereotypical gender lines not only in terms of their look but also because of the time consumed in creating that look (318–19). Indeed, Amy-Chinn argues that Spike crosses not only lines of gender but also of sexual behavior: "Spike occupies a series of paradoxical and liminal spaces" (313), she asserts. Picture him on his knees before Buffy in the musical "Once More, with Feeling"; he is open to being dominated (he calls himself "Love's bitch" ["Lovers Walk"]), and yet he can be a dominator as well, whether with his vampire crew, or Andrew, or females other than Dru and Buffy (such as Harmony). He is often a sex object, as when the Buffybot says, "He is evil. But you should see him naked. I mean, really" ("Intervention"), but he dies in a flame of love and self-sacrifice ("Chosen"). Spike, like the other hero-sidekicks, disrupts the categories.

Monroe of Grimm

Knowing Monroe

Despite the lack of a K to his name, Monroe of *Grimm* belongs to the character bloodline of Kuryakin, Spock, and Spike. Although Nick Burkhardt discovers he can see the usually hidden animalistic nature of Wesen and is attacked by more than one in the pilot, the Wesen Monroe becomes close friends with Nick. By the end of the third season, Nick is the best man at Monroe's wedding. Monroe is a Blutbad, the name of a creature, as he says to Nick in the pilot, "vulgarized by your ancestors as the Big Bad Wolf." The word "vulgarized" alerts us that Monroe is nothing so simple. The character is unusually complex, painted with detailed strokes through not only plot and dialogue but (among other things) setting, music, costume, camera work, and, of course, acting, by Silas Weir Mitchell. While illuminating Nick through their relationship, Monroe's complex presentation in the pilot and first several episodes can serve to begin the analysis of Monroe as a liminal hero-sidekick: Other/hybrid, eloquently intellectual and culturally aware, deceptively strong, emotionally deep, and gender-liminal.

Monroe appears halfway through the pilot episode, as Nick begins to fully enter the strange new world of Grimms and Wesen. Before he meets Monroe, we have already seen Nick shoot and kill Hulda, a Wesen that has attacked Nick's aunt. The attack occurs at Nick's home, in the night; the next day he has returned to searching for Robin Howell—his Riding Hood— the little girl in the red hoodie who has been abducted. On the hunt for the abductor, Nick emerges from a wooded Portland park to see a well-tended blue cottage with a yellow VW bug parked by it. A tall, dark, lightly bearded man in a rolled-neck sweater and jeans, a seemingly ordinary fellow, emerges from this cozy setting to check his mail—and as youngsters ride by on bicycles, he *woges*, showing a wolfish face, sniffing the air as the children pass. We have earlier seen a mailman with a different body type turn to follow the little girl Robin, so observant viewers know this new person is probably not the abductor, but Nick has not seen the mailman. He only sees that this other man is Wesen, and Nick rushes across the street to him as the man retreats to his house, already having woged back into human face. Nick reaches the door before the man can close it, and charges through the threshold. He throws the man down upon the staircase that faces the front door, and the camera emphasizes the moment by showing an extreme close-up of Nick's angry face as he shouts, "Where is she?" while the man—Monroe—recoils beneath him. The Grimm here is more ferocious than the Wesen. Nick will soon learn that his assumptions about this Wesen, this Other, are very wrong.

The moment of Nick's irruption into Monroe's place comes as one of two Campbellian threshold-crossing (or threshold-crashing) scenes for Nick and Monroe in the pilot,[4] and these scenes help balance the power between the hero and the liminal hero-sidekick. Having failed to find the girl in Monroe's home even with a phalanx of police officers searching (and having failed in his attempt to arrest Monroe), Nick returns alone in the dark. We see again the cozy blue cottage, a place out of a fairy tale, under the stars; within a well-lit picture window we see Monroe, wearing wire-rimmed glasses and carefully handling what we later learn is clockwork. Against the cool blue framing of this civilized sight is Nick watching hidden amidst the trees in the night: he is lit in red, and in profile he is the one who seems most like a predator at this point. He crosses the street and sneaks to the side of the cottage, observing as Monroe comes out to his backyard's wooden fence and urinates to mark his territory (an action that will turn out to be helpful later in the season, 1.21). As he does so, he sniffs, seeming to scent a stranger. Monroe's keen sense of smell is balanced against Nick's extraordinary hearing (which has already proven useful in the pilot as Nick discovered a dead girl's iPod, lost in the woods).[5] Both senses are ones that we in the audience share, but in these two characters they are so extreme as to be Other—yet another example of a quality that is different yet parallel between the two. Monroe disappears, and Nick is creeping by the side of the house again when Monroe crashes through the window above, just as Nick has earlier crashed through his door. Monroe grabs Nick and throws him against the red-brick side of his blue cottage,[6] growling, "You shouldn't have come back," echoing the treatment he has received at Nick's hands. The encounters have been equalized, and each has violently broken through a threshold into the other's world.

But then, as Nick tries to grab for his gun, Monroe woges back into his human face and *laughs* as he says, "Ok, ok, ok, lighten up—I'm just making a point." Monroe's face is lit against a dark, cloudy background as he adds, "C'mon, let's grab a brew. And by the way—you're paying for that window."

Monroe is not to be taken advantage of or intimidated; he is not afraid to find out more about a creature who is legendary to him: a Grimm. Later in the series Monroe usually drinks wine, but in this moment, "let's grab a brew" establishes him as a very unmonstrous, beer-drinking regular guy. (Beer turns out to be Nick's regular drink of choice). The astonished Nick follows Monroe inside, and we see them in Monroe's comfortable kitchen. Monroe seems neither fearsome nor fearful, but instead curious—though he makes it clear that he is aware of Grimms' reputations as Wesen-killers. However, Monroe—perhaps in part because of confidence in his own power as a Blutbad?—seems simply to be enjoying the encounter. With a half laugh, he says, "A Grimm—what do you know. I heard about you all my life—never thought I'd see one up close." As he hands over a bottle of beer, actor Silas Weir Mitchell, as Monroe, peers close into the other man's face, crossing another threshold by invading Nick's personal space and thus demonstrating his daring. Though stories his parents told about Grimms "scared the hell outta me when I was a kid," Monroe is not scared now. For viewers who have seen themselves as Other, Monroe's attitude may feel exhilarating.

In the latter part of the pilot scene inside Monroe's home, much about Nick and Monroe's relationship is established. Crucially, we see Nick getting to know a Wesen who is far from evil. If Wesen represent the Other (including ethnic/racial Others), such knowledge is key.[7] We also see Monroe beginning to teach Nick. Furthermore, we see Nick starting to draw Monroe out of his "lone wolf" zone of neutrality and into the broader moral connections that will bring them both great rewards and great costs. Unlike many Wesen (as we will later see), Monroe does not mind talking to Nick about the Wesen world, but he at first does not want to get involved in the rescue of the little girl. He tells Nick that he is not the abductor: "Look, I don't want any more trouble. I'm not that kind of Blutbad. I don't kill any more—I haven't in years." Monroe asserts that he has reformed himself "through a strict regimen of diet, drugs, and Pilates." Monroe is an enthusiastic vegetarian, and in later episodes we often see him dwelling over delicacies, seemingly displacing his memories of the "blood in your throat, and the taste of it" (4.19) with a focus on subtle flavors of very different sorts. He is certainly not a wolf with a belly full of maiden, a fairy-tale monster.[8] When Nick starts to ask about "all those things I've been seeing," Monroe stops him short: "We're not *things*. Look, I'm a clockmaker, for God's sake." He will not allow Nick to make Wesen merely Other; they are much more.

Nick is also surprised to learn that Monroe knows about the books— that is, the Grimms' handwritten encyclopedias on Wesen (though Monroe does not yet know of Aunt Marie's trailer, in which they are kept). This scene is the beginning of Monroe's teaching Nick about the Wesen world and about Nick's potential role in it. When Nick, wishing to escape his destiny and displaying some of the Campbellian hero's reluctance, asks, "How do I stop it?" Monroe replies, "You can't stop it. It's who you are."[9] As he says the words, Silas Weir Mitchell shuts the lid on a wooden chest, an act he repeats with another piece of furniture later in the scene: the actor is moving naturally through his character's home, but he is also shutting the door on Nick's past, just as earlier they crashed through into this new life. Monroe becomes Nick's primary guide into this world. He is the Virgil for Nick's Dante, in an underworld sometimes nearly as grotesque as the Inferno but laced with much more humor. In fact, some parts of the Wesen world are far from infernal—they are warm and loving. But Nick is yet to know that.

Monroe is hardly Virgilian, at the beginning of the series, in his sense of duty: He simply wants to be left alone. "I don't bother the other Blutbaden, they don't bother me," he tells Nick. He assumes that Nick similarly acts from self-interest, and that he has come to learn about the strange sights he has been seeing. But for Nick, it is not just about himself: "I'm here because of the little girl," he insists. And Monroe begins to respond to that ethical emotional call: "You still haven't found her yet?" he asks. Silas Weir Mitchell says, speaking for his character, "the journey has been about going from being this closed-off, hunkered-down, atavistic, solo, solipsistic, almost-person, to being pulled into the world—reluctantly, to be sure. But once [...] I started to see that maybe I could do good in the world, through working with this Grimm, that, to me, made the journey [...] worthwhile" (Nelson, "The Wolf" 29). In the pilot when Nick, believing Monroe knows who has the child, pushes him against the wall, Monroe says with quiet force, "Please don't threaten me"—but he goes with Nick to show him where she is being held. He acts as the guide here, as he so often does later.

Victor Turner wrote about liminal areas, often wilderness areas—deserts or dark forests—as places of testing. Nick will soon pass the test when he trusts his feeling about the identity of the murderous abductor—though Nick will not be the one to kill him. Monroe, for his part, guides Nick into the dark. With his head stuck out the window to sniff the trail, Monroe pilots Nick in the meandering yellow VW bug on a dark path amid the giant trees of the forests of the Northwest, to find the innocent child being held by a Blutbad who is not vegetarian. (The abductor Blutbad drives a dull-colored VW van, a distorted echo of Monroe's vehicle.) On the way there, the teacher/guide corrects the pupil a magical three times. He makes Nick wear wolfsbane to mask his scent; he has him leave the car on the picturesque bridge and walk through the water (to prevent detection, though it also serves as a baptismal border-crossing); and when Nick asks if he needs silver bullets, Monroe says, "What are you? An idiot?" In Monroe's last scene in the pilot, he once again demonstrates that he has yet to reach the moral status he will later attain. With the full moon shining down, he tells Nick, "I can't guarantee what'll happen if I go any closer—it's too dangerous. I might be on your side—I might be on his side—I might even go for the girl. I'm sorry"—and he leaves. But of course Monroe's declaration here is itself an attempt to prevent harm. And he has managed to bring his pupil to the place of testing.

It is worth noting that when Nick calls in his daytime partner, Hank, to join him in the woods at night, Hank parks his car in exactly the same spot on the bridge as Monroe had, and the cars on the bridge are given the same lighting and camera angle. Then Nick puts Hank through the steps Monroe had taught him—using wolfsbane, walking through the water (with the initiate, in this case Hank, once again asking what the bridge is for). These parallels underline Monroe and Hank's similar roles as partners to Nick (see Ch. 2). Furthermore, the scene shows that Nick is learning Monroe's lessons. Nick, the white police officer, is seeing a world of Others that he has never perceived, though it has been all around him; and he is comprehending it with the aid of Monroe.

In the very next episode, Nick asks Monroe to guard his hospitalized aunt, saying to the reluctant Monroe, "I trust you" (1.2). Their relationship is a pillar of the show's meaning. In the last season of the series, shots of Monroe's crashing through the window into Nick will be replayed as a memory told to regulars who have come to make up the family of characters in *Grimm* (6.7). They agree that without Monroe and Nick's meeting, none of them would be together as they are. The window scene in the pilot is a quintessential moment, representing Monroe and Nick's boundary-breaking relationship. In fact, the pilot as a whole represents in little space much of the nature of the characters and their relationships. If Monroe had not been so open-minded and curious, so brave, Nick would never have learned about Wesen from a Wesen point of view. If Nick had not been raised in ignorance, undoctrinated—and if his aunt had not died so soon after the accession of his powers, and if he had not been motivated by a desire to help—he might not have listened to Monroe. The growing, chosen good will of both characters eventually changes their world.[10] Furthermore, the threshold-breaking image recurs, in a different form, in the last episode of the entire series. After having saved the world from apocalyptic evil, Nick crashes back from an alternative plane into Monroe's (now Monroe and Rosalee's) living room, just as he crashed into it in the pilot—only this time, he is not entering angrily into the home of an imagined enemy but landing in the home of friends, with love awaiting. Having reminded viewers of the pilot five episodes before the finale, the producers thus tie together the entire series from beginning to "The End," as the episode is called (6.13). Breaking through barriers is central to the relationship of Monroe and Nick, and central to the meaning of *Grimm*. It seems only appropriate that a notably liminal character such as Monroe should be the guide here.

Following on from the pilot, in the next eight episodes, Monroe is given a remarkable set of opportunities for character development—especially for a character played by an actor with fourth billing in the series credits. In the second episode, as noted, Monroe protects Nick's Aunt Marie from an assassin as she lies hospitalized after an earlier attack against the older Grimm. Monroe struggles with his own doubts about protecting Marie, someone he knows has killed many Wesen—as opposed to Nick, who has just become a Grimm. With Marie apparently asleep, Monroe speaks aloud of his grandfather, killed by Grimms; but he also acknowledges that the grandfather "may have deserved it." Still, Monroe's eyes glow red as Marie's open and she says, "Take your best shot, Blutbad." At this moment of testing, an assassin appears outside her door; Silas Weir Mitchell's Monroe and Kate Burton's Marie share a look, and Monroe leaves to pursue the man. The assassin's clear-cut evil highlights Monroe's more liminal status and moves him toward heroism. But the episode is not just a morality tale. It also introduces a very human, relatable aspect of the character: Monroe's love of good food and drink. His passionate investment in good taste sometimes seems to be a displacement of darker desires. When Nick shows up at 6:30 one morning, we hear whimsical sounding, rhythmic music and see a shot of Silas Weir Mitchell upside down in screen perspective as he works his exercise machine in time to the beat. He is clearly being presented in a non-threatening way for a wolfish man. When Nick shows him a claw device used by bearlike Jagerbar Wesen and asks if he has seen one, Monroe replies, "Not up close, thank God. I think Jagerbars use them for disemboweling. Now I'm hungry." The lurching shift from disembowelment to hunger is so grotesque as to be humorous; it is also a reminder of Monroe's very present past. But Monroe does not go for breakfast meat; instead, he offers a bagel, and adds, "I'm going to French press some coffee, too—Guatemalan Highlands, craft roasted—very robust," and urges Nick to join him. His focus on these flavors is not only an indicator of his cultured palate; it is also a constant, life-affirming element of the character throughout the series. His protection of Marie and his eating habits are not completely separate matters: both are assertions of life.

For the first several episodes, Monroe does not appear until halfway through the show, but each displays more emotional and ethical growth in the relationship between the two men: more trust and more banter. The third episode, the unapologetically punny "Beeware," is noteworthy for the badinage between Monroe and Nick that helps establish the "broman[ce]" aspect of their relationship (as actor David Giuntoli calls it, "Unlocking"). The episode is co-written by Thania St. John, who often appears as a writer early in the life of a series with comedy/fantasy/romantic elements.[11] At this stage, Nick cannot automatically presume that Monroe will participate in his work. When in this episode Nick tells Monroe he needs his nose, Monroe replies, "Oh, I get it. So little Timmy's stuck in a well, you need Lassie to come find him? Boy, you really know how to butter a guy up for a favor." "I got a bottle of '78 Bordeaux in my trunk," Nick offers, and Monroe replies, "I could maybe catch a scent." (Even this humor reminds us, and Nick, of Monroe's resistance to being seen as an animal.) When Monroe later stretches back in the office chair of the woman they are seeking and says, "Maybe we could crack that Bordeaux while we wait," his body language and vocal tones (which for the first and only time have an odd echo of Don Knotts as Barney Fife) show his increasing relaxation with Nick.[12] In the next episode, "Lonelyhearts," Nick asks Monroe to go undercover—at least to the extent of hanging out in a bar to watch a suspect. Nick pays for the beer (and an onion ring or so). This is the last time Nick offers Monroe anything approaching compensation. In "Danse Macabre," rather than asking for help tracking a criminal, Nick asks Monroe to help him set an angry teenager on the right track—and the teenager is Wesen. Interestingly, it is Nick who persuades Monroe to reach out to his fellow Wesen, because the teen is a Rheinigen, or rat-like Wesen—not typically "drinking buddies" with Blutbaden such as Monroe. But Nick knows their common love of classical music: Monroe is a cellist (as we have seen in the preceding episode), the teen a violinist. No longer is the men's relationship simply a matter of chasing criminals, nor is it transactional.

Camera work and music have combined to emphasize the amiability of the wolfish Monroe, but the sixth episode clarifies that the character is not simple sunshine: his virtue is hard-won. In "The Three Bad Wolves," we learn something of Monroe's back-story as we meet Hap, a soon-to-be-murdered, clueless but genuinely friendly Blutbad who went through a "program" with Monroe years ago (the program is implied to be one that reduces violence) and who now asks Monroe to take him in after his home is mysteriously blown up. The decision to accept the hairy, ebullient, peppermint Schnapps-drinking Hap in his tidy home costs Monroe, but he makes himself undertake this act of friendship. We also meet Hap's intense, violent sister Angelina, Monroe's ex-girlfriend and the red-headed incarnation of temptation. Monroe manages to keep Nick and Angelina from killing each other, but he fails to keep Hap from being killed—because Monroe and Angelina cannot resist a night of hunting and sex in the woods across the street and leave the trusting Hap unguarded. The victim of revenge by another Wesen for one of Angelina's killings, Hap is killed in Monroe's home, normally a sanctuary of civility. Nick arrests the killer, fighting Angelina to prevent her from killing the other Wesen, and she disappears into the night, evading Nick's capture. But we see that, for Monroe, violence is always just outside the door.

While the first set of episodes emphasizes Monroe's growing altruism, the next set emphasizes his bravery (though both qualities are intertwined). In "Let Down Your Hair" (1.7), Nick and Monroe risk their lives together to rescue a feral Blutbad girl who grew up in the wild—a girl whose abduction Hank investigated years earlier. Monroe is threatened at gunpoint by the brothers of a criminal the girl killed as he attacked hikers. It takes both Hank and Monroe, each working with Nick but apart from the other, to bring the girl home. Though Hank still knows nothing of the Wesen world, Nick's two partners are being drawn closer together. By episode eight, "Game Ogre," Monroe, unseen, saves Hank's life, shooting a murderous ogre-like Siegbarste Wesen who has targeted Hank while Nick is hospitalized, having been beaten by the same Siegbarste. To save Hank, Monroe must retrieve an ogre-gun from Marie's trailer—and Nick gives Monroe the key to do so, trusting Monroe to go there alone before Nick tells anyone else that the trailer—the "National Archives of Grimmology," as Monroe later calls it (1.12)—even exists.[13] In the ninth episode, Monroe is badly beaten by unknown Wesen who mark his little VW with the Grimm-killer symbol, a drawing of the scythe of the Reapers who attacked Marie. He is thus joined with his friend the Grimm. The significance of the moment is highlighted by the setting: Monroe has been lured to supposedly repair a gigantic, public-facing clock on a columned building, and with the giant timepiece above, we see his beaten body below, by the tall white columns—a location that implies the establishment, the powers that be. Monroe later explains that there is a clear message: Monroe must not help the Grimm. As he says to Nick, "You start messing with the status quo, there are some people who might not be exactly sanguine about that. And what I am doing with you is definitely messing with the status quo." After a pause, Nick demonstrates his own ethical understanding of how much he has asked of his Othered friend, saying, "I'm not going to ask for any more of your help," and he starts to leave: he will not ask Monroe to risk his life. But Monroe replies, "Screw that. I'm not running," and he opens the refrigerator door (yes, one more opening door) and removes two beers, saying, "You ask me for all the help you need." And as he hands Nick a beer, the liminal hero-sidekick memorably adds, "I've never been much of a status quo kind of guy. The next time, we'll be ready for 'em." Nick takes the beer, quietly laughs, shakes his head, and clinks bottles, the two men framed reaching across the screen to each other, as they have had to reach across so much in their very different lives. Adding to the emphasis, this is the last shot of the episode.

Monroe has had his own sort of Campbellian hero's steps of reluctance followed by heroic deeds. Now Monroe and Nick are fully partners, just as are Nick and Hank; but Hank is the normal person and Monroe is the liminal one—"never [...] a status quo kind of guy."

Monroe as Other/Hybrid

Monroe's liminality is apparent in his status as Other/Hybrid, the first of the liminal hero-sidekick qualities—a status made very clear in the opening episodes. In fact, the series soon raises the concept of liminality very directly. Asked about a Murcielago Wesen, Monroe declares, "It's a legendary liminal being" (1.20). When Nick asks what that means, Monroe gives an explanation that does not cover every aspect of liminality but fits the show's particular context: "Well, it's two distinct states of existence simultaneous within one physical body. The duality of humanity" (1.20). He might be describing himself. Every hybrid incorporates the Other, and almost all Wesen are hybrids. During the opening credits for the series, we always see Monroe's two faces, human and Wesen: he is Other, and he is us.

If we grant that Wesen symbolically represent racial/ethnic Others, then the character relationship between Nick and Monroe described in this chapter works against racist assumptions.[14] From the start, Monroe implies that Wesen are in the position of a persecuted minority. In the pilot, he refers to Grimms as "profiling" Wesen, suggesting racial profiling. Taber, while praising the Monroe character, argues that other than he, Wesen are presented as "completely masculine and villainous, [... or] feminized and dangerous [...] or obsequious" (16), with racist implications. This reading overlooks a number of examples of Wesen characters who do not fit Taber's descriptors. In the first season alone, there is the lawyer father bear of "Beeware," who at first tells Nick to talk to him through his law firm but later helps Nick to stop a dangerous ritual; there is the "angry young man" violin prodigy of "Danse Macabre," mentioned above (1.5); there is the bold, strong young African American Wesen boxer who teases the older Nick and Hank and ends up an innocent victim in "Last Grimm Standing" (1.12); there is the battered woman who bravely tries to escape, the canary-like Wesen in "The Thing with Feathers" (1.16); and there is the well-known reporter who also fights for the Resistance and is described by Monroe as a sort of "civil rights activist," indicating the minority status of Wesen (1.18). This last character is also the ex-boyfriend of the most important other Wesen who does not fit Taber's categories: Rosalee, a Wesen about whom this book includes a whole chapter. Each of these characters is humanized (if I may put it that way) while still representing a very human variety of natures—something that works against racist interpretations. At the same time, Wesen continue to be presented as an oppressed minority in their Otherness and hybridity. Of these symbolic Others, Monroe is the most noteworthy.

Even within the Wesen community, Monroe is a liminal character. He crosses lines of time: Monroe is both traditional (a history-loving clockmaker) and forward-thinking ("not a status quo kind of guy"). When Blutbad Monroe and Fuchsbau Rosalee decide to marry, Monroe's parents vehemently object, in a distinct echo of those who object to interracial marriage. As early as the first season (1.21), Monroe has expressed fear of having a cross burned in front of his home, and after their wedding, that is essentially what happens (4.6), accentuating the idea of racial line-crossing (see Introduction). Members of the Wesenrein hate group responsible for the burning device—a group whose members are other Wesen—wear hooded robes that evoke the KKK. Monroe also refers to Wesen as comparable to another persecuted minority, Jews. He speaks of "Wesen pogroms" in which whole Wesen villages were killed (2.10). In the fifth season, with another Nazi-like group, the episode "Wesen Nacht" clearly alludes to the "Kristallnacht" perpetrated against Jews. Displaying Nazi-like banners and insignia, the fourth-season Wesenrein group kidnap, badly beat, and try to kill Monroe. They call him "impure," both for his marriage and his choice to help the Grimm, Nick ("Tribunal" 4.10). Monroe defiantly tells them, "Nothing in life is pure. It's not supposed to be" (4.10). He is hybridity elevated to philosophy.

Monroe, Intellect, Eloquence, and Culture

Monroe's philosophical attitude aligns him firmly with the second quality of the liminal hero-sidekick. Monroe is often eloquent, and he is certainly intellectual and cultured. When Hap borrows an old school t-shirt, we learn that Monroe went to graduate school at the Ivy League Brown University (1.6), though we never learn his major. (Silas Weir Mitchell's major at Brown was religious studies [Turnquist].) He is still in touch with former professors (5.16). But Monroe's love of history and culture goes far beyond the walls of a traditional education. He casually references and dissects historical events—the Paris Réveillon Riots of 1789 (5.6), the German Peasants' War of 1525 (5.11), the first-century battle of Teutoburg Forest (5.7). We see him having fallen asleep while reading *The Decline and Fall of the Roman Empire* (with an apt cover illustration of a huge wolf suckling Romulus and Remus) (1.21)—one of many touches of set decoration and props that add to the characterization. From the first season, we also see that classical music is part of his life as he plays his cello (1.4); shortly before they are engaged, he offers to play for Rosalee a passage from, as he tells her, Rimsky Korsakoff's *Scheherazade* (3.10). He loves not only music but poetry. He references Robert Frost with a Grimm-appropriate twist: "The woods are lovely, dark and deep—and full of dead bodies of all sorts" (6.9). With no twist at all, he touchingly recites lines from Yeats's "When You Are Old" to Rosalee (6.10). He refers to classical gods as if they are old friends— "Good old Dionysus—god of wine and orgies" (6.5). He has a living, loving knowledge of the Western cultural world.

Monroe's cultured love of poetry connects to a broader pleasure in language. He knows more than one language; he often helps Nick by translating German entries in the Grimm books in the trailer, and when Nick decides he must go to Germany to solve the mystery of the Grimms' medieval keys, Monroe is the one member of the group who accompanies him, at least in part because, as he says, "Ich spreche Deutsch, man" (5.11). He is interested in etymology, as his discourse on "waiting for the other shoe to drop" shows—no surprise, given his interest in history (6.4). But he is also sensitive to the construction of language. When Nick and his friends encounter a baffling prophecy written in an unknown language (or languages), Monroe explains its bizarre complexity by saying that it "appears to be alphabetic, logographic, symbolic, syllabic—I mean, we'd need our own Rosetta stone to crack this mess" (6.6). And there are very few characters who, when fighting off a zombie horde, would say, "One hopes they'll move" (3.1).

One might think that this display of intellect could not cohabit with pleasure, but Monroe's word-consciousness results in both plenitude and play. He seems to enjoy the richness and variety of language. When he first sees Nick and Adalind's new home, he says, "I think it's kinda homey ... in a kinda post-apocalyptic, neo-industrial, steampunk chic kinda way" (5.10). His use of "kinda" makes informal what would otherwise be a rather elevated phrasing, and Silas Weir Mitchell lingers over Monroe's enjoyable choice of each new adjective. Asked in the final episode whether a book passage refers to their nemesis, Zerstorer (the Destroyer), Monroe explains, "No, it's more generically in reference to unstoppable evil Zerstorer-like dark forces of the universe that precipitate apocalyptic events" (6.13); Monroe, whose family roots are in Germany, has a Germanic willingness to suspend the sense of a sentence. In trying to describe the odor emitted by a set of pubescent Wesen boys, he says the smell is "like a pungent, vinegarish— hmmm—glandular, musky, yeah—kind of like a chamber pot" (4.7). In the same episode he notes that the boys are linked to the Bruma—"that's Latin for winter solstice. How do I know that? [he asks himself]. I don't know."

Monroe does know, however, how to play with language. He enjoys changing the part-of-speech function of a word. When the recovering amnesiac Juliette tells Monroe she has been seeing ghostly images of Nick all around her, Monroe tells him, "I think she's kinda Nicked out" (2.17). When Nick is furiously jealous, Monroe warns that the Grimm "can't be going off half-, full-, or any other degree of cocked," with suggestions of both guns and sex hovering behind the words (2.13). When Monroe and Rosalee try to help Juliette and Renard fight off the effects of a spell that tortures them with unwanted sexual desire, Monroe explains that they are going to attempt to "reverse the pheromoniacal behavior," neatly combining the pheromones and the maniacal results (2.14). Greenwalt and Kouf's earlier writing associate Joss Whedon is famed for the playfulness of "Slayerspeak," and a similar sort of play can be seen here.[15] Greenwalt has said that Monroe is the easiest character to write for (Fahy 84). Monroe's linguistic skills demonstrate a kind of power.

But Monroe is noteworthy in using liminal language as well, with a marked mixture of formal and informal vocabulary. It is not the mixture of someone who does not recognize levels of formality, but rather a dancing, ludic movement by someone who enjoys crossing lines. For example, trying to comfort the tormented Rheinigen teen violin prodigy, Monroe says, "You were kicking some butt on that Brahms concerto, man—it was brilliantly executed—very fluid" ("Danse Macabre," 1.5). The brilliant execution argues with the butt-kicking—linguistically speaking. When Nick's girlfriend Juliette is abducted by a dragon-like Wesen, he says that Nick is going on a "quest—your princess has been taken by the dragon.... It is the ancient archetype of the whole relationship megillah" ("Plumed Serpent" 1.14). Archetypes, quest—and, yes, the relationship megillah. Monroe's peroration on liminality, mentioned earlier, moves from "the duality of humanity" to "the yin and the yang, the [pause] Ike and Tina Turner of it all" (1.20). Silas Weir Mitchell's pause in the delivery lets us take that enjoyable linguistic leap with him. Claudia Schwabe, in the *Channeling Wonder* collection, calls him "charmingly humorous" (306), and Monroe's *Grimm* sayings are listed online (Turnquist). When Monroe tells Juliette that "the dark does have its bright side," he is, in the moment, trying to comfort her in her frustrating lack of knowledge about Nick's world. But he also is playing with paradox in a way that perfectly expresses his own liminal nature (2.12). This power of expression is one of the great markers of the liminal hero-sidekick.

Monroe as Deceptively Strong

Despite the fact that he is a vegan and a cellist, Monroe is also deceptively strong. As he says to Nick in the pilot, he is "not that big," though he, like Spock, is taller than the central male of the series. Still, Monroe is hardly muscle-bound. But when in the second episode Nick asks Monroe to guard the hospitalized Aunt Marie, Monroe accidentally rips an attacker's arm off. The men who plan to assassinate Marie are human thugs, but when Monroe's presence drives them away from her and he follows them to the hospital basement, the two thugs attack him first, punching him and then kicking him when he is down. In response, Monroe slams one thug into the ceiling. The next is pulling a gun on him when Monroe jerks the gun arm off. In a Monroevian understatement, Silas Weir Mitchell stops for a moment to say, "Okay, that went a little too far" (1.2). Later in the episode we are shown the armless man on a gurney with an ice chest following behind, presumably containing the severed limb; in the next episode, Monroe asks Nick if they have managed to re-attach the arm. We are thus assured that Monroe has not killed. With the viciousness of the thugs' attack and Monroe's reactions, the producers seem trying to moderate the impact of the violence. But the evidence of his physical strength is indelible.

The series as a whole makes it clear that Blutbaden are among the most feared Wesen (see, e.g., 2.17, where merely the word "Blutbad!" is a fearsome warning). From time to time, Monroe's eyes turn red with the threat of violence—when arguing with ex-girlfriend Angelina (2.6), when Blutbad friends are being murdered (3.3), and especially when someone threatens Rosalee (e.g., 2.17, 3.16, 5.21–22). In a confrontation over a trunk full of Grimm books, he even kills the two men who murdered his Uncle Felix (5.10). Monroe in this instance is "Nature red in tooth and claw": We see his mouth bloodied after the kill. His normal behavior is a gentleness that he must choose again and again. His appurtenances—his Mr. Rogers sweaters, his modest VW bug—illustrate that choice. But when Nick has to fight the legendary Wild Huntsmen, Nick calls on Monroe—and Monroe suggests leaving Hank, the normal, at home (3.12, 3.13). When apocalypse threatens and Nick goes through the mirror to fight in another world, Rosalee persuades Monroe not to follow by saying they cannot lose both of them (6.11). From beginning to end, Monroe—like Spock and Spike and to a lesser degree Illya Kuryakin—can unleash physical violence. His physical strength is always there, but his choice not to depend on it makes him stronger.

Monroe and Emotional Depths (to the Death)

Monroe unquestionably has emotional depths as well; however, his depths are even less hidden than Spike's. It is true that when his beloved Rosalee is threatened, his eyes turn red with fury, but it is also not unusual to see tears in Monroe's eyes, whether because of love (4.10), death (5.10), or beauty (1.8). In his earliest appearances, Monroe seems charming but relatively detached emotionally. As his relationship with Nick grows—as described earlier in this chapter—so does the evidence of his deep emotions. His connection to Rosalee makes even more apparent just how much Monroe can care.

Evidence of this depth of feeling appears in Monroe's choice to endure death—like Spock and Spike before him. Their death and rebirth fits part of the pattern of the Campbellian hero's journey and is one of the reasons that these characters are liminal in the sense of being on the line between heroes and sidekicks. Spock's death is well-known to fans and scholars of popular culture: He sacrifices himself to save the ship (in effect, his family—especially Jim Kirk) in *The Wrath of Khan* (1982) and is reborn in the sequel film. Spike's death is also fairly well-known: He sacrifices himself in the series finale of *Buffy the Vampire Slayer* to save the world (especially Buffy) and returns in the next season of the spin-off series *Angel*. In each case, the return was at least in part extradiegetically motivated by the character's and actor's popularity. By the same token, the importance of the character is a reason to write the heroic death in the first place.

Monroe's death-and-return occurs within the space of one episode (as opposed to the sequel-straddling paths of Spock and Spike), but it unquestionably shows the character's emotional depths and (as with the other liminal hero-sidekicks) bravery. In the second season's very pertinently named "Over My Dead Body" (2.6), when Monroe's ex-girlfriend Angelina kills a contract killer who is trying to rape her, his employers force her to take over his job—only to discover that the target is Monroe. Those who hired the killer did so to use Monroe as an example, to send a message that Wesen should not cooperate with the Grimm. (If Monroe is a reformed Blutbad, Nick is a comparable Grimm—one who does not kill just because someone is Wesen, is Other—symbolically, one who does not kill because of race.) Those who represent the status quo do not want this sort of change, this sort of crossing of lines. Monroe conceives of a plan—with the strained cooperation of Angelina, Nick, and Hank—to convince the villains that he is dead. He asks the apothecary Rosalee—whom he has just started dating—to tell him how to concoct a mixture for a "dead faint." In it, he will not just appear but will be, to all intents and purposes, temporarily dead. Rosalee balks, warning that it is only too easy to permanently die from this concoction. But Monroe insists, making his motivation clear: He know these killers will come after all of Nick's friends in turn, including her. As he says this to her over the phone, the director includes a reaction shot for Angelina (Jaime Ray Newman), looking at him with the realization of how much Rosalee means to him: He is willing to die for her. He is also re-affirming his life-risking choice to work with Nick. Angelina will, later in the episode, give her life for Monroe, blocking a bullet meant for him, her last words—or word—a wonderfully unsentimental "Damn."[16] As she blocks the bullet,

Monroe leaps on the shooter, killing her killer. Here, as earlier in the episode, when Monroe literally lays his life down, surrendering to the "dead faint" on the narrow bed in the back of the apothecary shop, he acts out of love, his own possible last words used to reassure his friends as his consciousness fades. His difficult return (as Campbell calls it) is not as long as Spock's or Spike's but is marked not only by battle with villains but also by the loss of someone dear to him, a loss revisited in memory as the series proceeds (2.7, 4.13). The story of Monroe's death and return, then, provides a particularly intense demonstration of the depth of his feelings.

Monroe and Gender Liminality

As is the case for earlier hero-sidekick exemplars, emotion relates to the traditional markings of gender and, in the case of the more tender feelings, suggests the character's gender liminality. Monroe evinces many characteristics stereotypically seen as feminine. He is called "little Miss Monroe" for avoiding killing (4.19). He is normally associated with his domestic space, where Nick visits him; as a watch repairman—a job requiring delicacy of touch—he works there too. All the other male regulars work at a police station, so Monroe's domestic centering is the more noticeable. He is also, though not a chef, an exceptionally good domestic gourmet cook. In more than one episode, we are shown parallel scenes in which Monroe and Nick's girlfriend Juliette are cooking, and indeed, in one episode, they are both cooking for Nick: Monroe learns to his dismay that Nick is not coming for dinner as planned (2.20). This dinner plan occurs while Nick is actually living with Monroe, having earlier moved out of his home with Juliette. Monroe sometimes acts as if he is Nick's neglected girlfriend; on one occasion when the two are having dinner alone, Monroe asks, "What's my favorite color?" (1.10). Monroe has absolutely no embarrassment about the fact that his home is tidy and full of delicate possessions, including many antique clocks. We have seen him wearing rubber gloves, carrying a plastic bucket, and mopping up by hand (1.6).[17]

Of course, Monroe is mopping up the blood of a friend after Monroe left the friend unguarded to pursue a wild night with an old love—Angelina. Like Spike, Monroe moves back and forth in terms of both gender and sexual stance. In the series' fourth episode, mentioned earlier, Nick has asked Monroe to observe a pheromone-controlling Siegevolk Wesen in a bar, who is entrapping young women. As the Siegevolk enthralls a young woman, we see Silas Weir Mitchell smile nearby and drop his head atilt into his hand, equally entranced. Leaving the bar, he reports to Nick: "Dude, I can't be around that guy—he's way too potent. I almost bought him a drink" (1.4). Monroe is sometimes identified as Nick's partner—a secret partner, as if in a gay relationship of a few years back. Late in the first season, as they discuss the possibility of Monroe's accepting a dinner invitation from Juliette, Nick's sexual partner for the first three and a half seasons, Nick demurs: "Monroe, name one aspect of our relationship that we wouldn't have to lie about." And Monroe answers: "You're right—all the time we spend together—all the sneaking around—God, it suddenly just seems so wrong" (1.19). The conversation could be read as code for a gay couple—not that the series ever suggests that the two are actually in a sexual relationship; but *Grimm* is dense with symbols, constructed of code. The threshold-crashing scenes discussed earlier could be read as part of a long tradition of tales of sexual thresholds (such as for vampires—who do not, interestingly enough, appear in *Grimm*). It should be recalled that the paired threshold-crashing scenes suggest an equality, a give-and-take, in this relationship that is comforting to consider if we see Monroe as a character who plays with and stretches gender roles.

Monroe's father at one point says he thought that Monroe would never marry—a way of saying, in another time, that a man could be gay. Of course, his father says this during a phone call in which Monroe announces his engagement to marry Rosalee. Monroe's relationship with Rosalee is an impressively healthy, believable, slowly growing depiction of adult love. But its centrality to their story does mean that in the later years of the series, Monroe is less liminal sexually. He does, however, still exhibit elements of gender liminality. The Blutbad is still a clockmaker and cook; he still gets teary-eyed when his feelings are touched.

Conclusion: For the Time

There is much more that could be said about these liminal hero-sidekicks. One should note that none of the powerfully popular characters listed here is female, and it would be worth examining a parallel tradition in another standard gender (Willow? Starbuck?). One should also acknowledge that in the hands of lesser actors, these roles might have gone unnoticed: David McCallum (who, in his eighties, is now racking up fan mail as Ducky on *N.C.I.S.* [2003–]), Leonard Nimoy, James Marsters, and Silas Weir Mitchell are all extraordinary. Nevertheless, I would argue that the traits of the characters they were given—intelligent, culturally aware, eloquent, secretly strong, emotional, gender-bending and pleasurably Other—these character traits are essential to our attraction. What I would like to know is why we still seem to feel that they need to be the heroic sidekicks, rather than simply the heroes, of the story.[18]

Two

"I don't have a problem with it"

Killing, Sex, and the African American Cop—Hank

"If it's accepted that the black best friend is a stereotype, is a perpetuation of the marginalization of people of color in film, then it's something I don't want to be part of." So says David Oyelowo, the star who represented Martin Luther King, Jr., in the film *Selma*, in a 2019 interview. *Grimm*'s white male hero Nick Burkhardt acknowledges the wolf-like clockmaker Monroe as his "other partner" (1.15), but Detective Hank Griffin is his primary partner and his friend.[1] The actor who plays him, Russell Hornsby, has second billing in the series. He is one of two persons of color among the original six regular cast members. The role of the supportive African American buddy has been part of American television since *I Spy* (1965–68), but the character of Hank differs from the typical best friend, sidekick pattern in notable ways. While, as Donald Bogle and others have shown, African American males are sometimes categorized as either violent or tame, oversexed or neutered, Hank Griffin disrupts those categories. In the pilot episode, it is he, not Nick, who shoots and kills the child-stealing monster in the climax. While the character of Adalind Schade ends up having a child and making a home with Nick, Hank has sex with her first, in the first season of the series. Hank often makes sharp observations that help solve cases. He is the first non-supernatural character to be ushered into the secrets of Nick's world. All of these qualities present him as a figure of power. However, he is also presented as a character who has failed at love: he has been married and divorced repeatedly, and the two multi-episode relationships we see him engaged in during the series are both undertaken by his sexual partners for ulterior motives. The fact that the women's motives are to use Hank to get to Nick means that Hank is diminished, though the situation of this person seeking romantic love also presents a humanizing weakness. As a partner, Hank is never weak—in fact, he displays a rather dismaying willingness to shoot first and ask questions later. Hank's ultimate understanding of the supernatural world represents an acceptance of diversity, yet his methods as a cop should give us pause. Is this assimilation into a white-dominated institution? As Stacey Abbott and Lorna Jowett note in *TV Horror*, "the seriality of TV lends itself to moral complexity" (n.p.). Embedded in a narrative structure with some troubling implications for racial politics, Russell Hornsby's six-year turn as Hank Griffin provides a memorable performance of human complexity.

As the introduction to this book discusses, like many horror and fantasy fictions, *Grimm* operates on multiple levels. On the surface level of overt representation, one might note that the significant lack of diversity in the demographics of the city of Portland, where the series was produced, suggests that the producers' efforts at diversity of casting are laudable (especially in contrast with the casts of many police procedurals): The U.S. Census of 2010 (the series first broadcast in 2011) reported only 5.8 percent of the city's population was African American.[2] Other levels of meaning imply a more complicated picture. David Greenwalt says that the use of "metaphor" is purposeful (Fahy 86), comparable to his work as showrunner for the horror/detective series *Angel* (1999–2004). In the *Grimm* pilot, Nick comes into powers that enable him to see that some people, Wesen, have something like a beast within. Specific species of Wesen are connected to specific moral qualities, a troubling narrative pattern comparable to what Jeannette Covington describes as "assigning some black-specific trait (e.g., heightened disputatiousness, racial self-hatred, displaced aggression) to explain assaults and homicides" (157). Nick starts the series by just such illogical racial profiling. Immediately, however, Nick learns that he is mistaken to assume that because one is Wesen, one is bad: he wrongly accuses Monroe, who turns out to be not the big bad wolf who plans to eat the little girl, but instead a cello-playing vegetarian. Throughout the series, Wesen represent people who suffer the effects of racism. Nick's, and later Hank's, close relationships with Monroe and Rosalee, among others, symbolically show resistance to prejudice (as do Monroe's and Rosalee's relationships with Nick, since Grimms are traditionally hunters of Wesen). Yet at the same time, the story dismayingly presents a cop who is supposed to be justified when he kills, because he has the power to see who deserves to die.[3] There is thus a sharp dichotomy in the subtext. And into this dichotomy walks the character of Hank Griffin.

Officers of (Outside) the Law

Stephen M. Zimmerly, in *The Sidekick Comes of Age*, observes that there are many "memorable detective sidekicks" (16). Yet, in defining the characteristics of the sidekick, Ron Buchanan notes that such a character typically "does not solve the mystery or contribute significant clues" (17). From the beginning, however, Hank Griffin is presented as an astute detective—more than just a sidekick. While as a Grimm, Nick Burkhardt has hidden supernatural powers, nonetheless in the world of the police, Hank and Nick are equals. In the pilot, there is a murder followed by an abduction. When they are searching for the abducted little girl, Nick says they should follow the child's route as described by the mother instead of looking at a shortcut through the park. But Hank responds, "Yeah, kids always do what their mothers tell'em to do. I know *I* did." Hank thus leads them to her backpack and clues regarding her kidnapping—clues that ultimately show the murderer and kidnapper to be the same person. Near the end of the pilot, Hank recognizes that the person they have been questioning in his home has been humming the song ("Sweet Dreams") that a murder victim had been listening to as she jogged, and so he and Nick turn back to find the abducted girl. Hank's role in her rescue is far greater than that of the usual sidekick/friend. When evidence of another missing child surfaces after many years, Hank goes through box after box of files and discovers a flaw in the alibi of a man who turns out to be the criminal (1.7). After Hank learns of the Wesen world (2.3), he reviews a capital case from his early days on the force for which he was the arresting officer and uses a warrant for failure to do jury duty as a way to enter the real killer's home, revealing a collection of cannibalized bones (2.11). He discovers that Wesen victims of a peculiarly ghastly stomach-exploding death ate at the same poison-dispensing restaurant (though Nick had cast doubts on the suggestion) (3.3). When a Jack-the-Ripper-like killer answers their police captain's phone, Hank is the one who notes his use of the word "we" and leads to the discovery that the captain has been possessed (4.21). In an episode in which Nick says that the suspects are the wrong kind of Wesen, according to a photo taken during the attack, Hank points out—rightly—that it could have been a Wesen for hire (5.8). After a phone tip that leads to the captain's killing of an assassin, Hank is the one who realizes that it was a set-up (5.12). In virtually every episode, there is a scene in which we see Hank and Nick at the precinct, their desks perpendicular to each other, as the two detectives toss theories back and forth while they research at their computers. In *Where No Black Woman Has Gone Before*, Diana Adesole Mafe writes of the importance of the "subtle difference between a hero-sidekick pairing and a buddy pairing" (127), a difference that can be recognized here. As cops, Hank and Nick are fully partners.

But Hank also is a partner in the troubling extralegal aspects of their work, and in most cases, he "[doesn't] have a problem with it" (3.10). Questions of shooting outside the lines come up long before Hank knows about Nick's powers. In the pilot episode, Nick and his aunt (and adoptive mother) are attacked on the street by a Reaper, a scythe-wielding Wesen whom Nick shoots in self-defense (and aunt-defense). That killing is at the heart of the long-term through-story of the series. But the episode's central mystery of the killer who stalks girls in red hoodies is finally resolved through a shooting done by Hank, in a disturbing way. Nick has found the home of the killer with Monroe's help. After Monroe has left and Nick phones Hank to come to the scene, they question the mild-mannered postman killer (who has a disturbing collection of Hummel figurines)[4] and find no evidence. It is only after they have left his cabin in the woods that Hank comes to a standstill, realizing that he had heard the postman humming the song from the dead girl's MP3 player. On this slim hint alone, Hank and Nick burst back into the home, which now has its lights out. In the dark, the homeowner leaps on them; they fight, and he runs out into the night. Hank shouts, "Hold it," and, without pausing, shoots the fleeing man in the back. While Nick and viewers know that this is a monster, Hank does not have that certainty. The fact that he, not Nick, shoots means that Nick's hands are clean; the violence is displaced from the white cop hero onto the Black cop partner. In fact, in the first several episodes there are surprisingly few times that Nick kills. Hank's kill places him in a position of power—far from the typical Black best friend, sidekick stereotype. However, it also implicates him in a highly questionable police shooting—one for which he (not surprisingly) is never taken to task in this story world—any more than he probably would have been in the real world.

Ta-Nehisi Coates, in his remembrance of the unjustified police killing of a college friend, reveals after many pages that the killer was a Black police officer, pointing to the racism in the social structure, the structure of power (83). In terms of the psychology of the presentation of the character, Hank, like Nick (who shot the Reaper), is a figure of power and in that sense a racially positive representation—something still useful in this culture. For as Krista Ratcliffe says, "*race*, which is a fictional category, [is] possessed of all-too-realistic consequences. It has no scientific grounding but functions with tremendous ideological force" (13).[5] Hank, not Nick, is the character who kills the clear villain in the climax—the Big Bad Wolf, no less—in the introductory narrative for the series. If, however, viewers take the Wesen villain to represent the racial other, then the social symbolism is problematic. This can be seen as an aspect of what Derrick Bell termed, decades ago, "interest convergence" (523–24): The Black cop is assimilated into the white-dominated police force because it benefits that force as much as, if not more than, it benefits Hank. Hank in this shooting in the pilot is part of a structure that, from one view, protects innocent little girls; from another, condones shooting, with virtually no warning, of a suspect whom the police officer assumes (correctly, *of course*) to be the killer. There is a dizzying carousel of social implications, and it is difficult to know where to stop the wheel.

Again and again Hank participates in extralegal acts—some connected with his knowledge of the Wesen world and some not; some violent and some not. In the first season, Nick is nearly killed by an ogre-like Wesen, and Hank tells the hospitalized Nick that, many years ago, he purposely "lost" video evidence that could have provided an alibi for the criminal, asserting that the criminal arranged for a rough lookalike to provide the alibi. The criminal (whose guilt is established during the episode) is now killing those involved in his sentencing—the judge, the jury foreman, the district attorney—and Hank, as arresting officer, would be next. We learn furthermore that the district attorney participated with Hank in suppressing the video evidence; thus there is a conspiracy within the system by two of its members, who act extralegally based on their belief in their own judgment of the guilt of the accused (1.8). Hank's confession to Nick is an act of trust between partners and friends; however, it also, in effect, draws Nick within the "blue line" of police secrecy. Hank expresses guilt for his actions and determines to face the killer alone as a kind of atonement; in that sense, the series recognizes the problematic nature of his suppressing the evidence. The inevitably expanding consequences appear when the hospitalized Nick sends Monroe to follow Hank with an ogre gun (like an elephant gun), since of course the unwitting Hank cannot successfully take on an ogre alone. As a result, Monroe is drawn into the conspiracy when he has to (from a distance, unseen by Hank) shoot the ogre to save the detective. On the one hand, the well-intentioned Hank is saved; on the other, the extralegality spreads both secrecy and violence.

Hank does participate in many non-violent instances of extralegality. In "La Llorona" (2.9), a Halloween ghost story, Nick and Hank sneak out of custody an ex-police officer from Albuquerque, Valentina Espinosa, who has been arrested for impersonating an officer, having lost her job over her obsession with the ghost that killed her nephew. (It is worth noting that *Grimm*, having no regular Latinx character, features many in guest roles.[6]) With her help, they save the lives of three children. A late episode called "Blood Magic" (6.10) shows Hank, Nick, and Sergeant Wu condoning secret euthanasia committed by a Wesen doctor who specializes in helping to a peaceful death Wesen who are troubled by dementia—and thus unable to restrain themselves from harming others. An allusion to a well-known film about the way the system works legally—*Twelve Angry Men*—comes in the title of another episode about extralegality, titled "One Angry Fuchsbau" (the fuchsbau in question being Rosalee, 2.17). A Wesen whose pheromones enable him to both date-rape young women and enthrall jury members is the lawyer for a wife-killing Wesen when Rosalee serves as foreperson of the jury. When they realize what the lawyer is doing, Rosalee, Monroe, fellow Wesen Bud Wurstner (Danny Bruno), Nick, and Hank work together to interrupt the lawyer's latest attempt at date-rape and disempower his pheromonic influence over the jury. Monroe, in Blutbad form, frightens the lawyer as he is walking an enthralled woman back to his place; Bud "rescues" him and lends then retrieves the handkerchief that catches his sweat; Rosalee brews the apothecary's concoction that will undo the pheromones emanating from his sweat gland; Hank and Nick distract the lawyer with a never-to-be-reported police interview; and Monroe injects Rosalee's concoction into a toad which the Wesen lawyer then eats, disabling his evil powers and thus allowing the killer to be convicted. The episode as a whole is a humorous romp, with satisfying justice against wife-killers and date-rapists. It is one of many episodes, however, in which the characters, and possibly the viewers, become inured to the idea of taking justice into one's own hands—even when the hands belong to the police. Hank is unquestionably part of this pattern of action.

A variation of the pattern is one that involves the protagonists' judgment of certain characters, deciding to protect them from prosecution. In "Nobody Knows the Trubel I've Seen" (3.19), Nick, Monroe, and Hank encounter Theresa Rubel (Trubel), a violent young woman who fears she may be insane, but whom they discover to be an untutored Grimm. They protect her from a murder charge because they know she acted in self-defense against a powerful Wesen that others would have seen only as a young woman. In "The Taming of the Wu" (5.19), Sergeant Wu has unknowingly become infected with a virus that causes him to shift into a dangerous creature who kills a Wesen who attacks him. Hank and Nick hear the story and decide that Wu was acting in self-defense and that because the circumstances are inexplicable, they will not report his involvement in the death. In "PTZD" (3.2), the captain's brother Prince Eric has engaged Baron Samedi to turn Nick into a murderous, raging zombie. When he bare-handedly kills someone who attempts to knife him in a bar, Nick—upon returning to his normal state—wants to turn himself in. But by then his friends have lied to cover for him, and it is Hank who most emphatically dissuades Nick from presenting himself for legal justice. In each of these cases, it seems justice is being done, that the killing was justifiable. But also, in each of these cases (and more), Hank the cop joins in an extralegal decision to act as judge and jury.

Even more drastic are those cases in which the friends combine to kill. In "Over My Dead Body" (2.6), Hank has just learned of the nature of Wesen, and there is a charming scene (excerpted as a YouTube video) in which he and Monroe drink and Monroe shows him versions of the *woge*, the transformation. This bonding experience seems to be one reason that Hank, later in the episode, agrees to work off the books with murder suspect Angelina, Monroe's ex-lover and fellow Blutbad, in finding out who has put out a contract to kill Monroe. In the climax of the episode, Angelina, Monroe, Nick, and Hank fight the contract killer thugs. Nick chases and fights a Königschlange, a snake creature who was part of the plot against Monroe. We see Nick attacked by a monstrous snake; but Hank sees only a man, and only after he shoots does he ask if the man was Wesen. In this case, he has seen a man pull a gun on his partner, but the partners have already agreed that this interchange is "off the books"; they will not report the death. "Cry Havoc" (4.22)—from Hamlet's "Cry havoc, and let slip the dogs of war"—has the friends, again specifically disavowing their police status for the occasion, attacking a royal stronghold after the murder of Nick's mother and abduction of Adalind's child; they leave as many bloody bodies as are found on the stage at the end of Shakespeare's play. "Tribunal" (4.10) presents a Wesen hate group that is a cross between the KKK and the Nazis, a group which has abducted Monroe to kill him for marrying outside his "race." The friends rescue Monroe just in time, but to do so, they savagely kill. From early in the series, Hank—unlike Nick—wears his badge, his shield, hanging from his neck, easy to see, perhaps because as a Black man it seems more necessary to him to secure and clarify his status (and protection?) as a cop. Without it, he is unshielded. Here Hank and Nick remove their badges before they attack, making the extralegal nature of their action clear.

In all of these instances (and more), Hank is a character of strength and power who aims for justice—but who is shown to be a police officer acting outside the law to achieve it. Thus *Grimm* in some ways follows the pattern for the typical television police procedural, which "normalizes the systemic violence and injustice meted out by police and prosecutors who engage in abuse, particularly against people of color. [...] [f]raming wrongful actions as relatable, forgivable, acceptable" (Evelyn).[7] The series sometimes moves past the typical, however, in problematizing the pattern. As, time and again, he and Nick search through the Grimm books in the trailer, Hank does express disapproval of the violent extralegal actions of Grimms of the past (e.g., 2.8, 3.15). More notably in relation to his role as a police officer, near the end of the fifth season, Hank is kidnapped by another Wesen group, Black Claw, revolutionaries who plan an extralegal death for Hank and taunt him with having caused extralegal deaths before. They plant dead bodies in his home—Wesen whom Nick has killed, and for whom they now arrest Hank. Thus the Black police officer gets blamed for what the white police officer has done. The arresting officers (secretly Black Claw) spirit Hank away, and he says, "So we're not doing this by the book." Detective Baribeau replies, "Not exactly. But I'm sure you're pretty familiar with that. [...] Your partner killed two of our people. You don't think there's consequences for something like that?" (5.21). The chickens, as Malcolm X said, have come home to roost. The Black cop who is complicit in this broad structure of police-covered extralegality faces the accusation of those who have often unfairly suffered, and thus the series raises the issue. It sinks under the surface again as Hank is rescued and the revolutionaries are shown to be indiscriminately violent against those not of their own kind. But some viewers may not forget. And some viewers may have already been pondering the problem.[8]

It is worth noting that, by the end of the series, Hank Griffin, despite his mythological last name, is the only one among the regular cast of characters who remains a normal human—not a Grimm or a Wesen or a Hexenbiest (or Zauberbiest) or any other kind of preternatural being.[9] Thus the African American cast member is the person who represents mainstream humanity. Hank is humanized in many ways—his bad jokes and good repartee, his love of a good drink, his repeatedly referenced hatred of rats—and his reactions to dead bodies. These reactions are perhaps the more significant, given the extralegal deaths in which he is implicated. While Nick is normally phlegmatic in the face of death, Hank winces, curses, and whistles.[10] In *Primetime Blues*, Donald Bogle remarks on the power that African American performers have used to deepen their characters (468), and Russell Hornsby manages to suggest that Hank never becomes hardened to the sight of death. His human status also means that Hank is, in some ways, the bravest of the characters: He faces fantastically empowered, dangerous beings without any extra powers of his own. In that sense, Hank might be called—for those who followed David Greenwalt from *Buffy* to *Angel* to *Grimm*—the Xander of the group. Furthermore, Hank Griffin has perhaps an even more distressing love life than that character.

Sex and the Single Hank

As Donald Bogle says in the fifth edition of *Toms, Coons, Mulattoes, Mammies, and Bucks*, there has long been a "tie between sex and racism in America" (10). Hank, however, fits neither of the extreme stereotypes Bogle describes, neither sexless (2–3) nor oversexed (10–11). In the pilot episode, we discover that he has been married at least three times,[11] and references to those marriages are scattered throughout other episodes as reminders.[12] We soon find out that his second ex-wife was an anthropologist (1.2) who, we later learn, dragged him to foreign films (6.6); in another episode, we see where he bought her engagement ring (1.13); we learn that he went to Hawaii on his first honeymoon (1.10), and in the second season he takes his unseen ex-wife Nadine on vacation there. One is left to wonder why Hank's marriages failed, though of course marriage to a police detective is not easy. Hank from time to time gives Nick what seems to be good advice about relationships. Nonetheless, the recurring comments about his marriages establish Hank as unquestionably not sexless. "Love's a funny thing," says Hank, and Nick responds, "Then you must be laughing all the time" (1.9).

More significant than the referenced relationships, however, are the relationships that are depicted onscreen. Throughout the first season, Hank is unaware of the Wesen world. One of its members is the Hexenbiest, Adalind Schade, with whom he has a sexual relationship. Adalind is a young blonde lawyer who is described as "very pretty" (2.3). The relationship between Hank and Adalind could be considered racially progressive. Furthermore, Adalind is not a minor character. Though she appears briefly in the pilot, her impact was soon clear, and she was made a regular in the second season. In that second season she has an affair and a child with Renard, and later she becomes the mother of Nick's child and eventually his significant other. When Hank learns in the third season that Adalind is pregnant, he is greatly relieved to learn the child is not his. "Who's the idiot father?" he asks, only to learn it is his captain (3.18). One might argue that these story elements place Hank on a sexual level with his boss and his friend, the series hero.

However, as Darnell M. Hunt says in *Channeling Blackness*, "meaning is relational" (2), and other elements of the relationship are more problematic. Adalind does not enter a relationship with Hank because of attraction to him; instead, she does it, as she declares in the episode "Love Sick" (1.17), for the prince that, at the time, she loves, Renard, and at the direction of her mother, all with the goal of controlling Nick by threatening the life of his partner Hank. At this point, neither Nick nor Hank knows that the captain is half Wesen, and he maintains his secret by acting through Adalind, though she will soon come to act for herself. In an earlier episode, the captain slips a vial of Hank's blood from a recent departmental physical to Adalind to use in a spell. Hank, who has helped to save Adalind's life in the series' third episode, eats her gift of potion-dosed cookies and falls under her magical power. In the scene when Adalind gives him the cookies, he has yet to be enthralled, and their playful interaction is a charming one. "Maybe I should have a bite," Hank says, as she offers him her basket full. "Maybe you should wait until I'm gone in case you don't like them," Adalind replies. "I'm a brave soul," says Hank, as he tastes (1.15). Sexuality and food are here, as so often, connected. But his later response is under her control. Russell Hornsby's consumption of his cookies with coffee the next morning is emphatically, slowly sensual. He soon begins to dream of her; in an ambiguous scene, we see him, shirtless, walk from his bed to the adjoining bathroom where Adalind seems to have mysteriously appeared in a misty shower. When he opens the shower door, only the mist is left.[13] The episode closes with an unnerving image of Adalind's disembodied, ghostly hand stroking the face of the sleeping Hank. It is an image of control of an unwitting subject. Each episode of *Grimm* starts with an epigraph. The epigraph for this episode is "Soon he was so in love with the witch's daughter that he could think of nothing else. He lived by the light of her eyes and did whatever she asked" (1.15). The epigraph makes Hank's storyline central, but it is a story of being controlled.

As Hank's enthrallment progresses, he behaves in even more disturbing ways. An unreal vision of Adalind distracts him during a mission with Nick, causing them to lose track of two killers. As the story proceeds, Hank essentially stalks Adalind, sitting in his car outside her apartment and watching her through a picture window. When he sees her date another man, he abuses his position—though Adalind has earlier said that, before the potion, Hank did not feel right about dating someone who has been part of one of his police cases (1.15). But post-potion Hank grabs Adalind's date Peter on his way out and tells him to leave and not come back. "I'm a cop. And I do not repeat myself," Hank threateningly tells Peter (1.16). The scene flips the more typical racial dynamics of such an exchange. It is a display of unethical power from Hank, someone who is in authority; however, Peter is, like Adalind, working for the captain and has planned to evoke Hank's anger—all part of the system of control. By the end of the episode, Adalind has told Hank she will date him (her intention all along), and the episode closes with a wordless visual of the two at a brightly lit windowside table in an upscale restaurant, laughing and touching until the restaurant turns out its neon sign, while "Season of the Witch" plays non-diegetically to remind us who is directing the action—not Hank.

Ultimately, Adalind is prepared to take not only Hank's body but his life in service of the captain, the representative of white male privilege. The captain tells her when to sleep with Hank and stands in the room while she calls Hank to invite him for dinner. There is a shot of Hank and Adalind smiling at each other over, symbolically enough, Adalind's threshold. Then there is a shot of a table with red flowers and red wine, the food uneaten; then we see Adalind, who had welcomed Hank earlier in a strapless black top, now in the black leather jacket and boots associated with toughness, striding from the bedroom and out of her home, leaving the door ajar for Nick to enter later (as he both literally and metaphorically will). When Nick, Monroe, and Rosalee arrive, they find Hank stretched out on the bed, comatose, the iris of his eyes the same red as the roses and the wine. It is only because Nick fights and defeats her, destroying her Hexenbiest power, that Hank emerges from the deadly spell brought about by sex with a beautiful white woman.

The African American cop Hank, then, is presented as a sexual being, but his sexuality involves him in peril. Furthermore, in this relationship he is presented as unable to control his desire. He is also made a tool of the patriarchal captain and rescued by the hero Nick. On the other hand, Adalind is clearly a villain at this stage of the story, though her character begins its arc of change here too (a story for another chapter). In terms of the psychology of the character, Hank is blameless; but he is also, in this particular context, powerless.

The other major sexual relationship for Hank begins in the third season. While much of the racial content in *Grimm* is symbolic, in the episode "Eyes of the Beholder," racial and other social issues are both overt and symbolic. By the time of this episode, Hank has learned about Wesen (2.3).[14] Before the revelation, he has had glimpses of Wesen and has, like Nick at first, thought himself to be going crazy. Russell Hornsby very effectively performs a scene in which Hank consults an African American woman police therapist (2.3). He recovers his psychological equilibrium, but his unwanted romantic solitude is made clear. We have seen him preparing a TV dinner in his comfortable but lonely bachelor home, with the self-addressed sarcasm, "Ahhh, the good life" (2.12). Late in the second season he has gone on vacation with ex-wife Nadine and torn his Achilles "zip-lining in Kauai" (2.20). In the same episode in which we hear of Nadine, Hank, on crutches, refers to "a date with physical therapy." The term "date" is foreshadowing, because Hank becomes romantically interested in his physical therapist, Zuri.

The relationship with Zuri as it appears in "Eyes of the Beholder" is significant in part because it does not start with any connection to Nick. It is only years later (in both diegetic and real time) that the connection to Nick transpires. Thus in this episode the character of Hank receives notable development. The episode also embeds racial and other social issues. Zuri and her teenage brother Jared are African American. This ameliorates, for Hank, the problem that Robyn Citizen notes, of characters being "isolated from other members of their racial community" (qtd. in Mafe 123). Zuri is played by Sharon Leal, a strong performer noted for her skill (Bogle, *Toms* 424, 446). The episode explores issues of relationships between Blacks and police, between Blacks and whites, implications of mass incarceration of Blacks,[15] and threats against Blacks by gangs. Its climax twists expectations in an emotionally powerful way.

Zuri is mentioned (though not by name) in the preceding season, but we first see her in the third season episode preceding "Eyes of the Beholder." Hank, shown in physical therapy, jokes with his therapist, "You know you put me through so much pain it kind of feels like we're married," and she responds, "That sounds like you've been married before." His affirmative reminds regular viewers of Hank's seemingly hopeful, if unsuccessful, marital history. The interchange leads to Hank suggesting a date, which Zuri, standing behind a counter, puts off by saying that she likes to keep things professional. Russell Hornsby, as he asks, leans forward, smiling, arms wide open towards the counter; when Sharon Leal looks away briefly as she realizes what he is saying and offers her polite refusal, he immediately backs away physically, and his courteous words of understanding are belied by his facial expression, revealing a pained disappointment that longtime viewers presumably share. We later learn that Zuri's refusal is not based simply on professionalism or even lack of attraction to Hank, but a larger issue.

Near the beginning of the next episode, "Eyes of the Beholder," we see a young Black male teenager, Jared, in a diner, drawing a picture of the young, blonde, white waitress Joy, who is soon revealed to be his girlfriend. Thus an apparently positive interracial romance is casually established at the start of the episode. Jared has sneaked his sister's car out; as he heads home, he sees a mixed-race group of three attack an African American man and woman, diner customers, in the parking lot. All of them are gang members, we later learn, and during the attack we also learn they are Wesen. Jared yells a startled "Hey!" as if to interrupt the deadly fight. Then a Black gang member chases him, and Jared is seen racing out of the parking lot by a middle-aged white man, who reports part of the license plate to the cops sent to investigate the murder—Nick and Hank. Jared calls Joy to tell her what has happened, and she warns him against speaking to the police because of the murder victim's gang status. She indicates a socioeconomic class connection when she tells him, "You think they'll [police] be able to protect you? That's not how it works. Not in this neighborhood" (3.10).

When Hank and Nick follow up on information that the car is registered to a Tyler Z. Ellis, Hank and Zuri are both startled to see each other. She explains that she is Tyler; she goes by her middle name. With Sharon Leal delicately conveying her discomfort at having the police at her door, she allows them into her modest apartment, seemingly because of her acquaintance with Hank: Hank is not just an African American cop (whose interests might converge with the system), but someone she knows. Nick and Hank explain that they are investigating a murder from the location of which her car was seen speeding away. They learn that she lives with her teenage brother. She says he was home all night, but Nick points out that she had earlier said she was asleep and so could not know Jared's whereabouts. When Jared returns home to his sister's with bags of groceries, he drops the bags and runs at the sight of cops, and Nick and Hank give chase. The interaction between the innocent Black youth and the police is resonant, with Zuri following behind, held back by Hank while Nick tackles Jared to the ground. "Get off him! Get off him!" she shouts at Nick, and to her brother, "Jared, don't fight back! Don't lose your temper!" But to Hank, Zuri says, "Take your hands off me!" The scene seems meant to be fraught in terms of racial and police vs. civilian politics, and it is. It also, of course, clouds further a possible relationship between Zuri and Hank.

Taken to the precinct as a witness, Jared (Dalpre Grayer) almost weeps with fear at the idea of testifying. We learn that his only record of misbehavior is for running a stoplight as he escaped on the night of the murder. Hank and Nick also learn, however, that his father is in Oregon State Prison for life, for murder. With their mother dead, Zuri, as Hank says, "took on the responsibility of raising her brother." Thus the often disregarded extended costs of incarceration are illuminated.[16] Zuri takes her responsibilities seriously, and refuses to let her brother undertake the danger of testifying in a gang case, though Hank, apparently blinded by his determination to catch the murderers, seems to underestimate Zuri and Jared's concern: His identity as cop seems foremost in his mind. On the other hand, he has another concern: he points out that the "killer is still out there," and, indeed, two of the gang members attack Zuri and Jared at their home. It is only because Hank is on the phone with Zuri at the very moment of the attack, and because he has already memorized their address, that he is able to instantly order uniformed police to their home and save the brother and sister. In this moment, Hank—commanding a room full of uniformed cops and rescuing both Zuri and Jared—is a figure of power. This is in contrast to situations when a Black person has been unable to protect someone (as movingly described by Ta-Nehesi Coates, among others, 93–95, 143–45, and passim). Furthermore, earlier on the phone call, Hank has not abused his power; when Zuri asks if this is "a procedural call, or personal?" he answers, "whatever makes you more comfortable."

Under the circumstances, Zuri and Jared both agree to testify and are put in a safe house; Hank makes sure he is the officer with them. Once again, he does not pressure her sexually; instead, there is a friendly normality and a quasi-familial situation as she awakens to find Hank playing video games and joking with Jared. Zuri and Hank discuss their own youths, and Hank explains that his parents are "still alive, still together—still living in the same house I grew up in." His family's African American dream normality balances, in this narrative, the dead mother and incarcerated father of the Ellis household. When Zuri wonders whether she will be "enough" for Jared, Hank says, with a subtext of romantic longing effectively conveyed by Hornsby's face and vocal tone, "Well, when you have someone that loves you, that can get you through a lot of bad." He shows a version of what Hanif Abdurraqib, in *A Little Devil in America: Notes in Praise of Black Performance*, calls "the performance of softness" (251), which the writer connects to stretching the shape of genders ("trying to reach across the shallow expanse of gendered rigidity," 262).[17]

But when Jared learns that Joy is being held by the gangsters, the teen secretly leaves the temporary safe space. As he attempts to fight the gangsters for Joy's life, we learn that he is not only African American, but Wesen, as he shifts to his beast. Thus we know Zuri is Wesen too. It takes Hank, Nick, and—to their surprise—Zuri together to rescue Jared and the unwitting non–Wesen Joy, killing the three gangsters. And Nick agrees, at Hank's urging, to pretend Zuri was never there. Zuri is shocked to learn that Nick is a Grimm and that Hank knows about Wesen; she is, if anything, even more shocked that Nick, in his role of Grimm and cop, is willing to protect her, as Hank asserts. Thus the series presents a positive interaction between police and a person of intersectional minority status (Black, woman, single mother, Wesen),[18] but also acknowledges that this positive interaction is surprising.

In the aftermath, the question of romance emerges again. Zuri asks, "So you're ok with this?" She has apparently not wanted to date him because of the divide between Wesen and non–Wesen that represents the real world's racial divide. And Hank, explaining he has learned to adapt, says, "None of this changes the way that I feel about you." When she says, "It wouldn't work, Hank," he asks for a chance to prove her wrong, and "Take it slow, see what happens." He is making his case with a hopeful smile, taking her hand but not pressing her too hard. Though she says, "you are such a special man, Hank," she tells him that she can't. And when Hank says, "Zuri—I don't have a problem with it," she answers gently, in an unexpected reversal of status, "But I do." The pain of racial rejection is thus twisted onto the positive, progressive character who thought he was speaking from the position of presumed superior status—in parallel to a white position—and those who identify with Hank feel that pain.[19] The surprise might be even greater because of the relationship between Jared and Joy, which crosses both racial and Wesen lines. The emotional performances by Hornsby and Leal add to the power of this socially and psychologically complex moment. Hornsby makes Hank's walk down the hall from Zuri's apartment, as she watches, a very lonely one, though her face shows sympathy. The text warns us about presumption and shows us that, in many ways, racial and social experiences are not always what they are perceived to be.

There are more ways in which racism is confronted here. The generally accepted position that racism is wrong is maintained by most of the interactions of whites and Blacks in the series. However, there are those who feel (whether they announce it or not) that the "races" (that fictional categorization) are genuinely distinct in nature, not just treatment—and this belief is parallel to the differences between Wesen and non–Wesen (as well as differences among Wesen). Such a belief is strongly challenged when an admirable and sympathetic regular character like Hank is rejected on that basis. Perhaps the most straightforward interpretation of the story is that the main African American character is here suffering the effects of racism. But it comes at the audience in an unexpected way—ironically Black on Black racism; also, rejection of the supposedly more powerful "race" (Kehrseite, the non–Wesen) by the narratively subject race (Wesen). The twist, which shows as the twist of a knife in the gut for Hank, therefore has an emotional impact that echoes the racism of reality.

The third-season story of Zuri and Hank is such a meaningful one as it stands, that Zuri's return in the sixth season is unfortunately disappointing. At first it seems that she has re-entered Hank's life because of a chance encounter at a grocery store, and she has revised her view of relationships between Wesen and non–Wesen. She and Hank enter a sexual relationship, and they seem genuinely happy, though she spends considerable time asking Hank about "the Grimm." But we soon learn that she has joined Hank so that she can serve the secret revolutionary Wesen group Black Claw, which wants to control the world, decimate non–Wesen, and eradicate Grimms. Although the character of Zuri might arguably be involved in Black Claw, the seemingly genuine emotional respect earlier portrayed between Zuri and Hank is thus evacuated. It casts a shadow on the depth of feeling of the earlier encounter, which had seemed so poignant because it displayed disagreement between two people of integrity (though the audience's connection to Hank strongly implied Zuri's view to be wrong). With the new storyline, Hank's primary romantic relationship has become more about Nick than Hank.[20]

Conclusion: In Praise of Nuance

There is much more to the character of Hank; his role as an African American assimilated into the police world is at least as complex as his romantic status. His intelligence and skill as a cop and his witty use of language are effectively portrayed by Russell Hornsby, who studied acting at both Boston University and Oxford, and performed with Denzel Washington in *Fences* (2016). (He tosses off a Shakespearean speech, one of Hotspur's, during a bit of footage preserved in a gag reel.)[21] The strength of his portrayal is such that Hornsby was cast as the lead actor in *Lincoln Rhyme: The Hunt for the Bone Collector* (2020–), an NBC series based on the Denzel Washington role in *The Bone Collector* (1999). Hornsby's widely praised role as the father in the film *The Hate U Give* (2018) addresses racial injustice directly, but his character's representation in *Grimm* is important too. And in the context of his Blackness, Hank's gender and sexuality are presented with a nuanced subtlety that should be accorded more often to Black male characters. While the symbolism implicit in the narrative structure of *Grimm* is sometimes problematic, the psychology of the character Hank Griffin, as incarnated in Russell Hornsby, is compelling. The long-term form of television has perhaps offered the opportunity to make the best friend less of a simple stereotype than the film version David Oyelowo deplores. For those who choose to watch a series with a white male lead,[22] the *Grimm* character of Hank Griffin is much more than a stereotype.

Three

"I'm in control"

*Sergeant Wu, Wit,
and Sexual Ambiguity*

The character of Sergeant Drew Wu was not part of the original plan for *Grimm*. But when Reggie Lee tried out for the role of Nick Burkhardt's partner, Detective Hank Griffin, the producers were so impressed that they decided to create a character for the actor.[1] Reggie Lee (born Reggie Telmo Valdez) identifies as Filipino Chinese American and is thus the only Asian American regular on the show (one of two actors of color among the original six). Of his earlier work in *The Fast and the Furious* (2001), Lee comments, "I got to be the leader of a gang. And then I got to be the leader of a gang again—and again—and again. […] Then *Grimm* came, and this thing where I got to be a human being that wasn't bad, and it was wonderful" (Kade). Wu's character is part of the resistance to the sometimes racially troubling narrative symbolism of the series,[2] a resistance that is imperfect but important. Lee's Sergeant Wu is shorter and slighter of stature than all the other male regulars. In addition, his character is presented as lower in rank than the three other male regular characters who portray police officers. He is also the last among the regulars to learn about the supernatural world of Wesen. Nonetheless, Lee portrays a strong and relatable character, one that grows more powerful as the series advances—both diegetically and in terms of overall impact. Given an opportunity to comment on the series as a whole for a Season Six DVD featurette, regular Bree Turner said, "I love any episode where Reggie gets to shine, 'cause he's such a good actor, and so committed" ("A Grimm Farewell"). The character is created as much by Lee's intense acting as the writers' and directors' contributions. In a 2016 DragonCon panel, a comment on the character's importance was met with audience-wide chants of "Wu! Wu! Wu!" ("Grimm: Lowen"). A major element of the strength of the character is his dry humor. His verbal wit is pervasive; hardly an episode lacks a Wu drollery. Wu is not a figure of fun in the sense that he is an object of derision. On the contrary, the humor strengthens the character because he is the source of it; he controls it. Wu's humor seems to be part of a cop's or a soldier's emotional defense against violence; it also subtly recognizes systemic wrongs. His intelligence appears not only in his wit, but also his police work. His bravery leads him into danger. Eventually, because of one such dangerous adventure, he enters into preternatural powers of his own, which he learns to control through a fierce exertion of will. In fact, Wu becomes angry at himself when he fails to control himself. At one point he believes he is mentally ill because he has seen a Wesen; he commits himself into a mental institution and leaves after convincing himself that he can restrain his own mind. He is actually relieved to learn of the world of Wesen; for him, the fear of losing psychological control is greater than the fear of monsters. His control can furthermore be seen in the expression of his sexual orientation: Gendered male, he chooses not to employ all the signs of traditional masculine sexuality. One episode, "Mommy Dearest" (3.14), introduces a childhood friend whom others see as a romantic interest, but in the series as a whole Wu repeatedly presents himself in a fashion that is sexually ambiguous. Is this a racial stereotype of asexuality, a tale of unrequited love, a presentation of a recently championed choice on the spectrum of human sexuality, or a purposeful illegibility? In any case, it is a significant aspect of the vividly self-controlled character of the witty Sergeant Wu.

Diversity in Depth of Field and Story Arcs

According to the *UCLA Hollywood Diversity Report*, in 2017, the year of *Grimm*'s last broadcast, the "Share of Roles, by Race" for "Asian" actors in "Broadcast Scripted Shows" was 4.6 percent, thus under-representing this minority group (Hunt et al. 24). Asian Americans make up 5.6 percent of the population of the U.S., according to a 2017 U.S. Census estimate (U.S. Department of Health and Human Services). This statistic does not address the fact that, as Darrell Hamamoto points out, "'Asian Americans' [is] a political concept that in itself conceals the sheer diversity and fragmentation of the various Asian ethnic groups [...] Filipino, Asian Indian, Japanese, Chinese, Korean, and Vietnamese people" among others (xii). As numerous scholars have observed, race and ethnicity are not biologically real categories but are very real in terms of social impact (see, e.g., American Anthropological Association). Reggie Lee serves on the board of directors of the East-West Players, a group that strives to advance the work of Asian American performers (Zukimoto).[3] Because of his position as a rare representative of Filipinos in mainstream television, he is often interviewed. Of the "Mommy Dearest" episode, he says, "I've never seen a mainstream Filipino storyline in U.S. television, so I'm [...] really proud" (Chavez "'Grimm'"). Among television series with whites in leading roles, *Grimm* is thus progressive in terms of representation of Asian Americans.

Furthermore, *Grimm* is diverse in terms not only of stars but also of co-starring roles—what might be called "depth of field." There are numerous African American and Latinx co-stars (see Ch. 2, note 7). One of the most effective co-starring parts is that of Donna Reynolds in "The Hour of Death" (2.10). In this episode, the detectives try to rescue a young woman who has been abducted to be sold into sexual slavery—what has often been called "white slavery"—but instead of the television-typical slim blonde victim, Donna Reynolds is a young African American woman.[4] Nor is she light-skinned; she is medium-dark, modestly dressed, professionally employed, attractive without being thin, and possessed of two loving, church-going parents.[5] Effectively acted by Sapphire Lichelle, the Donna Reynolds role is just one of many meaningfully-cast co-starring parts that populate *Grimm*.

Less numerous but increasingly frequent are the Asian American co-stars. From Beth Furamusu as a street kid who talks to the police in Season One (1.10); to Sophie Soong as reporter Suzanne Li in the first three seasons (1.21, 2.14, 3.15)[6]; to Cathy Vu as the ophthalmologist Dr. Myers (4.3), Keiko Green as Nurse Fran (4.14), Stephanie Kim-Bryan as Good Samaritan Beth (4.17), and Scott Takeda as hotel manager Mr. Adams (4.22) in Season Four, to Karishma Ahluwalia as Detective Kate Masters (5.21, 5.22) in Season Five—and others—the presence of Asian American co-stars is noticeable. Particularly when it comes to the casting of Asian American Actors for roles with names like "Kate Masters" and "Mr. Adams," it seems that the producers are making an effort at representation. As Lee says, "Things have grown since the first year I started *Grimm* to now [2017]. The diversity has diversified" (Kade). A version of the "'contact hypothesis' of prejudice reduction" might seem to be at play here (Bogaert 10).[7]

Simple place-holding representation, however, is not enough. Story and character intertwine: A character needs a story to develop (see, e.g., Shimizu 18, Mukherjea 66, Hamamoto 8). Sergeant Wu is given more and more of a narrative as *Grimm* proceeds. As Lee says, "we're now no longer just filling a quota but we're moving the plot forward [...] part of the story" (Kade). In each season, Wu has his own stories, stories that increase in significance and in their honoring of the complexity of the character. At the very beginning, in Season One, the Wu stories largely amount to depicting him as an everyman experiencing collateral damage. Yet Lee makes them stories of very human humor. When Adalind enthralls Hank with love-potion-dosed cookies, Wu eats one and suffers side effects through multiple episodes. Because the potion was not meant for him, he passes out, convulses, breaks out in ferocious boils, and hallucinates (1.15). Rosalee is able to cure his immediate symptoms, but Wu still has an underlying problem. In the next two episodes, he begins eating everything from paper clips to carpet, passing out again (1.16, 1.17). He is briefly hospitalized and diagnosed with Pica, an eating disorder that the doctor says may be related to the stress of his job.[8] Rosalee is finally able to cure him. Lee makes the most of the comic opportunities here; the sight of Wu on his knees eating his own carpet is memorable. Lee proudly reports that Pip's Donuts (of Portland, where *Grimm* was filmed) named a prize-winning donut the "Dirty Wu" as a result ("Wu's Views"). While Lee clearly controls the physical comedy, it should be acknowledged that part of the humor is the loss of control for this normally professional character. Furthermore, his abjection is not part of a heroic encounter: Wu is in this season an ordinary person who gets in the way of larger forces. Lee's acting makes what could have been demeaning instead both relatable and funny.

All the succeeding seasons involve storylines that lift and deepen the character. Season Two involves more agency for Wu, though his stories are still often mainly about endangerment. In both the episode "Quill" (2.4) and "The Waking Dead" (2.21), Wu in his official duties confronts an abject person who falls on him—in the first case, a loathly, diseased woman; in the second, a zombie. Lee's believably horrified reactions drive the impact of these encounters. As he says, in these two scenes "you see [Wu's] vulnerability" (Cairns 143). Season Two also, however, includes "Nameless" (2.16); in this episode, Wu's exercise of his duties focuses on his intellect (about which, more later). Season Three moves to a much deeper story, wherein Wu confronts a woman from his past and a monster that unhinges his sense of reality. Wu's arc for Season Four centers on his learning the truth about the Wesen world. Season Five is a story of transformation for Wu, as he himself becomes a preternatural being. Season Six shows Wu confronting power—first arresting his police captain, then battling the apocalyptic Zerstorer. Through both story and performance, Wu is much more than diversity window dressing.

Status and Stature

Grimm is in part a police procedural, and according to Lee, "a sergeant is usually above a detective. [...] People get confused because [...] [the audience thinks] 'It looks like he's been ordered around by Nick and Hank, so he must be under them.' In reality, what a sergeant would do is manage detectives. Usually I'm first on the case and then I'll dole out the case" (Cairns 143). Wu can be seen ordering around other uniformed police (see, e.g., 1.14, 2.10, 3.1, 4.20). However, as Lee suggests, the show gives an impression that Wu is lesser in status. There is a pattern in which Nick or Hank will assert something that needs to be done and Wu will reply "yeah" or "yep"—which could be taken as agreement, or as an inferior officer accepting an order (see, e.g., 3.1, 3.19, 4.15). In the majority of episodes, Wu seems to be giving a situation report to Nick and Hank. The pattern is so regular that one might argue that Wu suffers from Uhura syndrome—the person of color (like the *Star Trek* lieutenant played by Nichelle Nichols) given a repetitious, limited activity to perform (cf. Mafe 122, 141). Of course, even at the beginning, Wu's wit enlarges these scenes (as will be discussed).

Of the five male regulars, Wu is one of four who are police officers—and the only one who normally wears a uniform. The captain's and detectives' civilian clothes suggest higher status. Wu is also the shortest and slightest of the five. Furthermore, Wu starts the series with a buzz cut; as his character grows through the seasons, so does his hair, in effect a traditional association of hair and power. (His cat, whether coincidentally or not, is named Samson.) In the first several seasons, when he wishes to speak to Captain Renard, he knocks and stands within the frame of the doorway (see, e.g., 1.14, 1.21, 2.5). Lee has Wu often hang in the doorway nonchalantly, half in (e.g., 3.22, 4.4), but the body placement seems to suggest lower status, especially when Hank and Nick are already seated in the office. After Wu learns of the Wesen world, he rarely if ever just stands in the doorway. Instead, he enters the hierarchical space, both physically and metaphorically.

Other elements of blocking and body language in the series show Wu in a lower status physical placement and a resistance to such status. Along with the crime sitrep, there is frequently a scene later in any episode in which Wu approaches the desks of Nick and Hank with either a laptop or a folder in his hand to provide an update; the two detectives sit while Wu stands, suggesting (in this context) a position lower in the hierarchy. In later episodes, he is more likely to be seated (5.6, 6.1, 6.8). Even in early episodes, Lee uses his body language to work against diminishment. As he searches Monroe's home in the pilot, he thrusts his arms out wide; elsewhere, he spins and walks backwards with arms out (1.10); as he orders other cops, he flings his arm out, pointing as he moves (2.22). Often he stands arms akimbo or with his hand on his gun belt (3.5). Lee is taking up more space, and thus his character does, too.

Enlarging past a smallness of status and stature is also reflected in the character's bravery in spite of fear. In Season One he declares a low tolerance for pain but does field work (1.7); in Season Three he makes clear that he has claustrophobia but forces himself to hunt through the sewers (3.5); in Season Five, when he hears a lycanthrope howl in the woods, he asks, "We going out there?"—but go he does (5.14). The episode "Hibernaculum" (4.17) features a high-speed, death-defying chase in which not only Nick and Hank but also Wu has his face dramatically lit in close-up as he drives head-on towards a criminal's car. Perhaps the most memorable of such moments comes in the season after the self-imposed mental hospitalization that results from his having seen the Aswang monster. Having since learned of the supernatural world, when Wu is lunged at by a violent Wesen, he punches him in the face, saying, "You're no Aswang" (4.10). Wu controls his fear.

Wit, Intelligence, and Mental Health

Wu certainly controls his language as well—not in the sense that he contains it, but that he wields it. While the character of Monroe is noteworthy for his effervescent, rambling, almost uncontrolled erudition, Wu is remarkable for his dry sarcasm—with the delivery often as important as the words themselves. Reggie Lee recognizes the idea of sarcasm as a protective control, an emotional defense: "When I first started the show, they hadn't really built a character yet. I went straight to the sarcastic mode because it was in the script. I did some research on sarcasm and found that most people that are very sarcastic are insecure. [...] That's their cover. [...] Wu is [...] saying 'I'll deal'" (Phillips). This "sarcastic mode" is so effective that there is a Twitter hashtag, #wuism, devoted to his remarks. In his very first moment on screen, the sarcasm establishes the character. This slight, uniformed person collides with the hero detective (who has stopped) and instead of being solicitous, rushes on, saying, "Sorry, Nick, guess I should have worn my airbag today." He introduces a rich white woman who has come to the station with a Karen-like complaint by saying, "She's got—how can I say this—smoke coming out of a lot of orifices" (1.5). Wu often deploys his wit in distancing the loathsomeness of the crime scenes it is his job to introduce. Pointing to a frozen corpse in a walk-in restaurant freezer, he says, "Prep cook found him between the petite escargot and the chocolate mousse, which makes him our special for today" (3.9). At the sight of the pustule-covered body of a cyclist, Wu notes: "Organ donor, but I think that ship has sailed" (4.16). Viewing the destroyed body of a professor of biochemistry, he says, with an edge of horror in the wit, it is "like somebody wanted to beat the lab to death with her" (6.8). There are many more such moments. All of them work outward, establishing Wu's relationship with the other characters (and the audience), and inward, reflecting a man who constructs a shield of wit.

In some cases, Wu's wit extends even further outward: It implicitly recognizes larger social issues. Perhaps the most memorable of such remarks comes in the first season. With an echo of criminals who sell animal parts for aphrodisiacs and health, the detectives discover that certain Wesen are selling human parts for similar purposes, harvesting homeless adolescents. When Nick, Hank, Wu, and Captain Renard find the shelves of dried human organs, the captain says, "Whichever way you look at it, it's still cannibalism." But Wu retorts, "Uh, I think it's pronounced *capitalism*" (1.10). In the same season, when they arrest privileged white male teenagers (also Wesen) who have been chasing a lower-class couple as a blood sport, Wu says, "At least they weren't doing drugs" (1.2).[9] Anyone aware of mass incarceration for minor drug infractions will find the comment the more memorable in its suggested excoriation of class privilege. Though Wu himself carries and sometimes uses a gun, his disapproval of wide-spread civilian gun ownership and, in particular, survivalist culture becomes apparent as they examine the computer records of a divorced father who has apparently abducted his daughter: "Guns. More guns. Here's a good one—how to build a self-composting latrine. That always comes in handy. Here's one for knives, Kevlar, and of course more guns. All sorts of fun and games for a nine-year-old girl" (2.7). In an environmentalist episode, Wu refers, with an anti-homophobic touch, to "crimes against nature—and I don't mean the Bible-thumping sex kind. I mean poaching, polluting, etcetera" (6.9). Without pedantry, Wu's remarks add to the progressive flavor of the series, while conveying both witty restraint and perceptiveness.

That intelligence is also at play in his work, both as a police officer and, later, as part of the "Scooby Gang" that surrounds Nick. In a Season One DVD extra, Lee asserts that Wu is "really good at his job" ("The World of Grimm"), and the episodes bear that out. We see him recognize on a dead face a white fluid that suggests death by drowning (1.10); we see him assessing an abductor's literacy as a reader of Thomas Paine (2.7); we see him identifying vintage vehicles to help locate a culprit (2.15); we see him finding a killer by means of fast food ("[A] French fry is like a fingerprint," 3.19). Perhaps his most multi-faceted display of intelligence comes in "Nameless," which centers on the software designers of a gaming corporation who have created a valuable new gaming platform/program. Wu has read all three of the novels whose title pages the killer leaves as clues, he demonstrates relevant expertise in gaming, he solves a message-laden Sudoku puzzle, he guesses a critical location, and finally, he solves the central mystery of motivation. A Rumpelstiltskin variation (the killer is named Trinket Lipslums), "Nameless" focuses on a young woman who does not keep her promise to a supernatural figure who has rescued her from difficulty. Wu recognizes that the clue books were all written by an author using a "nom de plume, pen name, pseudonym, whatever you want to call it"—such as Lewis Carroll for Charles Dodgson ("That's right, I took English literature"). The killer's game avatar (the champion of the Black Forest[10] game in question) is Nameless. The Sudoku numbers that Wu derives refer to a date (as Nick realizes) and time (as Hank realizes)—the three police officers working together seamlessly. But it is Wu who realizes that the time connects to a location, a restaurant called Nom de Plume—and the targeted game designer, with other team members already dead, remembers that there was a late-night IT guy she stood up for a date at that place and time, a man who had pressured her, saying he would fix their stalled computers if she went out with him. As she, Nick, and the captain wonder why this would make the man kill, the camera shows Wu's face in close-up: "Unless he helped you write the code," Wu says. Wu, standing, is looking at the seated, guilty-faced software designer Jenna Marshall, played by Camille Chen. Not only are we seeing an impressive display of intelligence by Wu; we are also, in the same emotionally weighty shot, seeing two Asian actors (one Filipino Chinese, one Taiwanese) in a crucial narrative moment. After this episode, it is all the easier to note Wu's sharp mind at work. Once he learns of the Wesen world, he immediately begins to apply that mind: he is shown repeatedly in late-night sessions at Aunt Marie's trailer, studying the Grimm books. Then he begins to apply his knowledge of Wesen to the solving of crimes (4.11, 4.12, 4.13, and on). He is gaining some measure of control through both intelligence and knowledge.

The depiction of Wu's issues with mental health is symbolically significant; these issues are interwoven with intelligence and control. Wu, a representative of a racial/ethnic minority, thinks this world is crazy because it is. As Silas Weir Mitchell (Monroe) says, " We're exposing the real truth—and that real truth is a Wesen truth" ("A Grimm Farewell"). In this complex text, Wesen are, as Mitchell says, "about inner truth"; also, they are on the one hand possibly (though not always) hidden danger and on the other hand oppressed minorities. Wu has two separate mental health narratives—the first season arc in which he is diagnosed with the eating disorder Pica and the third-through-fourth season ramifications of his encounter with the Aswang—but both bear symbolic meaning. Wu's eating disorder is the result of his lack of knowledge about Wesen: The damage is the result of his naiveté about the subsurface conflicts of the world. His second, more serious encounter with mental illness comes because he does see the horrible reality of the darkness of the world of the Aswang—and it devastates him to the point of a mental breakdown. He signs himself into a sanitarium. He is, for a while, and after much struggle, willing to believe that his mind has been out of control, his perceptions unmoored from reality. He tries to return to his police work, denying what he has seen.

But Wu is too intelligent not to notice the evidence of Wesen—the evidence of social problems—all around him. For a while, he attempts to inhabit his earlier sarcastic stance, saying that he will "believe anything" (4.1). Eventually, however, he reaches a point when he cannot find "any opinion that makes sense" (4.8).

Wu is not alone among major characters in having difficulties with mental health. When Nick becomes a Grimm and starts seeing Wesen, he doubts his sanity. Hank, also, after a close encounter with a Wesen, feels crazed and visits a therapist. Juliette bonds with Wu in a visit to the sanitarium when she tells him she thought she was losing her mind the year before and reminds him of a wild incident he witnessed. As for Nick's protégée, the Grimm Trubel, she was repeatedly institutionalized before anyone explained the Wesen she was seeing were real. She and Wu share a reciprocal moment about their nightmares (3.20).

Despite these notes of solidarity, Wu's mental state is worsened through long-term attempts by Nick, Hank, and the captain—in effect, the law enforcement establishment—to deny that Wesen exist, to deny that the social problems are real. They assert that they are protecting him, another symbol of a troubling paternalistic pattern (a pattern Hank does question). It is only when Wu demands confrontation that they finally acknowledge the underlying truths of their world, the "Wesen truth"—a truth that incorporates not just social problems, not just Wesen villains, but Wesen heroes, unrecognized. In "Chupacabra" (4.8), two heroic and believably workaholic Portland Latino doctors do volunteer work in the Dominican Republic. One, a Wesen, comes home to his loving wife sadly joking about Sisyphean tasks, not realizing he has a worse problem: He has been infected and has become a Chupacabra. Nick, Hank, Monroe, and Rosalee realize his condition and plan to treat him; however, Wu interrupts, only to see the full form of the Chupacabra. When the frightened wife declares that this is not her husband, Wu shoots at and almost kills him; Nick is able to deflect Wu's aim. Shortly thereafter, the doctor, realizing that it is too late for him, gives the only dose of antidote to his wife, to whom he has given the disease by having made love with her. Meanwhile, Wu has understandably gone out and gotten drunk, flashing back to scenes of the Aswang, and is put in the drunk tank. Nick and Hank release him—in more ways than one—and (in the next episode) take him to the trailer, in the dark of the woods, to learn more about the darkness of the world. Like Nick and Hank, Wu must go to the woods, the liminal space Victor Turner writes of, where Wu will cross over into knowledge. Even during the Chupacabra episode, Nick and Hank try to stall Wu, saying it is not the right time. Angrily, Wu says, "It never is" (4.8). Many who want change have been told that the time is not right. But he forces the time to happen, forces the truth. In the trailer, in the next episode, Wu, with shock and an edge of fury, confronts them with the fact that they lied to him about the Aswang, making him think he was insane when he was not. How could he know they are not lying now, he asks? Nick replies, "You don't. You just have to believe us or think that we're crazy" (4.9). In fact, craziness is ignoring the insanity of this world. In fact, Wu is completely, sharply sane.

Wu and Sexual Ambiguity: Freedom and Control, or Asexual Stereotype?

While in many ways steeped in social issues, *Grimm* does not often touch on sexual orientation. There are occasional comments that suggest progressive attitudes (such as Monroe's in "Double Date," 4.15, or Rosalee's in "Inugami," 5.17). But the regular characters Nick, Hank, Juliette, Monroe, Sean Renard, Rosalee, and Adalind are all cisgendered heterosexuals.[11] The depiction of Drew Wu, however, is more complicated in terms of sexual orientation.

Wu might be seen as a representation of asexuality. Anthony Bogaert, in *Understanding Asexuality*, says that the term refers to "a complete lack of sexual attraction and/or sexual interest" (7). Asexuals have only recently begun to self-identify, as indicated by the Asexuality Visibility & Education Network (AVEN), started online in 2001, perhaps the most prominent center for information. AVEN indicates variations in asexuality such as "gray-asexual," someone who "may experience sexual attraction very rarely, only under specific circumstances, or of an intensity so low that it is ignorable and not a necessity in relationship"; and Bogaert agrees on the need for complexity in definition (see, e.g., 23, 67, and esp. 85). Celine Parrenas Shimizu, in *Straitjacket Sexualities: Unbinding Asian American Manhoods in the Movies*, warns against "vilify[ing] asexuality" (5), and Jennifer Wojton and Lynnette Porter note that as of 2018, "neither representation nor discourse regarding asexuality has significantly expanded into popular culture" (124). Wu might be seen, in the Aswang episode (of which, more later), as romantically focused on a young woman, but as Bogaert and AVEN agree, "Asexuals are not necessarily *a*romantic" (Bogaert 10).

Is Wu asexual or sexually ambiguous? Bogaert describes stages of sexual identity formation including "recognizing one's own attractions" or lack thereof; "testing and exploring"; "labeling oneself" to oneself; and "public disclosures." His research suggests that "most asexual people" expect to be perceived with "public disdain" (86–87). There is certainly no "coming out" scene for Wu; nor do we witness him labeling himself with the term "asexual." However, he repeatedly makes comments about his own non-normative sexual behavior in the context of others' heterosexuality, a pattern that offers the possibility of a queer reading. In the first season, while Hank stares longingly at a hidden picture of Adalind, Wu asks him if he has plans for the evening. When Hank responds by asking if Wu has plans, the sergeant replies, "Sure. Going to curl up on that couch with my cat Samson, watch the *Apprentice* marathon, and have a bite to eat" (1.16). In the third season, Sergeants Franco (Robert Blanche) and Wu are seated in a squad car together eating sandwiches while Franco discusses his wife, saying she has "been mad at me for not eating healthier." Wu, with the driest of tones, says, "Sometimes my cat gets mad at me and all she needs is a belly rub." "My wife is not a cat," says Franco. "Doesn't mean it wouldn't work," replies Wu. The exchange is quietly humorous yet full of meaning. In this scene we are being directly reminded that Wu has no wife. However, rather than wishing for one, he seems to be suggesting that his situation is freer than Franco's, who has to eat a sandwich that is "not really" good. In addition, Wu seems to be drolly recommending the gentle sensual pleasure he can provide the cat to Franco in terms of his relationship with his wife. "You and your damn cat," says Franco, and then, "I'm just kidding." As Wu has said earlier in the series, "my life consists mostly of myself and my cat" (2.16). Wu is not labeling himself asexual; however, he seems to be not merely accepting but claiming benefit for being in a non-normative sexual situation. Self-identifying asexual audience members might see something of themselves in Wu, or they might be troubled by the fact that he is not "out" as an asexual. As it stands, he is a respected character who apparently has no desire for a sexual partner, but whose sexual orientation is not clear.

Furthermore, the possibility for seeing Wu as a positive representative of asexuality is complicated by his being an Asian male, since asexuality is one of a number of stereotypes applied to Asian males—and Wu does not escape some of those other stereotypes. Asian males are often stereotypically associated with skills at tech and computers (Hamamoto 179, Abrams, Kade). As early as the third episode, Wu provides self-aware mocking of this stereotype when Nick asks if the sergeant can intercept a cell phone text and Wu replies, "Of course I can. I'm Asian" (1.3). In almost every episode, he is seen displaying his computer skills. Associated with this is Wu's penchant for gaming, as seen in "Nameless" and elsewhere (e.g., 4.16). But perhaps the most frequently denounced stereotype is asexuality itself.[12] Shilpa Davé, Leilani Nishime, and Tasha Oren declare that "popular representations of Asian American masculinity [are] certainly plagued by stereotypes of [...] asexuality" (4). Hamamoto, who calls *Star Trek*'s Mr. Sulu an "intergalactic eunuch," emphatically complains of the "collective desexualization" of Asian American males (9, 14). Shimizu addresses the stereotype of Asian male asexuality through much of her *Straitjacket Sexualities* (e.g., 65). The presentation of Wu as an Asian male who is straightforwardly asexual, then, might lend itself to stereotyping.

It should be noted that in two *Grimm* episodes that make Asian characters central, there are representations of loving Asian heterosexual couples. "Inugami" (5.17) features a Japanese American couple and "Mommy Dearest" (3.14) focuses on a Filipino American couple. In the first case the couple had a young son tragically killed; in the second case, the wife is pregnant. In neither case is there suggested to be an asexual pairing. It is true that in "Inugami" there is an unfortunate exoticization effected by the use of non-diegetic music with stereotypically Asian tonalities. In fact, one of the weaker elements of *Grimm* overall is this tendency towards occasional exoticization by music, as can be seen, for example, for Jewish characters (4.4) and Mexican American characters (2.9). However, the Japanese-like music for "Inugami" is not sounded until late in the episode (at the first naming of the Inugami spirit), and the family—whose father joins the police in the chase—certainly avoids the stereotype of asexuality or passivity. The Tomases of "Mommy Dearest," as will be discussed, are even farther from this stereotype. As Erica Scharrer says, "For racial and ethnic groups that are infrequently portrayed on television, the depictions that do exist take on critical importance" (162). The presence of other prominent Asian American male characters who are in sexual relationships makes it easier to envision Wu's possible asexuality as a character choice rather than a stereotyping default by the writers/producers. In other words, because there is not just a lonely token character, there are options. Shimizu broadens the possibilities of interpretation when she asks about Asian male sexuality, "What would it mean to embrace these images previously deemed humiliating or to critique the manhoods we have available?" (83). In the episodes next to be discussed, Wu's intriguing sexual ambiguity is, by implication, such a critique of traditional masculinities—a queering of the character in the sense of being anti-establishment and offering the opportunity for imagined options.

There are two episodes that most directly relate to Wu's sexual orientation: the Aswang episode "Mommy Dearest," and the sixth season episode "Blind Love" (6.7). "Mommy Dearest" is the most important Wu episode for many reasons, particularly in terms of representations of Asianness and, possibly, asexuality. The title "Mommy Dearest" refers to a tell-all book by the adopted daughter of Hollywood star Joan Crawford, a tale of maternal abuse (also a 1981 film).[13] "Mommy Dearest" is the episode in which Adalind gives birth to Diana, but it is much more the story of Wu, his pregnant friend Dana and her husband Sam Tomas, and the

Aswang—the monster who is also Sam's mother who expects to eat his firstborn—another "Mommy Dearest." Reggie Lee has said that the producers "asked me, actually, 'Do you know any Filipino fairy tales?'—'cause that's my background, is Filipino Chinese," and he suggested the Aswang ("Something Wesen"). In part because of Lee's input, the character's "background is imbricated with his powers and perspective" (P. Smith).[14] Lee has also said, "It was like it brought the entire Filipino culture of the United States together just to watch the Aswang" ("A Grimm Farewell"). Constancio Arnaldo comments on Filipinos' "feeling invisible to the mainstream" and on television viewing experiences as "moments of diasporic intimacy" (29), and this episode counts as such. The element of migration in the Asian American experience is depicted in this episode more than once (cf. Davé, Nishime, and Oren 1, Mukherjea 65).[15] Sam, who has hidden his Wesen nature from his wife Dana, does not want his mother to eat their firstborn, and after Dana is first attacked by the mother-monster Aswang, Sam calls his brother in Manila to find out exactly where his mother is. After an establishing shot of busy Manila streets, the brother is shown at his business. Wu, in Portland, goes to visit his cousin Angelo, who apparently runs a Filipino restaurant. We hear the Tagalog language spoken and see references to Filipino foods. When Wu complains of using all parts of the pig including knuckles, Angelo makes a comment that bridges cultures: "Waste not, want not." This scene includes diegetic music of apparently genuine Filipino sources; the episode does not use exoticizing non-diegetic scoring. With Wu's cousin and Sam's brother, we see believable family dynamics on screen: disagreements, hugs, anger, laughter. And Wu's dream of his Filipino grandmother "Nanita" telling the story of the Aswang has an almost Lynchean flavor, as he sees first a nightmare image of Dana bleeding on the floor, then hears a woman's voice speaking Tagalog (translated onscreen) and opens a door to a Filipino garden where white sheets float, drying, and a bespectacled, brightly dressed, eloquent granny frightens the little boy Wu. The Filipino connections, stretching across countries, are beautifully displayed. The connections reach out to family and deep into the mind.

In this episode, Reggie Lee is clearly filmed as the protagonist, and the camera work might suggest the hero of a romance. As Dana is driven away after the first attack, Wu is shown standing in the street in profile, with the lights of the ambulance on his face; then the camera shows him at a greater distance, framed between the double trunks of the tree the Aswang has used to enter Dana's bedroom window. The tongue of the Aswang seems to flicker about Wu. He is made visually central and dramatic. Repeatedly in the episode, he is shown in close-up. After a confrontation with Sam at the hospital, Wu is again shown in distant profile, as if to accentuate his solitary state. The long shot down a hospital corridor is often used to emphasize a moment in *Grimm* (e.g., 1.1, 5.1), and here Wu gets that emphasis.

The episode balances delicately among possible interpretations, all of which are worth exploring. Wu might be feeling traditional heterosexual love for Dana, unrequited; or he might be experiencing the feelings of a romantic asexual, again unrequited; or he might be an asexual, caring friend (or a heterosexual or homosexual caring friend). This is the episode in which Wu and Franco joke together (described above). The joking scene could be taken as a reminder of Wu's asexuality, or as a way to remind viewers that Wu is alone. When they hear over the police radio the alert stating the address of the attack, Wu says, "My friend and her husband live there," making immediately clear the person to whom he is closer. Wu's cousin Angelo, in his restaurant, tells Wu, "I thought for sure she's the one you were gonna end up with," adding "Bummer" when he learns she has married, and "Double bummer" when Wu says they are still close. Angelo seems to see Wu as having an unrequited love for Dana; but Wu might be asexual or homosexual without his cousin's realizing it. Sam, for his part, reacts to Wu as to a rival. Though at first their interactions are polite, after Sam finds Wu and Dana hugging in her hospital room and the two men go out into the corridor to talk, Sam says, "She's my wife, not yours—just get over it. And leave us alone." Sam, like Angelo, may see Wu as being in love with Dana, though again, his perception may or may not be accurate. Alternately, this territoriality may be impelling Sam to cruelly taunt someone he sees as a closeted homosexual whose emotional closeness to Dana he, her husband, resents.[16] The long shot of Wu, left alone in the hospital corridor, emphasizes his solitary status in a way that suggests Wu's strong emotion yet leaves mysterious exactly what he is feeling.

Early in the episode, before the attack, we see Sam and Dana alone together in their home, and their playful emotional and physical closeness is apparent. There is never a suggestion that Dana secretly loves or desires Drew Wu. When Nick goes to the trailer to read about the monster that has attacked Dana, we learn that in Aswang families the eldest son is expected to let his mother feed on the fetus of his firstborn; therefore, young women were often acquired to be impregnated for the purpose. Ananya Mukherjea identifies the stereotypical "image of the innocent Asian woman mistreated, abused, or forced into sex work [as] a repeated motif in Western media" (69), and the cases described in Aunt Marie's books fit that pattern. Dana, however, does not. Wu tells Nick and Hank that he and Dana have known each other since they "were in diapers," and that if Sam tried to mistreat her, "Dana wouldn't stay with him." She senses the anger between Sam and the man she calls Drew, and instead of passively avoiding, she firmly addresses the subject with her husband. This scene comes after Sam and

Wu have had their confrontation, and Sam wants to end the relationship. But Dana says that Wu is "a good friend, and always will be." The words "always will be" show that she is asserting her choice, and Sam quite reasonably backs down.[17] It is true that Dana is ignorant of the knowledge of her husband's Wesen nature, but she is presented as both caring and strong.

As for Drew Wu, he directly says, "I really care about Dana," and ambiguously refers to "my past with Dana" as possibly affecting his judgment of her husband. When he visits her in the hospital as she is about to be released and Sam has yet to arrive, Dana tells Wu she thinks "it'll be hard to feel safe again." "But you will be," says Wu, stepping close. "I'll make sure of that." She hugs him and thanks him, saying, "You're such a good friend." Reggie Lee's acting here is intriguingly ambiguous. In the hug, his face hidden from Dana, Wu raises his eyes toward the ceiling. Is this a modest reaction to her thanks? Or is it a long-suffering response to being considered only a friend? Their closest physical interaction is unquestionably emotional, and yet the issue of whether or not Wu feels either sexual desire or romantic desire is left unsettled—or perhaps one might say, it is left for each viewer to settle. "Mommy Dearest" offers long-term viewers the chance to see Wu's not having a sexual partner as the result of faithful, unrequited love. On the other hand, it also leaves open the possibility that Wu is asexual or homosexual. In any case, it shows him as comfortable in presenting a non-normative sexual orientation that is bound up with gentleness and bravery.

Wu saves Dana from the Aswang twice, kicking down the door of the house on the second occasion. He in turn is saved by Nick, who shoots the Aswang as it crouches over Wu in a visually arresting shot that often plays a part in the series credits. (The credits also often show Wu with his gun raised, opposing the passivity of the Aswang clip.) The Aswang, the horror, is in Wu's face, and we see it in Lee's eyes. Of Wu in this episode, Lee says, "He's such a sarcastic guy who's always in control. I love that they've finally given him [...] some out-of-control issues[...]. [I]t rounds out the character really well" (Nepales). Though (as discussed earlier) seeing the Aswang and then having that sight denied by Nick and Hank convinces Wu that he should enter a mental institution, he is nonetheless presented as physically, emotionally, and mentally strong. Wu's scenes in the mental institution are searing, whether he is screaming at terrifying memories or quietly sitting with his pain. But he departs the sanitarium as he entered it, by choice: "Let's get out of here before they change my mind," he quips to Hank and Nick, as he re-enters the crazy world (3.15). Whatever his sexuality, it is not that of the pallid stereotype, but of a vivid, charismatic person.

"Blind Love" is another episode in which sexuality comes into play. In some ways it is French farce, comic relief in the midst of a darkly intense last season. But as is typically the case with *Grimm*, there is much going on in the humor. It is, for one thing, an episode that hinges on lack of control. The Scooby Gang of friends—Nick, Adalind, Juliette/Eve, Hank, Wu, Rosalee, and Monroe—are meeting for a weekend at the Columbia River Gorge Inn to celebrate Monroe's birthday. Randy, the son of a man Nick put in prison—a Wesen—is a waiter there, and in an extreme version of server's revenge, he spits in their champagne with the effect of creating a love potion that is both humorous (everyone is unrequited except Hank, who falls for himself) and fatally obsessive. Rosalee, who is pregnant, does not drink; Hank takes both his glass and hers, apparently resulting in his self-love, hilariously rendered by Russell Hornsby. Wu, for his part, falls for a server.[18] Juliette/Eve poignantly falls for Nick (who had been her longtime love); Monroe "loves" Juliette/Eve, Adalind "loves" Monroe, Nick "loves" Rosalee. One might note that the regulars who are persons of color are not paired with a member of their own group—though before analyzing further, one might also recall that Hank and Adalind have actually had sex earlier in the series. In any case, Wu's courtship of the server Holly is amusingly vehement. He quotes Shakespeare repeatedly[19] and wishes for the hotel manager to marry them, though Wu has to (as the camera and Lee's face clearly show) look at Holly's nametag to learn what she is called. At one point he tells her, "I've been waiting for you my whole life. The only one I've ever loved is my cat." While the regular characters here are deceived about their feelings for the love objects enforced by Randy ("I've been waiting for you"), none of them say anything else that is untrue while under the spell. Wu's comment about not having loved before, then, suggests that he did not love Dana romantically and he is possibly asexual. The status of deleted scenes is questionable, but those who explore the DVD extras will see Wu gently hugging and comforting Holly after he has emerged from the spell, while he honorably demurs from her seeming romantic interest just after he has saved her from being thrown off a cliff. Once again, Wu is a positive departure from traditional masculinity while being sexually ambiguous.

Power versus Control

Wu is able to save Holly from the villainous Wesen Randy (who tries to throw her off that cliff) because at this point of the series Wu has himself become a being of preternatural strength. In the fifth season, we follow Wu's transformation. Now knowing of the Wesen world, he joins Nick, Hank, Rosalee, and Monroe in pursuing a lycanthrope. In the world of *Grimm*, particular Blutbaden who catch a certain disease becomes Lycanthropes—the basis of the wolf-man legend. In the episode "Lycanthropia"

(5.14), a Blutbad son tries to hide his mother's lycanthropic condition. But when a car accident prevents him from being with her during the full moon, she kills two hikers. "My mother cannot stop herself," he tells Nick and his friends. She scratches Wu and transfers a version of the condition to him; the human version is so rare that it is not in the trailer books, nor have Monroe or Rosalee heard of it. Before he is diagnosed, Wu, unaware, kills too. But unlike the wealthy, white, privileged lycanthropic mother, Wu learns to control himself and apply his new, wild strength in battle. In earlier episodes, Hank has expressed envy of Wesen powers (3.2), and now Wu has them. It seems he gains both power and control.

The slow development, through half a dozen episodes, of this narrative arc provides impressive opportunities for both character and actor. Scenes of the arc are unified by non-diegetic violin notes, quietly and subtly applied by composer Richard Marvin. "Inugami" starts with a particularly surreal scene of Wu's transformation. With moonlight falling on him from his bedroom window, Wu violently tosses and turns and falls to the floor. There he sees mist coming in under the bathroom door. He crawls to it; it opens into a forest. He steps several paces into it, turns left, and runs; hearing the sound of his running feet, we shift to his point of view. Then we are again outside him and see him run, as a blur, to the right. Next morning he awakens and cautiously opens the bathroom door—but it is just a bathroom. He expels his held breath and laughs. We, however, see leaves and dirt on the carpet behind him. Once more Wu is caught in a scenario of trying to discern what is real. How can one have control without knowing what is real?

Perhaps in fear that they will question his mental state, Wu does not share this or similar unnerving experiences as he is going through "the change." We first see the face of what Lee and fans call "NeanderWu" ("Grimm: Lowen") on a night stakeout, when Wu, alone, reacts to a dog's growling at him by *woging*. Monroe and Rosalee later declare that he is not Wesen, but his transformation seems almost exactly parallel; it is clearly related to his emotional state and thoughts. After he first woges, runs, and falls, Wu is hospitalized with a concussion. When Nick and Hank take him home, Wu tells them, "I've had some really weird [dreams] lately. [...] I'm running through the forest—hunting—very real—and sort of primal—animalistic" (5.19). It is in this episode that he woges and kills a Wesen criminal who attacks him, later to realize that he is not dreaming at all. Once again, the seeming insanity is bloody reality.

In this same episode, we see Wu's anger when he sees himself as out of control in little ways, and his horror when he sees himself as out of control in killing. After Nick and Hank bring him home from the hospital, Wu plans to return to work immediately, but they convince him to take the rest of the day off. Preparing a sandwich, he breaks a mustard jar, cutting his hand. "Damn it! Stupid, stupid, stupid," he curses himself. This is one of the most clear-cut moments showing how hard Wu is on himself and showing his insistence on control. His body, however, refuses control: he watches his fingers turn into hairy claws. Soon after, he learns that his nightmare is real. Yet in the very next episode, he manages to learn control through painful practice. Staring at the mirror, he screams, "Show me what I am!" He punches the wall again and again until he woges and then, rushing back to the mirror, defies his own rage, shouting, "I'm in control"—and he is. Wu must lose control and regain it, again and again, to access power. In later episodes, he woges in battle, as we have seen Monroe, Rosalee, Adalind, and Juliette/Eve do. There are moments when his control slips (for instance, when he and Hank are fired by Renard). Still, overall, it could be argued that a character who represents a minority is keeping his powerful rage but controlling it for his own purposes.

Community, Complicity, Communion

Of course, in the world of *Grimm*, Wu's purposes are mainly in furtherance of the Scooby Gang, the community surrounding the white police detective supernatural hero Nick. Chapter Two, on African American Detective Hank Griffin, discusses at length the complicity of cops in extralegal activities. Here let it just be said that, once Wu knows about Wesen, he begins to participate in these extralegal actions, even extrajudicial killings. The first time is to save Monroe's life, and he insists that there will need to be more conversation to justify the actions (4.10). Later, he extracts from custody the Royal who kills Nick's mother and physically kicks the much larger man down, leaving him in a deserted warehouse for Nick to fight and kill (4.22), a much more extreme action. When the half-Wesen, half-Royal Renard joins the Wesen Black Claw, who plan to crush normal humans, Wu participates in the fight against them. In fact, he and Hank attempt to reasonably apply the law by boldly arresting the captain, whose fingerprints have been found at a murder scene, only to have the captain evade the law through a corrupt judge and district attorney. Wu's motives are generally good, but he becomes complicit in the extralegality that *Grimm* slowly complicates.

His entry into the special community can be seen as a kind of communion, and it is coeval with his entry into knowledge, power, and some degree of complicity. Several of the most enjoyable scenes in *Grimm* are the shared meals of the inner circle of friends, the communion through food and drink (see Ch. 8). The friends include Wesen and non–Wesen. Wu does not partake of these communions until after he learns of Wesen. After he helps save Monroe from the Wesen hate group Wesenrein, he shares in a celebratory toast at Monroe and Rosalee's home (4.10). Though he is not at Monroe and Rosalee's wedding (3.22), he is at the funeral Nick dreams of for Juliette (5.1). He comes to a dinner party at Nick and Adalind's (5.10). Most notably, in "Blind Love," he shares in a weekend of food and drink with a beloved community who take time to speak of their togetherness.

In the series' last scene of its regular characters, these people are called family. From this communal group come the people who hold the long-sought, fatally fought-for keys that open a box containing a mystically powerful object. Hank, Rosalee, Monroe, Nick, and Wu are at the center of the story. And near the end, these five all work together to contribute a record to one of Nick's Grimm books, one of those rescued from the trailer (6.9). Wu is one of those who have a voice, one of those who have control over the history, the story.

Conclusion: "I'm not going anywhere"

When Nick and Hank take Wu to the trailer to learn its secrets, Nick asks if Wu wants to forget it all and walk away. "I'm not going anywhere," Wu firmly replies (4.9). Reggie Lee's Wu is one of an under-represented, attacked minority,[20] but Asian Americans are not going anywhere either. Lee asserts that "the real draw for an actor is to find the humanity" ("The World of Grimm"). That complex combination of control and its lack is what makes a character human. Through the control of his wit and the struggle to control his mind and emotions, Wu is very real. And Wu's sexual ambiguity resists a reading of traditional masculine sexual roles. This chapter, with its many threads, is still only a partial exploration of Wu. Lee reminds us of another potential route to control: "It's time for us to take the reins into our own hands and tell Filipino stories. [...] It's time [that] our voices be heard" (Chavez, "Fil-Am").[21] In the out-of-control post–COVID world, that kind of control, at least in mainstream television, is yet to come. Meanwhile, Wu is not going anywhere.

Four

"I never choose sides"

Prince-Father-Captain Sean Renard and the Gothic Hero-Villain of Patriarchy

"Renard can brood with the best of them. Renard will brood over breakfast. I mean, that man will just brood from the time he gets up until the time he goes to bed. He broods in his sleep," declares Renard actor Sasha Roiz (Nelson, "Royal" 98). Renard's brooding is one of many qualities he shares with the Gothic hero-villain. The Gothic hero-villain has long represented dangerous elements of patriarchal power. There could hardly be a character more marked as a representative of patriarchy than Sean Renard, who is not only a prince but also a police captain and, notably, a father: a member of a ruling structure, an enforcer of the legal structure, and someone defined by the root meaning of patriarchy—fatherhood, in its extensive and various applications. As such, he is often—but not always—the antagonist in the series. In the pilot, Detective Nick Burkhardt trusts and obeys Renard as his police captain, but the audience sees the captain planning the death of Nick's aunt: Renard is part of an unseen power structure, a secret prince with extra influence in the magic world Nick is entering as a new Grimm. However, the captain is always distinct from that power structure as well: He is a bastard; furthermore, he is half-Wesen, the son of a king and his witch mistress. He is thus an outsider in more than one sense—appropriately for a Gothic hero-villain. He must struggle for power rather than assuming it, and his struggle reveals the darkness in patriarchy. Renard's upbringing leads to a sharp duality in his public and private selves, illustrated by the contrast between his handsome face and the monstrous visage he rarely reveals. He also exists in duality with the hero, for whom he serves as a foil. During those times when he is trying to build a working relationship with the Grimm, he displays intelligence and bravery. But his obsession for power leads to a sequence of varying affiliations—the police, royalty, the Resistance, Nick's group, and Black Claw, who successfully run

Renard for mayor of Portland (with larger long-term designs). Both his resistance against injustice and his desire for power inform his choice to accept this role (as it may for many a politician), even after he learns that the preceding candidate has been murdered so Renard may take his place. Nick and his friends are able to stop the plot but must come to an agreement to return Renard to his role as police captain. Through all this, Renard is the most unequivocally traditionally masculine of these characters, as well as being completely heterosexual, always with an aim towards dominance. Yet Renard—despite his Gothic glamour—is shown as unloved and essentially alone. In this series, the ultra-masculine heterosexual man who aims for dominance is not rewarded with romance. In the end, a genuine connection with a comrade-in-arms (Martin Meisner), his strong love for his daughter Diana—his most literally patriarchal relationship—and an apocalyptic threat to humanity at least partially redeem Renard and adjust his perspective. Demonstrating the insufficiency of the traditionally gendered heterosexual male, this morally gray character illustrates both the threats and temptations of patriarchal power.

"I was doing it for you": The Gothic Hero-Villain

Scholars such as Ellen Moers (*Literary Women*) and Sandra M. Gilbert and Susan Gubar (*The Madwoman in the Attic*) long ago connected the Gothic with fear of patriarchy.[1] The Gothic hero-villain is a "sinister patriarchal figure" inhabiting that world (Miles 131). He is a man of mystery, a wealthy aristocrat ("malevolent aristocrats," in Botting's phrase, 3). He is, of course, associated with a Gothic setting that suggests his frightening power. His dark, brooding good looks make him the fraternal twin of the Byronic hero. He may be a "scheming, wicked older man who wishes to seduce [a younger woman] for his own ends" (Horner 116). He is usually an outsider, marked by illegitimacy (Stoddart 114), "racial alterity" and otherness (Cavallaro 163, 115). Captain Renard bears all of these qualities.

In the pilot episode, we learn that the captain who appears concerned for Nick's welfare is not what he seems; his desire to kill Nick's aunt is part of a larger mystery. We soon discover that, more than an aristocrat, he is a prince. In the first episode that uses the term "your Highness," he is also connected to a ritualistic priesthood which serves his royal needs (an element quickly dropped, 1.12). Standing before a portrait in a museum, he tells the Hexenbiest Adalind Schade, "We owned this in the seventeenth century and lost it along with a lot of heads in the revolution" (1.15). We gradually learn of the seven royal families (who are aware of the Wesen world) and how valuable a Grimm is to a Royal (1.18). When the hero's beloved Juliette falls into a Sleeping Beauty coma, only the prince, Renard, can wake her (2.2). His wealth is apparent. His clothing shows his status (designer suits, camel-hair coat), as does his home: first a penthouse apartment, then a house that costs "a small fortune" (4.5). The setting the captain is earliest and most thoroughly identified with, however, is the police station that he at one point calls his home (4.4). In the pilot, we see a large, arched entrance hall and, in dim light, multiple flights of wide stairs with carved banisters. That is where we meet Sean Renard, emerging from the darkness. The exterior shows stone archways over twenty feet high, a courtyard, further archways and broad wooden doors: It is actually the historic Portland U.S. Customs House (1898–1901), as close to Gothic in feeling as one can likely get in Portland, where the series was filmed. The building suggests the power of the man. Greenwalt and Kouf lend power to his literal home as well. Both his apartment and his houses are modern in design but filled with museum-quality artifacts and paintings such as a portrait of an aristocratic Renaissance man over the modern fireplace. In the episode in which we learn of the seven royal families, a scene in the captain's apartment ends with a view outside his window-wall of the river and city beyond, and a dim vision of the captain through glass, standing tall, his shape crossed by reflected lights of the cityscape. Then there is a cut to a shot perhaps a hundred feet away, showing that his apartment is atop the tall building, with the broader view suggesting his ambitious scope (1.18).

Early in the series, the makeup department added gray to Roiz's hair, thus fitting him to the image of the dangerously attractive older man who uses a younger woman—as we see from the pilot, in which his tool is Adalind Schade.[2] He first sends her to kill Marie (Nick prevents her); later, he tasks her with getting a valuable key from Nick. Renard's scenes alone with her imply sexual manipulation, especially one in which he, in his usual suit, suddenly appears while Adalind, clothed only in a towel, is drying her hair. In the previous episode, in the museum scene, he has touched that hair and run his hand down her shoulder. Now he moves so close to her (a breath away from a kiss) that she is left with a strand of hair down the middle of her forehead as he departs. It is a suggestive disorder (1.16). In the next episode, "Love Sick" (1.17), the title seems to apply to Nick's partner Hank, whom Adalind has bewitched (for leverage on Nick). But the title also applies to her. With an attempt at insouciance, she acknowledges her love for Renard to her mother (see Ch. 9). She has long said that what she is doing is risky (1.3). After she loses her powers in a conflict with Nick, Adalind says to Renard, "I was doing it for you" (1.17). For his part, he rarely seems more cruel than when he responds to the weeping Adalind, "You're useless now. Just another pretty girl" (1.17). Using her "for his own ends" is part of the villainy of the Gothic hero-villain.

Otherness—a quality most of the main characters of *Grimm* can claim in some degree—is, for the captain, embedded in his Gothicness. There is otherness on the surface, from an American perspective, because of his cosmopolitan nature. He is foreign-born and speaks many languages on-screen, Roiz fluently managing French, German, Russian, and Latin (e.g., 1.4; 1.18; 3.9; 2.18). He has a sophisticated knowledge of culture, coming in second only to Monroe in that regard. But his secret otherness truly makes him an outsider. His imposing physical presence suggests power. Yet as the son of a Hexenbiest, he is half Zauberbiest, and when he transforms, parts of his face are monstrously distorted, abject. When Adalind returns to town in the second season, she tells him (during an episode pertinently titled "Face Off"), "I want you—the real you," and, smiling, he shows her that monstrous visage as they tear into their sexual encounter (2.13). Renard has all the major parts of the Gothic hero-villain.

This combination, however, creates a character who is both within and separate from patriarchy. His upbringing (about which we learn gradually) makes this status clear. He is both a bastard and, in the terms of this series, a half-breed (of "racial alterity"). His half-brother, the crown prince Eric (James Frain), tells Adalind that Renard's mother was *one* of the king's mistresses (2.8). Renard tells Nick, "You should know that his mother tried to murder mine and me." "That would make for an awkward Christmas," replies Nick. "I wouldn't know. I was never invited," says Renard with bitter calm (2.22). Though his cousin Prince Viktor (Alexis Denisof) later says, "My uncle does love his bastard son" (4.1), and the king himself tells Juliette that it was the queen, not he, that pursued Sean and his mother (4.22), the king seems to have done little to protect him. Renard comments on a spell his mother used to hide him from the pursuing Royals (6.12). It is not surprising, then, that Renard's character is marked by lack of trust and a reflex for self-preservation. When he enters his own apartment, for example, he holds a gun under the coat over his arm (1.18). He never appears in a scene with the king, though other princes, and even Adalind and Juliette, do. The production designers created an Austrian castle frequently used for the series,[3] but this prince is never seen in the castle.

"You walk in two worlds": The Duality of Public and Private

From the beginning, we see Renard as both the public, rule-following captain, and the private, above-the-law prince (a duality incarnate in his two faces). The captain is the one who gives press conferences (1.5, 1.7, 1.13, 1.21, and on into the following seasons). He is therefore conscious of public policy and sentiment: "We don't need the city scared to use public transportation" (1.3) or "I've got a dead popular teacher at an expensive private school; I'd like an answer before politics screw things up" (1.5) are typical remarks. Two of the most frequent types of scenes are meetings in his office and Sorkinian hall-walks with detectives Griffin and Burkhardt, discussing cases. We see him staying late and taking care. He leads with seeming integrity, telling Hank and Nick for example, "I'm not going to protect a dirty cop, but you make sure you're right" (1.6). His insistence on following protocol can sometimes be frustrating to Nick and Hank, especially before they know he understands the Wesen world. When he insists on handing a Wesen case to the unknowing FBI, for instance, the agents end up dead (2.1). He avoids publicly stretching the rules (as opposed to privately breaking them). Sometimes he uses his seeming respect for authority to accomplish his own ends. In the second episode, while he is still trying to kill Aunt Marie, Renard has been forced to put a police guard on her in the hospital after a deadly attack. But, as he explains to Nick, "With no hard evidence of a second attack, I couldn't justify the expense [of keeping the guards] to the chief without it looking like we're giving preferential treatment to police families" (1.2). His apparently straight-arrow behavior gives him the opportunity to send another assassin after Marie. In another episode, with a pretense of professional courtesy, he tells Hank to question a Department of Corrections employee at home—which, Renard knows, will lead to evidence of the man's involvement in a criminal fight club, an enterprise in which Renard had until recently participated (1.12). When Adalind returns to town, Renard uses the excuse of questioning her about her mother's death to hunt her down for his own purposes (2.12). You are what you pretend to be, the adage says; and in many ways Renard is a good cop. As he says to certain Russian visitors, "Here the police are not useless" (3.9). We even see evidence that he wishes to do well. When Nick wants to go after state marshals who have taken custody of a mild-seeming but deadly Wesen, Renard tells Nick he must let the marshals take the man but he will call to tell them death threats have been made so that they will themselves increase security. When Renard learns that they have been killed nonetheless, we see him privately gesture his frustration (5.2). But he will not publicly deviate from the role of rule-following captain; it is too important as a cover for him, as a matter of self-preservation—and it is also a role he seems to enjoy inhabiting.

At the same time, the prince engages in wildly extralegal and illegal activities. He frequently wears black leather gloves as part of his upper-class armor—gloves that let him avoid leaving fingerprints (1.17, 2.12). When a "Reaper of the Grimms" comes to town hunting Nick without Renard's princely permission and fails to be sufficiently apologetic,

Renard uses the man's scythe to slice off his ear (1.4). Whenever he feels threatened, he kills without hesitation, whether the threat is death or exposure—which, in his world, can lead to death. His attempt on Marie's life has already been noted; as he later tells her sister (Nick's mother), she was a Grimm and she had a key; Grimms are generally considered enemies of Wesen, so she was fair game, though he has since changed his views (2.18). When someone who is paying him tribute gives him a veiled threat, the captain gives him one chance to reform, then watches coldly as, under his orders, a hell-hound assassin starts to tear the man apart. While the man shrieks and dies, Renard coolly walks away (1.12). In "Love Sick," a royal cousin comes to town and sends his chauffeur-cum-assassin Woolsey to fetch Renard at gunpoint. Woolsey tells him he will have to drive, and Renard says that it is better than having to die. Woolsey responds that Renard shouldn't rule that out. He adds, "It's nothing personal, sir." "I know, Woolsey—but I'm taking it that way," says Renard. "Your privilege," Woolsey concedes. Having brought Renard to an empty factory—clearly a possible location for assassination—his cousin presses him, and Renard knocks Woolsey to the ground and shoots the cousin in the head with Woolsey's gun. When Woolsey, from the ground, says that the other Royals will kill him, Renard and Woolsey echo the earlier badinage: "It's nothing personal," says Renard. "I know, sir. But I'm taking it that way." "Your privilege," says Renard with a small smile, and the camera cuts away before he shoots (1.17). The echoed language emphasizes the reflecting action: Renard does to others what they try to do to him.

Renard's secret violence is frequent; his deception is constant. He must pretend to be ignorant of threats he recognizes, and somehow lead his officers to respond to them. His managerial strategies demonstrate his power within the patriarchal system. When, for instance, Nick reads aloud a medical report on escaped convict Oleg Stark, it would be clear to Renard that Stark is a Siegbarste, an ogre-like Wesen. Stark is pursuing vengeance on Hank as his arresting officer, and Renard's order that Hank endure protective custody is the more insistent because he knows what Hank faces (1.8). He pretends ignorance of the killer Edgar Waltz as police hunt him, even though he knows him to be one of the Verrat, enforcers who work for the Royals (1.18). He also deceives Waltz, keeping Nick's identity as a Grimm secret for as long as he can. Renard hoards information as part of his protection and power. He is the only person to enter and search through Nick's book-filled trailer without Nick's permission—the main source of Nick's informational power, and a symbol of his private self. Renard's uninvited entry is a good representation of their relationship. When Nick brings one of these books to Renard to translate the Latin, Renard wonders aloud if Nick has many more—but he knows (2.18).

It is therefore an extraordinary moment when Renard decides to reveal his royal status to Nick. Renard has by then stolen Nick's key (add theft to lies and murder). He does so, however, only to give it back, as proof of his good intentions towards Nick. Unknown to Renard, Nick has already learned that Renard is the prince in town, but at the cabin in the woods originally seen in the pilot, Renard also reveals his Zauberbiest nature. That Renard has never let Nick see his Wesen face before attests to the captain's emotional control. Here, he reveals himself during a fight, so it may or may not have been intentional; but reveal himself he does (1.13).

This revelation, however, does not lead to a new era of openness. The illegality and extralegality continue, now with more coordination between the captain and those few police officers who know the Wesen score (see Ch. 2). When Prince Eric comes to Portland and has Nick kidnapped and turned into a zombie-like creature, Nick kills a man who attacks him. Renard organizes the cover-up for Nick, even stealing the security video that shows the fight. Despite what some viewers might have suspected, he never uses it against Nick. When Nick wishes to turn himself in, Renard shows him the video and Nick recalls seeing the man's knife before killing him with his bare hands. Renard tells Nick, "This is one of those times when you walk in two worlds. You know why you did it, you just can't explain it— at least not in a court of law" (3.2). This speech conveys much of the philosophy behind Renard's duality. Whether it suffices as justification for all his actions is another question.

"I understand he's not exactly traditional": Renard as Foil of Nick

When Prince Eric has zombie Nick placed in a coffin, he mockingly says, "Good night, sweet Grimm"—which is also the title of the episode, the second season finale. The words, as many will know, echo those addressed to Hamlet as he dies. The title of the Season Four finale is "Cry Havoc"— words of vengeance from Hamlet. In the world's most famous revenge tragedy, Hamlet avenges both father and mother. In *Grimm*, Nick's mother has been murdered (much more gruesomely than Gertrude). The phrase in Hamlet is "Good night, sweet prince," and I would argue that, mocking though he may be, Eric is granting Nick equivalently elite status. Sean Renard and Nick Burkhardt are thus, in different ways, princes; and they are foils in many ways.

Perhaps most striking are the parallels and variations in Nick and Renard's mothers. Both mothers are supernaturally powerful and loving but strikingly absent. Diane Long Hoeveler, following Moers, calls the "absent mother" a standard element of the Gothic (xiv). Nick's mother "died" when he was twelve; when her husband was murdered in a car crash, she decided to pretend to be dead to keep her enemies away from her son. Similarly, Sean's life was upended when he was thirteen. He tells Eric, "I believe I was thirteen when my mother pulled me out of French literature class in Geneva and whisked us out of the country to keep us from being murdered by your mother" (2.22). Thus both boys entered puberty with the threat of or confrontation with death. Renard's mention of French literature class suggests his protected earlier status; it would seem both he and Nick were removed from relative innocence at the same stage of life. Renard's mother stayed with him longer; she relocated to Portland in part to be close to the wise Hexenbiest Henrietta (4.11). But as adults, both men are rarely able to contact these absent mothers. Renard's mother, the accomplished, wealthy Hexenbiest Elizabeth Lascelles, seems to mistrust letting her whereabouts be known, presumably for fear of the Royals; Kelly Burkhardt, Nick's mother, is often on some Grimm quest, dealing death rather than fearing it. Each woman, however, materializes when told her son is in deadly peril. Elizabeth endangers herself to save Sean's life after he has been shot (4.1); Kelly endangers herself when Juliette (newly a Hexenbiest) tells her Nick's life is at risk. Kelly is killed by the Royals who have so often threatened Elizabeth. In fact, they kill Kelly in order to get Renard's child—the child born of his "Face Off" sexual encounter with Adalind. In desperate circumstances, he has given her to Kelly to keep her from the Royals. Months before Kelly's death, when Elizabeth learns of her grandchild, she wants to know where Kelly and the child are. Trying to find out, Renard tells Nick, "I don't want my mother to kill your mother." Nick, with apparent sincerity, responds, "And I don't want my mother to kill your mother" (4.6). (Kelly has already killed Adalind's mother). These mothers illuminate the reflections and distinctions between the two men.

Renard and Nick are also foils in other ways. They both have powers of superior strength and extensive knowledge, though Renard's has been absorbed over years and Nick's comes mainly from study in the trailer and tutelage by Monroe and Rosalee. Both men have been underestimated (as Viktor says to Renard, 4.12). Of Nick, Eric says, "I understand he's not exactly traditional," and Renard replies, "Neither am I" (2.22). Both are willing to try to work with someone very different. But Renard's difficulties with trust lead to serious problems with relationships, whereas Nick's ability to trust eventually extends his power through relationships. This applies to their drastically different attitudes about killing (see Ch. 5). Overall, Renard highlights Nick's strengths, while their position as foils shows both Renard's heroic and villainous sides.

"If you and I can overcome our differences, we will make history": Affiliations of Power

Renard, with his patriarchal upbringing, uses affiliations for protection and power. We first see him associated with the police, as has been discussed. We learn of his connection to royalty ("In the old days I would have had you drawn and quartered") before we learn of his bastardy (1.12). Princes Eric and Viktor, for their own ends, claim at various points to be willing to enfold him into the family (2.22, 4.12). Renard himself, as noted, kills a royal cousin when threatened; he also orders the assassination of Eric after Eric kidnaps Nick (3.1). When Prince Kenneth (Nico Evers-Swindell) takes over, he physically beats Renard (who is not at his best) and demands fealty or death. By the beginning of the next season, Kenneth is dead and being used as a scapegoat for killings that Renard performed (while possessed). One investigator states, "Apparently he's [Kenneth] some kind of royalty," and another adds, "If you care about that sort of thing." "Not really," says Renard, with amusing irony for the benefit of regular viewers (5.1). His statement also, however, marks his moving on from the attempt to use his affiliations with royalty as a source of power.

Even while using his royal status, Renard has also engaged with its Resistance. We see him on secret phone calls with Resistance members starting in the second season (2.4), and he has a Resistance spy in the castle (recurring character Sebastian [Christian Lagadec]). When he meets with Resistance leaders, he eschews his usual suit and wears a man-of-the-people waffle-weave sweater. In trying to convince them to work with him, he lays out his advantages: "My blood gives me access to people that we need. I understand Wesen in a way that many of you can't. And I have a Grimm" (3.8). His speaking of Nick as a possession demonstrates that his connection to Nick has always included a plan for his own power. As he says to his impatient and soon-to-be-dead cousin, "Some of us actually put some thought into what we do before we do it" (1.17). When Nick points out that Renard is, like his mother, working for the Resistance, Kelly says, "I'm not in this for myself. He's got too many strings" (3.17). Eventually, in the fourth season, Renard discards the Resistance as well, after telling one of their leaders that they have a mole. Meisner (Damien Puckler) later tells him that the Resistance holds his daughter Diana, and Renard subsequently accepts a lethal attack on them for her retrieval. Renard is eminently transactional in his associations.

For a time, as he attempts to consolidate power with Nick, he becomes close to Nick's inner circle. As noted, Renard takes the calculated risk of revealing himself to Nick shortly after Hank has learned of the Wesen world. Temporarily, the motley group works very successfully to solve crimes with a unique combination of police, Wesen, and Grimm power and knowledge. Renard's personal bravery is never in question (despite his pragmatism and self-protectiveness), and he risks his life with Nick's group more than once. Notably, he joins them in rescuing Monroe from the Wesen hate group that plans to kill him for intermarriage. Director Peter Werner shoots Nick, Renard, Hank, Rosalee, Wu, and Juliette in a power walk down the halls of the police station, an emphatic inclusion in the group. They find Monroe about to be killed after a vote by the Wesenrein group in Oxbow Park (an allusion to a 1943 film about lynching, *The Ox-Bow Incident*). They save Monroe and celebrate with a champagne toast "to your honeymoon," as Renard says; it should be recalled that Renard is himself a child of a mixed union (4.10). On another noteworthy occasion, Renard, Nick, Hank, Wu, and Monroe are ambushed by Black Claw, and Renard once again risks his life as part of Nick's group—before Renard is himself associated with Black Claw (5.1). But by the end of Season Five, Renard fires Hank and Wu and puts a shoot-to-kill order on Nick. He does so because of his next affiliation.

In the third season, after his friends have covered up his killing of a man while in a zombie state arranged by Prince Eric, Nick goes privately to Renard's office to talk. "The man I killed—" and Renard interrupts, "accidentally killed." "Well, that's not the point. I killed him." Renard impatiently responds, "Yeah, I know. And you're bothered by it." Nick, with a hint of indignation, replies, "Yes, I am. I'm beginning to remember." Then Renard, the half-Zauberbiest, speaks up: "Let me ask you something, Nick. What's really bothering you—the fact that you killed somebody, or the fact that you killed somebody who wasn't Wesen? Because God knows you've killed plenty of them. That's what you Grimms do, isn't it? Now excuse me. I've got a meeting with the mayor. When you have an answer, let me know" (3.3). He leaves Nick in stunned silence. It is perhaps the captain's finest moment, as he raises the question of civil rights as a member of a minority group speaking to a Grimm, a cop, who is a lethal enforcer. It is one of those moments when *Grimm* raises the issue of extralegal police killings through the powerful presentation of a character. It should also be acknowledged that this character is far from perfectly virtuous—but to ask this question, does he have to be?

This scene shows what seems to be a genuine feeling on the captain's part, and it is one reason for his decision, much later, to join Black Claw, the revolutionary Wesen group. As noted, we first see him working against Black Claw with Nick's group. They learn that Meisner is locally in charge of the Black-Claw-fighting organization Hadrian's Wall (HW), which includes Eve (the transformed Juliette), Nick's protégée Trubel, and Katrina Chavez, a Wesen FBI agent. HW is integrated; Black Claw, we later learn, is Wesen only—an important distinction Renard once would not have accepted. But he is drawn into Black Claw very gradually. While he is fighting the group, he starts to learn of its strength; he learns of more and more Wesen who are involved in it. Black Claw wants to take control and to subjugate or kill all normals. When the police arrest and investigate the notably named Black Claw operative Billie Trump, for instance (who works with a man named Cruz),[4] Renard says of her parents, "So we have a normal, middle-class mother and father who are backing their daughter's involvement in a radical, violent Wesen organization" (5.17). Here he is sarcastic, but he is also absorbing information about spreading attitudes. Apparently he comes to believe that, as Monroe's friend Xavier says, "There's no stopping them" (5.7). His pragmatism and search for power come into play.

While Renard is taking in information, he is himself unknowingly being manipulated into Black Claw. He is approached, as police captain, to become a public supporter of Portland mayoral candidate Andrew Dixon, who seems to be a genuinely good potential mayor. The campaign's press secretary Rachel Wood (Anne Leighton), over multiple episodes, seduces Renard. The series makes clear that she, not Renard, initiates the affair. When a Black Claw operative assassinates Dixon, and, after an anonymous tip, Renard kills the assassin during an attempted arrest, it is Rachel who reveals the plan. Dixon was to be killed so that Renard could be a hero and win the election in his place. She and another member of Black Claw unroll a Shepard Fairey–style poster of Renard's face, and Renard's first response is, "You've got to be kidding" (5.12). He does not initially accept their offer; neither, however, does he try to pursue murder charges against the woman he is sleeping with. Instead, as his whole patriarchy-soaked life has taught him, he weighs the drawbacks and benefits.

There is a poignant moment in a later episode when Rachel comes to Renard's office to pressure him to run for mayor. "Maybe I'm happy where I am," says the captain (5.14). He is in an office where we have seen him operate with intelligence and effectiveness for the greater good as well as for his own desires; in fact, it always seems that the captain believes his being in charge would improve the world. (Modesty is not his keynote.) He even, in a shadow of their connection, consults Hank and Nick about whether he should run; however, they have by then learned something of Black Claw's plans and so decide not to speak openly. This lack of trust means that a final opportunity for influence is lost. But their lack of trust is the result of years of Renard's own guardedness.

In the end, several motives lead Renard to join Black Claw. His affair with Rachel—which, it becomes clear, was planned by Black Claw—facilitates the process, but it is not a motive. The first motive is his unceasing desire for power, and his assessment that Black Claw will win ("You need to be on the right side of history," Rachel tells him, 5.14). They have offered to advance his political career far beyond Portland. The second motive is his genuine wish for racial justice (though he will later more fully understand that Black Claw wishes to replace one inequality with another). Finally, Black Claw offers to retrieve his stolen daughter for him, and it is this that pushes him into decision. In some sense, power links all these motives. There is an image, often used in the credits, from a first season episode in which mystical coins grant their bearer an addictive power over others (they once belonged to Hitler, 1.13). While briefly possessing the coins, the captain in a dream raises his arms wide to a cheering crowd below his penthouse balcony. With Black Claw, his dream at last seems to be about to come true.

Even as the dream happens, however, he maintains some sense of reality—a pragmatism that will eventually enable him to return to his useful position as captain. On the night of his election win, he tells the full-Zauberbiest leader of Black Claw, Conrad Bonaparte, "I obviously wouldn't be here without you." Bonaparte replies, "No, but you won the election legitimately." "I won. Let's just leave it at that," Renard wryly replies (5.21). Renard comes to realize he is in another patriarchal organization with a different patriarch (see Ch. 9) and a different prejudice. Furthermore, as he tells Adalind, he and she "do not have complete control here" (5.20). For a time, he throws himself into the attempt to create a Black Claw world. After Bonaparte dies at Renard's own hand, and after Nick's group convinces Portlanders that Renard has abdicated the mayorship, Black Claw tries to pressure Renard into continuing. For a plenitude of reasons (to be discussed later), Renard at last repudiates them. He is unaffiliated and—almost—alone.

"If I didn't know better, I'd be in love with you": Renard as Unloved

For someone who tries so hard for far-reaching connections, Renard is a peculiarly lonely person. Only his mother (who is almost never there) and his daughter (who is, for years, lost to him) seem to really love him. As for romantic love, after he dismisses Adalind in the first season, none of his affairs involve love. In "Over My Dead Body," an episode constructed with a set of parallel romances, the glamorous blonde aristocrat Mia Gaudot pretends interest. With his typical mistrust (too often justified), he has her tailed, and stops her as she is about to abandon him in her private jet (2.6). Rachel, as noted, seduces him on orders, not from personal desire; she is simply doing a job. On the evening of his electoral victory, even though he and Adalind are publicly a couple, Adalind refuses him and he returns to Rachel. But after valedictory sex, she tells him it is over—first gently, then—when he seems to want to persist—with frigid coldness: "Get out" (5.21). He has nothing, not even friendly affection, from her or any other sexual partner we know of. Her brutal rejection is comparable to his coldness with Adalind after she loses her powers; it is a transactional relationship.[5]

Renard also has a relationship of sorts with Juliette. First they obsessively lust for one another as a result of the kiss that awakens Juliette from her coma, both the coma and the obsession coming from a spell by Adalind. Renard, trying to maintain a relationship with Nick, and, perhaps, out of some genuine integrity (or a desire for self-control) fights this obsession. But later, when Juliette unintentionally becomes a Hexenbiest, she turns to him. He attempts to advise her but when she asks to stay with him, he resists, saying that it will put him in an awkward situation with Nick. Finally he agrees to let her stay if she opens a magic book for him by cutting herself and bleeding on it, a job he cannot do (4.15). In other words, this relationship, too, is transactional. When they ultimately have sex, there is no affection. He has returned, angry and beaten, from his confrontation with Kenneth. She touches Renard's cut lip, saying, "Does that hurt?" When he says yes, she adds, "So will this," and he says "Good," whereupon they ferociously kiss (4.17). He wakes up to an empty bed—as he always will.

His major and most fraught relationship, however, is with Adalind. Some of this relationship has already been outlined; after he rejects her, Adalind goes to Europe and seduces Eric. She is working for Eric when she returns to Portland and has sex with Renard to deflect the magic lust for Juliette that Adalind herself has vengefully created. It is not clear whether or not her feelings are anything more than sexual at this point, but her consequent pregnancy brings them together again. She chooses (with the help of Meisner and Kelly Burkhardt) to rejoin Renard with the baby, and they are briefly reunited. But when the Royals come after Diana (who has not only royal blood but extraordinary magical power), Renard makes another mistake borne of lack of trust. He pretends to give the child to Prince Viktor, to Adalind's anguish and fury. He does not let Adalind know that he has instead given her to Kelly for safekeeping, with the help of Nick's friends—who also mistrust Adalind and keep the secret. The choice is understandable but an irretrievable error for their relationship. Adalind pretends to return to him in order to manipulate him so she can regain Diana; she follows orders from Viktor. As they hide out (in a luxury hotel), she invites Renard to sleep with her, and afterwards, he tells her, "If I didn't know you better, I'd be in love with you" (3.21). Her face flickers in this noir moment, but she proceeds with her plans, using him and deserting him as coldly as he once did her. Years later, when he has joined Black Claw, they enable him to return Diana to Adalind. At the end of the episode, there is a shot of the six-foot-five Renard that emphasizes his broad shoulders as he looks down on mother and daughter rejoined, the sense of power palpable in his stance. In Adalind's face there is a hint of fear because she knows Renard will use Diana to control her (5.18). Their relationship is infected with mistrust and manipulation.

This manipulation leads Adalind to a pretense of being part of a happy family with Renard, Diana, and Kelly, her son with Nick, with whom she is now in love. Both Diana and her daddy push Adalind towards renewing their relationship (see Ch. 9). Scenes of Adalind's resistance are sometimes tense and sometimes humorous. On the night of his election, Diana magically draws her parents together, and they come close to having sex—except that Adalind realizes what is happening. "You really think that I just all of a sudden decided you were the hottest guy on earth and couldn't wait to take my clothes off and hop into bed with you?" "Well, I *am* the new mayor," he offers. Roiz's performance of this moment makes it both laughably ridiculous and faintly touching: All his life, Renard has thought that such status and power would bring him happiness, and he has still to learn that it will not. His sexual pressure (among other things) will eventually lead Adalind to say "I hate him" (6.3). His longest romantic relationship most clearly reveals that his lack of trust and pursuit of power prevent him from experiencing love.

Wounds and Water, Trust and Transition

Hoeveler, referencing Brontë's Rochester, observes that "gothic heroes all endure very real beatings and wounds, not merely symbolic ones, and in the receiving of these wounds it is as if they have earned the right to overthrow their fathers and establish a new [...] family" (20). Renard seems to fit this pattern at least to a point. In the fourth season he undergoes a rehearsal for his ultimate wounding when he is possessed by the spirit of Jack the Ripper. In the final season he is haunted by the ghost of Meisner past in a rather Dickensian fashion, experiencing a relationship that is not transactional. Furthermore, through the last two seasons, he comes to know someone he cares for more than himself: his daughter Diana. As he and Nick's crew together struggle to protect her and all humanity from an apocalyptic threat, he receives his ultimate wound when he dies for Diana. But when the world resets, he may have a chance to change.

At the beginning of the fourth season, Renard, having been shot in the chest, is declared dead just as his Hexenbiest mother arrives in the operating room. She saves him, but—as Adalind later explains—when he comes back from his brief time dead, a spirit attaches itself to him. Months later, when Renard rises from his empty bed after sex with Juliette, his wounds are bleeding again (not for the first time). He cries "No!" and punches his mirror, which breaks (a typical sign of fracturing identity); he flashes back to his operation. Then one of the eeriest scenes in the series occurs when his bedroom wall opens to a bright blue sky with the sun behind. Giant, red, bloody, black-clawed hands reach out to him; he falls back, mouth wide open in shock; he yells and tumbles to the floor. What happens to Renard in private often suggests that he is undergoing more than others comprehend. Through the ensuing months the others will realize that he is possessed by the same spirit that controlled Jack the Ripper. The captain's horror when he understands that he may have been randomly killing is not just a display for others; he expresses it when alone, as well (4.21). Jack's kills are a distorted, extreme version of Renard's own. He awakens, again and again, in—as Henrietta observes—places associated with water. One Lynchean scene opens with Renard floating in a suit in a swimming pool at night. The first shot shows him not only face down but upside down, in relation to the screen—appropriately for his disoriented life. He is the hanged man, poised for transition. The blue light of the rectangular pool almost fills the screen, with Renard in the center. We hear what we might if our heads were under water; we see his face under water as he opens his eyes and mouth. Then he splutters up and swims out, grasping the edge, panting (4.20). Renard in the water is suffering as he confronts a concentrated version of the evil he has engaged in, at the same time he is cleansed. In the season's penultimate episode, he says to the others, "Maybe it's best I do remember," and allows them to treat him (4.21). The treatment, though he does not know beforehand, involves their not only dosing him but shooting him with rubber bullets, convincing the spirit that the body is dead—in short, putting him through another death from which he is painfully reborn. But this experience is not cathartic enough for the captain; the patriarchal power of Black Claw tempts him back into those claw-like clutches.

When Black Claw, led by Bonaparte, invades HW headquarters near the end of the fifth season, Bonaparte tortures Meisner as Renard watches. We have seen Meisner, from the second season, as Renard's comrade-in-arms. Both have been persecuted by Renard's family. Meisner killed Eric and birthed Diana: he was the sole helper to Adalind as they hid in Meisner's family's cabin in the woods after Renard entrusted him with helping her escape the Royals. Renard and Meisner have worked together for the Resistance—even roomed together in a pungent hole-in-the-wall with a sewer exit they were forced to use. Later, as the king tried to steal Diana away in a helicopter, Meisner revealed himself as the pilot and threw the king out over the sea. Once Diana is handed to the Resistance, only

Meisner bothers to tell Renard that Diana is alive and his father is dead. When Bonaparte and Renard step over the dead bodies in HW headquarters, Meisner tells Renard, "You chose the wrong side, Sean." "I never choose sides. You shouldn't either," says Renard. This is a naked desire for power and self-protection without the pretense of ethics. He still invites Meisner to join Black Claw, but Bonaparte insists Black Claw is Wesen only and proceeds to torture Meisner till his eyes bleed. Again and again Renard tells Bonaparte to stop. When he does not, Renard finally shoots Meisner in the head. "You are compassionate," Bonaparte says; but to him, it is no compliment: "That's dangerous for all of us" (5.22). When Nick, Trubel, and Eve find the body, Trubel weeps, saying, "I thought Meisner was Renard's friend." "Sean Renard has no friends," says Eve. This is their understanding of him, but viewers know he is more complicated. The two sides of Renard struggle in the scene of Meisner's death.

In the next episode, in the next season, the haunting begins. Renard sees blood on his hands; he hears Meisner's voice saying, "You chose the wrong side, Sean," and sees his bloody eyes in the face of Sgt. Franco (6.1). He hears bullet casings fall and looks down to see the gun he used (6.2). Then, after Nick and friends push him out of the mayoralty, he sees Meisner himself, come back to haunt him—in his home, in his office, in the parking garage. Dead Meisner allows himself more of a sense of humor; when the angry Renard throws coffee at him, it simply splashes on the window-wall: "Talk about coffee going right through you!" Meisner chortles (6.4). He also takes great delight in pointing out to Sean (as he in friendship calls him, unlike most of the other characters) that others are seeing him talking aloud to no one (6.4). Meisner wears exactly the same shirt, suit, and tie as Renard, planting the idea that he may be merely Renard's conscience. He forces Renard to come to grips with the fact that Meisner's death is the result of his betrayal. In the third episode of the haunting, Renard calls up and visits the pawn shop of an old acquaintance, Steiger, to learn if he is really haunted or simply losing his mind (a question that occurs to a fair number of characters in *Grimm*). Steiger asks for a magical price, and Sean offers a ring: "This was my father's. And his father's before him."[6] Renard is giving up a talisman of the patriarchy to find the truth. And of course, the haunting only troubles him because he does, after all, harbor compassion. He must strip naked to be tested. He has his answer when Steiger turns out to be Meisner, and the pawn shop to be empty.

Viewers, too, know the haunting is real when, in the next episode, dead Meisner saves Renard's life after he begins his renewal. A leader of Black Claw comes to Renard's office and pressures him to continue their political plans, but Renard finally rebels and kicks the man out. It is then that Meisner asks Renard, "Do you trust me?"—and it is a supremely important moment for Renard. Yes, he does trust the man he has killed, his true friend. Meisner warns Renard that the man from the office and an accomplice are waiting to kill him in the parking garage. Meisner blurs their eyes as Renard kills them. When Renard asks Meisner why he saved him, the answer is, "This time, you chose the right side, Sean." Life cannot be just self-preservation, or power for the sake of self-preservation; there is an ethical color to every action. Renard is hardly an angel of light, but he is beginning to see.

Diana, Power, and Love

As in life, there are simultaneous, various threads of development for characters in *Grimm*, and perhaps the most important thread for Renard is spun by his daughter Diana. There is a moment in the third season after he has given her to Kelly that no one but the audience sees: Renard in a bar alone with a whiskey, listening to Miles Davis ("Flamenco Sketches," from *Kind of Blue*). A Hitchcockian shot from under his table emphasizes the scene, showing, in reverse, a white paper napkin with the word DIANA handwritten on it in pen. Renard's feeling for his daughter is real. It has begun before her birth; Roiz shows it in Renard's face when he secretly watches, with great seriousness, an ultrasound (3.5). The feeling shows in his quiet smile when, alone, he hears over the phone from Meisner that "It's a girl" (3.14); and when he finally holds her, he gazes at her, seeming spellbound (3.17–3.18). The next chapter discusses the problem of male protectiveness, but Renard's protectiveness is unusual in that it leads him to let his daughter go. It is also mixed with a love that grows as he comes to know Diana upon her return.

Certain aspects of Diana and Renard's relationship are discussed in the last chapter, but other aspects connect more directly to Renard's own journey. His relationship with his extraordinarily powerful daughter is a mixture of exasperation and adoration. When we see him put her to bed in his own home for the first time, he says, "I love you"—something we never hear him say to anyone else (5.19). In the same episode, he begins to recognize her power as a shield: When Bonaparte says they will kill Adalind if she refuses to join Black Claw, Renard replies, "Well, you may not want to tell that to Diana" (5.19). Bonaparte's attitude of extreme patriarchal control will later lead to his death. Renard also recognizes the danger of Diana's power: after she has killed Rachel, he angrily tells Adalind that he wants to have a talk with Diana "about killing people" (5.22). When she tries to magically push her parents together, Renard is more susceptible—perhaps because he would not object to rekindling the relationship. After Bonaparte almost chokes Adalind to death and Diana sees the marks, she magically guides Renard's hand to kill Bonaparte just in time to save Nick's life. This action, too, might be easier for Diana to accomplish because of ambivalence in Renard about Nick and Bonaparte, who has brought about Meisner's death and almost killed Adalind. Is he coming to wish Bonaparte's death? In some ways, Diana undercuts Renard's power; in other ways, she can be seen as an extension of it.

It seems that Renard comes to realize the importance of guiding Diana towards ethical behavior for the sake of their own safety—and in reinforcing ethical behavior in her, he gradually comes to reinforce ethical behavior in himself. He confirms (6.4) that she caused Bonaparte's death because, as Adalind puts it, she "just wanted her daddy to be a hero and save Mommy" (6.1). When Diana says with a sigh that "Mommy loves Nick," he replies, "And I love you," and accepts it when she concludes, "I guess we all love each other then" (6.4). When Nick and friends force him to give up the mayorship, an important part of the deal for him is that he gets to raise his daughter (6.3). For Renard, Diana represents both power and love.

Because Diana is threatened by the apocalyptic Zerstorer, he joins forces with the rest of the group once more, all of whom are fighting for her safety as well as the security of their whole world. He thus has the opportunity to apologize to Adalind. Telling her they did one thing right—Diana—he adds to his apology, "I wish I'd never heard of those damn keys or Black Claw" (6.13). When Trubel sees him and angrily says, "You're supposed to be on our side now?" (echoing Meisner), Adalind tells her, "A lot has changed," and Trubel says, "Yeah, I know. I wish Meisner knew." "Trust me, he does," says Renard, sealing the connection to the friend who helped him change. (Trubel simply unsheathes her machete and stalks away.) At one point we see Renard offering, like most of the other adults in this small group of heroes, to enter Zerstorer's dimension to save Eve and Nick—a man he has recently tried to kill—because it is for the greater good. Renard has, after all, always looked to the big picture. But his relationship with Diana awakens him to the importance of the individual: he experiences non-transactional love at last. In "The End," we see him die trying to save her, her name his last word.[7]

Conclusion: "Even You"

When the world resets and everyone lives again, Nick lands in Monroe's living room, shocked to see them there. Joyfully, he exclaims, "You're all okay. Even you—" those two words being addressed to Renard. As Renard stands there, looking a bit befuddled, he is holding onto Diana, the person who has pulled him into human connection. Renard is among those that Nick calls family: "Everyone I ever loved and anyone who ever meant anything to me—my family" (6.13). We can assume that Renard fits into the second category, but he does at least fit in. In the "20 Years Later" sequence that follows, the adult Diana speaks of "Mom and Dad" to her half-brother Kelly, Nick's son, leaving us to wonder whether or not Renard has maintained that role; perhaps Diana has two fathers. Perhaps Renard has grown out of his Gothic darkness, his fearful, untrusting patriarchal desire for power. We do not know. There is, quite believably, more than a touch of the patriarchal in each of the main male characters, but the hero-villain Renard has most clearly illustrated the dangers of immersion in such gendered attitudes. His final position as a family man is not a complete moral resolution, but another way to pose the problem, since patriarchy, after all, begins at home.

Five

"You know, Nick— he's a sensitive Grimm"

Nick Burkhardt, Emotional Engagement, and Male Melodrama

"I think watching my hairdo's storyline will be the most compelling. That first season haircut—what the hell was going on? You tell me. There was a flatiron involved. I'm not kidding," laughs David Giuntoli, portrayer of the Grimm, Nick Burkhardt, in a final season DVD feature ("A *Grimm* Farewell"). Visual, physical presentation of a character certainly plays a part—perhaps a more important part than we might want to admit. I confess that after watching the first couple of episodes of *Grimm*, I turned away from the series, specifically thinking that the hero was too blandly handsome for my taste. I have no doubt that the hairdo played its part in my decision. In the back of my mind, I believe I saw his looks as a sign of the kind of support of the status quo that Kimberlé Crenshaw (among others) warns against.[1] I turned back to *Grimm* only after my colleague Mary Alice Money convinced me, a season or so later, that the blandness seemed to have been purposeful, meant to contrast with a later "roughened up" version of the character. In Nick's very first scene, his police partner, Detective Hank Griffin, takes a photograph to capture Nick while he is "still young and innocent," a framing that suggests that showrunners Greenwalt and Kouf did plan for a roughening to come. And the character does grow deeper and darker as the series proceeds. His look slowly changes, with his hair eventually creeping back from his forehead and his face more and more often shadowed with stubble. His changing look—as is often the way with fiction—represents that changing character. Nick begins as a relatively naïve man of benevolent, if simply defined, intentions; he grows to become much more knowledgeable about the world and the people in it, and much more complicated in his own motives. Nick is the white, heterosexual hero at the center of a fantasy/police series. He is given elements of traditionally masculine presentation—but that presentation allows protective coloration for the character, whose open-minded, transgressive relationships and emotionally engaged male melodrama provide a shifting flow of experience that works against what might be the expected pattern of a dominating male superhero. He thus offers some viewers the chance to join him on the journey from flatiron naiveté to the shadowed uncertainty of a more mature look—and view of the world.

"Nick, do you see things the rest of us can't?" Seeing and Masculine Power

Central to Nick's nature as a hero is his special sight. He does not enter into his ability to see the hidden bestial aspect of Wesen (and his special hearing and strength) until he is around thirty years old; indeed, his first few sightings make him doubt his sanity. When his dying aunt comes to town to tell him of his heritage, he is already working as a police detective. His roles as a Grimm—a kind of superhero—and police officer will both overlap and conflict.

In the pilot episode, many elements of the character are established. Nick is an intelligent, hard-working, kind man, liked and respected by those around him. Young, hopeful Nick lives with a woman for whom, in his first scene, he has just bought an engagement ring.[2] His story, as Linda Williams would say of the melodramatic protagonist, begins in innocence (65). Like the typical hero of melodrama, he is good-looking. He and his partner are clearly friends who are both devoted to and good at their detective jobs—in this case, the entirely virtuous one of finding a missing girl—a hoodie-wearing variation of Red Riding Hood. But there is much more to the world than these police officers know. Early in the episode, Nick starts seeing bizarre visages take the place of the faces of certain people, and he learns that these visions are true.

Nick's world is turned upside down, and body placement in the pilot reinforces what is happening to the character: Three times he is physically thrown. First, early in the episode, his aunt and he himself are attacked in the night by the Wesen Hulda, a "Reaper of the Grimms," on the sidewalk in front of his home, where aunt and nephew have gone to talk in private about her coming death and his arriving powers. Police officer Burkhardt shoots and kills the scythe-wielding Hulda, but Nick shoots from the ground, having been literally "knocked on [his] ass" by his first conflict with a Wesen. This Wesen seems simply evil. Later, his police captain tells Nick he will need to see the department therapist after this, his "first shooting." In other words, Nick as a cop has never killed before; his first act of fatal violence happens as he becomes a Grimm. Becoming a Grimm means entering a world of deadly harm. The second time Nick is toppled in the pilot happens midway, in an encounter with Monroe, the Wesen who will become his best friend (along with his partner Hank), but whom Nick first sees as a suspect—the wolf-like creature he believes has taken the child. The chapter on Monroe discusses their double throw-down at some length; for now, let it be noted that Nick's incipient, mistaken understanding of Wesen is demolished as surely as he is overturned by Monroe. He learns (and later learns more fully) that Wesen are not all wicked monsters but can be admirable instead. Finally, the end of the episode finds Nick crashing yet again, this time having been penetrated by the poison of a Hexenbiest, a witch-like beauty whose secret face is that of an ancient, distorted hag. The Hexenbiest in question is Adalind Schade; the chapter on Adalind also analyzes at length this scene of Nick's fall. Like Monroe, Adalind will become important in Nick's life—first as an enemy, later as the mother of his son, and finally as a representative of loving partnership. She will thus lead to Nick's biological combination with a Wesen. Taken together, Nick's three falls demonstrate emphatically that his world has been upended. In at least two out of three cases, they will turn out to be Fortunate Falls.

Nick's world is upended because he sees things differently, and his aunt—also a Grimm—helps him understand his new vision. But Aunt Marie does not simply impart oral history; she also bequeaths him her silver Airstream trailer, filled with handwritten books of lore accrued by Grimms through the centuries (as well as rare potions, weapons, and devices). The trailer becomes Nick's refuge, a private place where, in a sense, he receives help from Grimms who have gone before him, through their writings and relics—to which he in his turn adds. This is a place where he allows only those closest to him to enter[3]; it represents his most secret self, to be shared with only a few. The trailer's books aid him in understanding but also contribute to one of the major problems of the series. In the pilot, Monroe refers to Grimms as "profiling" Wesen. If we accept that Wesen represent racial/ethnic Others and we consider that Nick is a police detective, then the show presents its hero as using racial profiling—a seriously problematic implication. The books in the trailer, in Nick's private space, identify specific types of Wesen as having specific moral characteristics—descriptions which lend themselves to racial profiling (see Introduction). Furthermore, if we accept that Nick can see the inner nature of a person, then he, the cop, feels justified when he shoots, even if others cannot see the evidence—a deeply troubling piece of symbolism. It will take Nick's lived experience as a character (along with other characters') to at least partially undermine this implication.

Five—"You know, Nick—he's a sensitive Grimm"

Nick's evolution comes through his relationships with others. Nick is at the center of a varied set of characters, each of which is analyzed in a chapter of this book. Though they are all vividly developed in terms of their own natures and stories, they nonetheless also all exist in relation to Nick: his Wesen friends (such as Monroe and Rosalee); his lover-partners (Juliette and Adalind); his cop buddies (such as Hank and Wu); his police captain (Sean Renard); his two mothers (Kelly Burkhardt and Marie Kessler); characters that he mentors/parents (such as the younger Grimm Trubel and Adalind's daughter Diana). Much of Nick's nature is described in their chapters (especially the one on Monroe). Most of these characters were born into the world of Wesen. In some fantasies, everyone knows there are dragons; that is not the case in the world of Nick Burkhardt (or Harry Potter or Buffy Summers), and that is part of their struggle.[4] That is one reason that their core group of knowing friends is so important. And it is one reason their narratives are so resonant, suggesting dangers in the world that not everyone recognizes. Nick Burkhardt is presented first of all as a good and in most ways ordinary man who comes to clearly see hidden perils all around.

"I'm okay with just some coffee": Nick as "Normal"

Nick is presented with many cultural markers of normative masculinity. Early in his relationship with his Blutbad friend, Nick says, "Look, I was different growing up, and I have a feeling you were too, Monroe" (1.5). We learn that after a fatal car crash,[5] "For the first few years, I wished I was in the car with [my parents]" (1.20), and after the crash, his Aunt Marie frequently moved the two of them around—for safety, though he did not know so at the time (3.19). While Nick may have grown up as the perpetual new-boy orphan, as an adult he wears standard masculine traits.[6] He favors beer over wine (the latter being the preferred drink of his gourmet friend Monroe); in fact, one of the DVD features includes a montage of Nick opening refrigerators to pull out beer (see, e.g., 2.13, 5.9; "Gag Reel"). He also reports on one occasion that he "had to drink a lot of mezcal and eat a worm" to win an Elvis lamp (2.18). He is a black coffee guy. When Monroe offers him quinoa blueberry pancakes, his response is "I'm okay with just some coffee" (2.14). We never see him drink tea. He also says that he cannot cook (2.17)—in distinct contrast to Monroe. In addition to fighting well, he seems to enjoy paying attention to his weapons and tools. He mentions cleaning one of his oversized Grimm guns (2.7) and, with Monroe's help, practices with his weapons in the woods (1.19). When he needs a knife, of course he has one in his pocket (1.16). We see him shirtless, sweating away as he uses a large hammer on an outsized tunnel door, yelling, "Son of a bitch!" when he has trouble with the job (5.9). He is a sports fan, particularly of hometown Portland teams the Timbers and the Trailblazers (2.18, 1.17). Speaking of Nick and Hank, Juliette asks, "Don't you guys ever talk about anything but work?" and Nick replies, "Yeah, sure we do. You know we lost eighty dollars on the Blazers game last week—that got very emotional" (1.17). Then after a pause, with mocking emphasis, he adds, "*Men.*" Both the series and the character recognize the gender markings with self-conscious, amused distance.

Juliette's comment about "talk" relates to another set of masculine markers for Nick. Calvin Thomas writes of male anxieties of production particularly in the context of language (e.g., pp. 8–10, 13–18, 28). Nick is far from the extreme version of the "strong, silent" type, but he is relatively quiet, especially in contrast to the ebulliently verbose Monroe. Nick enjoys throwing out funny lines (as will be discussed later), but he is not very verbally expressive about his feelings. In the pilot, when his aunt is being carried off in an ambulance and Juliette says, "I love you," he does not reply in kind. It is not unusual for him to leave the "I" out, saying merely "Love you" (e.g., 1.12, 1.20). He does not speak those words on-screen to Adalind, his second romantic partner and the mother of his child, until the last episode of the series. When he traumatically loses his powers and Juliette asks, "Can you talk to me?", he answers, "I don't know" (4.1). When he reunites with his protégée Trubel after thinking she may have been dead, she weeps and speaks with strong emotion, while he simply agrees quietly that he had thought they might never see each other again—though Adalind has earlier told Trubel that Nick was "out of his mind" with worry about her (5.6). He is also shown struggling to put into words his entries in the annals of the *Grimm* books (e.g., 1.18, 3.6).

There is a device of body language associated with Giuntoli's performance of Nick that clearly links to this pattern of guarded expression. It can be repeatedly observed in the fifth season, in particular (after Nick has undergone some severe losses): When Nick is involved in an emotional talk, he is positioned to be looking straight ahead rather than directly into the eyes of his conversational partner, thus protecting himself emotionally. For instance, Nick and Monroe have a conversation while the two men are standing on the roof of Nick's new loft home, with a brightly lit night cityscape of Portland before them. As they discuss Nick's relationship with Adalind, they look out at the view rather than each other, only occasionally stealing glances. This conversation of emotional uncertainty ends with a remark from Monroe that might, in its suggestion of sexual prowess, reassure some viewers uncomfortable with the uncertainty (while others might embrace the weirdness): "But dude, seriously, it is so weird that you slept with both of them while they were each other" (5.10).[7] In the next episode, the same body position is used. Nick decides to tell Monroe that he has slept with Adalind, but he does so while they are in a car together. Though they occasionally indulge in a partial, quick head turn, they mainly focus their eyes on the road (5.11). Similar positioning happens when Nick is in a car with Eve (the transformed Juliette) and she tells him about having slept with Rachel Wood (5.17). Adalind, who is now sleeping with Nick, for a time had suppressed the Hexenbiest within her but has kept secret the fact that her powers have returned; when she and Nick finally have an open conversation about her powers, the two are seated on the end of their bed, both facing forward for much of the talk (5.19). The body positioning shows Nick's discomfort (what some would consider to be stereotypically male discomfort) with communicating on matters in which he will be expressing his own emotions—though, as will later be discussed, he is often good at attending to others' emotions.

One other pattern for the character represents a noteworthy version of normative male avoidance of emotional expression: Nick has a habit of walking out. In the second season, Juliette suffers from amnesia and forgets her relationship with Nick, so Monroe lets Nick live with him for a time. When a dinner between Nick and Juliette goes badly and Monroe asks Nick to talk about it, Nick angrily walks out (2.20). Admittedly, he is under the influence of a supernatural creature at the time, but his underlying behavior tendencies prevail. In the third season, Nick becomes the victim of another supernatural being and goes on a rampage as a zombie. Afterwards, when Nick and Juliette are discussing his objections to the cover-up his friends plan for the consequences of his rampage, Nick walks out again (3.2). Perhaps most notably, he walks out after learning that Juliette has become a Hexenbiest and has told his captain of her condition before telling Nick (4.14). Though Nick is unquestionably shocked by Juliette's change he is wounded that she has revealed her problem to Renard first. At this moment, he seems more concerned with his own feelings than Juliette's very serious problem (which is the way they both see her condition at this point). His emotions are understandable, though hardly altruistic—hardly heroic. And rather than staying to talk, he strides out into the night despite Juliette's pleas. Though he soon tries fervently to communicate with her, this initial decision to walk out has major repercussions for their relationship. He continues the pattern later. After Juliette is presumed dead and Adalind has just had baby Kelly (her child with Nick), Nick tells Adalind of Juliette's "death" when he is placing the baby in its crib, looking down at the child. Realizing what Nick must be going through, Adalind thanks him for taking care of her and the baby. Nick can muster no more than the faintest of nods before he walks silently out the door and into the room he once shared with Juliette. Nick's pattern of walking out fits with stereotypical male avoidance of expression of emotion; at the same time, however, it suggests that there is much emotion for him to suppress. None of these are extreme behaviors, but they add many small strokes to a portrait of normative male ways of being.

Nick's "normality" is also conveyed through his personal physicality. Of the five regular male characters, Renard, Hank, and Monroe are all taller than Nick. Only Wu is shorter. Thus Nick is presented as average in height. He has a body of ordinary, healthy muscularity, in contrast to the muscle definition of the frequently shirtless Renard or Hank. It is not unusual to see Nick stride purposefully (e.g., 2.22, 3.19, 6.12), and he sometimes, in particularly happy moments, even has a bit of a bounce (e.g., 2.6), but his walk is usually unremarkable. So are his clothes: Attending a dinner for a police ceremony, the captain shows up in what appears to be a designer suit, while Nick, with his generic dark suit and blue shirt, wears a brown belt—hardly a fashion plate (2.8). When a beautiful dragon-like Wesen meets him, she says, "You're not exactly what I expected [...] Grimms are bad-asses" (1.14). Similarly, a stolidly vicious Gelumcaedus Wesen tells Nick that his grandfather's stories of Grimms frightened him, but "You don't look so scary" (3.7). Nick, who lives in a very nice middle-class house (partly paid for by his veterinarian girlfriend) but who cannot pull together a hundred thousand dollars in twenty-four hours (5.10) is consistently presented as a normal, middle-class man—with secret superpowers. Repeatedly, the series raises the idea that such a person may be underestimated (e.g., 2.13, 2.22, 5.22).

As the audience is getting to know Nick, he is presented as a straight-arrow cop—and that attitude is presented as normal in his world. When Rosalee speaks of getting false documents for her activist ex-boyfriend so that he can leave the country and escape an assassin, Nick does not want to hear about the illegal papers (1.18). When Rosalee and Monroe want to help a pregnant woman and her partner who are two of the last of an endangered Wesen species, Nick objects that "He may have killed a guy," and Rosalee responds, "but the baby is innocent." By the end of the episode, Nick will have helped deliver the baby and shot the killer who hunted the couple and their child (2.19). During an attack by a zombie horde, when Monroe says, "You might have to shoot a few," Nick answers, "I can't—they're innocent victims" (2.22). In contrast, after he himself has become a zombie and killed with bare hands a man who attacked him with a knife, Nick insists, "If I killed somebody, I have to turn myself in" (3.2). It takes the unanimous persuasion of his small secret community to convince him otherwise, to convince him that he too is an innocent victim. When a Wesen father tries to protect his daughters by confessing to a crime he did not commit, Nick tells him, "We'd rather leave here with who's really responsible" (3.4). When he confronts a Wesen who claims to see the future and eats babies to prevent their growing up to be serial killers, Nick tells the baby-eater, "If I wasn't a cop, you'd be holding your head in your hands"—that is, Nick is tempted to indulge in the Grimms' traditional response, decapitation (6.4). At one point, Nick's Wesen friend Bud Wurstner, trying to recoup the mistake of almost revealing Nick's secret identity to the unknowing Juliette, tells her that a Grimm is just a term for a "good cop" (2.4). Bud's explanation is an attempt to tie Nick to an ideal normality.

"He really tries to protect you": Nick and Protectiveness

The problem is that a good cop can also be a Grimm. We are presented with the normal good guy deciding to take actions that should be abnormal but are presented as acceptable because he and those close to him see dangers that most cannot. Chapter Two discusses and categorizes serious extralegal actions, including killings, undertaken by Nick and his crew. The first time Nick kills a Wesen, Hulda in the pilot, Nick follows police procedure, and Hulda has a record that supports Nick's truthful story. Later in the first season, however, when Nick is attacked by two other Reapers of the Grimms, the fight ends with Nick calling Monroe and asking him to "bring a shovel" (1.19). This is the second time Nick illegally deals with a dead body (though not the last). In the preceding episode, he directs Monroe to get rid of one that was killed by a friend of Rosalee's because Nick knows Monroe and Rosalee will otherwise be targeted by assassins and, in fact, the dead man was an assassin. Nick explains to the killer of the assassin that he is "saving my friends" (1.18), protecting them. He and his friends more than once put their badges aside to save Monroe (e.g., 2.6, 4.10). And as Monroe says to Juliette, "He really tries to protect you"—a remark that simply irritates Juliette (2.12). Nick also acts extralegally, and sometimes without violence, to save others besides his friends. On Halloween night, he and Hank sneak the jailed former detective Valentina Espinosa out of her cell to help them save three children who would be killed by La Llorona, the ghost, by midnight (2.9). At the end of the second season, they take Al the zombie tow truck guy to the Spice Shop so that Rosalee can save him. When Hank asks, "Can we [legally] do this?" Nick answers, "Hell if I know," but he risks the extralegality and thus helps to save the lives of Al and dozens of other afflicted people (2.22). As Michael J. Diamond asserts, "In Western societies [...] the underlying cultural images for masculinity generally continue to mean being rational, protective, aggressive, and dominating" (29).

About *Grimm* specifically, Nancy Taber argues that "Nick's role as protector to Juliette in particular but all civilians in general" results in subordination of those protected (19–20). Many of us would like our heroes to be protective, but protectiveness can easily slide into domination.

Perhaps the most grisly extrajudicial killing comes when Nick stabs Prince Kenneth, the man who has killed Nick's mother (4.22). After Kenneth is arrested based on planted evidence (a severed head) because they do not have evidence of the real crime, Wu drops him at a deserted factory where Nick is waiting. Nick emerges eerily from the shadows as Kenneth (in his evil British accent) mocks both Nick and his dead mother, throwing in a taunt about having slept with Hexenbiest Juliette as well. Even so, our hero naturally does not strike the first blow. Their fight is brutal; we have earlier seen Kenneth beat the redoubtable Sean Renard (4.16). After Kenneth picks up and starts striking blows with a metal bar, however, Nick uses an ancient Grimm blade to stab the man in the neck. Between clenched teeth, he grits out, "For my mother" as blood spurts in a long red arc. This is no longer protectiveness; this is vengeance.[8] It may be satisfying for some (given Kenneth's melodramatically clear-cut evil and Nick's mother's virtues). Nick is, though, in this moment, as enmeshed in patriarchal structures as he is ever shown to be. It is not a pretty sight.

Nick's presentation is complicated, however, and often his protectiveness takes the form of genuine kindness, frequently towards people from whom he can expect no return. This kindness comes in gestures both small and large. In the second episode, he quietly hands a handkerchief to a weeping young Gilda, the Goldilocks character who has broken into the wealthy Rabe family home. In the fifth episode, he asks Monroe, who is among other things an amateur cellist, to reach out to an angry young Wesen violinist who has been expelled from high school. In the twelfth episode, he offers to fight in Monroe's place in a death match into which Monroe has been forced. When Juliette's college roommate Alicia comes to stay with them to escape from her physically abusive husband, the marks still on her face, Nick makes sure to say aloud, "This isn't your fault, you know" (3.9). Similarly, in the following season, he sits down with a little boy after his abusive ex-stepfather and uncle attack the child and his mother, telling him, "I want you to know that nobody should do that to you" (4.4). He pats the arm of a lonely widow who has been the victim of a spiritualist scam (4.12). After Sgt. Wu learns the truth about Wesen, Nick tells him he can "go to the trailer any time [he] need[s] to," and apparently trusts him enough to give him a key (4.11). Time and again Nick soothes frightened Wesen witnesses, telling them some variation of "I'm not gonna hurt you" (5.5). Perhaps most notably, he helps the almost invincibly untrusting, angry young Grimm Theresa Rubel, aka Trubel. He tells Juliette that Trubel "just needs a warm bed, a roof, and a little understanding"—and despite Juliette's misgivings (3.20), he persuades her to give a home to Trubel for some months, by the end of which time she is almost a daughter to him. This particular act of kindness will, in the end, save the world (see Ch. 10). Often, Nick's kindness is openly linked to his attitude of protectiveness (e.g., 3.20, 4.2).

Nick's position as a sometimes simply kind and sometimes paternalistic, even violent protector (or sometimes both) is moderated in effect by being placed against various foils. In the second season, an unknown and frighteningly fierce Grimm tortures and kills Wesen criminal suspects and alarms Nick's Wesen friends, even kidnapping and threatening to kill the guiltless Bud Wurstner. This "new Grimm in town" secretly contacts Nick to tell him he is not Grimm enough, making the comparison direct. He is discovered, however, to be no Grimm but a police intern, the amiable-seeming Ryan Smulson (Michael Grant Terry), who has appeared in three episodes to disarm the audience, and who in fact is a Wesen himself. He had devoted a wall of photographs in his home to worship of Nick, emphasizing his status as foil (2.10). But his attempt to reflect Nick omits Nick's kindness and restraint. Nick's sanity and desire to stay within the law is highlighted in contrast. Another foil is Sean Renard, secret prince, and the public face of Nick's precinct, his captain. Both Nick and Renard have power in the world of Wesen, but Renard, in his role of bastard member of the royalty, is much more likely to act illegally (in secret) and kill without qualm whomever he perceives to be a danger (see Ch. 4). Trubel, too, the Grimm that Nick mentors (or parents), is another foil much quicker to violence than Nick. We see her, for example, decapitate a Wesen and then kick the head away without a change of expression (4.21). Nick teaches Trubel that there are good Wesen, but she has spent years being terrorized by them, with no one to believe the truth of what she saw. She therefore tends to be much more reactive than Nick. When she joins the anti-revolutionary group Hadrian's Wall (which, it should be noted, includes Wesen members) and Nick asks what she does for them, she tersely responds, "What Grimms do"—meaning, kill Wesen (5.6). Nick's much more nuanced approach is put in relief by comparison. Perhaps most memorable of the foils is Nick's mother. When she re-enters his life at the end of the first and beginning of the second season, she is shocked to find that her son is friends with a Blutbad and a Fuchsbau (2.1); indeed, she begins by attacking them. She is a more hardened warrior than he. When Nick tries to protect his mother by, for instance, warning her that the corpse she is about to examine is mangled, she coolly places her thumb and forefinger in two bloody holes to gauge the size of the bite that killed the man (2.1). On later occasions, he has to restrain her from killing first and asking questions later (a technique that can prove uninformative). "Thinking is going to get in the way, Nick," she warns him (3.18). But she does finally let him use diplomacy first. All of these foils (and more) establish a spectrum of behavior that places the protective Nick in a less violent, less patriarchal, less presumptuous position on that spectrum.

"I was supposed to protect her": The Failure of Protectiveness and Power

Importantly, however, the series also shows that protectiveness does not always work; paternalism is not enough. Despite his repeated assertions, Nick cannot save his beloved Juliette from every danger; in fact, she is often attacked in their own home. In the eighth episode, an ogre-like Wesen beats Nick, who has just followed Juliette's telephoned request to start boiling a pot of water for dinner preparations. After the fight, Nick, knocked to the floor (yet again), gasps out to the arriving Juliette, "Run!" But she grabs the pot and flings boiling water in the almost invulnerable Wesen's face, forcing him to retreat. It is Nick, not Juliette, who ends up in the hospital. In a later season, when a Wesen bounty-hunter comes to their home to kill Nick, he races home only to get there too late. Juliette, who has (unknown to Nick at this point) become a Hexenbiest, has dispatched the murderer herself when he tried to kill her. "I swear to God," Nick tells Juliette, "it's never gonna happen again" (4.12). The impossibility of such a claim by any man is obvious in the series' context. Just as obvious is the man's self-deceiving desire for his claim to be true. Juliette replies, "You can't protect me, Nick. That's something I'm going to have to do for myself." In like fashion, in the fifth season, when Nick is living with Adalind, she points out the limits of Nick's protection. Juliette has returned to the scene as the even more powerful Eve, who kills twenty Wesen at once (5.6), and Adalind fears Eve will attack her. Nick tells Adalind, "I'm not gonna let her hurt you," but Adalind is having none of it, reminding Nick of the extent of Eve's power (5.7). Furthermore, she points out another potential failure—and a very common one—of patriarchal protection: "People change their mind, Nick"—as many an older first wife might agree. The limits of Nick's protection can also be seen in regard to his quasi-daughter Trubel and his son Kelly. At the end of the fourth season, Nick, under a pile of attackers, cannot help Trubel; he has to tell her to run (as he once told Juliette). He will then not see her for months. It is not the first failure: "I was supposed to protect her," he says to Hank when she is in danger much earlier (3.20). On yet another occasion when Trubel is in jeopardy, Hank tells the frantic Nick, "This is why I don't have children" (4.2), clearly placing Nick in a paternal position. And in the fifth season, HW warns Nick that his son may be taken. "I'm not gonna lose my son," he sternly asserts; but at least temporarily, he does (5.19). The wish to protect may be possessive, or benevolent, or both, but, through Nick, the series shows that to imagine unassailable protection is delusional.

In other ways as well, Nick's experiences encourage viewers to relinquish the idea of the big daddy who takes care of everything. Nick must confront not only the failures of his protection but also the loss of power, both as a Grimm and as a cop. At the end of the third season, approximately halfway through the series, Nick loses his Grimm abilities. This hexed loss comes as a result of having sex with a woman who wishes to disempower him: Adalind magically takes the form of Juliette, becoming the Delilah to Nick's Samson. Without fully exploring the complexities of this event (discussed at greater length in Ch. 9), it can be noted that the tale of the male's diminishment through having sex dances through millennia of stories. It is during this time of loss that he has his eyes examined by an ophthalmologist who comments on some swelling in the eye and, to Nick and Juliette's startlement, asks, "Nick, do you see things the rest of us can't?" (4.3). He may, it transpires—like some women—have extra cone cells in his retinas. The doctor laughs when Nick says no, noting that "since no one can really see the world the way everyone else sees it, people of special vision tend to be unaware of it." But Nick, of course, is quite aware that his vision is usually special. Even without his special powers, Nick does not surrender to depression (though he occasionally expresses frustration). Instead, he depends on and collaborates with others, especially Hank, Trubel, Monroe, and Rosalee, to do his work. As Juliette points out, Nick was a very good detective even before becoming a Grimm (4.1). Nick and Hank have been exceptionally successful at closing cases in part because of Nick's special sight (2.2). But because he has real friends among Wesen and because he has fostered Trubel, he still has eyes on the Wesen world even when he can no longer see it for himself (e.g., 4.3, 4.4, 4.5). Nick has always worked well with others, but during this period of his life he must depend on them in a way he never has before. He is in this phase even further than usual from a hypermasculine superhero.

At the end of the fifth season, Nick suffers a different loss: his power and position as a police officer. Captain Renard and Nick publicly, physically fight, and Nick is jailed in a situation that could lead to his death. The first episode of the last season is titled "Fugitive," and for a while, Nick lives outside the protection of the law. Once more, it is his community of friends that allows him to survive and succeed—that and his intelligence in using the magical tools at his disposal. But again, it is important that the story has the character confront the possibility of loss and exclusion. Specifically, in this stage of his life, Nick is threatened with extralegal violence by Wesen who feel they have been—indeed, who often have been—treated unfairly in the past. The Wesen Black Claw organization lays the ground for a revolution, planning to slowly, secretly take control of the government and then show their true selves. Unfortunately, they also plan to kill any Wesen who do not join, and to subjugate or kill normal humans and Grimms. Hank is arrested based on planted evidence of the sort he and Nick have used, and Nick is extrajudicially judged, echoing the way he has extrajudicially judged others (5.22). When Nick is captured and tortured in the North Precinct police station where Wesen have taken over, the Wesen shout at him about relatives that have been killed by Grimms; no one makes any claim of wrongdoing by Nick himself (5.22). Black Claw's extralegal violence is a distorted mirror of Nick's: Nick has always attempted to be just and has never killed indiscriminately, like many Grimms of the past. The series thus maintains a distinction between their extralegal actions and the hero's; but it does bring the parallel to the surface. And in the weeks that follow (or months, if the summer hiatus counts), Nick is without the tools of research and authority that he normally possesses as a police officer. Trubel offers him a way out: to leave Portland to fight alongside her with HW (6.2). But with a glance at Adalind, he refuses. He has in the past fought on even without his powers as a Grimm; now he chooses to fight on even without the power of the law behind him. (He is reinstated in episode 6.4.) In both cases, he displays his heroism. But it is also significant that both cases remind him, and us, of his vulnerability and imperfection as a hero and as a cop.

"You really want to tally up the dead?" The Restraint of Killing

Nick has, with Monroe's (and his other Wesen friends') help, come to understand the falsity of the narrative that says all Wesen are killers deserving death; for his part, he has to work against the narrative that says all Grimms kill Wesen indiscriminately and therefore deserve death at the hands of Wesen. In fact, it is a very important part of Nick's character that he kills very seldom for a superhero in a police procedural. Alissa Burger and Stephanie Mix say that Nick "very rarely kill[s]," and "only when they pose an otherwise unstoppable threat to others, the community, or the world" (21). In the first season, there are approximately 56 killings within the space of the 22 episodes.[9] Nick, however, that fearsome, male super-powered force of justice, kills only four of the 56.[10] He does not even kill the Big Bad Wolf in the pilot; instead, Hank does. The numbers creep up only slightly in the ensuing seasons. Nick kills six in Season Two, ten in Season Three, and again six in Season Four. In Season Six, which lasts thirteen episodes and includes an apocalypse, Nick kills six. Only in Season Five does the tally go markedly higher. This is the season during which a Wesen ally tells Nick they are fighting a "war" against the racist revolutionaries of Black Claw (5.1), and twelve of Nick's kills come in the finale episode, when Nick's home is invaded and all of Nick's friends are threatened with death by Black Claw. Perhaps not coincidentally, this season also starts with the birth of Nick's son, making the stakes for paternalistic protection higher; as Prince Kenneth tells Juliette, "Now that he's going to be a father, his protective urges have shifted" (4.19). Often male violence uses the woman as excuse; lacking that, the child as excuse will do. That sentence is a flippant oversimplification but does express some part of the complex of motives at work. It should be remembered, though, that the fifth season is an aberration. Overall in this hyperbolic fantasy world, as a cop and as a Grimm Nick is marked by his generally consistent choice to avoid killing when he can.

It is also significant, however, that other members of Nick's inner circle—especially the males—sometimes substitute for him in killing. Hank's position in the pilot has already been noted; it is perhaps not surprising that as Nick's partner, he is also involved in killings (see, e.g., 1.13, 2.6, 3.10, 4.8, 5.5). Monroe, too, sometimes kills one of Nick's targets (e.g., 1.8, 2.6, 3.13, 4.10, 5.10). Others of Nick's associates (Wu, Renard, Juliette, and Rosalee) do so less often. These deflected killings mean that the character of the main white male is portrayed as less violent, more likable.

It is unlikely that many other viewers have conducted a tally of Nick's kills, but it is likely that viewers will have absorbed a sense of Nick's restraint. Therefore, when he uses death threats to extort information, we are unlikely to believe those threats—though those he threatens do believe. Thus, in an early encounter with the Eisbieber Bud Wurstner and his friend John Oblinger, who have alarmed Juliette by their spying on her and Nick, Nick sounds at the end almost like an angry father: "I'm not gonna kill anyone [...] unless they threaten me or my girlfriend. [...] I'd hate to have to come back here" (1.11). He questions a hospitalized gang member who refuses to give any cop information about her boyfriend's killer: "Right now I'm here as a cop, but I can come back as a Grimm" (3.10). She takes this to be a death threat, but we know otherwise. He terrifies her, but it is only for her own safety (and others'). When Monroe is kidnapped and about to be killed (gruesomely staked and burned alive) by the Wesenrein, Nick brings in for questioning the sister of Jesse Acker, a cop who secretly belongs to the Wesenrein, and Nick, Renard, Hank, and Wu pretend that Nick will kill her if Acker does not tell them where to find Monroe. He believes it, though the audience presumably does not. But neither as a Grimm nor as a cop does Nick ever kill in cold blood.[11] That is one reason that, as the seasons proceed, his reputation as different from the usual Grimm begins to spread among local Wesen (e.g., 1.10, 4.8, 6.5). When Renard bitterly asks if Nick really wants to tally up the dead, perhaps they should have (5.21). For a normal human the numbers would be shockingly high, but for a Grimm, the numbers are evidence of an intention to avoid violence.

"Do you hear something?" Hearing and Emotional Engagement

While Nick, then, has many normative masculine traits as a superhero and a man, these traits are often moderated. Furthermore, he has a superhero ability that is relatively unusual and represents unusual emotional engagement: his hearing. Nick not only sees what is invisible to others; he also hears with extraordinary acuity. In the pilot, shortly after his first vision of a Wesen, his sharp hearing ("Do you hear something?") allows him to discover a clue—an iPod dropped by a murder victim, playing "Sweet Dreams"—a musical selection that suggests the entry into a world where reality is more uncertain than it once was. Nick often employs his hearing to aid him in a hunt, but it also enables him to help people, to reach them. In "Stories We Tell Our Young," for instance, when Wu and his crew of uniformed police believe that young Daniel Keary has run away from the site of a violent death of a priest in a church, Nick hears the sound of nine-year-old Daniel's breathing and finds him fearfully hiding in a cabinet. Nick's manner of speaking demonstrates his ability to understand and respond to the child's emotions. Placing himself on a level with the child, Nick says, "You're safe now. Want to come out?" When Daniel shakes his head, Nick adds, "Your parents are in the next room. Want them to come in?" Nick's use of questions rather than orders offers the child a sense of control. Then, as the parents are fetched, Nick says to the boy, "All right, I'm gonna untie that rope from around your wrist, okay?" Nick signals his intention rather than simply moving his hands towards the frightened child, and again he gives Daniel the opportunity to refuse. Nick, in short, is a very good listener; he listens to all the clues of the situation, not just the physical sounds.

The words Nick may say more often than any others are "Are you okay?" He says them as a result of that special, thorough listening, that emotional engagement. He asks Hank, "You okay?", and when Hank says, "I'm fine," Nick follows up with "What kind of fine?" (1.21). When Juliette has become a Hexenbiest but has yet to tell him he asks, "Are you okay?" She puts him off, but we later see the two of them lying in bed, one after the other wide-eyed with worry in the night (4.10). When he and Adalind have been living together for a time, he asks her, "You okay? You seem kind of quiet," and she explains that it was the day of her mother's birthday—then adds that she ought to know Nick's, too. He lets her know he already knows hers (and lest the scene seem too sentimental, she deduces aloud that he knows because he arrested her once, 5.10). When Nick has magically taken the form of Renard, and Renard's daughter Diana has magically flung Nick across the room and back into his own form, a worried Diana asks, "Is Daddy okay?" But Nick thinks to ask the little girl who has just thrown him (onto the floor once again), "Are *you* okay?" (6.4).

Nick also often hears unspoken messages from those around him. When Wu, Hank, and Nick are about to enter the sewer tunnels for a criminal investigation, Wu says to Nick, "You're not claustrophobic, are you?" Nick correctly understands that *Wu* is claustrophobic and responds with "Not really. Look, you don't have to go down there" (3.7). When Monroe, during his first Christmas living with Rosalee, initially puts up and then takes down his usual extravagant decorations, he says to Nick and Hank, "I guess Christmas just means different things to different people." Nick immediately knows what Monroe is really saying: "*Rosalee* didn't like it!" (3.8). On her first night staying with Juliette and Nick, Nick hears the clues in Trubel's voice (she thanks them specifically for the Chinese food, and no more) and he waits for her on the porch, assuming she is planning to leave in the night. Surprising her there, he shows her that he understands more than she expects; after giving her the reasons he thinks she should stay, he hands her the black chess knight that is her talisman—something found at a crime scene, something he has guessed is hers. He then goes back inside, leaving the door open for her both literally and metaphorically. And their relationship truly begins. In the next season, when Monroe warns that a lycanthrope is afoot, Nick and Hank take Doyle Baske[12] to the station only to discover that he does not change with moonrise. When Monroe and Rosalee declare that Doyle is not the lycanthrope, there is a vivid close-up of Giuntoli's face, highly lit, head tilted, as he says, "It's his mother." Long-term viewers know the importance of Nick's own mother to him. Giuntoli expresses Nick's total, sympathetic comprehension of this other son's feeling for his mother—the wish to be a protector of that mother, and the danger therein. However difficult Nick may find it to verbalize his own emotions, he is very good at listening to the emotions of others.

"No! No! No!" Nick and Male Melodrama

When, in the second season, the amnesiac Juliette cannot remember Nick, Monroe and Bud try to cheer him up by watching a televised soccer game with him. But it does not work, and with an apology, the glum Nick walks out, beer bottle in hand. Bud comments to Monroe, "I'm just kind of surprised that a Grimm can hurt like that. But you know, Nick—he's a sensitive Grimm" (2.18). Nick's hurting, his suffering, extends throughout the series, and it is an aspect of the character that links him to melodrama. Like many relatively recent critics, I do not use *melodrama* as a pejorative term. Agustin Zarzosa "challenges the long-standing definition of melodrama as a system that aims at making visible a defunct moral order" (3). Considerably earlier, Linda Williams has argued "that the sexual, racial, and gender problems of American history have found their most powerful expression in melodrama" (82). The "dialectic of pathos and action" (69) that Williams uses to define melodrama applies to *Grimm*, and the series explores some of the problems that she identifies. Michael Stewart carries the argument further by claiming that contemporary television includes series that are "morally hesitant and ambivalent melodramas" (18). Central to the pathos and action, central to the moral hesitation and ambivalence, are the protagonists, the characters, of *Grimm*. The earlier discussions have already conveyed some of that complexity, but another melodramatic aspect of the main protagonist, Nick, seems particularly pronounced: the "sensation scene" (Williams 59). These scenes involve (as the term suggests) high emotion and often the suffering of a wronged character. As Williams explains, melodrama is not limited to "women's films" (42), but the fact that she has to make that argument reminds us that many make such a connection. I would argue that Nick's sensation scenes not only help establish his moral status (good but not perfectly innocent); they also help situate the character across stereotyping gender lines, avoiding rigid masculinity: "Nick—he's a sensitive Grimm."

In *Grimm*, there is an absent father who is never missed: Reed Burkhardt, Nick's father, who died when Nick was twelve. He is rarely named and never described.[13] In this regard, Nick differs from the typical Campbellian hero who searches for the father. Nick, indeed, works to come to terms with his mother—or, rather, mothers—and they inhabit important "sensation scenes" with him. In the pilot, the scene in the dark in which Aunt Marie tells Nick of his Grimm destiny is not only the Campbellian hero's call to adventure (which Nick is, in true monomythic fashion, reluctant to accept)[14]; it is also a sensation scene. There is a shot of the two figures in the bottom right quadrant of the screen, street-lit in the dark, their lighting and screen placement hinting at their vulnerability. A large tree stretches branches over them, suggesting the connection to the forest of harsh fairy tales, so often shown in this series. Marie, delivering the first emotional blow, tells him she may have only weeks or days to live. Then, as the second blow, she says, "There are things you don't know. Things about your family." "*You're* my family," he insists. (*Grimm* is, in some ways, a family melodrama.) Then she asks if he has been seeing things, adding, "When it happened to me, it knocked me on my ass. I couldn't move for a week." She is telling him he is a Grimm—"the misfortune of our family" (which, we learn, comes to some family members, not all). As the third blow, she instructs him, "I know you love Juliette, but you have to end it and never see her again. It's just too dangerous." As the shock and confusion cross his face, the emotional blows devolve into physical ones in just the way Williams predicts (57–59): They are attacked by the Reaper who wields a scythe like Death. It is another shock to see the bald cancer victim Marie pull a sword from her cane and fight, before Nick pulls his gun and shoots the monster. As Marie lies bleeding on the sidewalk, she strikes the final blow, telling him his parents' car crash was not an accident but murder. She pulls from her neck a chain with a key that will launch a quest and hands it to him. And with an exclamation of "What?!" Nick steps fully over the line into his new Grimm world. Soon we see Nick in one of *Grimm*'s many long hospital corridor shots that seem to suggest the distant, cold outside world in contrast to the pained emotion of the person lost there. Nick's hands shake as he draws a picture of the monster he saw—the first of many such drawings—and the shaking hand confirms the sensations he has just endured.

For good measure (and in case anyone missed the pilot), Marie will die in Nick's arms in the next episode—right after having physically fought off, from her hospital bed, an assassin dressed as a priest. Though she kills the assassin, the effort is too much for her; Nick arrives only in time to hold her up as she dies saying "Remember who you are. Trust your instincts and nothing else."[15] They share a long last look, and she passes with a death rattle.

Nick's sensation scenes with Aunt Marie have established that he is a reluctant hero who sees himself as a normal man, not someone with a supernatural calling; they also establish that he is a loving person. But Greenwalt and Kouf have given Nick another mother to love and lose. The last two seconds of the first season reveal, in one word and a stunned face, that Nick's mother is not dead after all—a genuinely melodramatic twist. In the opening episodes of the second season, Nick undergoes multiple sensation scenes with his mother Kelly, all of them quite different from the ones he experienced with Marie. When he learns that she purposefully left him when he was twelve, he is angry; he recoils at her attempt to touch him (which only comes several minutes after she is revealed; she wants to examine an enemy's body first). But soon understanding that she stayed away from him for his safety, he takes her to his special place—the Airstream trailer. He learns that she and Marie bought the trailer together;

his two mothers provided him with a womb-like space of safety. Richard Butt writes of maternal melodramas that focus on loss of maternal connection. He discusses Lady Dedlock and Esther Summerson of Dickens's *Bleak House*: "Having found her mother, [Esther] immediately loses her again" (32). This is exactly what happens to Nick. In the trailer, they fully reconcile. She tells him, "I never wanted this [being a Grimm] for you"; none of the family members know ahead of time whether they will have the gift (or curse), and it comes to different individuals at different times of life. Then she must tell him that she has to leave on a quest of her own, to destroy magical coins whose dangerous effects Nick has already seen. For his part, Nick gives an unusually (for him) long speech, hesitant with emotion: "Look, you know, I have seen a lot of things. And ... I cannot judge the decisions that you had to make. But, you know, I just wish I didn't have to grow up without you." "So do I," she responds, and they weep in each other's arms. It is Kelly who breaks it off first, patting him on the back in a signal to stop (2.1). This is a scene of pathos, though they soon will move into action. Furthermore, as in the rooftop conversation with Monroe mentioned earlier, there is a closing here that safely re-connects Nick to normative masculinity: His mother proudly notes that he is the Grimm who mailed two Reapers' severed heads back to those who sent Reapers after him. (He does not explain that he did neither of the decapitations and killed only one of the Reapers—though attentive viewers may recall.) But Nick has unquestionably expressed the pathos of loss—for the preceding eighteen years, and for her coming departure.

As with Marie, Kelly has a similar sensation scene with Nick in the succeeding episode (helpful for any viewer who missed the first). Again in the trailer, she tells him, "I don't know what'll happen with Juliette. But don't make the same mistake I did. Don't leave the people you love" (2.2). This advice, quite believably the opposite of her sister's, carries heavy emotional weight with Nick—and in fact, in the long run strengthens the community for which he serves as the center, though it causes some havoc along the way, including, indirectly, Kelly's own death. For now, Nick heroically embraces the independence of his mother: "I thought about you every day for my entire life. And having you back in it? I don't see how I could ask for anything more." "I'll come back if I can," she says; and she does. This scene is replayed shortly before Kelly's death; the showrunners thus acknowledge its emotional effect.

Nick's dealing with the loss of his mother (first, her living absence in his childhood; here, her departure; later, her death) is an extreme version of a loss every successfully individuated adult goes through in one form or another. To put it another way, we can relate. It is the extremity that creates the melodrama (the term "excess" is often used for such scenes),[16] and the

Five—"You know, Nick—he's a sensitive Grimm"

extremity is marked in part by the fact that Nick is notably more verbose than usual. There is a Nick-Kelly sensation scene, however, in which Nick is reduced to screams. At the end of the fourth season, Kelly, deceived by Juliette into thinking that Nick's life is at risk, comes back to Portland and is killed by Kenneth and his royal thugs. In traditional fashion for a Grimm, they decapitate Kelly; they leave her head in a cardboard box for Nick to find. Trubel calls his attention to the box, blood seeping from one corner. There is a noticeable stream of ambient, low background sound in the scene that is cut off when Nick opens the lid of the box and he, and we, see Kelly's severed head. For a moment, the muscles of Giuntoli's face contort in silent revulsion; then he says, "No. No"—and finally he screams loudly, harshly, "No! No! No!" to end the episode on a ringing note. A screen screamer is usually female, but not here. With Kelly's actual death off-screen, there is no question that we are focusing on *Nick*'s emotions as he unjustly suffers (as the melodrama hero must).

It is Juliette who has led Kelly into this trap (though she did not know it would lead to Kelly's death). In the very next episode, Juliette receives her punishment in the course of an equally if not more vehement sensation scene. Juliette returns to their home to tell Nick she did not mean for Kelly to die; Nick almost strangles her, then stops himself, saying, however, that he is "done"—with loving her, it seems, as well as with fighting. Juliette, on the other hand, declares that she is done with neither, and—with her recently acquired Hexenbiest skills—is about to kill him when Trubel returns to the scene and shoots Juliette instead (with a crossbow). Near Nick's dead mother's head, his daughter-figure kills his lover. Juliette dies in his arms. And once again, Nick weeps. One might begin to suspect that it is a bad idea to leave Nick—whether as a mother or a lover. Nick's suffering seems to have been repaid with their deaths. However, Juliette will return, not having been truly dead; and Kelly will return as a powerful spirit who will help Nick save the world—not to mention a different kind of return through her namesake grandchild. For now, Nick will not, despite his fury, take revenge by killing Juliette. Instead, Trubel shoots her for him, when Juliette is about to kill him and thus clearly justifies the shooting. Despite Juliette's wrongdoing, the series suggests it would be wrong for this hero to kill her—but someone who is in a way an extension of himself kills her instead. Thus the season finale's exceptionally packed sensation scene displays the ambivalence that Michael Stewart notes.

A very different kind of sensation scene takes place between Nick and the woman who was once Juliette but is now called Eve. The scene occurs when they first exchange words after her return. Nick has been told that he can meet Eve in a public place, an upscale restaurant in downtown Portland. When he arrives, it seems to take him forever to cross from the door of the crowded restaurant to the table at the back where Eve awaits. The scene is cut so that he seems to be walking enormous distances, though later shots indicate that the restaurant is of normal size. His walk to meet the notably-named Eve seems to suggest subjective time, a reflection of Nick's agitated emotions (cf. Williams on *Way Down East*, 73). His angry comments splash off Eve's marble face; she is a seemingly emotionless being, and Nick's emotions are therefore the more acutely displayed. Certainly the traditional gender markers of emotion and rationality are exchanged between the man and the woman in this scene. And in fact, Eve will turn out to be the more powerful of the two. By the end of the scene, pathos will again shift to action: Eve will kill a Black Claw villain without a touch, and Nick will dispatch his henchmen by fist and knife, saving the other people on the scene. Nick's anger at Eve has been given another object; but he has thus begun to work with Eve, work with the woman who is no longer part of him.

There are many, many more sensation scenes in *Grimm*. Not all of them center on Nick, but many do. Each has its individual purpose. But as a whole, they press against gender restrictions of the hero. These scenes of emotion accumulate. Along with them, other aspects of the character add to his complexity and freedom. I would not go so far as Zarzosa and say that melodramatic "characters gain the freedom to excise themselves from the series in which they participate" (133)—at least not in this case. But touches of abjection and humor humanize Nick even as he endures melodramatic suffering.

"Infected by your being what you are": Touches of Abjection

Before she changes, Juliette expresses repugnance when she realizes that Nick has slept with someone he thought was Juliette but was instead the magically transformed Adalind. (Juliette here echoes Nick's failure to respond to a partner in crisis, since Nick has in effect been raped; see Ch. 9.) Juliette tells Nick that she may no longer be able to tolerate their lives being "infected by your being what you are" (3.22). As Calvin Thomas states, "activity, invulnerability, mastery" (11) are seen as male traits—these being in contrast to the boundary-crossing abjection associated with females (see Ch. 6; see Kristeva). Juliette's term "infection" is one example of abjection associated with Nick (especially in the context of his virtual rape), removing him from simplistically male categorization. There are others. At the end of the second and beginning of the third season, a monster spits an ugly fluid into his face, turning Nick—like many others—into a zombie-like creature. The spit itself is abject, and its effects can be seen as entering both Nick's body (with his gruesome pallor and coldness) and his mind (with his bestial ferocity). These qualities do not quickly disappear; instead, over coming seasons, we occasionally see Nick return to the pallor. But he seems to have been able to absorb the abjection and made use of it—for example, going without breath for a long time underwater, or resisting strangulation. His abjection, then, is something to be accepted. A much more amiable and domestic abjection is his willingly changing his baby's diapers—yet another way Nick resists older gender demarcations (e.g., 5.6). A very curious sort of abjection can be seen in a pattern of other characters consuming Nick's blood. Adalind bites Nick's lips and, swallowing his blood, loses her powers (see Ch. 9). Later, Juliette and Renard swallow Nick's blood as part of a potion to help them extinguish out-of-control, magically induced sexual desire. They do not know they are ingesting his blood, and he says with dismay that he wishes he did not know either (2.14). The abjection of this blood exchange has unusual implications: Renard and Adalind will later have a child; still later, Nick and Adalind will have a child; in the interim, Juliette and Renard will choose to have sex. Nick is in a weird sense the paterfamilias of this curious group, by blood connection.[17]

There are other abjections that relieve Nick of the status of "invulnerable" male, but I will mention one more as particularly significant. One of the admirable elements of *Grimm* is that, when there is a bloody fight, the series often shows the physical consequences—the mess left behind. Barbara Walker writes about patriarchal males' avoidance of cleaning up abject materials such as vomit or blood (34). In *Grimm*, more than once, Juliette faces this task. But there are two men in *Grimm* who clean the blood as well: Monroe (after his friend Hap has been killed, 1.6) and Nick. In the night after Trubel has chopped the head off a Wesen who tried to kill Renard, we see Nick's yellow-gloved hands squeezing out a cloth stained with blood as, on his knees, he works with a bucket in his home. "Let me do this," he says, when Juliette finds him. "Not alone," she answers (4.1). This moment comes shortly after he has lost his Grimm powers. Like most women, I have done my share of cleaning, and I find this a meaningful scene. Nick's acceptance of abjection—cleaning the blood after the kill—makes him more of a whole person, not just the hero half.

Yet another humanizing—as opposed to masculinizing—quality of Nick's is his expressive humor. While Wu is noteworthy for his witty sarcasm, Nick's humor often takes the form of a genial teasing—a kind of humor that depends on relationship. In the pilot, when Hank essays a few bars of "Sweet Dreams," Nick cheerfully responds, "I didn't know you couldn't sing." When Monroe complains that they talk about nothing but police business and gets Nick to ask his favorite color, Nick says, "Well, I feel so much closer to you now" (1.10). Another of Nick's varieties of humor emphasizes relationship: the comedy duo of Nick and Hank. Seemingly spontaneous trading of lines by the two partners, immediately sensing each other's intent, repeatedly warms a scene, whether it is in a limo escorting Monroe and Rosalee on the way to their honeymoon, or in the hospital with a recuperating Wu (4.10, 5.19). The melodramatic sufferer also sometimes mocks the melodrama: "Does anything not end in death?" he asks Monroe and Rosalee (and they simultaneously respond "Uh—not that I know of / Mmm—not really," 2.13). There is a strain of physical comedy in the series in which Nick fully participates. His interaction with Monroe before their first dinner with Juliette is mentioned in this book's first paragraph. The two men are trying to hide the supernatural nature of their collaboration while still letting Juliette become friends with Monroe. Nick and Monroe's secret fist-bump and their half-disbelieving, self-congratulatory faces are disarmingly ridiculous, especially after the awkward coat removal and stiff handshake that start the evening. Little gestures light the comedy throughout. In "One Angry Fuchsbau" (echoing *Twelve Angry Men*), Hank, Monroe, and Nick stand in a Bergsonian repetitious row, nervously waiting for Rosalee; Nick is the one who moves his jittery arms as whimsical music plays and Rosalee enters.[18] The smallness of the gestures belies the degree of amusement provoked. In the sixth season, when Nick magically transforms to the shape of Renard (in an episode directed by Giuntoli), there is an entire physical comedy routine, with Nick forced to strip to his underwear, Giuntoli's embarrassed gaze pushing the other actor/characters to gaze elsewhere—so that when he executes a perfect pratfall as he succumbs to a slow-acting potion, falling on his back as the magic takes effect, we in the audience see him through a corridor of faces turned away from him (6.3).[19] These are far from being the only examples or even the only types of Nick's humor. In general, however, Nick exists with humor in a way that avoids hierarchy, sometimes even abasing himself—and Giuntoli is extremely effective in such moments. As he does in a much more serious context in the pilot, this character comically falls down. This hero joins the rest of us on ground level.

Nick's Magic Stick: "It can't be just a stick!"

The quest implicitly given to Nick in the pilot through his aunt's key is fulfilled in the fifth season when Nick and Monroe retrieve a magical artifact from the Schwarzwald, the Black Forest of Germany that lies behind so much of the *Grimm* storyworld. In more than one way, this artifact is a symbolic representation of Nick's character. The artifact is also a running joke in the fifth and sixth seasons, reflecting the disarmingly humorous aspect of Nick's nature—while being, at the same time, of enormous importance.

Over eight hundred years ago, a group of seven Crusaders, all of them Grimms, decided to hide from the royal families a mysterious something that these knights thought the Royals should not possess. They forged seven keys to open the treasure chest in which the "precious" thing (to quote Kelly Burkhardt and echo J.R.R. Tolkien) was hidden (2.1). Medieval metallurgy forged a part of a map on each of the keys. Over the centuries, many died in the struggle to possess the keys and find the extraordinary treasure. Because of others' trust in him, by the fifth season Nick holds five keys, and with the help of his friends (especially Monroe), he figures out the location of the treasure. Their discovery is the result of an easy, comfortable coequal exchange of ideas—a true collaboration (see especially 5.10–5.11): Hank, Wu, Monroe, Rosalee, and Trubel all participate along with Nick. Monroe, who speaks German, claims the right to go with Nick to the Schwarzwald, the land of Grimms' fairy tales, where the "precious" is hidden.

The episode in which Nick and Monroe discover the treasure chest is visually interesting in more than one sense of the word. The show cuts back and forth between Nick and Monroe searching an underground catacomb in a sunken church in the dark, silent forest, and a Portland park in bright sunlight where chaotic crowds of people react first to a political rally and then, with shrieking noise, to an assassination. Meanwhile (oh melodrama), in the forest, Nick demonstrates his ability to see things differently—through his intelligence, not just his Grimm abilities. With a hint from Monroe about thinking like people of the time, Nick suggests turning out their lights to see in the dark, thus revealing the glowing skulls of the seven ancestral Grimms, arranged in the catacomb to hide the treasure chest. The scene of their discovery is quintessential Nick/Monroe (see Chapter One). The two men then escape the crowd of angry Wesen locals who have discovered Nick is a Grimm, Monroe being bitten along the way, and they return to the U.S. But they do not leave darkness behind.

Back home in the basement of the Spice Shop, the treasure is given an introduction that helps convey its symbolic implications. Nick, Monroe, Rosalee, Hank, and Wu each are given one of five keys (Monroe has recommended lock-picks for the two remaining slots), and Nick solemnly hopes aloud that what is in the bronze casket is worth the lives lost (including his aunt and Monroe's uncle). Choral-sounding music rises with the readying of the keys—only to bathetically stop when, even after the locks click, the lid will not open. There is a final barrier, a sealant around the lid. As Monroe (barely holding on through the pain of his wound) guesses, it takes Nick's blood to open the seal. This blood use places Nick in the same category as Hexenbiests in the Grimm world, whose blood can be used to open magically sealed books (e.g., 6.10); it is also another touch of abjection for the hero. When at last, after all the centuries, Nick opens the lid, and they take out the ancient cloth inside and unfold it, there is yet another moment of bathos as a dark, slim piece of wood, about seven or eight inches long, appears. Monroe says, "It's a stick?" Hank replies, "Looks like a stick." Wu continues: "A really old stick." And Rosalee protests, "It can't be just a stick!"

It certainly is not just a stick. The showrunners have risked making the resolution of the quest into a laugh without having lost the larger meaning that eventually is revealed for this "really old stick." Diegetically, it will be the catalyst for apocalypse, and symbolically, as noted, it will represent the hero. In this first stick scene, Hank proposes, "Maybe it's some kind of important stick that belongs to a bigger stick that means something," and he is exactly right. Rosalee suggests that it may be a religious artifact, and Wu, that it may open "the gates of Hell" in Portland, and they are right, too. First, however, they learn—as Monroe collapses from blood poisoning and Nick grabs his wounded arm while happening to have the stick still in his hand—that it is a healing stick. Its powers are such that it will later retrieve Juliette/Eve from the brink of death and Nick from beyond the brink. Hence some of the reason for keeping it out of the wrong hands becomes clear.

Nick's magic stick is almost embarrassingly, laughably phallic. The show seems well aware, and the characters seem to be in on the laugh in at least one sense: repeatedly, as the stick is shown to a new person, they are underwhelmed by its appearance. Nick and the stick—which he begins to carry on his person—become more and more clearly identified, and if we recur to the idea of the normal-seeming, underestimated male—someone we can laugh at—who actually has secret power, then parallels to the stick are clear.

The symbolism extends further, however. It turns out that the stick is a small piece of a large staff belonging to the Satanic Zerstorer, who will have absolute power if he can complete his staff. But Zerstorer must have the stick's owner choose to give it to him of his own free will; he cannot take it. This treasure has through the centuries been connected to the traditional church and the royalty—the patriarchy incarnate. It was taken from and kept from those patriarchal forces by the seven Grimms, in an act of independence from patriarchy. While Grimms have sometimes worked for the Royals, these seven acted by their own conscience, instead—just as Nick has always done ("This one has a badge and a conscience," says Renard, 1.10). His small power—his magic stick—is both separate from and potentially connected to that larger patriarchal staff.

It should also be noted that Nick, as he keeps the stick longer, becomes more and more dependent on it, especially after it returns him from the dead. Like Tolkien's "one ring," it begins to exert an addictive effect. Heavy breathing, lightheadedness, sound distortion, and his recognition that "It felt like I needed it" make its drug-like qualities apparent (6.2, 6.3). Patriarchal power would indeed be difficult to give up.

By the series finale, Nick has been melodramatically tormented with the deaths of all those close to him, at Zerstorer's hand. Zerstorer offers to resurrect them if Nick will relinquish the stick. He tells Nick, "You might want to ask your children [i.e., Kelly and Diana] what to do" (4.13). Thus the paternal, familiar desire to protect is here the source of damnable temptation for Nick. As Chapter Ten explains in greater detail, Trubel—resuscitated by Zerstorer as a demonstration for Nick—argues with Nick against giving in to Zerstorer, taking the traditionally male rational position against Nick's traditionally female caring for his loved ones, which is in this case entwined with paternal protectiveness. The ghosts of Kelly and Marie appear to add their voices to Trubel's. They tell him that the strength of family will save him—but they do not mean for him to place family above all; he is to draw on the strength of his ancestors to make the right choice, fight the right fight. He must consider the good of all, not just the good of his own. He, Trubel, Marie, and Kelly—three women and a man—conquer the evil Zerstorer and take his staff. In the end, Nick—always a good listener—listens to his mothers.

The imagery is not finished, however. The fight over, it occurs to Nick that, with control of the staff, he can save the lives of his loved ones. But the ashes of the dead Zerstorer create a swirling, shining portal into which the staff starts to be drawn. Though it is perhaps no necessary adjunct, the female-to-male symbolism does seem to operate here. Because of his determination to save his loved ones (who are scattered on the ground around him), Nick will not let go, even though it seems he is being sucked through the portal into Zerstorer's alternate world; he gives himself over to the swirl for the sake of his family, keeping hold of the staff. But when he emerges, he is not in Zerstorer's hellish home world. Instead, the world has re-set, and he is at Monroe and Rosalee's, with all his people alive and well. The scene of his return is closely reminiscent of the conclusion for Jimmy Stewart's character George Bailey in *It's a Wonderful Life* (1946), with the circle of family newly appreciated by the hero who has undergone the experience of a world without them. Like the ordinary-but-also-special George, Nick, overcome by emotion, fumbles joyfully as he tries to explain what coming back means. (There are also repeated references to Schrödinger's cat, but that's another story.)

Nick's sometimes laughable, sometimes underestimated magic stick has for a time been kept from the larger, more dangerous patriarchal staff by his and his ancestors' choices. In the end, Nick allows his stick to merge because he now controls that staff—a conclusion that may seem too optimistic and still problematic for some. A benevolent, regenerate male holds the staff of patriarchy? In fact, we never see Nick use the staff after he kills Zerstorer. But, kept among other weapons in the new trailer's new weapons cabinet, twenty years later the staff of power passes back and forth between the hands of Nick's male and female children in the last scene, ready to be used in the hunt for evil.

Conclusion: "Don't take this the wrong way"

Nick Burkhardt, who may on the surface seem to be a traditional man and a traditional cop, is instead a much more complicated character. His intelligence, his humor, and his loving nature—not to mention David Giuntoli's good looks, which become more apparent once past the original haircut—make him attractive. (Giuntoli has gone on to star as a romantic protagonist in the television series *A Million Little Things* [2018–]). His virtue becomes more and more visible as he suffers through melodramatic torments almost always connected to his concern for loved ones, as he confronts his own limitations and even experiences some degree of abjection. His emotional engagement seems to cross traditional gender lines; he is a "sensitive Grimm." Although he has the power of a Grimm and of a cop, he chooses to restrain himself, in the great majority of cases, from killing. He is flawed enough (as in the brutal killing of his mother's murderer or his walking out on the newly transformed Hexenbiest Juliette) to make him more believable. Because this series (like most television) rarely uses a first-person point of view, we normally have the equivalent of what students of literature would call an omniscient narration to confirm that Nick's decisions are almost always right. More than once in the series, Nick says "Don't take this the wrong way" when he is about to state something important to him (e.g.,2.22). We might say the same of the character as a whole. Given that a series with a white male lead may include in its audience some more traditional viewers, it is possible that Nick's character might draw some of those viewers forward. Will it change how we think such men *should* act or reinforce how we think they *do* act?[20] If Nick is taken as closer to an ideal, then he provides viewers a goal. But if we believe that he is a normal man, and normal men are underestimated and justified in their paternalistic protectiveness; if we believe that he is a normal cop, and normal cops almost always see the truth and show restraint—then he is an excuse for what is, not an image of what might be. As Linda Williams says, melodrama has us recognize both "how things are and how they should be" (48). Whether or not we take this character the right way is ultimately up to us.

Six

"Women become aware sooner than men"

Marie Kessler, Kelly Burkhardt, and the Crones of Portland

The first important female character we see in *Grimm* is a witch, and the second looks like one.[1] Most female characters in this series are set apart from the police world of the central male characters, four out of five of whom are police officers. Yet many of the women in *Grimm* are quite powerful. They are numerous and morally various; they are also not teenagers but adult. As Sheldon Cashdan says, "Female characters figure [...] prominently in fairy tales. [...] [T]here are many more witches than ogres, and appreciably more fairy godmothers than fairy godfathers" (28). In *Grimm*, when witches—Hexenbiests—transform to exert their power, they present the faces of ancient, deformed hags. The women in the dark fairy tale world of *Grimm* connect to an even more ancient tradition of "'primordial characters'" (Rodney Needham qtd. in Hutton ix). Barbara Walker, in *The Crone: Women of Age, Wisdom, and Power*, reminds us of the powerful archetype of the older woman—traditionally one of three female archetypes: the Maiden, the Mother, the Crone—birth, life, and death; "Creator, Preserver, Destroyer" (21). In a wide-ranging historical examination, she argues that while the Maiden or Virgin aspect and the Mother aspect have been absorbed into patriarchal religion, the Crone aspect has been distorted and demoted from the prehistoric time of matriarchal Goddess worship.[2] She distinguishes matriarchal and patriarchal religious figures in part by the latter's avoidance of abjection (34), following the same sorts of gendering of abjection that Julia Kristeva and Barbara Creed discuss. Walker (among others, such as D.J. Conway and Jane Caputi) emphasizes that the Crone herself has multiple aspects: that of the older Wise Woman (Sophia or Sapientia), often encountered as a healer; but also the figure of death, whom she calls the Terrible Crone—a human memento mori, related to Hecate (50), the Celtic Caillech (77), or Kali (78)—often depicted as the Huntress. As Walker says, "She is the one we most need to understand: not the pretty Virgin, not the fecund Mother, but the wise, willful, wolfish Crone" (13). The image of the wise, powerful, dangerous Crone was gradually transformed into that of the evil Witch—with particular force in the Middle Ages. Recent writing has renovated some of this archetypal content. *Publishers Weekly* named the fall of 2019 as the "season of the witch" (J. Bennett C20). Witches are being reclaimed, in books, movies, and television, such as the rebooted versions of *Charmed* (1998–2006; 2018–present) and *Sabrina the Teenage Witch* (1996–2003; now *Chilling Adventures of Sabrina*, aka CAOS, 2018–2020). Books on Goddess worship abound. Artist Rachel Feinstein titled her 2020 retrospective "Maiden, Mother, Crone" (La Ferla C17). Many people may also be familiar with the Virgin/Mother/Crone triumvirate through the *Game of Thrones* novels. Jack Zipes asserts that the wicked witch "stereotype is the result of misogynistic cultural processes that have transformed goddesses into witches" (65). Ronald Hutton includes four major definitions for *witch*, the latest being "a symbol of independent female authority and resistance to male domination" (x). This definition signifies an inheritance from the Crone. In *Grimm*, numerous regular and recurring female characters exhibit strength and complexity in multitudinous ways, but awareness of various aspects of the Crone archetype can connect and illuminate their power.

The triumvirate of female archetypes including the Crone has become popularly known through recent incarnations of Goddess worship and reclamation of witch imagery. Hutton offers a highly specific historic tracing of the evolution of the witch as conceived in the fifteenth century at the start of widespread European witch hunts. He declares that witches of that time were not (as was suggested in the nineteenth century and popularized in the early twentieth by Margaret Murray) secret followers of a pagan religion (120–121). He does, however, note remnants of ancient beliefs that survived. Furthermore, in his conclusion, he asserts: "The modern concept of witchcraft as a pagan nature religion, standing for a wild and green spirituality of feminism, [...] personal liberation and self-realization, itself based on nineteenth-century scholarship, has produced a constellation of successful, viable and [...] thoroughly worthwhile religious traditions" (278).[3] These traditions often correlate with the triumvirate that Walker and others study. From a certain perspective, these archetypes might be seen as essentializing, as limiting (see, e.g., Sempruch 14, 34). The later chapters in this book, giving fuller examinations of major female characters, should work against the idea that these characters are essentialist in terms of gender.[4] There are many ways in which *Grimm*'s female characters do not match these archetypes. *Grimm* is, after all, not a scripture or an academic tome, but a popular text, and a lively one. However, echoes of these archetypes in their various forms—in particular the Wise Crone, the Crone of Death, and the Witch aspect of the Crone—sharpen the impact of the characters.

Taken together, there are many significant female characters who relate to this imagery. Nick's aunt and mother, the Grimms Marie Kessler and Kelly Burkhardt, are perhaps the most notable Crones in the story. Along with Trubel (a younger Grimm) they help him save the world at the end of the series. These three are recurring characters (with Trubel recurring very frequently). There are aspects of the Crone in all the regular female characters: the sometime Hexenbiests Juliette Silverton/Eve and Adalind Schade, whose faces turn aged when they take on the aspect of the Witch; and the Wise Woman magical apothecary Rosalee Calvert. Other recurring female characters are in various ways Crones. Adalind's daughter, the significantly named Diana (a child we see become adult) also participates in the pattern. There is a group of witches of notable age: Adalind Schade's powerful, conniving mother Catherine; Renard's worldly, wealthy Hexenbiest mother Elizabeth Lascelles; and the ancient, beautiful Hexenbiest counselor Henrietta. Then there is a set of Wise Women/Hunters who actually are connected to law enforcement: Harper, the smart, tart medical examiner; the determined, secretly Wesen, FBI agent Katrina Chavez; and Deputy Sheriff Janelle Farris. There is, in addition, a set of recurring characters of more problematic presentation, including the aged baby-seller Frau Pech; the queen of the Schwarzwald Roma, Stefania Vaduva Popescu; and the Mexican American Wise Woman Pilar. Overall, these female characters are numerous enough to represent an appropriate spectrum of morality, yet they also represent either the wisdom or the deadly power of the Crone—or both. As Eve Bennett says, in modern fantasy/science fiction television, representations of substantial older female characters are unusual (189). While *Grimm* can be seen as flawed in its racial/ethnic presentation, it is much more effective in terms of gender representation, especially in its intersection with age, as can clearly be seen in the Crones of Portland.

The Kessler Crones

The pilot episode of *Grimm* contains one of the most interesting images of the Crone, because it shows us the negative, patriarchal vision and then shifts away from it. This is a vision of Nick's Aunt Marie Kessler. It is a lengthy, multi-shot, darkly engaging passage establishing the importance of the Crone in the series from its start. Kate Burton gives genuine gravitas to the role of Marie. Without knowing who she is, we see a bald older woman as she drives alone through the town. We see her entering a house alone, limping with a cane. The man we already know to be our hero, Detective Nick Burkhardt, comes upon her as he slowly enters this house in the dark: we see her holding a large knife. Certainly, she seems a frightening figure. But then Nick says, with obvious pleasure and surprise, "Aunt Marie!", and they hug. She has been chopping up not victims but vegetables in the kitchen, with Nick's beloved Juliette, and Marie whispers as she and Nick hug, "We need to talk." This moment is a synecdoche for the shift from the negative to the positive view of the Crone, from the patriarchal to the matriarchal. At first, Marie seems to be a threatening figure, the Hansel and Gretel witch or the Baba Yaga who could eat you up. But instead of—or as well as—the one who eats, she is the one who feeds; her knife is for nourishment, and she whispers to share wisdom. Her appearance is the result of terminal illness, not an outer sign of inner depravity. Now dying of cancer, Marie raised Nick after he, at age 12, lost his parents because of a car crash. She is thus both the Crone and the Mother. She has come to inform him of his heritage as a Grimm, and she leaves him that Airstream trailer full of handwritten books to guide him—her magic bookmobile. Before she dies, she is repeatedly attacked by Wesen and she violently fights them off; when she is hospitalized, a doctor notes her many battle scars and asks Nick what line of work Marie was in. "She was a librarian," he answers, in a moment that combines the best of the series' restrained humor, mystery, and reversal of stereotyping expectations (1.1). She is capable of dealing death, and she is herself a figure of death who returns, in the last episode, after having died in the second. But through her gift of knowledge she is primarily associated with the Wise Crone, the one Walker calls the "owner of the sacred lore" (27).

Marie's sister Kelly, Nick's mother, is wise as well, but is more emphatically the Huntress. In Season One, the last word that is heard, the last word Nick speaks, is "Mom?"—and he says it as a question. After eighteen years of presuming she was dead, he has come, in the middle of a battle, face to face with his mother—a stunning cliffhanger ending for the first season. Nick does not engage in a Campbellian hero's search for the father; instead, he grapples with the existence of his mother. Pursued by deadly enemies, she gave her son to her sister Marie for safekeeping, deciding that the best way to keep her enemies from Nick was to pretend to be dead. Thus Kelly has chosen to turn her back on mothering, for the sake of saving her child. Instead she has developed the aspect of the Terrible Crone, the bringer of death, as a Grimm. As Walker says, "the Huntress character belonged originally to the Goddess's third persona, the dangerous Crone" (23), and Kelly is an impressive Huntress. As with Marie, the writers use Kelly's introduction to play with our perceptions. In our first visual of her as an unknown character, we see black boots, black coat, black gloves, and a switchblade; we cannot tell the gender. Even when the camera pulls back to reveal a dark-haired woman who appears to be in her fifties, we do not know who she is; but we see her calmly examining a dead body on a hotel room floor; and later in the episode, we see her fight with swift efficiency. She saves her son from a Wesen predator who was one of his father's killers. She stays with Nick for a few episodes to help him battle a particularly vicious enemy, and she gives him practical battle advice. Her wisdom comes mainly from experience, and once they re-connect, she shares her experience with Nick, not only in the trailer she bought long ago with her sister, but also in the field. As she explains what it is like to become a Grimm, she tells him, "Women become aware sooner than men"—a statement of fact in their storyworld, but also a statement that is resonant in terms of gender and power (2.1). Dynamically portrayed by Mary Elizabeth Mastrantonio, she is clearly a woman of action more than a woman of lore: She is, as her introductory episode titles her, the "Woman in Black" (1.22), the Crone of Death. At one point she says, "I don't trust anybody I'm not close enough to kill" (3.17). Mastrantonio's low voice and cool, sometimes even cold, facial expressions convey her fatal power. Walker argues that the Celtic name Kelly is related to the name of the Hindu goddess Kali (78), which would mean that the name is an apt one for Nick's deadly mother. The name's gender ambiguity is suggestive as well: As her introductory visuals imply, Kelly is not limited to traditionally expected gender actions.[5] When she tries to revisit a more expected kind of mothering, making breakfast, Kelly burns Nick's toast; but she kills his enemies (2.1, 2.2). The character of Kelly Kessler Burkhardt does illustrate the fatal aspect of the Crone. And the Kesslers' literal and spiritual sisterhood illustrates another kind of strength.

Witches, Healers, and Hunters

For the major characters, along with the Wise Crone and the Warrior Crone, *Grimm* presents versions of the Witch aspect of the Crone. Alissa Burger and Stephanie Mix assert that "the representation of the witch is an inherently feminist one, in its negotiation of witchcraft as a power which enables its users to exercise their agency" (12). The Witch is in this series visually connected to the Crone. As noted, when a Hexenbiest shows her secret face, it is the face of an ancient hag; when the Hexenbiest essence is driven from a person, it also presents as an aged, hag-like spirit. There is thus a suggestion of secret, fearsome power in each of these women. As they often have for men, age and power connect for women here. Both of Nick's lovers are—on and off—witches.[6]

One of the most interesting characters in the series is the Hexenbiest Adalind Schade (pronounced, in English, as *shade*, with appropriate connections to darkness). Briefly seen in the pilot, the character as written and as strikingly portrayed by Claire Coffee became central to the story. She is the first witch we see, and Nick's first sight of the *woge* transformation. Her eventual romantic relationship with Nick parallels the Slayer-vampire attraction of Buffy and Angel or Buffy and Spike (among many cases of a protagonist drawn to a lover from the dark side). She is skilled at potions and has no hesitation in using them to do harm, to control others she sees as her enemies. She is a lawyer—another kind of Wise Woman—but notably, through Adalind, the Witch combines with the Mother, in a circuitous journey. The ghastly but humorous misery she endures to regain her powers—the abjection of Adalind—is curiously endearing.[7] There is a period in the story when Adalind seems to have become subsumed by motherhood; she declares that she does not even want the power of being a Hexenbiest anymore. But after a time, she combines in herself the Witch and the Mother in a powerful fusion—one successful choice for a woman, but not the only one depicted in the series.

Another successful but very different choice is made by Juliette Silverton, who also reflects multiple aspects of the Crone. Like Shakespeare's Juliet, she starts as the romantic heroine, Nick's beloved. But even when she is Nick's girlfriend, the woman who lives with him, she is also more: She is a veterinarian—a woman of science, a modern Wise Woman. Once she is introduced to the world of the Wesen, she starts helping to solve Wesen problems by applying her scientific knowledge. When Nick loses his powers, he is only able to regain them because Juliette has the courage to undergo a spell in which she takes the form of Adalind. As a consequence of the spell, she becomes the dark version of the Witch, cruel and casually fearsome. She can exert extraordinary power even without a potion. In one of the most horrifying acts of violence in the series, she torches Aunt Marie's trailer, the center of wisdom. It is an act that the others consider unforgivable. Actress Bitsie Tulloch spoke of the pleasure of playing such a different and powerful character ("Grimm: Lowen"). "Killed" by Trubel, Juliette returns after months away, reborn and rechristened as Eve, having been translated into an almost emotionless figure, a superpowered death-witch who works as an agent of Hadrian's Wall—a hyper-efficient Huntress. As Eve (another archetypal name, of both the woman who tastes knowledge and the mother of all)[8] she is ironically no Mother, but a new woman, and the former veterinarian is now even more of a Wise Woman, as well, often connected to computers as unfeeling as she is. She goes through yet another death and resurrection to change again, reconnecting with emotional elements of the earlier woman she was (4.22). Tulloch incorporates touches of Juliette's quirkiness as she returns from the coldness of Eve—another case of the significance of humor in the series' characters. She emerges, like Adalind, as a character who is a combination of phases she has undergone. Throughout the series Juliette/Eve has refused marriage, and towards the end she, as a powerful, knowledgeable, and yet caring Witch, makes clear that she lives for a purpose beyond the personal. The two main Witches make very different life choices, illustrating options beyond traditional gender limits.

Juliette/Eve and Adalind are both befriended, at different points, by Rosalee Calvert. Rosalee is no Hexenbiest; as noted, she is Wesen, a Fuchsbau friend of Nick's. The woman who can be a beast is named for a flower. However, from the outset she is presented as a character who knows darkness. She is introduced as someone who was addicted to drugs for years and is now living sober. She has returned from Seattle to Portland to bury her brother, whose murder Nick solves, and she announces her intention to go back to Seattle. But soon she finds that she is able to save Sergeant Wu's life because of the knowledge held in the books of her brother's shop, and the knowledge she gained training as an apothecary with her parents. Her exercise of this knowledge (as well as her growing connection to Monroe) draws her to stay in Portland. Rosalee is capable of fighting (she saves Monroe in her first episode) but is primarily a version of the Wise Woman. Again and again, she serves as a healer, and Bree Turner conveys determined caring without a touch of the saccharine. Rosalee employs both chemistry equipment and old-fashioned cauldrons as she brews her healing potions. She uses health-making herbs but also fits into the magic/Witch tradition that Hutton identifies as *pharmakides*, as in pharmacist—those who use recipes of magic (55, 103). Though she is no Hexenbiest, her apothecary advice could certainly have gotten her burned as a Witch in the wrong place and time. Like the witches of *Grimm,* Rosalee has a secret second face, in her case the face of a beautiful animal. In the Wesen community, she is known as a confident, authoritative maker of potions. Although Wesen in general fear witches, Rosalee's skills ally her with her witch sisters.

Rosalee gives her loving friendship to another character as well—the young Grimm who calls herself Trubel. Theresa Rubel arrives on the scene fresh from a Washington state mental institution, having escaped attempted rape on the road to Portland: She has had no one to tell her what a Grimm is, what Wesen are, and she doubts her own sanity. She is as far from a Wise Woman as can be. But Nick, Hank, Monroe, Rosalee, and Juliette help her come into her own (as does Wu, once he knows about Wesen), and she becomes unquestionably the "willful, wolfish" Huntress—or, as Trubel calls it, "the Hunter" (3.20). She is another Woman in Black. In fact, more than once she enters a scene shot in such a way that it is not clear whether or not we are seeing Nick's mother. Trubel, who becomes almost like a daughter to Nick, is very like his mother in her hunting ferocity (see, e.g., 4.21, 4.22). She, Kelly, and Eve share the image of the darkly hooded woman, the death-dealer, the Terrible Crone—though Trubel is still young (twenty-one when she first appears). Certainly primarily the Hunter, Trubel also literally runs towards the books from the trailer when she first encounters them and is repeatedly shown studying them; she comes closer and closer to being a Wise Woman as she gains experience. Jacqueline Toboni's effective depiction of Trubel's bluntness, combined with her deep gratitude and affection that have survived monumental abuse, make her yet another character whose force is humanized by a complex combination of elements. While she connects to this gendered archetype and is herself gendered female, Trubel has fewer traditional gender markings than any other character except Monroe.

Even younger than Trubel is perhaps the most terrifying character in the series: Diana, daughter of the Hexenbiest Adalind and the half Zauberbiest, half Royal Renard. From before birth—for we observe Adalind's pregnancy—Diana is connected with images of spiders and skulls. She is powerful even from within the womb and threatens to become a danger to all. Her characterization is, for quite a time, eerily ambiguous—a difficult portrayal successfully managed by young Hannah R. Loyd. The name Diana refers to a goddess with multiple aspects: the deity of the moon; the Huntress; and Hecate, the hell-queen of Witches. Diana is all of these. Hutton reports that Jakob Grimm (yes, that Grimm) writes of a medieval cult of Diana; while Hutton argues against the idea of the cult's continuity, he notes that scribes for medieval witch trials referred to the name of Diana as an object of worship by Witches (136–37).[9] Potentially the demon child, Diana is rescued from patriarchy (in the form of her grandfather, the king) and raised lovingly to understand the right.[10] She has an unsettling ability to comprehend lore: Late in the series, Rosalee, Juliette/Eve, Trubel, and Adalind work together to decipher the meaning of an ancient text; when Diana arrives, she is able to see even more (6.2). Diana is a child Witch of uncanny wisdom, but our last view of her, in the series finale set twenty years later, is as a powerful Huntress. Considering both her young and her (brief) adult representations, she is yet another who integrates multiple aspects of the Crone.

The Elder Crones

It is an indicator of the representation of female power in *Grimm* that major characters spend much more time dealing with mothers than with fathers.[11] Dee Wallace, known not only for *E.T.: The Extra-Terrestrial* (1982) but also for playing a werewolf in *The Howling* (1981), effectively portrays the werewolf-like Monroe's mother Alice in a fashion that seems at first to be too repressed for a Crone; but in the end, she demonstrates some qualities of the Wise Woman in the psychological insight she uses to hold her family together after the surprise of Monroe and Rosalee's intermarriage. Similarly, Rosalee's mother Gloria Calvert (Bryar Freed-Golden) displays wisdom as she reconciles with her daughter after a break of seven years. On camera, she does not employ the specialized knowledge of a Crone, but we know that in the past she has taught her daughter the skills of an apothecary. These two older women partake of the Mother and to a lesser degree of the Crone. Nick's two mothers have already been discussed as Crones. In the world of *Grimm*, some Crones are older than others. Three such particularly noteworthy recurring-character Crones are the Hexenbiests Catherine Schade, Elizabeth Lascelles, and Henrietta. Two out of three of these are mothers of regular characters. All are formidable. Each is beautiful; each hides a powerful inner hag.

Catherine Schade, played with astringent panache by Jessica Tuck, is the blonde mother of blonde Adalind. Like many significant characters in *Grimm*, she makes her first appearance in a way that is set up to be misread. She makes her entrance in Crone-Hexenbiest form, appearing in Adalind's apartment unannounced, and a startled Adalind woges back, so that at first it seems Catherine is a threat. When instead Adalind addresses her as "Mom," the interpretation flips as the two women hug. But in fact, Catherine *is* a threat for Adalind, in many ways. She in effect sells her daughter for the use of Sean Renard in order to pay off a debt: She expects Adalind to have sex with Hank in order to magically endanger his life and thus coerce Nick to relinquish a special key. We learn by the episode's end that Adalind has acted out of love of Renard, to help him. She has prostituted herself, but Catherine has prostituted her own daughter. It also becomes clear that Catharine has had sex with Renard long before. Love, however, is not something Catherine approves of. When she asks Adalind (early in the episode) if she still loves the captain and Adalind asks why that matters, Catherine replies that she has taught her daughter well (1.17). In her well-appointed home, Catherine surrounds herself with mirrors—appropriately enough for someone so self-centered and transactional. The captain/prince warns her to stop looking in the "mirror, mirror on the wall," connecting her to the evil Witch in *Snow White* (and perhaps Adalind to the princess).[12] When Adalind loses her powers as a result of trying to please her mother and her prince, Catherine—rather than comforting her daughter—rejects her, magically slamming the door behind her. The mother is willing enough to raise Adalind and pass on her witch lore in hopes of sharing success but is not willing to protect her in failure. She can be directly contrasted with Kelly Burkhardt, who parted from her son only to save him. When Nick and Kelly are searching for Adalind (after Adalind puts Juliette in a coma), Kelly goes to Catherine's home to interrogate her. Their conversation turns into a fight which Kelly wins, accidentally killing Catherine. But in true Wise Crone fashion, Catherine has left behind a potion for the captain that Rosalee is able to reformulate in order to help save Juliette. Catherine's fate suggests that those women who serve the patriarchy—here, most overtly, Royals such as the captain—end up less powerful in spite of natural and cultivated abilities. She is a Crone who represents some of the darker elements of the type, part of the spectrum that the series displays.

Another memorable mother and Hexenbiest-Crone is Elizabeth Lascelles, the mother of Sean Renard. The wealthy, intelligent, beautiful blonde Elizabeth, almost courtly in manner, was the mistress of the king of Austria. That king's queen drove her out. She has clearly been smart and brave enough to save herself and her son and to teach him self-preservation—though she may also have taught him not to trust. She both has used and been used by the patriarchy; she walks a delicate balance, and normally keeps herself apart even from those she loves. Renard is surprised when she phones to thank him (after he arranges the death of his murderous half-brother). We hear of her many times before we see her. Like several other intriguing women characters, she is given a purposefully misleading entrance, reminding us to question our interpretations. When Renard is shot and lies near death, we see from behind a slim woman walking towards his hospital room, her long blonde hair swinging. She looks for all the world like Adalind, the mother of Renard's daughter; but she is, instead, Renard's mother. She appears her son's age but is much older. She saves her son's life using a magical snake, traditionally an image of dangerous wisdom—a method she tells him can only be done once for either of them, implying the danger she has undergone for his sake. Both wealthy and generous, she buys him a new, more secure home, so that he is better protected after she is gone. At this point in the story Nick has lost his powers; Elizabeth is willing to help him regain them because she believes it will aid the grand-daughter she has never met—Diana, who is being cared for by Kelly in secrecy. As Elizabeth once cared for Sean Renard in hiding, now Nick's mother does so for Elizabeth's grand-daughter—a mirroring that reflects positively on Elizabeth. It is she who discovers that Adalind has used an ancient Witch's hat (from the days of the witch hunts and the *Malleus Maleficarum*, Elizabeth says) to transform herself into Juliette, trick Nick, and destroy his power. "To beat a Hexenbiest like Adalind, you need a Hexenbiest like me," Elizabeth says. She thus reminds us that not all Hexenbiests are morally equivalent (4.3). We finally see her gray-haired Crone self as she stirs a cauldron

Six—"Women become aware sooner than men" 131

in Rosalee's shop. Fully the Wise Woman, she consults one of Catherine's old books and devises a method for Nick to be magically repaired by having Juliette reproduce Adalind's actions, including taking on Adalind's shape and making love with Nick. Elizabeth coolly explains the possible dangers but just as coolly points out that there could be equal, unforeseen dangers if they do nothing. The cultured voice and graceful body language used by actor Louise Lombard suggest a relaxed control that comes of long knowledge tempered by experience. Elizabeth Lascelles is hardly a humanitarian, but she loves her family and treats honorably those who treat her well. She is another Crone, another powerful woman at yet another point on the moral spectrum.

When Elizabeth escaped with her son and brought him to Portland many years ago, she did so in part to be close to another wise and powerful Hexenbiest-Crone, Henrietta. Henrietta, like other Witches in *Grimm*, only looks old when she woges, but she is older and wiser than Elizabeth. When Juliette asks Renard how old Henrietta is, he replies that he has never asked and she shouldn't either. Before we meet her, we are prepared by Renard's comments to know someone special, and she is. Henrietta is also the only recurring Hexenbiest character who is Black. She is never given a last name. One might say that that is because, like Elvis or Beyoncé, she only needs the one; one might also contemplate a more uncomfortable naming possibility relating to her Blackness—and she is, judging by what American audiences would consider to be a lack of accent, African American (in contrast to the British-accented Elizabeth). Naming questions aside, her power is made clear before we ever meet her—in part by Renard's comments, and in part by her ability to do magic from afar—such as her re-ordering on the page the numbers and letters of her written address, to keep it secret. Like Catherine Schade, Henrietta lives in an elegant house on a hill, the doors of which she opens and closes without touching. When she first appears, she is descending a staircase, her physical position conveying her elevated status—a status that actor Garcelle Beauvais suggests Henrietta is well aware of. Her posture, her direct gaze, and her firm voice imply self-confidence. She is dressed in glamour, in all senses of the word. It is Henrietta that Juliette consults (on Renard's advice) when she has, to her horror, turned into a Hexenbiest. In a room of Victorian formality, Henrietta displays mysterious powders and glass devices, magically drawing blood to test Juliette. Like Rosalee, she is a pharmakides, a magical practitioner with the knowledge of an expert doctor, and she too consults her books. Of all the Hexenbiests, Henrietta is presented as the wisest. She briefly mentors Juliette (something Adalind later enviously complains of when she and Juliette are in conflict). She helps Juliette to know her new self by abruptly startling her with her, Henrietta's, Crone face, instigating Juliette to reciprocate with a woge of her own. She knows before Adalind does that Adalind is pregnant. She knows, too, how extraordinarily powerful a Hexenbiest Juliette is becoming, and how impossible it would be for her to return to her earlier condition—something she openly tells Juliette, the doctor delivering a true diagnosis. When Nick, equally as horrified as Juliette, comes to insist that Henrietta must be wrong in her diagnosis, Henrietta displays her power against the Grimm by briefly enthralling him, kissing him, then releasing him. All three of these beautiful elder Hexenbiests—Catherine, Elizabeth, and Henrietta—are comfortable with sexuality. (Only Catherine's sexuality is presented in a negative light.) It is to Henrietta that Renard comes for counsel when he fears that he is being possessed by a Jack-the-Ripper-like spirit. It is all the more horrid, then, when Henrietta is one of three important women characters to be killed in the space of three episodes—the other two being Kelly and Juliette. When I lectured on these season-ending events at an academic conference with an audience largely unfamiliar with the series, I asked if they could guess who was the first of the three to be killed. It was with neither satisfaction nor surprise that I heard them correctly guess it was the Black character. At that point we did not know that she would be the only one of the three not to return in this fantasy series, either alive (as Juliette does) or as a spirit (as Kelly does). Her death does not help mitigate the racial/ethnic problems of presentation of the series. Henrietta's life, however, is part of *Grimm*'s presentation of power and wisdom for older women.

Crones of the Law

Much younger than the elder Hexenbiests but still older than typical women on television, especially fantasy series, are the next three characters, all of whom are connected to the law in some way. While there are no female regulars who work in the police department at the center of the male regulars' lives, there are three notable recurring characters who do work in law enforcement: Harper, Chavez, and Farris. Medical Examiner Harper (who, like Henrietta, has only one name) appears in almost a dozen episodes. A doctor who seems to be in her forties or fifties, she fits in the Wise Woman category of Crone. Into the third season, she provides sharp analytic advice to Nick and Hank.[13] Actor Sharon Sachs makes the most of each encounter: her delivery is emphatic without being over-the-top, suggesting an assured professional. She presents her information with touches of wit, joking with Hank, for instance, in "Beeware" about a bee the size of LeBron James (1.2), or displaying a miniature autopsy of a secondary victim: a rat in whose stomach she finds crucial evidence (1.5). We learn a bit of her backstory: She worked in Kenya after medical school. As the series proceeds, we even see her outside the autopsy room and drawn into the magical storyline: During an autopsy, she touches the Coins of Zakynthos (which appear repeatedly in the series) and, like the main male characters, she is drawn to them and, shortly after, pistol-whipped by an assassin who is searching for them. Harper is not only older but also heavier than a standard television fantasy female. She is humanized, not marginalized, as a wise older woman.

The second of this group is FBI Special Agent Katrina Chavez. Like many strong female *Grimm* characters, she has an ambiguous introduction. Unlike Marie, Kelly, Catherine, and Elizabeth, there is no visual mislead, but audiences are led to suspect that Chavez is a morally culpable character. As an FBI agent, she investigates the beheading of fellow agent Weston Steward, which happens in Nick and Juliette's home—a killing admitted to by Trubel, in self-defense. We already know that Steward is a Wesen working for the Royals; we learn that Chavez is also Wesen, and we know that many Wesen mistrust Grimms. Soon we see Chavez kidnap Trubel and invite her to work with her in a secret organization—while warning Trubel not to tell anyone of the encounter, before Chavez releases her. When Nick's mother is killed and Trubel has to shoot Juliette to keep her from killing Nick, the last shot of the season is of Chavez outside the house, saying "Get her." Whether she is after Trubel or Juliette is unclear. It is only months later that we learn Trubel had already joined Chavez. In fact, we learn that Chavez is willing to give her life—and does—in this "war," as she calls it (5.1). The secret organization she works for (alongside her job with the FBI) is Hadrian's Wall, in which various kinds of beings—Grimms, Wesen, Kehrseite—fight against the all-Wesen Black Claw. A shot of an FBI ID shows that Chavez, a slim and attractive woman, identifies as Hispanic and is in her forties. Thus, like Harper, she represents, in addition to gender, other intersecting categories of marginalized persons (age and weight or age and race/ethnicity). In a bit of backstory, we learn that her diplomat parents were assassinated, leading to her desire to join the FBI. Elizabeth Rodriguez acts Chavez as business-like, tough, cool, and smart; she fits into the Huntress category of the Crone figure. In her later episodes, Rodriguez manages to hint at a warmth underneath the toughness—for example, when she is tied up in the basement of the Spice Shop, facing the angry Rosalee, Monroe, Hank, Wu, and Nick, all of whom believe she may have killed Trubel, and Chavez reiterates Wu's comment: "Somebody's gotta start trusting somebody" (5.1). It is this interchange of trust that leads Nick and his friends to knowledge of Hadrian's Wall. Appearing in about half a dozen episodes, Chavez dies in the first episode of the fifth season, thus becoming the fourth strong woman character and the second woman of color to die within four episodes (if we cross the summer hiatus). Like Henrietta, she does not reappear, but unlike Henrietta, Chavez is remembered repeatedly by other characters as they gradually come to know her organization, Hadrian's Wall.

The third in this group, Deputy Sheriff Janelle Farris, also fits into the Huntress aspect of the Crone. She is perhaps the youngest of the three, possibly in her thirties, but no younger. Actor Toni Trucks identifies as mixed race, so Farris, like Harper and Chavez, represents two marginalized categories. Farris appears in only two episodes, but she is important in each of them; fans also remember her as someone who seemed to be a potential love interest for Hank (see Ch. 2 note 19). She is more, however, than a love interest. In her first appearance, she seems a capable and intelligent officer; she discovers a related case unknown to Nick and Hank. She politely insists on her equality on the job; when Hank offers to take her shovel as they search for evidence in the field, "I can dig," is her response (4.6). She is investigating a kidnapping when she is knocked unconscious and kidnapped herself. This episode features Wesen worshipers of Kali-Ma, but it does not present Kali-Ma in connection with positive Goddess worship; instead, there are stereotypical villains and stereotypically ethnic music (see Ch. 3). Farris is shown as a careful investigator but, at the end of the episode, lacking knowledge of the Wesen world, she is a rescued victim. Her next appearance offers her more scope. It is an episode that focuses on racial injustice, the unsolved murder of a Native American man. We learn a bit of Farris's backstory: Her ex-husband was a member of the same tribe. She is able to introduce Hank and Nick to a tribal leader to help the investigation. Furthermore, she enters a kind of liminal status: She witnesses a spirit that has possessed the murder victim's teenage son (a spirit connected to his mother's tribe, the Ojibwe), and Hank presses her to acknowledge what she has seen, admitting he and Nick have seen it too. The spirit, possessing the son, kills two of the three men who murdered the father in a hate crime; though Hank, Nick, and Farris discover who the third killer is, they cannot legally prove his guilt, a weighty moment in the series—especially for Hank, who has also been briefly possessed by the spirit. In the end, the spirit possesses someone else and kills the killer. It is only in the last moments of the episode that we learn that it is Janelle Farris who has unknowingly been possessed, as she looks in confusion at her bloody reflection in a forest pool. On the one hand, her having been possessed by the spirit suggests a lack of agency for her. On the other hand, the episode has made clear that she, like Nick and Hank, very much wished to see the killer punished; so she enacts the justice they wanted, perhaps a wish fulfillment for her—and thus, in a sense, a participation in magical agency. It also in effect implicates her in the extrajudicial killings performed by law enforcement in *Grimm* (see Ch. 2)—implying both complicity and community with the other cops. Furthermore, the episode leaves her in a liminal status between the unknowing Kehrseite world and the world of those who know Wesen. This status suggests that she is on a path to greater knowledge. Had the series lasted longer, this Huntress might have reappeared.[14]

Crones of Stereotype

While *Grimm* generally presents adult women as interesting and often admirable, stretching traditional gender roles as they evince aspects of the Crone, nonetheless in three cases there are flat, racially/ethnically stereotyped recurring Crone characters: Frau Pech, Stefania Vaduva Popescu, and Pilar. Frau Pech (Mary McDonald-Lewis) is an old-world Witch, a wrinkled Hexenbiest baby-seller with a heavy Germanic accent. Her ethnicity is vaguely central European, stereotypically old-world. She first does business with then later threatens Adalind and magically steals the appearance of Adalind's body, thus offering Adalind and her co-conspirator the opportunity and justification to have Frau Pech killed, to be used to restore Adalind's powers. That co-conspirator is Stefania Vaduva Popescu, none other than the "Queen of the Schwarzwald Roma"—so of course she is a double-crosser who plans to turn the pregnant Adalind over to the Royals, who want her magic child but not necessarily Adalind. Another character with a (different) heavy accent, she is played with eye-widening flair by Iranian American Shohreh Aghdashloo (later known for her work in *The Expanse*, 2015–). The scenes she acts with Claire Coffee's Adalind are often humorous and sometimes ghastly, but the character is little more than a Roma cliché. Despite the use of the preferred term "Roma," she is a stereotypical child-thief in "long skirts […] scarves and gold earrings" (McClain 129). In the end, she is shown (like Catherine) as servicing the Royals: This queen is ultimately subservient. Pilar—yet another one-named woman—is essentially a Mexican American version of the "Magical Negro" stereotype.[15] It should be acknowledged as progressive that Pilar and Juliette often converse in Spanish (the language of Juliette's grandmother), which implies respect for ethnic/racial diversity. Angela Tenga suggests that Pilar helps convey a theme of connection to ancestry and past (35). Also progressive is that in her first episode, "La Llorona," Pilar appears with an unstereotypical Mexican American father character and participates in a context of neighborhood support for that father (2.9). However, in most of her appearances she simply gives metaphorically couched advice to Juliette (who is dealing with long-term partial amnesia). Pilar seems to have magical knowledge without effort. This mysterious ability is in contrast, for example, to

Henrietta or Rosalee, who are depicted as working with powders, mixtures, and books—or any other of the Wise Women, who earn their knowledge. Actor Bertila Damas injects warmth into the part; indeed she sometimes conveys a wry restraint at Juliette's unwillingness to listen (this being before Juliette knows of Wesen). Pilar also has a bit of backstory when she describes her childhood fear hiding from El Cucuy in Guadalajara (3.5). But in the end, there is not much for Damas to work with. Unlike almost all the other Crones, these three are not resonant characters, and they are perhaps the most harmful in terms of racial/ethnic impact.

Conclusion: A Diversity of Crones

There are a number of other interesting adult female recurring characters in *Grimm*. Angelina Lasser, Monroe's ex-girlfriend, memorably played by the Academy Award-winning Jaime Ray Newman,[16] is discussed in Chapter One; Zuri Ellis, played with appropriate complexity by Sharon Leal, is discussed in Chapter Two; and there are more. But the Crones discussed in this chapter demonstrate the variety of women characters that *Grimm* presents in the course of its six seasons. *Grimm* never suggests the good/bad, Virgin/Whore dichotomy that has often trapped those gendered female. The variety of presentation encompasses diversity of many sorts, from morality to body size, from career to family ties; and, to a lesser degree, of race/ethnicity. Significantly, there is also diversity of age, as the Crone connection implies. The show does not rest on youthfully dewy good looks—though most of the actors are conventionally attractive. Does the fact that most are conventionally attractive, even when they have a Crone inside, suggest that women have to hide their wisdom? Perhaps, but again and again, in *Grimm* the Crone is revealed; the power is made known. Whether a Witch with an inner hag, a Wise Woman, or a Huntress—or all three—the Crones of Portland are characters worth getting to know. In the next chapters, five of them will be visited at greater length.

Seven

"Smoking that hat"

The Shape of Power for Fred/Illyria in Angel *and Juliette/Eve in* Grimm

When *Grimm* first aired, there was only a single female actor among the six regulars.[1] Her character was the hero's girlfriend, Juliette Silverton. In the first season, she was presented as an almost parodic damsel-in-distress, in a Perils-of-Pauline style scene, tied up in a cart on the railroad tracks—a mockery of old gender roles (1.14). In fact, the parody seems to have been purposeful: Before the end of the episode, Juliette punches the villain—another woman—in the face and escapes (with the help of Nick and Monroe). Nonetheless, this Juliette is a very simple person compared to the complex being we see developing over the course of the six seasons of *Grimm*. She goes through four distinct stages of existence and two different names: the kind, intelligent, red-headed Juliette; the dark-haired Hexenbiest fury still called Juliette; the cold soldier Eve; and the later Eve (Juliette/Eve), who incorporates emotion in agency. The actor who plays her reflects such changeability in the real world: she also changes names. She begins the series credited as Bitsie Tulloch but by the end, she is Elizabeth Tulloch. The significance and depth of the character's changes, both in bodily presentation and psyche, can be illuminated by comparison to a character in a different but related series: Fred/Illyria of *Angel* (1999–2004).

David Greenwalt, who served as co-creator and showrunner of *Grimm*, also served as co-creator and showrunner of *Angel*. Though the *Angel* character of shy Winifred Burkle (Amy Acker) transitioned to the powerful character of Illyria after Greenwalt left his showrunning duties at *Angel*,[2] the compound character has significant similarities to the transitional character of Eve in *Grimm*, who started out as Juliette. Both Fred and Juliette begin as intelligent women—Fred a research scientist, Juliette

137

a veterinary doctor—who are depicted with heterosexual relationships (Fred with teammates Gunn [J. August Richards] then Wes [Alexis Denisof], Juliette with Nick). Both, however, go through an abnormal death and emerge as much more powerful beings who no longer have the same gender presentation, emotional affect, or sexual interests. The former god Illyria is last seen on screen facing possible apocalyptic death with chosen family in *Angel*'s finale; Eve, on the other hand, is shown surviving such an apocalypse, part of another chosen family that is facing an open future. The very names of Juliette and Eve suggest a shift from representing the romantic to representing womanhood more generally. Late in the series, Eve tells her erstwhile significant other Nick that she does not live for happiness; she has chosen to live for a larger purpose. This speech expresses a positive theme in the character that is implicit in earlier actions.

While Fred is transformed into Illyria against her will, Juliette makes a choice that ultimately results in her becoming Eve. Hexenbiests on *Grimm*—women of power—are shown transforming themselves by means of an ancient witch's hat which emblematizes both female and male qualities. Juliette is warned that there may be unpredictable consequences to accessing this power, but she makes the choice in order to help in the fight against darkness. She herself becomes a dark witch for a while and as a result is shot and then forcibly re-programmed as Eve. After again dying (or coming near death) in battle, she is re-born once more, eventually emerging with the ability to make her own decisions. She decides that her fight—in effect, her career—is more important than romance or children. Yet, at the end of the series, she is nonetheless part of the chosen family. While Illyria is an almost complete rewriting of Fred, Eve is finally a transformed character who bears within her some threads of the earlier Juliette, who, year after year, refused Nick's offers of marriage. She thus displays a forceful evolution of identity rather than an evacuation of it. Juliette/Eve demonstrates the unpredictable results of our choices and their impact on our identities while evincing an internal continuity of character. Fred is felled by the disease of Illyria, but Juliette smokes the hat, the dangerous drug of power.[3]

Narrative Contexts

David Greenwalt worked with Joss Whedon on *Buffy* and then co-created and ran *Angel* with him for three seasons. As scholars such as Elizabeth Rambo, AmiJo Comeford, Jes Battis, and others have noted, the few female regulars and recurring characters in *Angel* tend to have limited life spans. Cordelia Chase, Fred Burkle, Darla, and Lilah Morgan all end up dead; Detective Kate Lockley is fired and disappears; Wolfram & Hart's Eve is excised by romance[4]; and Harmony Kendall is rarely more than a peripheral figure of fun. Cordelia suffers multiple forced supernatural pregnancies—in effect, rape without intercourse—and Darla, Cordelia, and Fred all die as the result of being used for the gestation of a supernatural being, the latter two having been chosen for this "honor" because of their exceptional qualities (see Potvin). In contrast, *Grimm* is replete with women regulars and noteworthy recurring characters, both human and Wesen. Many of these characters fit into the category of the "wise, willful, wolfish Crone," as Barbara Walker defines it (13). They are all either wise women or warriors; some are both. There are enough of them that they can represent a spectrum of moral qualities, and not just along the sexual line most typically used to measure a woman's morals ("Are you honest?" Hamlet asks Ophelia [3.1.103], meaning "Are you chaste?") Each of the regular and most of the recurring females have a complex past. Rosalee, for instance, was a drug addict; Trubel was placed in an insane asylum; and Adalind's arc curves even more sharply than that of *Angel*'s Cordelia: Cordelia may have begun as a high school bitch queen, but Adalind started with attempted murder. That there are enough women characters to have moral variety is (it is worth repeating) one of the real virtues of *Grimm*.

Fred and the Damsel in Distress

We experience the characters of Fred/Illyria and Juliette/Eve within these larger narrative contexts. Thus, for instance, when the Wolfram & Hart lab scientist Knox speaks of Illyria being "hatch[ed]" from Fred, and Angel calls it a "gestat[ion]" ("A Hole in the World" 5.15), long-time viewers may well recall Cordelia's three separate experiences being supernaturally impregnated—the last experience, giving birth to the fully-grown, world-dominating Jasmine, leads to Cordelia's coma and eventual death (see Comeford 159, Battis 113). But Fred/Illyria's individual character arc is certainly significant. In biographical order—as opposed to series plot order—Winifred Burkle is raised by loving parents in Texas and goes to graduate school in physics at UCLA. There, because of her brilliance, she seems a threat to her male faculty mentor, who therefore gets rid of the competition by sending her to the hellish dimension of Pylea—not the worst metaphor for an unhealthy faculty-student relationship. In Pylea, where humans are enslaved, Fred manages to escape the slavers and live hidden in a cave, where she becomes slowly less sane but continues to write formulas on the cave wall. When Angel and company come to the Pylean dimension with the purpose of rescuing Cordelia, Angel saves Fred, too: "Handsome man saved me," are Fred's first words to Angel ("Through the

Looking Glass" 2.21). On their return, Fred at first leaves with her parents, but, recognizing a biological pattern relating to a case, she realizes the team is in danger and returns to save *them*. From that point she gradually recuperates and becomes a full team member, specializing in science. Much of her screen time focuses on heterosexual romance: first with Charles Gunn, the African American young man who had his own team of vampire fighters before he joined Angel's, and later with Wesley Wyndam-Price, the British former Watcher who specializes in occult knowledge. Fred's strength is clear. When, for example, Jasmine, the Power that Was, takes over almost all the world, it is Fred alone of Team Angel who sees Jasmine for what she is. That Fred does so is at first a chance of the touch of Jasmine's blood; but it is no mere chance that keeps Fred fighting alone until she can awaken others. When Angel and company are given the L.A. offices of demonic law-firm Wolfram & Hart in the fifth season, Fred hangs up her Dixie Chicks poster and takes over her division, insisting that they "work the damn problem" ("Conviction" 5.1). When Spike realizes he is a fading non-corporeal, it is to Fred, whom he calls "the science queen," that he says, "Help me."[5] When Wesley and Fred do field work and Wesley makes an impressive two-gun move against the bad guys, gunless Fred says sarcastically, "Yes, thank you, Wesley, I'd love a gun" and asks if he realizes how "patronizing" he has been when he says he should have protected her ("Lineage" 5.7).

It is not surprising, then, that when Fred is infected by the ancient god-king Illyria, she gets out of her sickbed and goes to the lab to fight back, directly declaring to Wesley, "I am not the damsel in distress" (5.15). But in terms of the structure of the narrative, she is exactly that. She says once more to Angel, "Handsome man saves me," recalling her Pylean days; she refers to the six male characters around her as "my boys," an unusually maternal expression coming from Fred. She is unable to save herself, and though her boys find a way to save her, they choose not to do so, because they learn that thousands of others would need to die—something Fred would not want, they say. Thus Fred becomes another sacrificial woman, dying for others by a choice the men make,[6] presuming (however correctly) she would agree.

Illyria and Heterosexual Romance

Fred is evacuated to make way for the god-king Illyria. The smart human woman is replaced by something that looks like a female comic-book hero. Roz Kaveney, Jes Battis, Cynthea Masson, Nikki Faith Fuller, Bronwen Calvert, Matt Hills and Rebecca Williams, and others have discussed the Fred/Illyria transformation in various ways. Calvert points out that "gender [is] problematised in the appearance of a nominally masculine or even genderless character (a 'god') as a leather-clad female" (184). It is worth noting that Illyria, a name that Shakespeare fan Whedon took from *Twelfth Night*, comes from the Shakespeare play that perhaps most pervasively explores gender roles. In Illyria, we are presented with the spectacle of a being identified as formerly genderless or male, being forced to exist in a female body, and not being very happy with its limitations. Illyria speaks of the limitations as human, but we are viewing the body as female. On the other hand, we get to see this female form trounce all the male warriors in the show, as they try to control and test Illyria. Calvert writes of the continuity of the character as residing in embodiment and its negotiations. In her existentialist analysis, Masson reminds us that Fred's soul has been annihilated, and Battis says that Illyria therefore "embodies loss" (129). Following Calvert's emphasis on embodiment, and for additional reasons, I too will refer to Illyria using the female gender. All these scholars examine her choices to deal with this world[7] and move forward in the end as part of Team Angel. In various ways, they comment on Illyria's relationship to Wesley, and Fuller emphasizes the emotions involved.

I would go a bit further and argue that the relationship can be seen, despite the gender queering, as a heterosexual pairing. At first Illyria appears so distant from humanity that a romantic relationship would seem absurd, but that gradually changes. For example, Illyria is troubled when Wesley speaks to Spike and, she says, Wes "showed no regard for my presence" ("Power Play" 5.21)—he didn't notice me. After appearing as Fred for Fred's parents, Illyria tells Wes, "You loved this and part of you still does. I can feel it in you. I wish to explore it further"—though Wes recoils ("The Girl in Question" 5.20). And of course, in the series finale, she rushes to Wes's side to be Fred for him as he dies. Many have noted that it is her concern and grief for Wes that leads her to join Team Angel for the final fight. The structure of the situation thus suggests that Illyria is saved by the love of a good man. As writer and fifth-season showrunner Jeffrey Bell says, "Illyria is finding herself falling for Wesley because she used to be inhabited by Fred" ("Not Fade Away" Commentary 5.22). While there are many other elements of the character that are worth discussing, the element of heterosexual romance is one that I think does obtain.

Juliette, Knowledge, and the Rejection of Heterosexual Romance

It is noteworthy that the ultimate version of the Juliette/Eve character turns away from heterosexual romance. The character certainly does not begin at such a place; her very name suggests Shakespeare's most famous romantic heroine and in the pilot, her lover Nick (a character more like Buffy than Angel) is called Romeo by partner Hank.[8] A deleted pilot scene shows her working in a café, but before that could air, Greenwalt and Kouf had decided to make her a veterinary doctor, a career that denotes strength of intellect and determination.[9] By the second episode she is leaving Nick in bed early in the morning, telling him she is going to operate on a bulldog—a scene and comment that might suggest gender dominance. However, if we examine Juliette in this first character stage by using the lens applied by many essays in Juliette Kitchens' *At Home in the Whedonverses*, we might note that while we do sometimes see her at work in the veterinary hospital, she is much more often shown in the home she shares with Nick, and her role as romantic interest is dominant in the early episodes.

Her character at this stage is hardly sentimental, however; it is instead enlivened by touches of humor. Some of Bitsie Tulloch's best acting comes in those moments. When Juliette tells Nick she wants to learn to shoot and he responds, "A gun?" Tulloch's rapidly timed delivery of "No, a bow and arrow" effectively conveys the give-and-take of a believable relationship (1.15). When a scientist asks if her request to use his lab is top secret, she replies with a glint of amusement: "Not top secret, more like middle secret" (1.21). When Monroe, Rosalee, and Elizabeth declare that she is the missing ingredient to the spell needed to regain Nick's powers, director Tawnia McKiernan shoots the double phalanx of characters—Nick, Rosalee, Monroe, Elizabeth—looking at Juliette as she emerges, unwitting, from the dining room. With Trubel stuffing her face in the background, Tulloch, Lucille Ball–like, has Juliette make a slight rubbery twist of the lips to emit from the left side of her mouth the one word "What?" (4.4). Actors and director thus play against the conventional prettiness of Juliette's usual presentation in a way that humanizes the character with humor.[10]

Early in the series, conflict between Nick and Juliette is based on the fact that he has recently discovered the Wesen world; he is able to see the various species hidden within apparently normal human beings. She turns down a proposal of marriage, saying she thinks he is keeping things from her. He believes she would think him insane if he tried to explain—and in fact, he is shown to be right. When she is scratched by a cat belonging to the lawyer Adalind Schade, veterinarian Juliette takes it lightly. But Nick, knowing Adalind to be a vengeful Hexenbiest, fears for Juliette's life and so makes a desperate attempt to get her to take the situation seriously by trying to explain the dangers of the Wesen world. Unconvinced and resisting magical treatment, Juliette falls into a coma at the end of Season One, and spends the first episodes of Season Two as Sleeping Beauty, eventually awakened by the kiss of the nearest prince, Nick's police captain. She spends much of the season either comatose or amnesiac—none of which seems to advance her as an exemplar of feminist power.

In her magical memory loss, she forgets romance, but not her career: She forgets about Nick, but she never forgets her abilities as a veterinarian—something that actually does give her one kind of power. And her memories of Nick gradually return. Magic-induced feelings of lust for Renard, who kissed her awake, lead her to recognize the existence of magic. At this point of the character's development, she repeatedly seeks information about the supernatural. In one visually memorable moment, Rosalee moves to physically and emotionally stand by Juliette as Juliette asks Nick's best Wesen friend, Rosalee's boyfriend Monroe, for information—and after this expression of solidarity, he reluctantly gives it (2.16). In a culmination of her initiation to knowledge, three of Nick's Wesen friends—Rosalee, Bud Wurstner, and Monroe—reveal themselves to Juliette—an act of great trust on their part, requiring them to will her to see them (whereas Nick can see them whether or not they choose). Thus Juliette, by choice, becomes a Kehrseiteschlichkennen—a normal who knows about the other world—just at Fred chooses to stay with Team Angel. When a character is being initiated into Nick's world, Nick seems to enjoy almost ceremonially opening the doors to the weapons cabinet in his Aunt Marie's trailer, but Juliette opens those cabinet doors herself without Nick present—appropriately for her agency in crossing the threshold (2.17).[11]

Once Juliette crosses that threshold, she enters a stage during which her own skills as a veterinarian (similar to Fred's as a physicist) and her growing knowledge of Wesen are effectively combined. Wesen are based in part on characters like those in the Grimm fairy tales, but also on other folk tales from around the world. As such, Wesen are almost uniformly animal-related—the wolf; the fox; the beaver; and when Amy Acker guest stars, she is a Spinnatod, a tragic arachnid. The unusual natures mean that Juliette's veterinary knowledge can help (and, like *Buffy* and *Angel*, *Grimm* often centers on the search for knowledge). Thus Juliette is able to help stop the serial killing of Blutbaden through her knowledge of "breed-specific" "gastric dilatation vulvulus" (3.3). She is able to prevent the execution of a young boy by the Wesen Council because she recognizes that he is suffering from an obscure protozoan infection rather than a supernatural hereditary evil (3.6). She comes up with an effective method of administering a mass treatment for zombie-like symptoms (3.1). As actor Bitsie Tulloch said during a Dragon Con panel, she was happy her character got to be a member of the Scooby Gang, the term used for the friends in *Buffy*—a term other actors in *Grimm* used as well ("Grimm: Lowen"). Juliette happily invests in the combined work of the group—though she still puts Nick off when he once again brings out the engagement ring (3.22).

The Return of the Ring

From the first to the last episode of *Grimm*, the traditional diamond engagement ring appears again and again to symbolize problems in traditional gender relationships—first in connection with Juliette, then in connection with Adalind (see Ch. 9). The initial scene with Nick shows him emerging from a jewelry store with an engagement ring in his hand, as his partner Hank photographs him. Hank says he is just testing new camera equipment, but the camera-within-a-camera metatext of Nick's first close-up calls more attention to the nature of the moment as part of a story, as does Hank's later calling Nick Romeo.[12] Attention is brought again to the ring as Nick leaves work: the ring box falls out of his jacket pocket, and Hank throws it to him. This ring already seems ill-fated—appropriately enough for characters called Romeo and Juliette and a series that focuses on the dark side of fairy tales. And in fact, Nick, interrupted by attacks on a little girl, on his aunt, and ultimately on himself, is unable to offer the ring to Juliette in this episode. Later in the first season, Juliette teases him about not being late for their anniversary, and, in the same episode, finds, with a smile, the ring box in his sock drawer. Near the end of the episode, she is waiting alone at the candlelit dinner table. When he finally calls, she is seated on their bed, holding the ring. He tells her he loves her, but she responds only with a brief inarticulate sound before clicking off, dropping the phone from her hand, and staring seriously at the ring box (1.12). All of these images speak rejection, failure. By the time he does propose, holding out the ring to her in the sixteenth episode, she tells him she loves him and wishes she could marry him someday, but feels she cannot because she believes he is keeping secrets from her. (Of course, he is.) She is unwilling to enter a marriage uneven in power, as would be the result of their disparate knowledge. Love is important to Juliette, but she is not willing to disempower herself to secure it, to formalize it.

At least once a season, at roughly the same point, the story returns to the ring, always showing the attempt at traditional marriage as unsuccessful for Juliette and Nick. In the eighteenth episode of the second season, Juliette is attempting to recuperate from her amnesia, and in a touching moment that closes the episode, she recalls Nick's proposal. It helps prepare for the reconnection of their love that will come at the season's end, but again does not lead to a formal engagement; they both speak of renewing the relationship slowly. In the seventeenth episode of the third season, Nick comes to the dining room with the ring in his pocket, ready to propose, when they are interrupted by his mother knocking at the door with the fugitive Adalind, carrying her baby Diana. In hindsight, given Nick and Adalind's later romance, the interruption seems almost fated—especially considering that the episode's title is "Synchronicity" (a subject on which Juliette discourses in Jungian terms). But the ring's failure is not merely fated. In the last episode of season three, while preparing for Monroe and Rosalee's wedding (and a marriage that is fully successful), Nick pulls out the ring box again, and once more Juliette tells him to put it away, saying they can return to it later. They never do. In the normal human way of things, her feelings are mixed, but in the end, reluctance about marriage predominates.[13]

The last instance of the ring as reflecting the relationship between Nick and Juliette—and the larger recognition that traditional marriage should not be the automatic preference—comes in the fourteenth episode of the fourth season. In this episode, Juliette has already become a Hexenbiest and she is finally, fearfully, revealing her condition to Nick. Upon seeing her hag-like, woged face, Nick assumes it is Adalind, not Juliette—that Adalind has taken Juliette's form again. But Juliette convinces him that she is herself by telling him about his first proposal, pointing to the couch where she sat as he offered her the ring. She is using her knowledge of the ring to identify herself—her old self. She is no longer that person. Indeed, considering her reluctance to accept the ring, it seems she never did fully embrace the kind of relationship that it would seem to represent for Juliette and her Romeo. Furthermore, she tells him that the sickness she felt when she was in the process of becoming a Hexenbiest led her to believe that she might be pregnant. Then Nick responds to her Hexenbiest condition using the language of an unwanted pregnancy, telling her they will "get rid of it." They have this loaded discussion in an episode that centers on a grotesque fertility ritual, an episode titled "Bad Luck." The episode's context seems to warn against unthinking investment in the traditional package of marriage and procreation (while still offering the alternative of Monroe and Rosalee as a thoughtful pairing). Instead of becoming pregnant, Juliette is becoming invested in a dark and extraordinary power. While Nick visits Henrietta to unsuccessfully seek a way to change Juliette back, Juliette tries on the ring once more. But as she does so, her hand changes to that of the gnarled Hexenbiest, and, struggling, she pulls the ring off—an effective moment of symbolism. When he returns, she confronts him with her belief that their relationship is now impossible and walks out. She is, in the end, the most powerful Hexenbiest in the storyworld. Both because of what seems to be fateful timing (synchronicity?) and her own underlying resistance, Juliette does not choose the ring, does not choose the traditional path.

Juliette as Non-Traditional Hexenbiest

Juliette's second major phase, her becoming a Hexenbiest, has indirectly come as a result of her choices, her agency. Burger and Mix assert that "the witch figure is a litmus test of cultural perceptions of and responses to women's power and, particularly in the case of wicked witches, women's anger"; they focus on "its negotiation of witchcraft as a power which enables its users to exercise their agency" (12). In terms of this fourth-season "transformation," they assess Juliette herself as "a much more complex negotiation of the Hexenbiest's power [than Adalind]" (23).[14] When Monroe and Rosalee marry, they become objects of persecution by racist groups because of their intermarriage between Wesen species. At this point, Nick has lost his powers because Adalind has taken the form of Juliette and slept with him. Adalind transforms by using an ancient witch's hat she has inherited from her mother. The hat is placed over a cauldron in which the Hexenbiest has placed a special brew, and as the steam rises, the hat stiffens and grows erect. Adalind places her mouth over the tip and breathes in, holding a breath of the smoke at a time, and morphing into Juliette. The hat combines female and male imagery (not to mention a particular kind of smoking) as the woman uses it for power generated through appearance and deception. Setting aside Adalind's motives, after they have sex Nick is left, like Samson, bereft of his powers and unable to protect his friends Monroe and Rosalee. The group learns from Elizabeth that Nick can regain his powers if Juliette will smoke the hat, take the form of Adalind, and sleep with Nick. At first Nick and Juliette demur. They have been told that there could be unintended consequences—but that doing nothing might also have unintended consequences, in particular for Nick. Later, standing in the glare of a flaming symbol of race-hatred by which Monroe and Rosalee have been threatened, Juliette declares that she wants to get Nick's powers back (4.6). She decides to risk herself for the sake of greater power to do good.

They succeed in regaining Nick's powers, but their choice ironically leads to evil, as well. It is some weeks after she smokes the hat that Juliette discovers with horror that she herself has become a Hexenbiest. She exhibits more power than any other Hexenbiest. But as her power grows, her empathy shrinks. She is arrested for assault after sexually taunting and hurting a man in a bar, and in jail, she tells Nick that she revels in this new power. She initiates sex with increasingly problematic partners: the morally mixed Renard and the evil Prince Kenneth, who orders Nick's mother's death. (Since Rosalee and Adalind both initiate sex with morally good partners, the problematizing seems to center on Juliette's partner choice, not the sexuality.) She nearly kills Monroe when he, Rosalee, and the others try to give her a rare and difficult-to-produce potion to suppress the Hexenbiest within her (something she had earlier desired). She becomes enraged when she learns that Adalind is carrying Nick's child, the result of their intercourse when Adalind took the form of Juliette. (Stacey Abbott echoes Tim Minear in calling the *Angel* plots operatic [*Angel* 14], and we could certainly apply the term to *Grimm*.) Burger and Mix identify Juliette's angry actions as "punishment" for Nick's unknowing unfaithfulness with Adalind, "an outlet for her rage and previous powerlessness" (23). This is one of multiple possible motivations that the show suggests—reflecting human psychological complexity. "I am on top of the world," Juliette tells Rosalee; then later in the same episode, "I am in hell," she says to Nick (4.19). Juliette experiences pleasure, fear, and horror at the thought of the change. She may be reacting to the realization that she is not a ring-on-the-finger person; she is something, someone, altogether different. She at first recalls that the change was the result of her choice, knowing there could be unexpected consequences (4.14) but later blames others for her condition (4.17), later still embracing it. Jailed, she says to Nick, "Deep down, I do blame you for what's happened to me, and part of me loves you for it. [...] I like this power, Nick. [...] You really think that you can just take off your clothes and crawl into bed with me again?" With her hand on his, she woges into hag-face for those final words (4.18). She is complicated psychologically, but her change is not just theoretical, not just mental; it lives in her body (as for Fred/Illyria). Her embodiment as the hag-witch is a reversion/revulsion from the conventionally pretty Juliette, and here she uses that shape as a threat.[15]

Another kind of confrontation of embodiment and destructiveness comes in the first of the two most memorable actions of rage by the dark Juliette: She torches Aunt Marie's trailer. In a series with many shocking turns, this is one of the most shocking. The trailer has been a home, the center of knowledge and secret community. A relatively modern space, it is filled with ancient tomes, weapons, and potions. The little silver shape sits in a fairy-tale forest of gigantic, aged trees. Its combination of the fairy-tale with the modern is a representation of this storyworld as a whole. And Juliette wrecks it. We see not only the fire but the burnt pages of the books in the aftermath—the ruined word as damaged flesh. The other Hexenbiests in the series are uniformly depicted as valuing, even revering, the books and tools that have been passed down through the centuries; as discussed in Chapter Six, this attitude is an aspect of the Crone figure that *Grimm* connects to witches (in terms of both visage and actions as Wise Women). But Juliette is a different kind of Hexenbiest. Rather than being born, she has been made—an extremely unusual creation, and all the more powerful as a result (as Rosalee explains, 4.10). When she woges, though her face is just as wrinkled and malformed, her hair is not gray like the others.[16] It seems she has the power of the aged Crone, but not the wisdom. She is thus separate from other Hexenbiests. Her transformation is a ragged one.

Alone, she joins forces with the royal family, who seek Adalind's magic child by the estranged bastard prince, Renard. Because that child is secretly being cared for by Nick's mother, Juliette arranges for her to come to the home Juliette had shared with Nick, where Kelly is beheaded by the Royals. (In another moment of extreme abject embodiment, we see Kelly's head in a box, seeping blood.) There could hardly be a more dismaying representation of a female's sudden access to power than Juliette's. And at this point in the series narrative (4.20–22), the showrunners kill three notable women of power: first Henrietta, the ancient, beautiful counselor Hexenbiest; then Kelly; and next, Juliette herself, who is shot by Trubel as Juliette is about to kill Nick.

Eve as the Cold Soldier

Had the series ended at this point, the story would have been, to say the least, unsatisfying; the women of *Grimm* would have been in similar condition to the women of *Angel*.[17] Over the summer hiatus, showrunners Greenwalt and Kouf insisted at Comic-Con that Juliette would not return. But half a dozen episodes into the fifth season, we see for the first time the *Alias*-wigged, body-suited powerhouse Eve, also played by Tulloch. She bears a striking resemblance to the character of Illyria.[18] In addition to the catsuit and the ability to fell a dozen supernatural opponents at a blow (or rather, the twist of a wrist), Eve has the same lowered vocal range, "minimal movement" (as Calvert says of Illyria, 184–85) and limited emotional affect; she even has the same head tilt.[19] But where Illyria has only "fragments" of Fred's memories ("Shells" 5.16), Eve tells Nick that she "remember[s] everything" (5.7) Roz Kaveney has noted the parallel between vampires and Illyria—the demon taking over the body; Eve carries the parallel further, at least in sharing the continuity of memory. Nonetheless she insists that she is a completely different person, and Nick soon asserts the same, as do the others when they encounter her. Unlike vampires such as Angel or Spike, Eve denies responsibility for the actions of the earlier self Juliette. Her emotionlessness is a drastic differentiation from the rage that drove the Hexenbiest version of Juliette. The original warmhearted Juliette was red-headed; the Hexenbiest Juliette was dark-haired[20]; Eve's frequent use of wigs and costumes heightens the idea of femininity as performance and her as genderless. (While Nick, like Angel, has a cabinet of weapons, Eve has a cabinet of wigs.) Eve now works for the organization Hadrian's Wall,[21] devoted to fighting a secret Wesen revolution that is being plotted around the world with the intention of conquering normals. Trubel's membership in the group lends moral validity to Eve's current work and new self.[22]

Eve declares that fighting in HW has given her purpose; in this sense she has continuity with her earlier character of Juliette, who not only worked as a veterinarian but applied her skills to dealing with Wesen as well. When asked why they call her Eve, she says, "Because I'm starting over" (5.7). But there are troubling aspects to her transformation. The beginning of each *Grimm* episode has an epigraph, and for Eve's introduction, the epigraph is "I have been bent and broken but, I hope, into a better shape." The apparently dead Hexenbiest Juliette was hidden away to be broken, as Trubel says,[23] in order to turn her into a weapon for the sake of good.[24] Early in that process, when she starts to attack a captor, he hits her in the face. We see a man—Meisner, someone accepted as a good guy—emerge from her cell repeatedly after sounds of violence. The epigraph for the episode in question comes from Dickens's *Great Expectations*; it is a line stated by Estella, who has used Pip cruelly but in the end feels for him. However, Dickens implies that Estella has suffered domestic abuse as the wife of another man, so the epigraph adds to the disturbing context of Juliette's rebirth as Eve. Though, unlike Fred in *Angel*, Juliette seems to have endorsed this new identity and to have retained memories of the old identity, the change for the woman is still fraught. Both Nick and Eve speak of the need to bury Juliette, and early in the season, Nick dreams of a burial that never happens.

Nevertheless, like Illyria, Eve slowly becomes more and more integrated into the team—not only the Initiative-like, government-supported, underground-cell-based HW, but also the Scoobies: Nick, Hank, Rosalee, Monroe, Wu, Trubel (who floats between the two groups), and the renovated Adalind.[25] It is at this stage that Hank asks her, looking askance, "You thinking about smoking that hat again?" (5.16). Eve is valued as a comrade, but at first, as little more.

Juliette/Eve and Agency

At the end of the fifth season, Eve is mortally wounded and enters yet another phase of existence. In this phase, she moves beyond the weaponized, militarized woman to a place of greater personal agency. She no longer takes orders. Throughout the series, characters have been searching for seven keys that lead to a treasure hidden by seven Grimms during the Crusades. With all the Scoobies working together, Nick and Monroe retrieve the treasure—which turns out to be a wooden stick. After some understandable underwhelming, they discover it has the ability to heal; it saves first Monroe and then Nick from death. Nick keeps it carefully hidden, but he brings it out to save the wounded Eve. Those who have seen the original *Blade Runner* (1982) may recall the android Pru's (Darryl Hannah's) death throes; Eve's reaction to the stick is similarly inhumanly orgasmic, unlike Monroe's or Nick's. Once she is saved by Nick's magic stick (yes, a symbol; see Ch. 5), Eve accesses feelings she had forgotten, and she temporarily loses most of her powers. She declares in confusion that she feels herself to be both Eve and Juliette. (We might call her Juliette/Eve.) Nick lifts her broken body and calls her Juliette (5.22). It seems as though, as in the case of Fred/Illyria, we may once again have a powerful female socialized by the love of a man.

But the *Grimm* narrative takes us to another place. Nick has, in the seven-month absence of the presumed-dead Juliette, begun a relationship with Adalind, the mother of his son. Subsequently the Hadrian's Wall headquarters in Portland has been destroyed in the battles associated with Eve's death-and-rebirth as Juliette/Eve, and Nick and Adalind have taken the homeless Juliette/Eve into their home. No longer cat-suited or bewigged in the last episodes, she wears unremarkable clothing and is brown-haired. Juliette/Eve awakens one morning to find Adalind's daughter Diana watching her. Director Aaron Lipstadt focuses a strong light on Juliette/Eve's face as she looks at the little girl, and the scene is silent for several seconds. The solemn, vulnerable openness of Tulloch's expression displays a very different character than the Eve of earlier days. When Diana asks if she wishes she had Nick back, Juliette/Eve tells Diana, in childlike terms, that it would not be right for her to have a relationship with Nick, even if sometimes (using Diana's words) her "tummy hurts"—even if sometimes she has regrets (6.7). More importantly, Juliette/Eve later declares to Nick in very adult terms that she is not making choices based on their relationship and that he should not feel guilty because she has endangered herself. When she says so, she has entered a hell dimension to try to save them all and he has followed her; he thinks that she is trying to redeem herself and blames himself for her having become a Hexenbiest in the first place. But she does not allow him to claim what has been her choice—a decision made to support the good fight, even in the awareness that unforeseen consequences would come—her culpability in his mother's death, her power, the loss of their relationship, and more. Through the years Juliette never chose to be married to Nick, and the sense that she has, deep down, always had a different kind of purpose emerges in the speech she gives to Nick in the other world.

First, in echo of Fred's saying she is not a damsel in distress, Juliette/Eve says, "I don't want to be rescued, Nick. I came here for a reason" (6.11). She reminds him that he, the male, not she, has parental responsibilities. He tells her, "You're here because of me. None of this would have ever happened to you if you hadn't met me," but she reminds him that it was her decision to become a Hexenbiest—which led to both violence and power. She admits that she did unforgivable things but insists she is a different person. "None of us are who we used to be," he replies, and she tells him it is a good thing: "I have a strength and a purpose that I never had before. I know you're here because you loved me once and you feel responsible [...]—but you can't change any of it—and I can't change any of it. And if you could, would you really want to go back to the way things were just to be happy? Happy doesn't interest me anymore, Nick. It just gets in the way" (6.11). This speech is much longer, and its very length declares its importance to the character (not to mention the mist surrounding her as she speaks).[26] Juliette/Eve seems in this near monologue to be declaring that her primary focus is the mission[27]; her declaration that "happy doesn't interest me" could, in context, be read as a rejection of romance. We might, in other words, say that she is not interested in love and marriage, but in her career. Unlike Illyria, Juliette/Eve is not driven to fight because of her feelings for a man. She makes her choices with an underlying purpose to do right, and the dark stage she has gone through when first a Hexenbiest only highlights that fact, much as happens for most of the characters in *Angel* other than Fred—and a few in *Grimm*, as well.

Conclusion in Community

Despite her impressive speech, Juliette does not proceed to take down the apocalyptic bad guy; four other characters do that: Nick in combination with Trubel, his dead mother, and his also dead aunt. But Juliette/Eve, unlike Fred/Illyria, ends the series as part of a family with a future. Not only is she gathered in along with the others during the penultimate scene; she also, three episodes earlier, hangs out with them at Monroe's weekend getaway birthday party in a way that it is hard to imagine Illyria could ever do with her chosen family. Juliette/Eve's character does less to explore gender queering than Illyria's does, but it plays in the perhaps equally uncertain waters of ordinary human social life. And there she stretches the patterns of gender: She is a powerful woman who has made mistakes and nonetheless has friends. No longer costumed as a superhero (or a supermodel), she nonetheless has extraordinary strength, honed through trial. Ultimately, Juliette/Eve's choice to be a woman of purpose without romance, marriage, or children is all the more significant because it is presented as one option among many, an array of chosen purposes for different women. Fred wants to stay and is deprived of her choice; but when Juliette smokes the hat, she makes her own path and, in the end, becomes a more complete self.[28]

Eight

"I've seen this before"
Rosalee Calvert and Practical Magic

The final broadcast episode of *Grimm* was introduced by two fan favorite actors before the actual episode began: Silas Weir Mitchell (Monroe) and Bree Turner (Rosalee). Turner was not one of the original six regulars; she first appeared in the fifteenth episode and joined the cast full-time for the first episode of the second season, enlarging the number of women regulars to two. The second Wesen friend for Nick, Rosalee was installed as a love interest for the immediately popular character Monroe, but she is much more. Apparently in her thirties, she is nonetheless clearly a Wise Woman character and thus an aspect of the Crone archetype. From her first episode she actively serves as a healer. She trained with her parents as an apothecary and the "Exotic Tea and Spice Shop" she inherited from her brother Freddy is actually an apothecary shop, with thousands of medicinal herbs and hundreds of books. There are two major depositories of special knowledge in the series: the books and bottles of Aunt Marie's trailer—now Nick's; and the books and bottles of Freddy's Spice Shop—now Rosalee's. Knowledge thus crosses gender lines. It also crosses traditions: Rosalee uses both ancient lore and modern science to heal—whatever gets the job done. She is equally transgressive in her relationships, becoming friends with more than one Grimm and marrying someone of a different Wesen species/race—a marriage that turns out to be a model of caring and equality. Physically brave but pragmatic, physically attractive but not polished, Rosalee is a very relatable character. She also resists the gender stereotype of enmity between women by being at the center of relationships with the other two female regulars, Juliette and Adalind.[1] With her ability to connect, she builds friendships and community in a way that correlates with a measure of political power; it is she who is connected to the Wesen Council. Her past struggles with drugs and with her own family only make her more human. As a former drug user who is living clean; a generous friend;

a loving, beautiful, but not glamorous woman with a healthy emotional and sexual relationship with her partner; and a medical professional with vast expertise and quick wit, she is that rarity, a fully good yet genuinely likable character. Rosalee is one representative of a woman of power, of the young Wise Woman, a Crone in training.

Rosalee's Introduction

Greenwalt and Kouf give Rosalee a very thorough introduction in her first three episodes. She is brought in after Monroe's character has become established. Nick has earlier encountered Frederick Calvert, the Wesen owner of the Spice Shop, while investigating shady drug dealings in the tenth episode; in the fifteenth, Freddy is murdered by Wesen users of another substance (a drug for Wesen, though not humans). His sister Rosalee comes from Seattle to Portland to claim the body, wanting nothing more than to leave immediately. In her younger days she was herself "hooked" and, with Freddy's help, left Portland to remove herself from the temptation of old connections. When Nick takes her to the Spice Shop, director Rob Bailey brightly lights her sorrowful face as she looks at the place where her brother died. She drops to her knees by the bloodstains on the rug. Bree Turner poignantly moves her head as the character *woges* into a beautiful foxlike creature, suggesting the depth of her emotion.[2] At this moment of vulnerability, Nick speaks to her and she sees, startled, that he is a Grimm—a being she thinks of only as a Wesen-killer. When he reaches out to her, she quickly moves back in fear. But by the end of their conversation, she has heard him tell his partner (by phone) that he thinks she is clean; and he asks her to get in touch not only if she has information, but also if she needs anything. "You're not at all what I expected," she says with great seriousness; and the second true friendship between Grimm and Wesen has begun, because Rosalee is open-minded enough to judge for herself—not just by what is "expected."

Soon Nick brings Monroe to the shop to help examine its contents, and Monroe, who knew Freddy, offers his condolences—and by his presence, another piece of evidence for Nick's bona fides. When, later, Rosalee is attacked by the killers (who have returned to the shop for more of the drug), she escapes by jabbing a box-cutter into the hand of one—her first action of physical bravery on-screen. She goes to the police station to look at mug shots with Nick late at night and expresses sympathy to him for his having to keep his life as a Grimm secret from those he works with; as both a Wesen and a former addict, she knows about such secrecy. But for a Wesen to sympathize with a Grimm is unexpected, to say the least. It is another marker of Rosalee's open-minded, open-hearted nature. When Nick offers to give her police protection, she asks instead for the man she calls his other partner—Monroe. Monroe tells her he is sorry she is shutting down the Spice Shop, because it is one of the few places for Wesen to gather. It is to Monroe that she speaks of having trained with her parents as an apothecary; so we begin to learn of her status as Wise Woman.

When Nick sends Sergeant Wu to the shop to check on them, Wu collapses and bursts into horrific boils as a result of a magic potion. Nick rushes to the scene and wants to hospitalize Wu, but Rosalee tells him the doctors would not recognize the problem and Wu would die. In this scene, Bree Turner has Rosalee speak very forcefully, and she uses a gesture that will become a signature physical expression—her hand out, fingers splayed in emphasis. She evinces a medical professional's command. "I've seen this before," she insists, and—ordering Monroe around the shop to retrieve the correct ingredients—she concocts the antidote, convinces Nick, and saves Wu—the first of many she will save.

When they carry the unconscious Wu back to his apartment, Nick asks for more information about finding the drug addicts, and Rosalee, with a self-conscious glance at Monroe, confesses that she was hooked for seven years. (The condition of the addicts in the episode makes clear what Rosalee has escaped.) She tells Nick he needs a dealer to buy tickets to an Island of Dreams—a Trauminsel, as Monroe calls it, a Wesen crack house—and, that evening, risks herself by finding one of her old dealers to buy two tickets. Monroe, who has by now accompanied Nick on several jobs, goes along to enable Nick to enter a Wesen space, but Nick tells Rosalee, the recovering addict and victim's sister, that she has done enough and should stay in the car. Rosalee, of course, will not stay in the car. When one of the killer addicts fires his gun in a struggle with Nick, the crowd of users rush out of the building, Monroe chasing the second killer—only to find the killer pointing a gun in his face. But in that moment of shock, we see Rosalee hit the killer in the head, felling him to the ground with a brick. At the episode's end, Monroe brings her a thank-you bouquet of flowers, finding that she is setting up the shop again—while waiting for the trial, she says. Drawn by her calling as a healer and by her new relationships, Rosalee never leaves.

In her second and the series' seventeenth episode, "Love Sick"—an episode important for all the regulars—Rosalee saves yet another character. In "Island of Dreams" she saved Wu with magical medication and Monroe with a brick; in this episode, she saves Nick's partner Hank. She also, as a side dish, saves Wu once again, since he is suffering new effects of having eaten a cookie dosed by the witch Adalind and intended for Hank. Rosalee is the one with the knowledge and intelligence to be able to deduce that

Eight—"I've seen this before"

Wu's symptoms are the result of a sorcerous side-effect. Now fully enrolled in helping Nick, she and Monroe search desperately through the books in the Spice Shop to find the spell Adalind has used on Hank. While Monroe eventually falls asleep, Rosalee perseveres and discovers the spell. And when they find Hank comatose after having had sex with Adalind (it'll do that), it is she who realizes the stakes have changed and tells Nick he must somehow get the blood of a Grimm into Adalind. He does so by—in the midst of a physical fight—kissing Adalind as she lies on the ground beneath him, leading her to bite his lip. Hank is freed in that moment, as she loses her powers. This single action sets in motion a myriad of plots and themes for the series. It would not have happened without the counsel of the Wise Woman Rosalee. Of course the Wise Woman is also left with the problem of explaining to the reawakened Hank what she and Monroe are doing in Adalind's bedroom with him. Wisdom in *Grimm* is not two-dimensional.

Rosalee's third appearance, in episode eighteen, gives further background and even more fully establishes her worth. In "Cat and Mouse," we see a Wesen man chased across the country by other Wesen and then escaping after being shot outside the Portland bus station. When Rosalee enters the shop for the morning, he grabs her from behind, putting his hand over her mouth. But she quickly dispatches him, using self-defense moves any woman might employ. Immediately, though, she discovers that it is her old lover Ian Harmon, who had come to get a false passport from Freddy (not knowing of Freddy's death). Rosalee calls Monroe to ask him to assist as she removes a bullet from Ian, demonstrating not only her skill but also her trust in Monroe. Though she has never operated on a bullet wound, she shows Monroe her father's old black medical bag, affectionately patting it, and says that she has watched her father remove bullets many times: she has seen this before. With Ian unconscious, she tells Monroe (who knows of Ian as a reporter) they can trust him because she was with him for a year and a half. When Monroe calls Nick for help, Monroe identifies Ian as "a civil rights activist slash freedom fighter" because Ian works for the Resistance against the seven royal families who have for centuries secretly exerted power over Wesen. Ian's stature adds to Rosalee's: she was the significant other of a hero. After Nick comes to the shop, he recognizes Ian's face as that of a man wanted for murder and pulls his gun. Rosalee, her hands outspread, steps between Ian and Nick, showing her physical bravery yet again, and yet again speaking assertively. She explains that her parents, grandparents, and brother were part of the Resistance, though she had thought the struggle, centered in Europe, was too far away for her to confront. Now they acknowledge that the struggle has come to America, and she convinces Nick to help Ian. When, later in the episode, the assassin holds a gun on her and threatens her life, she suffers through his political pontificating at length before he accuses her of failing to understand—to which she replies, with visible disdain, "I'm sorry—I wasn't listening." She then, with quick wit, spontaneously takes part in a deception started by Monroe and Nick that allows them to distract and overpower the assassin. Part of the deception rests on the assassin's racist/speciesist prejudice against Fuchsbau—which both Rosalee and Ian are, but Monroe is not. The ability of the Grimm, the Fuchsbau, and the Blutbaden to work together is an important part of the successful resolution. But that resolution also rests on Rosalee's medical skill, loyalty, bravery, and intelligence—topped by a touch of snarkiness. In the space of three episodes, we have come to know much about the character of Rosalee Calvert.

Wielder of Lore and Science

Rosalee's work as an apothecary not only functions in many plots but also serves to develop her character: She is a very specific kind of Wise Woman. Barbara Walker discusses one aspect of the Crone as the "healer [...], wise-woman, arbiter of ethical and moral law, owner of the sacred lore" (32). She also asserts that "medicine was almost exclusively in the hands of old women for countless thousands of years" (127). Despite her relative youth, this image of the Wise-Woman healer meshes well with the character of Rosalee. The apothecary in the story-world of *Grimm* functions as the major healer for the Wesen community. Rosalee's Spice Shop is a primary set for the series, and its shelves of various labeled jars of ingredients and rows of thick books physically represent Rosalee's work. Ronald Hutton describes beliefs as early as fourth-century BCE Greeks in magic potion-makers called "*pharmakeis* (masculine) or *pharmakides* (feminine)," terms clearly related to pharmacist, and "*rhizotomoi*, 'root-cutters,' who appear [...] to have worked a magic, and in modern times also a medicine, based primarily on herbs" (55). He also writes of the later European "'healing woman,' the 'woman doctor,' the 'herb woman,' the 'learned woman,'" in his study of the witch (85)—the witch, in Walker's view, being an aspect of the Crone (see Ch. 6). In more recent images, Justyna Sempruch says, "the herbalist-witch represents clearly [...] a fantasy of the superwoman, the feminist heroine of the 1980s and 1990s" (14). In the mythology of *Grimm*, Rosalee is, as a Wesen, part of the supernatural world; she is not precisely a witch, but a witch-adjacent Wise Woman healer who works herbal magic.

The term *lore* suggests the transmission of tradition, and Rosalee participates in that. Knowledge she has gained from her parents has already been mentioned, and it is noted later in the series as well (e.g., 2.6). She uses the space and tools inherited from her family. Her work has elements of cookery, thus connecting with traditional visions of women. More than once, Rosalee and others refer to the list of her ingredients for her concoctions as "recipes" (1.17), and Hutton also uses the term in the context of "the practical purposes of magic" (103). Natalia Andrevskikh discusses the idea of food symbolism and fairy tales. She argues that while some modern scholars have presented food preparation as an imprisoning image, keeping women in the kitchen, there is an older way of viewing women and cooking that connects to "female empowerment and sacred knowledge" (147); she references Baba Yaga and her cauldron (148). Time and again Rosalee saves the day by cooking up something in her alchemical apparatus or her witchy, cauldron-like small pots. Her mortar and pestle are symbolically both male and female; she is not restricted to one kind of power (e.g., 2.15). It should be remembered, too, that Monroe is notably the better cook of the two. Rosalee is not just an earth-mother or numinous figure of mystery. Sempruch warns against "confining women to the mysterious and not quite human other" (58), and it would have been easy for *Grimm*'s showrunners to make the main female lore-keeper just that. But Rosalee uses lore that comes from a specific human heritage.

The books she uses so often might, in fact, be connected by some to a logocentric masculinity—but she makes them her own. She often turns directly to the spot on the shelf where the needed volume stands (e.g., 2.4, 2.19). The Spice Shop's multitudinous books look like nineteenth-century printings of medical tomes, with old-fashioned, captioned line-drawing illustrations (e.g., 2.17, 2.20). In other words, they seem to come from a time when few women would have been doctors. They are in clear contrast to the volumes in Aunt Marie's trailer, all of which are handwritten by various Grimms—male and female—through the ages, in multiple languages, with hand-drawn illustrations.[3] The Grimm books seem closer to lore than the Calvert family's collection of published materials—though, specializing in Wesen medical treatises as they do, the Calvert books are hardly standard fare. In terms of these sources of knowledge, as is often the case in *Grimm*, gender lines are crossed.

Indeed, this Wise Woman herbalist apothecary often couches her diagnoses in terms of science, a stereotypically male realm. When a Wesen who blinds and sometimes kills his victims blinds Nick, Rosalee explains that the reason she has to dig out the killer's eye with a spoon (yes, a cooking instrument) is that they are making the equivalent of a vaccine from antibodies (2.15). When they need to stop a Wesen lawyer from unduly influencing a jury on which Rosalee serves as "foreman," she notes that they will be giving him a "pheromone vasectomy" by super-stimulating a specific gland (2.17). When they are trying to cure a horde of angry zombies, she realizes that they can give the treatment as an inhalant using (as her friend and fellow scientist Dr. Juliette Silverton points out) the Williamson Ether synthesis (3.1). When they try to help a beautiful frog-Wesen who unintentionally kills by the touch of her skin anyone who is sexually attracted to her, Rosalee successfully theorizes that they can depolarize her membranes (4.16). None of this is to say that *Grimm* can be used as a science text, but rather to argue that the series connects the Wise Woman herbal healer with the traditionally masculine territory of the scientist.

Though she sometimes doubts herself (as one would hope for any sane diagnostician), Rosalee nonetheless normally speaks with great confidence when she is in her role of apothecary healer. She often orders others to help her, starting with her first episode, when she tells a doubting Monroe exactly where to find the chyme extract—even though she has not been re-acquainted with the Spice Shop for long. She orders Nick to put exactly six drops of her medicine into the eyes of the comatose Juliette, and he trusts her enough to do so (while Monroe and Nick's mother hold off the alarmed hospital staff, 2.2). With her characteristic bold hand gesture, fingers outspread, she directs Nick, Hank, and the former arson investigator Orson as they prepare a substance to permanently douse a fire-creating Wesen, and they swiftly obey (4.13). It is perhaps less effective when, in a cabin in the woods with a Wesen going into labor, Rosalee orders Monroe and Nick to "bring me a lot of stuff [pause] we don't have" (2.19). But she soon begins directing them to participate in what turns out to be a TV-successful birth. Overall, when the apothecary Rosalee is involved in healing, she is the figure of authority.

Creator of Community and Communion

While Rosalee as healer is the person in charge, it is the mutuality of her relationships that is her other greatest strength. She is transgressive in her open-heartedness and open-mindedness. She is physically bold in her interactions. She is relatable in her unglamorous appearance and pragmatic attitude, as well as her humanizing backstory. All of these qualities support her success in connecting with people: with friends, with customers, with her community, even with the secret Wesen political structure. The predominant connection, however, is the one that led to having Bree Turner and Silas Weir Mitchell introduce the series' final episode: Rosalee and Monroe's admirably balanced and loving relationship, including eventual marriage.

From her first appearance, Rosalee is willing to be transgressive in her relationships. Her initial reaction to Nick is a quiet version of the fear

Eight—"I've seen this before"

most Wesen exhibit in response to the sight of a Grimm, but she quickly accepts the possibility of working with him. In fact, before the episode's end (as noted), she finds common ground in their difficulty of leading a hidden life—an emotional leap of faith in relationship that surpasses even Monroe's early bemused willingness to help Nick. Because of her friendship with Nick, she even, eventually, becomes friends with Adalind, a Hexenbiest—a kind of being most Wesen fear and detest. Rosalee's dawning romance with Monroe, too, is a kind of transgression. Chapter Two discusses the symbolic racial/ethnic romantic issues between Wesen and non–Wesen, but (as will be discussed further), the series makes it clear that some in this storyworld see sexual relations between different kinds of Wesen as miscegenation. Rosalee, however, makes her own judgments and reaches past boundaries.

She reaches out physically as well: her inter-relationships are marked by physical boldness. She hugs more than any other character in the series. We even see her hug Nick's fearsome mother, Kelly, who (having at first physically attacked Monroe and Rosalee because they are Wesen) now accepts this curious friendship amongst the three and gives Rosalee two quick pats on the back—perhaps to signal the end of the hug. After Kelly leaves, Rosalee and Monroe discuss whether the effectively ambiguous expression on Mary Elizabeth Mastrantonio's face was a smile (2.2). Whether or not it was, the scene—along with many other less fraught moments of hugging—shows that Rosalee's embraces are not sentimental signifiers. Her physicality in expressing connection is part of her bravery, not merely a stereotypical female attempt to please.

That bravery is made even clearer in the context of her physical boldness in moments of confrontation. The moment in which she, in her first episode, saves Monroe's life by using a brick to hit a villain, is memorable in and of itself; however, viewers are reminded of it again and again when Monroe fondly recalls the incident—culminating in his recapitulation of the story during their wedding vows (3.22). It is far from an isolated event, however. In her third outing, as noted, Rosalee effectively fights off someone she thinks is an attacker in her shop, using physical moves of self-defense that have nothing to do with her being Wesen—a very relatable scene (1.18). In the second season, she holds down and injects violent zombies (2.21–2.22). On the evening that she and Monroe become engaged, they earlier exchange "first-time" stories—the first time of woging; and she tells of biting her teasing brother's ankle (3.12). When Adalind's dead Hexenbiest mother is to be cut up for potion parts, Adalind cannot face doing it, and Monroe demurs on grounds of being vegan. It is Rosalee who cuts into the not-desiccated-enough corpse (4.19). And when a cowardly friend participates in a set-up by Black Claw to try to kill Monroe and their friends, she punches the man in the face, holding him back from escaping as she phones to warn of the danger (5.6). Rosalee's warmth is reflected in her physical boldness; the punches are the other side of her hugs. She does not make physical connection from a place of fear.

While Rosalee is physically bold, she is not making the moves of a superhero or a martial arts whiz; she typically makes the moves of a normal human (except, perhaps, for that ankle bite). She is relatable not only in her physical interactions but also in her appearance. Bree Turner is a beautiful actor playing a beautiful character in Rosalee, but it is a beauty clothed in normality. In her second episode, when she and Monroe try to help Nick fend off Adalind and save Hank, Monroe says that as a Hexenbiest, Adalind is "not exactly lovable" but "kinda hot." Then after he and Rosalee exchange a glance, he adds, "If you go for that obviously hot thing—which I don't" (1.17). Putting aside the likelihood that Monroe has not just improved his romantic chances, the passage says something about Rosalee's physical presentation. Often, Rosalee appears in plaid shirts of the sort easy to spot in the Pacific Northwest. She first appears in a plaid wool jacket; she sometimes even sleeps in plaid (5.10). Bree Turner was pregnant early in her time as a regular, so she often wore concealing sweaters—a style that did not drastically change through the years of the series. In fact, her clothing style reflects that of the often cozily sweatered Monroe. She does not look like a woman who has stepped from the pages of a superhero comic. She looks like someone a viewer might meet in real life.

Her being attractive but not extraordinary parallels her being highly moral but not saintly. Rosalee repeatedly espouses an understandable pragmatism that sometimes sets her apart from her friends, while it may place her closer to the attitudes of many viewers. Julie O'Reilly, in *Bewitched Again*, argues that in turn-of-the-twenty-first-century television, "supernatural women enact a high degree of selflessness" as a payment "for claiming power" (190). That abdicatory selflessness does not characterize Rosalee. Rosalee the Wise Woman is powerful without being superpowered—except to the degree that being Wesen gives her supernatural power. Her status is liminal, with her relatable normality usually predominant. That includes her pragmatism. When, for example, Nick is abducted by members of the Royals who have put him, unconscious, on a plane bound for Austria, Juliette, Monroe, and Hank are all for heading overseas to save him. But Rosalee reminds them of the economic power and defensive capabilities of the Royals; she has seen enough of the world to know that their quest would be virtually impossible (3.1). When Nick discovers a young boy who seems to be a Grausen—a youngster who will grow up to cause monstrous evil—Rosalee calls the Wesen Council, even knowing that the child will probably be killed. She warns Monroe of the danger if the Council were to find out that they had not reported the possible Grausen and had been dealing with a Grimm; she tells him she has no intention of going to his funeral. (For his part, Monroe calls to tell Nick of the Council representative's arrival.) When the weeping Adalind shows up for a hug from Rosalee after her child has been taken—in fact, after Rosalee and Monroe secretly helped abduct the child to get it to a safer home—Rosalee reminds Monroe that Adalind has regained her powers, so "Having her pissed at us is not such a great idea." When Monroe asks, "Can we just make her feel better for now?," Rosalee replies, "Till we can get rid of her" (3.19). Given Adalind's earlier willingness to kill Aunt Marie and Hank, Rosalee's response is both amusing and understandable at this point in the series. Yet viewers have already started to see more in Adalind, so Rosalee's remark also has a taste of acerbity that complicates the flavor of the character. Perhaps the clearest example of Rosalee's pragmatism comes at the end of the fifth season, when Nick sends his friends down a hidden tunnel to escape their enemies while he fights them. When he unexpectedly closes the tunnel door, telling them to run, Trubel and Juliette/Eve want to turn and fight alongside him. But Rosalee tells them Nick has bought them time, and they should move on. Rosalee has more than once risked her life to save a loved one (e.g., 3.2, 4.10). But she is Wise Woman enough to see the world in practical terms.

These chiaroscuro touches of character correlate with elements of Rosalee's backstory. In the age of the opioid epidemic, Rosalee is a drug addict in recovery. Her introductory episode focuses on drug users and her reconnecting to that world. In a later episode, speaking to her friend Juliette, she obliquely suggests a cause for that drug abuse: "It's not easy to admit being Wesen [...]. I did everything I could to deny what I was. I hid it, hung out with the wrong people. You have no idea how badly you just want to be normal" (3.9). Even to Juliette, she does not directly speak of her drug use. She later has a similarly oblique conversation with Adalind (now also her friend) (5.12). Nick and Monroe have learned about Rosalee's drug use in her first episode; Hank learns of it later, when Nick asks Rosalee for information about Wesen gangs engaged in the drug trade (3.10). Repeated letters and calls from an old partner in addiction make clear that there are consequences for such a path. Tony, from her drug days, finally comes to the place that represents Rosalee's power: the Spice Shop. He arrives while Nick and Monroe are out of the country. Rosalee and Adalind together fight off his violent assault, which is directed at both the women and Rosalee's Wise Woman medical drugs. There are limits to the depiction of Rosalee's drug problem: All the internal struggles are spoken of as in the past, not as part of her current psychology, not as part of the daily fight that addicts typically endure. But the past continues to be present in Tony and in Rosalee's expertise on an underworld that she has seen more of than her friends. And the cause she cites for her drug use—feeling she is the outsider—her desire to be normal while she feels she is not—is itself quintessentially normal.

Another element of her backstory that many can relate to is her difficulties with family. In the third season we learn that Rosalee has not spoken with her mother and sister for seven years because she failed to attend her father's funeral (3.11). They are unaware that Rosalee was in jail at the time for shoplifting—another result in the web of consequences for her drug use. When her mother invites Rosalee to dinner on the anniversary of her father's death, Rosalee asks Monroe to accompany her. Her sister Diyetta has moved back home to help their mother, and when Monroe asks if they should bring something to dinner, Rosalee tells him, "A bottle of wine would be nice for my mom—and a quart of Jack Daniels for the martyr." (Rosalee is effectively depicted as more blunt with Monroe than she usually is with others.) After they arrive, Rosalee and Monroe sit for some time in the car before she can make herself approach the house. When she does, Bree Turner uses another of Rosalee's signature physical moves, a fast, forward-leaning walk that expresses her intensity—though when she reaches the door, her finger stops before touching the doorbell. (Monroe helps her move it the last quarter inch.) The reunion dinner is a successful presentation of a family fiasco. Diyetta snipes at Monroe's being a Blutbad ("Did you really just play the Wesen card?" Rosalee asks) and Rosalee, in reaction to her sister's declarations of superior virtue, angrily agrees, "I partied my little ass off, up and down the coast." By the end of the evening all the pain is out in the open (reflecting the episode's other story of a covered-up military rape). Rosalee and her mother hug, and Diyetta lovingly threatens to kill Monroe if he hurts her little sister. Rosalee and Diyetta's parallel substance dependency is revisited (though with a light touch) when Diyetta gets so drunk on the night before Rosalee and Monroe's wedding that she spills red wine on the wedding dress (3.22). Family closeness is never really clean. But its warmth is real and helps to portray the realness of Rosalee.

Rosalee's connections are not limited to her family. She is repeatedly shown taking a personal interest in her customers. One episode makes such a relationship central, placing Rosalee on the edge between medical advisor and friend in a case of euthanasia (6.10). Monroe, in her first episode, described the Spice Shop as a gathering place for Wesen, and more than once, a crowd of Wesen gathers there at a time of community stress (e.g., 2.14, 5.6). The showrunners deepen the sense of community by having actors repeat co-starring roles from earlier episodes—even when they just contribute a line or two in the crowd scene. In these scenes, Rosalee is the owner of the space and the one the crowd has come to for advice: She is the Wise Woman. "You trusted my brother, you can trust me," she tells them on the first such occasion (2.14). And they do trust her. Because she is in relationship with them, she has the power to help guide the community's action.

Rosalee is also connected to the larger Wesen community in the form of the Wesen Council. She thus participates in some degree of political power. She seems, in effect, to represent the local Wesen to the far-off European center of Wesen law. Like many women in the not-too-distant-past of Western democracies, she has come to her position through the power of older male relatives. When a trio of Portland Wesen break the cardinal rule of secrecy by publicly woging to disguise themselves to rob banks (and eventually kill), local Wesen panic for fear of witch hunts (or Wesen-hunts). It is Rosalee who calms the panic by telling the crowd she knows whom to contact on the Council. The Council, it should be noted, does not hesitate to mete out capital punishment, so most Wesen (such as Monroe) dread to deal with them. Rosalee privately tells Monroe that her "father had an uneasy alliance with the Council. [...] And Freddy took over for my dad, and I was supposed to take over for him" (2.14). She notes that her father even served on the Council before her birth. She now holds the contact information and goes through a formal ritual of recognition by phone. Her phone call eventually results in the Council's execution of the killer thieves who endangered the Wesen community by risking their secrecy.[4] Over the seasons, Rosalee interacts with the Council when it seems Portland events would have implications for the larger Wesen world (e.g., 3.6, 5.7). Sometimes the interactions reflect the power of her connection; at least once, the interaction results in a threat from the Council against her and Monroe (4.12). Overall, these episodes show Rosalee in a political role. Bree Turner, in an interview near the end of the series, said, "I would have liked to have seen Rosalee's political career," noting that something of it had already been shown, and adding, "I feel like it's very much a part of how the writers wrote for her in terms of her activism and her compassion for the disenfranchised in her community. And I would have liked [...] her [to] be president of the Council" (Huddleston n.p.). In some senses, Rosalee might be seen as a community organizer.

Her closer connections are even stronger. Some of the happiest scenes in the series are dinners or drinks at Rosalee and Monroe's, sometimes including Wu, Sean Renard, or their friend refrigerator repairman (and Eisbiber) Bud Wurstner, and normally involving Hank, Nick, and Juliette. Music, food, and information are shared with equal zest. These dinners are, in effect, rituals of communion (see Ch. 3). Rosalee becomes close friends with Juliette, inviting her to be her maid of honor: It is Rosalee who brings Juliette into full knowledge of Wesen by being the first to woge for her (2.21), and she advises Juliette on problems with friends as well as health.

When Juliette is trying to find out more about Nick's secret life, Rosalee more than once helps Juliette persuade Monroe to reveal information (2.16, 2.20). Rosalee also makes the unnerving effort necessary to reach out to the almost feral young Grimm Trubel when she first appears, having spent her short lifetime being repeatedly attacked by Wesen and having no one believe her. In the first scene for Rosalee, Monroe, Trubel, and Nick, the two Wesen are clearly nervous, holding onto each other for comfort. But by the scene's end, Rosalee is gently touching Trubel on the shoulder, a small hint of hugs to come (3.20). She even, after many years of distaste and detestation, becomes friends with Adalind. In the fifth season, Adalind tells Rosalee she is her only friend (5.2).

One of the most quietly enjoyable moments of the series comes when Rosalee calls on her female friends for support. Because Nick has lost his powers, he and Hank ask Monroe to help them in seeing certain Wesen malefactors, but Monroe is concerned about leaving Rosalee alone in the shop since they have recently been threatened by the Wesenrein hate group. As they speak, Juliette opens the shop door and says "Hi" to Rosalee's clearly expectant "Hi," and apologizes for being late, saying she had to pick up ammunition. Upon the men's surprise at her bringing a gun comes the entry of Trubel with another "Hi" and this time, two "Hi" responses in chorus, from Rosalee and Juliette. The three women—whose gathering has clearly been arranged by Rosalee—stand together, and Rosalee says to Monroe with a smile, "You're good to go" (4.6). This is an example of what Bree Turner refers to as "a little girly power unit" (Dolenga n.p.). These are friends who will put themselves on the line for each other, and here Rosalee is the center.

Rosalee's closest connection, though, is undeniably with Monroe. Silas Weir Mitchell's Monroe is possibly the most beloved character of the series, and to be his partner requires someone of noteworthy quality (for both the character and the actor). Interviewers typically comment on the actors' chemistry (e.g., Briede). Furthermore, the showrunners give the relationship space to develop. Both characters have not only familial backstories but also romantic backstories : We not only hear of but get to see Rosalee's admirable Ian Harmon (the Victor Laszlo of the Wesen Resistance) and Monroe's vivid, beautiful, dangerous ex Angelina Lasser (see Chapter One). While Rosalee and Monroe decide not to speak about past romances (2.4), it is clear that these are two experienced people. This is, as Bree Turner says, a genuinely "adult" relationship in many ways ("Something Wesen"). As adults, they take their time in becoming intimate—but they do not take so long as to reach television-delayed-gratification absurdity (consider *Bones*, 2005–2017). When Nick introduces Monroe to Rosalee, and Monroe says he was Freddy's friend, she tests his truth by woging, to see if this friend of a Grimm can actually be Wesen. She grabs his arm and their woge-and-response, their shared gaze at their secret faces, holds a kind of intimacy.

Each of their early encounters is memorable, but one may particularly convey the humanity of their connection. "Over My Dead Body" (2.6) opens with four parallel scenes of dining, each of which is emblematic of the relationship involved. The amnesiac Juliette cooks for Nick, using a recipe that she only knows he likes because the recipe card has a note in her handwriting; Monroe cooks for Rosalee, tasting his vegetarian cuisine with obvious pleasure while classical music plays; Angelina is treated by a lout to chicken fingers and beer in a country music dance hall; and Prince/Captain Sean Renard sits in an elegant hotel room (with a servant visible) at a white-clothed table with no food, opposite a glamorous associate of another royal family. Monroe and Rosalee's is the interaction that is given the fullest presentation. When Monroe says, "Can I just say—you look beautiful," Rosalee responds with a glowing smile, "You look beautiful too." Both happily absorb without difficulty this avoidance of objectification. When they talk about Monroe's beloved clocks, Rosalee, to paraphrase Rodgers and Hammerstein, laughs at his jokes too much—a tonally appropriate moment. After dinner, they bond over a shared, esoteric musical taste. When Monroe puts his valued garage sale find on the turntable and says she probably will not know the musician, Rosalee instantly says, "Hugues Nuages! The Austrian zitherist!" With giddy delight, they lob bits of information back and forth about the zitherist's extra fingers and missing leg. The usually articulate Monroe, saying "You're—I'm, I'm, ah, hell, I'm"—moves in for a kiss. I will interrupt this moment to note that writer Spiro Skentzos was having great fun here: "Nuages" was a signature song of the Romani-French jazz guitarist Django Reinhardt, who lost the use of a leg and two fingers in a fire, and whose career was promoted by jazz aficionado Hugues Panassié.[5] This scene is at once playfully self-conscious and emotionally rich. And my interruption reflects another, since Angelina bursts into the house before Monroe can complete the kiss. As Angelina and Monroe argue, Rosalee silently departs—a departure that will last for several weeks as Rosalee cares for a sick aunt and Bree Turner has a baby. But this scene is impressive enough to carry the relationship through the absence. The actors, writers, and director somehow manage to make Rosalee and Monroe's date both over-the-top and grounded.

The moment when Rosalee tells Monroe he is beautiful too suggests something of the respect and equality of this relationship. This attitude is observable in small things as well as large. When Monroe and Rosalee are on the phone giving Nick the phone number from a shop record in order to identify a purchaser, they both start speaking at once, but Monroe stops and lets her finish: It is she who discovered the number, after all (2.1). Both of them have independent careers that require a high degree of expertise: she, the apothecary; he, the clock and watch repairman. Monroe works at home or on-site; she has her own space; but we sometimes see them sharing the same work table in her shop (3.11). Early in the series (in fact, in the episode of the memorable "Nuages" date), she asks him to help in the shop, and they work together more and more. The relationship only improves with marriage—and it is never saccharine, even when Monroe quotes Yeats at her. The poem is "When You Are Old," and Rosalee is both touched and yet immediately worried about her "changing face" (6.10). Their interactions speak the language of the well-married. When Rosalee throws him out of the shop to avoid conflict with an old enemy, he returns, calling himself an idiot. If he had not returned, *she* says, he "might have been a little bit of an idiot" (4.13). When Black Claw operatives in a pickup watch their house and Monroe angrily confronts them, the pragmatic Rosalee becomes angry with Monroe in turn, saying it won't help if he gets himself killed, "thank you very much!" Then she goes inside and writes down the license plate number—and he says he is glad "at least one of us wasn't being stupid" (5.21). Rosalee and the audience—but not yet Monroe—will confirm in the episode's second part that she was pregnant when she counseled caution, undergirding the emotional complexity of the scene (5.22).[6]

Rosalee and Monroe's equality and respect play out in terms of their sexual relations, as well. Early on, the two make tentative moves towards each other. In the fourth episode of the second season, Rosalee is infected by a Wesen disease that lowers inhibitions and increases libido, and she initiates an enthusiastic make-out session that ends when Monroe discovers her illness and she collapses (2.4). But her initiation of intimacy is not limited to occasions excused by being, in effect, under the influence. When she returns after weeks of absence, Monroe comes to pick her up early in the morning at the bus station with a rumpled Nick in tow and a bouquet of flowers in hand. Rosalee walks straight up to him and plants their first real kiss, noticing neither Nick nor the flowers. She also is the one who closes the deal on their spending the night together for the first time. After a dinner during which Monroe seems to have approached then backed off from the subject, picking up the dishes to wash, Rosalee puts her hand on his neck and says, "Why don't we do that in the morning?" (2.22). "You are so hot," Monroe says as she woges. Their sexuality continues to be shown after their marriage, as well (including an encounter that combines a circus costume and a wolf howl, 3.16). Their sexual relationship seems adult in the best sense of the word.

The emotion between Rosalee and Monroe is accentuated by Bree Turner's occasional use of peculiarly melodic vocalizations. The often slightly humorous and very human effect of these sounds can hardly be conveyed on the printed page. But when Rosalee says a low-toned "Whoa," on finding out that Hank knows about Wesen (2.4); or emits a swerving, extra-syllabled "hello" when Nick—temporarily living with Monroe—interrupts what might have turned into Rosalee and Monroe's first night together (2.19); or when that high-pitched note of joy comes out as she announces plans for Monroe's birthday celebration (6.7)—these are unpredictable touches of the actor's art that feel like moments of life.[7]

Their lives are certainly not always light. The transgression that is their mixed marriage brings painful challenges. First they must deal with the "ignorance" (as Rosalee calls it) of Monroe's parents, who physically recoil at the idea of a Fuchsbau daughter-in-law (3.12). Later the brick Rosalee used to save Monroe is remodulated as a brick thrown through the Spice Shop window by bigots. Monroe is kidnapped by the Wesenrein species-purity hate group and almost killed, after seeing the burnt body of a fellow victim of symbolic racism. When their friends come to the rescue, Monroe and Rosalee together kill the leader—another Blutbad—as he tries to kill Monroe. In this scene, both Rosalee and Monroe are ferociously Wesen: The two tear out their enemy's throat with their canid teeth. This scene is perhaps Rosalee's clearest entry into the abject. On the other hand, some of the most touching moments of the relationship happen when Monroe undergoes post-traumatic stress and Rosalee comforts him—using, for his sake, the humor of a clock metaphor (4.17).

Conclusion: Imperfect Joy

The relationship between Rosalee and Monroe, in short, is a truly engaging depiction of a marital partnership. But it is not all there is to Rosalee—the Wise Woman, healer, Grimm counselor; the shop-keeper, life-saver, friend, community leader, and wielder of practical magic.[8] The consequences of her drug use, her suffering at the hands of racists, the discord in her family all clarify her empathy and make her more real. Imperfect and human, Rosalee sees and understands much. In her compassion, connection, and wisely used power, she paradoxically inhabits a positive female archetype and yet comfortably steps past gender lines. Her alignment with science, her political leadership, her sexual initiative, her physical bravery, her avoidance of self-abnegation, her loyal friendships with other women all work against female gender stereotypes that are still too present in the world. The series makes clear that hers is not the only path a woman may follow; it also makes clear that her path is both strenuous and admirable. In the pilot, Nick is given a key by his aunt; "Guard it with your life," she says. We gradually learn that this key will only work in concert with other keys. These keys will provide access to an object of magic that no one can describe. In *Grimm*, such keys bring both treasure and danger. Nick gives his key to Rosalee for safekeeping; and when he acquires another, he gives it to her as well. The final three keys are brought to her shop, too. She is the one that knows about working in concert; she is the one you can trust with your secrets and your life. Rosalee is the keeper of the keys. She stores them nearby, under a floorboard in her shop: Magic can be hidden in the most ordinary of spaces. And Bree Turner's Rosalee conveys the happy imperfection needed for practical magic.

NINE

"I just drank my mother"
The Abjection of Adalind Schade

When Adalind Schade says, "I just drank my mother" (4.20), the words suggest the idea of symbolically consuming the knowledge and power of an earlier generation; but in *Grimm*, the words are also meant in a much more grisly, literal fashion.[1] Adalind, like her mother, is a Hexenbiest. She is a beautiful young woman who, when she *woges*, presents as the Hag aspect of the Crone that patriarchy made: the witch. Her surname connotes darkness; as Barbara Walker says, the Crone is sometimes called Queen of the Shades (50). Adalind is the first Wesen perceived as such when Nick begins to come into his powers; with her, he loses his Grimm virginity. Representing the patriarchally debased aspect of womanhood, Adalind has been trained to serve the patriarchy: A lawyer, Adalind does clandestine work for the royal family, partly at the behest of her mother (who is indebted to them) and partly because she is in love with Sean Renard, bastard prince of that family (and the son of a Hexenbiest). After Nick destroys Adalind's powers and her mother throws her out, Adalind takes magical vengeance on Nick through Juliette and, indirectly as a result of that magic, becomes pregnant by the prince. Her royal pregnancy gives her bargaining power, and she uses it to recover her Hexenbiest abilities. But that recovery requires a full-on experience of Kristevan abjection. Some moments of Adalind's experience are horrific and some are grotesquely humorous, but the result of her abjection is a strange kind of cleansing. She has paid a price (in part as an object of the audience's derision), and she is thus to some degree rehabilitated. She becomes more empathetic, starting with her child, whom she had originally declared an intention to sell. Her determination to recover her power is also impressive, and it eventually results in her daughter's becoming powerful as well. Later, in order to take Nick's powers from him, she has sex with him in the magically formed shape of his beloved Juliette. It is an encounter that reflects the rape-like experience through which he took her powers—one of a number of surprising parallels between the two characters. The structure of their relationship has significant elements of romantic comedy and even screwball comedy, a genre linked to gender issues. To safeguard the child resulting from that encounter, she ingests a potion to suppress her power—the potion made from her mother's dead body. Adalind's willingness to give up her power for the sake of her child could be seen as a troubling self-abnegation, especially during the part of the series when she is in effect confined to the fortress-like home she shares with Nick: She is a peculiar version of that nineteenth-century gender nightmare, the Angel in the House. The contexts of her presentation show that motherhood can be seriously problematic. Yet Adalind once again recovers her powers and, now disabused of her belief in the royal patriarchy, uses those powers for friends and loved ones worth trusting. Her intelligent, determined character suggests that sexuality does not have to diminish a woman's strength, and that motherhood and power are not mutually exclusive.

"You were my first": Sex, Structure, and Horror Rom-Com

Two strong characters who seem not to wish to be together but keep displaying hints of attraction: this is the well-known heart of romantic comedy.[2] Both the story structure and the character portrayals lead to Nick and Adalind's eventual conjugation (as fans call it, *Nadalind*). There are even elements of screwball comedy, including physical conflict/slapstick, fast-paced dialogue, disguise, and occasional farce; this is a genre that in the early twentieth century anticipates (though it also often ends by retracting) gender equality (Gehring, e.g., 1–3, 19, 61). But romantic comedy's greater emphasis on serious emotion is the dominant note. The first Adalind scene in the series is also the first Nick scene—one of many connections between the two. We initially see Nick emerging from a jewelry store with an engagement ring for his girlfriend Juliette in his hand, but several scenes before we see Juliette, we see Adalind. First we hear the sound of her laughter as she speaks with a friend. Then we see a good-looking blonde woman in business-like clothing (black suit and white blouse), seemingly about Nick's age, thirty. When Nick's partner Hank complains about Nick's eying Adalind, Nick claims to be simply profiling her: "wears Armani, makes low six figures, drives a BMW, and is falling for a senior partner at her law firm." But when Hank moves away, Nick keeps watching Adalind with a smile; she sees him watching and smiles back. This is the first moment between the two, as he stands there with an engagement ring in his pocket.[3] Then

Adalind woges. A woge typically occurs when the person is experiencing some sort of emotion: Adalind is responding to that first interaction before she knows him. Then they both experience knowledge of each other: He sees (and we see) a gray-haired, wrinkled, distorted hag face with salient teeth; she sees (presumably) the infinitely dark eyes of a Grimm. Years later, he tells her "You were my first" and explains that he had never seen a woge before; but his phrasing suggests a sexual encounter, and Adalind agrees that he was her first, too: she had never seen a Grimm (5.3). In the chronology of Adalind's life, he is certainly not her first sexual encounter, nor she his. But they are each other's "first" across the Grimm-Wesen divide, and they are also each other's first sexually charged encounter in the series—a horror version of the meet-cute. As she woges, Claire Coffee's performance of Adalind's open-mouthed smile becomes a serious, slightly fearful look; she briefly shares a glance with him before she woges back and looks away, while he still stares, stunned.

She stuns him again at the end of the pilot. Nick is by the hospital bedside of his unconscious, dying Aunt Marie; he is speaking of his love for Juliette and vowing to fulfill his duty as a Grimm when he looks up and says, "You!" Adalind has once again interrupted an expression of his love for Juliette. Nick instantly recognizes Adalind, now dressed in a white doctor's coat and about to inject his aunt with venom. He reaches out and grabs her arm to stop her: They are already having a physical confrontation in their first real meeting (and let Freudians play with their struggle over the syringe). In the struggle, Adalind injects Nick instead, securing her escape. We see him tumbling down, horizontal, with his eyes slowly blinking and his mouth open—an almost sexual image. The camera shows her sideways across the screen, from his point of view; she is the sign of the world's changing, as she woges once more, her mouth open in apparent defiance and frightful power—but as Kristeva says, the abject can also attract (55). More and more loudly, we hear the heavy guitar and drums of an ecstatic cover of the Eurythmics' "Sweet Dreams" (the original version having opened the episode, to serve as soundtrack for the first incursion of Wesen violence) as she walks into the night and strips off the white disguise. Nick has literally fallen for Adalind. Whether or not the showrunners planned it,[4] the pilot instigates the relationship.

One could describe the hospital scene as the first, or at least a foreshadowing of, a series of dueling sexual assaults that pass back and forth between Adalind and Nick, each clouded with shadows of desire that complicate the violence. The effect is similar to the invitation extended to the vampire, whose bite is also sexual (see Creed's Ch. 5). At the same time, Adalind and Nick participate in a sort of noir and horror version of the romantic comedy (*Grimm* does blur genres). In her second appearance, the two join in rom-com dialogue clashes, with a rudeness that borders on humor. As Hank and Nick investigate the deaths of her lawyer colleagues, she tells them to call her Adalind—"all my friends do." "All your friends are dead," Nick slices back, alarming Hank (1.3). When Nick asks why someone wants her dead, she replies, "You're a detective—figure it out." Later, seated, facing each other, he taunts her until she woges and lunges forward—and he smiles; their physical confrontation is an adumbration of their fight in "Love Sick" (1.17). When she disappears (to escape from the killers), he runs through the halls calling not "Ms. Schade!" but "Adalind!" in a surprising touch of intimacy. When Renard tells her to draw Hank into a relationship, Adalind asks why she should not go for Nick instead (1.15). When Nick is trying to explain to Juliette why Adalind is trouble, his responses lead her to ask, "Did you have some kind of relationship with her?" (1.22). After Adalind has left the country and returned, in search of the special key Nick's aunt gave him, she is jailed (by her own design) and from behind bars, asking for that key, she tells him, "Under different circumstances, I think that you and I could have really had some fun" (2.12). Throughout their conflict, in true (if dark) rom-com fashion, moments of sexual attraction flare.

Darkness comes in incidents of barely hidden or even open sexual aggression—perhaps most notably in "Love Sick." In this episode Adalind is once more trying to get the key for Renard. As do all *Grimm* episodes, this one starts with an epigraph: "Forgive me for the evil I have done you; my mother drove me to it; it was done against my will." Adalind and Catherine Schade are the mother and daughter in this episode; the epigraph thus prepares us to consider some measure of forgiveness for Adalind. There is quite a lot to forgive. She has bespelled Hank with blood cookies; he will sleep with her in this episode and fall into a coma that would, without intervention, lead to his death (see Ch. 2). Hank later says it seems as if she roofied him (1.18)—in other words, Hank is a victim of sexual assault. In an earlier episode Adalind expressed indignation when a man pressured her for sex, but now she has been asked to essentially prostitute herself by both her mother and the man to whom her mother is indebted—Renard. More to the point, he is the man Adalind loves (as will be discussed later). Taught by her mother to disregard love and use her body to manipulate, Adalind ironically prostitutes her body for love of Renard. Thus (though she is complicit in a way that Hank is not), both she and Hank are sexually abused in this scenario.

In order to save Hank from his deadly coma, Nick learns that he must somehow get his blood into Adalind—an image that echoes the vampire in its abjection, horror, and sexuality. Early in the episode, Nick is shocked to see that the woman Hank is dating is Adalind; Nick confronts her privately

Nine—"I just drank my mother"

in a stairwell, grabbing her arm as he did in the pilot, their faces lit in intimate close-up. Adalind defiantly refuses to be warned off. In the climactic scene, the confrontation is even more intense. Nick says, suggesting the simmering growth of the conflict, "I think it's time we settled our differences—violently." Thus, though she makes the first move, he invites the violence (in fact, he has said he is willing to kill her, to save the man she is willing to kill). They fight at length, towards the end rolling over and over each other, she in woge strength. As he lands on top, she reverts to her non-Wesen face and he kisses her—presumably expecting what happens next: She bites his lip ferociously to make him stop, but instead he continues until his blood has flowed into her. We see the ghostly shape of the hag-spirit, the Crone power, leave her with an echoing shriek. Nick's mouth is bloody, but hers is more so. Actor Claire Coffee conveys a pitiable vulnerability in Adalind—voice shaking, usually shiny hair realistically mussed, as she says, "You killed me." "You don't look so dead," says a confused Nick. *La petite morte*, the little death, is the French term for orgasmic sex; and death has been used by the poets for centuries as a metaphor for sex, that other boundary-crossing experience. Sex is also, of course, often used as a way to exert power rather than to make love. Adalind declares, "I'm nothing now—I don't have any powers. You've taken everything. I'm just like everybody else—I'm nothing." Later in the series Adalind will be able to live well without magical powers; for now, she is devastated. But not for long.

Rejected by her mother and her prince, Adalind leaves and eventually regains her powers while she is pregnant. The pregnancy is not the direct cause of her power, though it is related (on which, more later). When Nick and others conspire to take her child Diana from her, another prince, Viktor, offers to return Diana if Adalind will take Nick's powers in a reflection of what he has done to her in "Love Sick." This time, however, the sex will go beyond an assaultive kiss. In the pilot, Adalind stole Juliette's place; now she counterfeits her body, using a spell to make herself Juliette's exact double. It happens in the third season finale, the episode of Rosalee and Monroe's wedding, and it is a distorted mirror of that wedding. Adalind appears as Juliette in lingerie and "a romantic mood," enticing Nick to bed. He awakens to find her watching him, a reverse-gender example of the Mulveyan gaze. She is the person in power in this scene of sexual theft. Burger and Mix argue that Juliette later feels anger and jealousy because Nick sleeps with Adalind (23), and that interpretation seems likely; but it should not be forgotten that Juliette is not the primary victim here. Adalind in effect rapes Nick—as he has virtually raped her. The expression on actor David Giuntoli's face when Nick realizes he has slept with Adalind, even before he realizes he has lost his powers, shows a sense of loss that does not seem to be just about his relationship with Juliette. In each case, there is a very thin veil of magic separating their actions from real-world rape, making it more possible, in combination with the emotional murkiness of their relationship, for some viewers to move past. But the darkness is there.

In the following season, Renard's mother, the wise Hexenbiest Elizabeth Lascelles, analyzes Adalind's spell in order to reverse it, calling it an entwining twin spell. She says that it "ties them together in unpredictable ways"—an assessment that proves true for the rest of the series (4.3). By the time Elizabeth says this, Adalind and Nick have shared ferocious physical pain and then seen through each other's eyes—she in a dungeon in Austria, he in his home in Portland—to the bewilderment of each (4.2). Although Adalind has her powers and Nick has lost his, Adalind is for a time unable to use hers: She is trapped in a Hex-proof cell by Prince Viktor. They are thus paralleled again.

Because Rosalee and Monroe are threatened by a Wesen hate group, Nick and Juliette decide to get Nick's powers back—but to do so, they must recreate and reverse Adalind's actions. That is, Juliette must magically embody herself as Adalind and then sleep with Nick. (Coffee, when performing Juliette transformed into Adalind, holds her arms slightly stiffly as she walks, effectively imitating Bitsie Tulloch as Juliette, 4.6). Nick is at first not enthusiastic; when told to think of it as a costume, he says, "a costume of Woman-who-tried-to-kill-me" (4.6). Eventually, however, we see the Adalind-shaped Juliette roll off Nick in bed, a smile on both their faces, in a shot often replayed. In this version of the repeated interaction, sex may seem a happy weapon for good. But even here there is complication: Juliette is now part of the entwining twin spell (you sleep with whoever your partner has slept with), and she later carries some of Adalind within: Juliette eventually becomes a Hexenbiest.

There is thus a kind of character chiasmus between Adalind and Juliette. Adalind has tried to kill Nick's substitute mother, Aunt Marie, in the pilot; Hexenbiest Juliette does participate in setting up the death of Nick's mother Kelly (4.21). Juliette steals Diana from the Royals; Adalind fights to get her daughter back (4.22). After Adalind leaves the Royals, Juliette moves into Adalind's hotel room; after Adalind has Nick's baby, she moves into Juliette's house (4.22, 5.2). Adalind even drives Juliette's old car—not to mention her boyfriend (5.3, 5.11). As Adalind says to her baby, it is "ironic" that the car "belonged to a woman who tried to kill me—'course, I tried to kill her too" (5.3). There is no question that Adalind is supplanting Juliette; however, by the end of the story it seems they both have moved where they should be—whether or not they really knew what they wanted at the start. They discover themselves through each other, through playing the parts of each other—a version of the disguise device of screwball comedy. And the horror rom-com pair Nick and Adalind discover themselves through reflecting each other's experiences as well.

In fact, Nick, like Juliette and Adalind, must transform himself into another to finally make sure he and Adalind can be a couple. The one he must transform into is Renard, Adalind's former love, who has—with the help of the racist Wesen group Black Claw—forced Adalind and her children to live with him in order to advance his political career (on which, more to come). "Oh Captain, My Captain" is a joyfully farcical show used to resolve some very dark story lines (6.3). But it also shows Nick undergoing the same physical pain and emotional stress Adalind and Juliette did in transforming. He does not suffer similar long-term effects, but he endures the threat of them: For a while, he cannot transform back. His friends fear that he is in fact Renard. The test that proves him true is answering the question of where he and Adalind had their first kiss.[5] That answer expresses an important part of his identity. And part of the bargain he makes with Renard is that Adalind will leave Renard and be with Nick. This final shape-change thus proves an interior truth, arrived at after long journeying.

That journey is central to both the characters of Adalind and Nick (and to Juliette in a way as well—her way out). We never saw the courtship, the growth of relationship, for Juliette and Nick: They are presented as a fully formed couple, living together. For Adalind and Nick we observe the relationship emerge—an automatic advantage to the interest of their story. For an evil witch and a lawyer, no less, Adalind is a real romantic. This is, after all, someone who in her twenties fell in love with a prince. Because Juliette "dies" at the end of the fourth season and Nick and Adalind's son Kelly is born at the beginning of the fifth, their relationship opens up. We see Nick making ham sandwiches and Adalind happily eating them as they try to civilly cohabit after Adalind's C-section. When she says she is allergic to raw tomato, Giuntoli as Nick playfully puts a whole slice in his mouth, keeping her safe. When, in the same conversation, he says he is thinking of selling the house and that she and Kelly can come, if she likes, she answers "Sure" with a mouthful of sandwich, and adds, "This is really good," which provokes perhaps the first Adalind-directed smile from Nick (other than smiles born of anger). While for years Adalind has dressed almost exclusively in black, in this scene (and many fifth-season scenes) she wears white, the color suggesting her changed role. They begin a quietly pleasant conversation on the relatively safe topic of foods, both actors making clear how delicately the characters are stepping. Food often suggests sensuality or sexuality; just as often, it suggests home. Both subjects seem at play here.[6]

Succeeding episodes carefully lay further relationship groundwork, with rom-com touches. In the next, we witness their rather flirtatious conversation about "first times"; this occurs as they pack to move into a new home—their own space, one never shared by Juliette—though Nick has selected it, choosing, while Adalind convalesces, a loft that has qualities of a hidden fortress for his son and that son's mother (5.3). Later in the episode, Adalind—dressed in inelegant, light-colored, string-tied pajamas rather than her earlier black negligées—asks Nick to sleep in "our room"—that is, their son's and hers—because she is afraid. Coffee then has Adalind hop back and turn away, saying, "I'm sorry—this is too weird" in what seems a thoroughly awkward fashion—though one wonders if Adalind is purposely revealing her vulnerability to persuade. In any case, Nick answers, "I think we're beyond weird at this point" as he rises, picks up his bedside pistol, and goes to lie, wide-eyed, beside her in bed (5.3). In the following episode, there is a humorous scene of their trying to deal with a crying baby who stops at the sight of a cell phone. When Nick suggests they get him his own phone, Adalind responds with mother-wisdom, "Not till second grade" (5.4). We later see them sharing a supper that this time she has cooked, as she tells him that she taught herself because her mother was not often around to cook; he tells her that he was twelve when he lost his mother, and she replies that her father left when she was four, again tracing parallels. After thanking Nick for what he is doing as a father, she adds, "I don't like having to rely on you. Not just you, I don't like having to rely on anybody," and explains that she has heard she could get a job with her old law firm, something she will pursue later. Having declared her independence, she asks him to sleep in "our room" again. He is silent, but later we see that the plan has become accepted practice. Adalind is moving them into a family structure.

We subsequently see that her desire not to impose on him extends to not buying new clothes; in a rom-com-ish scene, he has to bring her one of his shirts when she is in the shower, since she has no clean clothes. He tells her to use his credit card to buy clothes. She answers, "Eeuhh—I feel a little awkward doing that." "Well, not having clothes is awkward," he replies. In the same show, when he returns home after a long day, each of them notes the other's needs—do you need help with the baby?—are you tired?—and she tells him, "I was worried," her eyes looking down as she puts some baby gear away. "About Kelly?" he asks. "No, you," she answers, with a face of trepidation. His own face serious, he steps closer and pulls her into a hug. In the reverse shot, we see that her eyes are wide and her lips are open in a look compounded of both surprise and worry. It is perhaps the most important turning point in their relationship—not a moment of violent sexuality, but of affection and trust. Coffee and Giuntoli's acting skills are absolutely essential to conveying this development of the characters. The moment's importance is only confirmed when, moments later, Nick hugs another woman—the wounded Trubel, his quasi-daughter, who has shown up on their doorstep. Adalind is now part of a family.

Adalind and Nick's relationship, however, is far from unromantic *agape*. In the "Wesen Nacht" episode, Trubel and Adalind have a private conversation, and Trubel asks if Adalind is in love with Nick. The usually articulate lawyer slides down to sit on the floor, answering, with a slight laugh, "Huh—eeah—uh—That, no, that would be—that would be just too, I mean that would really, too, I just, I, well, I don't even know what that would be" (5.6). Adalind may not let herself know, but Trubel does. Coffee delivers Adalind's quietly embarrassed, half-smiling babble in a completely believable way that makes the real answer obvious. As Trubel says much later, she knows Adalind loves Nick, before he does (5.20). The next episode brings their first kiss: Seated at the table with Nick, Adalind moves in first, though he moves immediately after (on initiating sex, see Ch. 8). Coffee is in this scene wearing what appears to be her lightest make-up ever, with uncurled hair and loose, light-colored clothes. This is Adalind au naturel. This is Adalind with Nick. After they kiss, they question themselves, and Adalind says, "I don't think there's anything safe about us"—a Hexenbiest loving a Grimm; a forbidden love of the Buffy/Angel (or even Bella/Edward) sort—but grown-up. Hank once called Nick Romeo, and Nick had his Juliette (1.1); forbidden love certainly did not work for Nick and the changed Juliette. But then Adalind is a much more experienced Hexenbiest than Juliette was, and Nick has had earlier experience loving (though unsuccessfully) a Hexenbiest. Furthermore, there is the chiasmus again: Nick tried to get used to being with Juliette after she gained uncontrollable power, whereas he now is becoming accustomed to Adalind while she has voluntarily suppressed her power. Most importantly, these are two different people, who want to earn their way to a happy ending with each other. By the time Adalind's power emerges again, they will have taught each other to begin to trust.

They embark on a relationship that is, as Nick tells Monroe, "strangely normal" (5.10). They have marital give-and-take in their dialogue ("What if there's a lot of water on the other side and you drown?" "Not helping" 5.9). Coffee even employs a gesture of silent communication that she has Adalind use with Nick, a kind of reverse nod in which her chin goes up first, then down (e.g., 5.2), seeming to suggest resignation, affirmation, and understanding all at once. They have a dinner party for their friends at what Adalind calls their "Fome—it's a cross between a fortress and a home" (5.13). (Hank avoids the cookies.) Nick does not tell her he loves her until the series finale, but Adalind says it to him in the series' 99th episode, and she is the one who initiates sex (5.11). The next morning, she asks him if he is all right—an unusual but reasonable question, given that he has been flashing back to their earliest encounters. He asks the same of her. But by the fifth season's fifteenth episode, it is implied that they are frequently having sex.

Sex is now a matter of trust between them. When Adalind gets her powers back in response to a direct physical threat to her and Rosalee, she fears Nick will discard the baby and her (as Renard did, as her father did) or even kill her (as Hexenbiest Juliette feared). Rosalee urges Adalind to tell Nick herself; eventually, Rosalee feels she must tell Nick. Rosalee, Nick, and Monroe agree to keep silent in hopes that Adalind will eventually tell him herself. In the meantime, he apparently stops having sex with her. One might recall—*Nick* might recall—Juliette's direct threat to him after she becomes a Hexenbiest, placing her hand on his and asking if he would dare to come naked into her bed, as she woges into a snapping-teethed hag (4.18). When Adalind stops the legal work she is doing at the table, diplomatically hints her invitation, and kisses Nick, saying "This is not ending here," Nick looks at her with a gravely serious face. It is not necessary to invoke the *vagina dentata* or fear of castration (apropos though those may be) to suggest that he, a Grimm, might be afraid to go to bed with a Hexenbiest who is keeping secrets. But it is a mark of the trust that has grown between them—in spite of the fear that leads her to keep her secret—that go he does. Their sexual relationship resumes. And afterwards, she tells him a secret—Renard's having contacted her about Diana's possible return (5.18). Then, in the next episode, after waking in the night to see him holding their son, she trusts him with the secret of who she fully is—a Hexenbiest, a woman of power, again (5.19).

The Curse of the Ring

The child of parents who use or abandon her, Adalind, once she experiences being a parent, puts her children first. Thus she leaves her home with Nick to re-connect with Diana: "I feel how badly she needs me" (5.19). She leaves Nick a letter giving the children as the reason she is going; but her magic reveals an added, underlying message: she is protecting him, too. When she does join Renard, now a candidate for mayor backed by Black Claw, he tells her, "You and I do not have complete control here. Welcome home" (5.20).

This is home as designed by patriarchal power—as is clearly shown by the symbol of the cursed ring she will wear. The notably named Conrad Bonaparte is an older man, the Wesen head of Black Claw in Portland (and elsewhere) who apparently lives in the mansion Renard and Adalind now occupy with Diana and Kelly. It is he who insists that Adalind marry

Renard. In a scene that evokes historically earlier patterns of marriage, it is the patriarch Bonaparte who places a diamond ring on Adalind's finger as a sign of her "wedding"; her planned marital partner, Renard, does not offer her the ring. Instead the patriarchal figure joins her with Renard for reasons that have nothing to do with romance. He hints that Adalind should service Renard sexually, and when Adalind objects, Bonaparte calls her stubborn and turns her to stone. As for many a woman, her sexual choices are disregarded in this match. She tells Bonaparte that he hurt her "a lot," but it is his final threat that is overpowering: If she ever takes the ring off, "it will be extremely painful—for your children" (5.21). Trapped in a set-up that is designed for men's political and economic power and uses children as pawns, Adalind agrees. We hear Coffee swallow hard as Adalind says of the cursed ring, "It's very nice." It represents the imprisonment of old forms of marriage, and Adalind's forced, hollow endorsement represents a situation many women have faced. In this show of dark fairy tales, Bonaparte says, "You are a princess and Sean will be your prince. People love a fairy tale"—but this is a fairy tale that *Grimm* will repudiate.

Adalind later tells Nick, "I'm afraid to take it [the ring] off without knowing how to break the spell." Nick responds, "we'll find a way to break it" (6.1). The world has to end first, but Adalind and Nick do reject old-style patriarchal marriage. In the finale's original timeline, after Adalind dies, Nick takes off the cursed ring and flings it into the mud. When time is re-set, in the main characters' last scene, he holds her hand up, seeing that the ring is still gone. For Juliette, he had repeatedly offered a ring that was not right for them (see Ch. 7), and she never took it. The shot of Nick and Adalind with her hand free of the ring emphasizes their freedom from cruel tradition. Combined, the trope of the problematic ring for Juliette and Adalind shows a questioning of old ways. We learn from the series' final scene, set twenty years later, that Nick and Adalind's different style of relationship has endured.

"You still love him, don't you?": *Dupe or Manipulator of Patriarchy*

Adalind's eventually successful romantic relationship with Nick is not the only one for her we see depicted on-screen; she also has extended relationships with Renard and his half-brother Prince Eric (she refers to having sex with Hank as "working," 1.17). In the pilot, we learn that she acts under orders of Renard; but in a later scene in a museum (1.15) and one in her bathroom (1.16), Coffee and Roiz's body language suggests Adalind's attraction to Renard and his exploitation of it. When her mother asks, "You still love him, don't you?" Adalind declares that love doesn't matter, coolly indicating that she has a new "beau" at the captain's behest (1.17). But by the episode's end, she declares with tears that she "did it"—she tried to kill a Grimm (Aunt Marie), slept with a man, and fought another Grimm— "for him," for love of Renard. When she is doing his bidding, Renard cajoles her, calling her "incredibly powerful," but when she has no magic, he calls her "useless" (1.17). (He will later revise that judgment.) Her mother subsequently tells him he "played with her heart" (2.1). At this point, Adalind has believed in the fairy tale prince that Bonaparte describes and she later rejects.

Her next step, however, is not real independence but a turn to another prince. Adalind goes to Austria and seduces Renard's half-brother Eric, introducing herself at the bar of an opera house with jaunty, teasing references to betrayal, Wagnerian tragedy, Grimms, and his brother: "Then I would say you are well-versed in betrayal," Eric replies ambiguously, who nonetheless enters into an affair with her (2.8). Adalind at this stage has no magic power; even when her goals are questionable, her determination is admirable. Beautifully coiffed and dressed in black, as she sits in an elegant room with Prince Eric, she tells him of her relationship with Renard: "I was young, he was charming—that's a volatile combination," suggesting she has moved on emotionally, though that later seems less clear. She also openly tells Eric she has a "wish list" of her own. When he says, "I didn't think you came all the way to Vienna to listen to the zither," she replies, "I happen to like the zither" (2.8). This remark comes two episodes after the moral touchstone characters Monroe and Rosalee bond over their shared love of an Austrian zitherist, and thus is one of many subtle character touches that bring Adalind into the light of likability in spite of her wrong-doing. Adalind employs her looks, her charm, and her sexuality to get what she wants. But that Adalind actually becomes fond of Eric we learn later, when she delicately blots away a single tear of blood while she watches news of his death (3.3). She is nothing if not complicated. This fondness suggests that she is still drawn to and sees herself connected to the patriarchy.

Earlier, soon after their affair begins, Eric sends her as his emissary to Portland, and we see evidence that Adalind also still has feelings—very mixed feelings—for Renard. Using a potion she acquires who knows where, Adalind has placed Juliette under a spell in revenge for Nick's taking her powers; as she tells Renard, Nick has taken something from her, so she has taken something from him (2.7). Juliette can only be awakened from her Sleeping Beauty coma by a prince—but when Renard awakens Juliette, the spell shifts into catastrophic, increasing lust—part of Adalind's revenge against him for rejecting her. Adalind returns to Portland with an entourage; the camera first shows her red stiletto heels, ready to stomp. After doing some damage to Hank, she tells Renard to "be a good little prince" and get the special key from Nick for Eric (2.12). She later tells Renard that, though she cannot undo the lust spell, she can stop him from being so "pent up" (2.13). To the accompaniment of enthusiastically twanging guitar, they have sex out in the wild, in the night, she insisting that he show her his true, half-Wesen, abject face. Coffee speaks in a cat-like, almost growling tone as she says, "I want what you would never show to her" (the episode is called "Face Off," 2.13). Adalind here is clearly happy to have sex with a man she once loved, even while she is having an affair with his brother. Whether or not she still loves Renard is unclear, but later in the episode she coolly thanks him for "last night." Even if she still has feelings for him, she will no longer risk herself for him: She heads back to Vienna and Eric. In the last shot of the episode, we see her smile as she looks at a positive pregnancy test, heralding the birth of Diana. It may be true that when at her lowest, she ran to another prince and the patriarchy for protection; but she here seems to be manipulating both princes for her own ends.

Manipulating the patriarchy, however, is a dangerous game. Though she may have planned to trade away the child to get her powers back, through the course of her pregnancy, she becomes emotionally attached (see Ch. 11). "So weird to think of myself as *us*," she says with a smile right after the baby is born (3.15). She magically regains her powers but no longer wishes to give up her child. She fights the Royals, fleeing with the Resistance, to try to keep her baby. Ultimately, she risks her life for the first person she loves unconditionally—Diana. In fact, Renard, Nick, and his friends also try to keep Diana from the Royals, but they do not trust Adalind enough to tell her their plans. Thus Adalind believes the Royals have Diana when in fact she is being cared for by Nick's mother, Kelly. Adalind acquiesces to Prince Viktor's demand that she take Nick's powers by sleeping with him, which she accomplishes by transforming into the shape of Juliette. She is employing her body for the sake of her child. Afterward, she literally flies to the patriarchy: We see her alone on a plane with a determined look on her face, believing she will retrieve Diana. Adalind is unaware that the Royals, the patriarchy, have nothing to give her.

Adalind later tells Prince Viktor she did what he wanted "for my baby" and that "it wasn't fun" (4.2). In yet another parallel between Adalind and Nick, her sexual behavior is made uncomfortably public, as Viktor asks her, in front of two employees, "How was it, by the way?" Similarly, Nick's sexual behavior and deception are discussed by a car full of his friends, to his clear misery (4.1). They are both, in some sense, victims of the Royals, the major representatives of the patriarchy in *Grimm*.[7]

At one point, Adalind obsequiously listens to King Frederick, pretending to agree with him so she can be with the Royals in their search for her magical daughter. With oily duplicity, he tells her she is too important to be left alone (4.15). Later on, Adalind, still trying to get Diana back, works with yet another prince, Kenneth. He shows her exactly what her place is in their system: "So you're the Hexenbiest mother of the child everyone is so obsessed with"—he categorizes her by race (Hexenbiest), gender and role as parent. When she asks, "Does anyone care what I think?" his patriarchal answer is a resounding "No" (4.19). But at least she now knows it. As Renard says early on, "Sometimes Adalind has a mind of her own" (1.17), and she comes to understand the world—including the patriarchy—more and more clearly.

"You just can't get Hexenbiest blood out of anything": Abjection and Humor

An abject romantic comedy heroine is not a typical figure. In *Pride and Prejudice*, Elizabeth Bennet gets mud on her skirts, but Adalind is something else again. Adalind is not solely, simply rom-com, but that is one of the character's aspects. Julia Kristeva has highlighted the nature of the abject and its connection to gender—the unsettling disturbance of boundaries established by symbolic law; wordless mother nature versus the categories established by man. Barbara Creed refers to Barbara Walker in Creed's application of Kristeva to the monstrous-feminine (e.g., Creed 74). Samantha Pentony has connected Creed's theory (based on horror film) to fairy tales such as we see in *Grimm*. Walker emphasizes distinctions between most patriarchal and matriarchal religious systems, saying, "Clergymen [...] never helped clean up blood, vomit, pus, or feces. As usual, such [abject] services were left to women" (34), and she adds, "The same mixture of fear, avoidance, or even contempt that a patriarchal society applies to pregnant [...] women may be applied to old women" (36). Old women; pregnant women. More than any other major character in *Grimm*, Adalind is identified with the abject, and more than any other, she is depicted as pregnant and mothering. Furthermore, she has been shown since the pilot to have an inner old woman—as does every young woman, if she lives long enough. Adalind—birthing mother, Crone, and witch—is a character ripe with the abject.

Adalind is connected with the abject in instances throughout the series, but most particularly while she is pregnant.[8] The abjection is tied not only to the pregnancy itself but to Adalind's determination to regain her power. In the eighteenth episode of the second season, we are shown the night sky above the glittering city of Vienna as the camera moves down to focus on Adalind, in a skimpy, glamorous negligée, hugging the toilet and vomiting. She vomits because she is pregnant. She is called to the door of her expensive hotel room by Frau Pech, an exceptionally ancient and hag-like Hexenbiest whom Adalind is using as an agent. The usually elegant Adalind's discomfort is amusing, and her discomfort is far from over. Frau Pech tells her that she is to meet the queen of the Scharzwald Roma, Stefania Popescu Vaduva.[9] The two arrive at Stefania's luxurious tent home and, after formal greetings, Adalind is grabbed by two of Stefania's sons and forced to endure an examination to test the child's blood using a gigantic modified metal speculum. As Stefania calmly says, "It's standard procedure—which unfortunately you have to be awake for" (2.18). Adalind's screams are muffled by the sound of music made by hundreds of Roma surrounding the tent. This is Adalind's second quasi-rape, though it has more of the medical about it. She emerges determined to get "the most for my baby" and demands as her price not money, but a return of her powers (2.18). At this point she seems to see the child as no more than a tool to power.

Frau Pech prefers that Adalind sell the child for money and threatens Adalind, saying that she could be worth more dead than alive; and indeed, Frau Pech tries to make a bargain with the Royals behind Adalind's back (2.21). After this threat, Adalind, frightened and angry, calls Stefania, who promises to "talk to" Frau Pech: i.e., she initiates a plan to kill Frau Pech so that Adalind can be imbued with her Hexenbiest powers. Rather than a purification ritual for the abject (per Mary Douglas), Stefania explains that Adalind must undergo the *Contaminatio Ritualis*—the ritual of contamination.[10] We then see, over multiple episodes, a sequence of images of abjection that are both horrific and humorous. Adalind cutting eyeballs out of the dead, Adalind shifting dirt by hand, Adalind stitching up the Hexenbiest corpse and being told to bite off the bloody thread—all of these are required in the ritual for the return of her power. Kristeva says, "When a woman ventures out into those regions [of abjection], it is usually to gratify, in a vary maternal fashion, the desire for the abject that insures the life (that is, the sexual life) of the man whose symbolic authority she accepts" (54).[11] But Adalind chooses this abjection for her own sake, not for a man's.

The contrast between the horrific activities and the well-dressed, conventionally pretty, clearly disgusted Adalind is the center of the humor. In response to new abject tasks, her repeated, whiny plaint of "Really?" gives the audience a chance to laugh (2.18, 3.1). It also places her on the side of the normal; rather than being the source of the abject in these scenes, she is subjected to the abject, immersed in it. Her clothes become filthier and filthier, bloody and dirty. When Adalind is told she has finished one of the tests and says, "Thank god," Stefania says, "I wouldn't" (3.1). The moment is comical and connects to Walker's point about religion; but Adalind is at a different place than Stefania in that moment, not as far from the audience as the killer queen who has stabbed the living heart out of an old friend. At the same time, Adalind pursues the ritual in her determination to regain her power in full knowledge that she is defiling another woman's body and benefiting from her death. This is the purpose for which Stefania has cut out Frau Pech's still-beating heart. She later brings in Adalind, who emits a gasp and retracts her head. Stefania, smiling, says she'll have to throw away the carpet: "You just can't get Hexenbiest blood out of anything," she says to the once-and-future Hexenbiest (3.1). When Stefania subsequently tells her the heart must be buried with her hands, Adalind says, "Of course it must" (3.1). Coffee portrays moment after moment of laughable loathing and repulsion.[12] But when ghostly Hexenbiest hands touch Adalind and her eyes glow, her face shows triumph, and abjection enters her again. Soon, Stefania says, "I think she [dead Frau Pech] likes you" (3.2).

Coffee has stated her surprise that her character is so well-liked by fans ("*Grimm*: Myths"). One likely reason is that we enjoy seeing her abjection. She has in the past used her abject inner nature against others, but now she is paying. Another reason is that, horrifying as Adalind can be, she fights for her power—and in doing so, she has never directly, intentionally killed. She participates second-hand in the death of Frau Pech only after the Frau has threatened her life. More specifically, Frau Pech is killed by Stefania only after Frau Pech performs a magic spell to take over Adalind's body, dosing Adalind into unconsciousness and extracting her blood: We see Adalind morph into the aged shape of Frau Pech and Frau Pech assume the smoothly naked shape of Adalind with a smile that Coffee performs to chilling effect (2.22). Frau Pech's death directly follows from this body-theft.[13] Adalind's earlier attempts at killing were just that—attempts; and they were attempts against those she perceived as enemies, such as a Grimm.[14] This latter point leads to a third ameliorating reason: Of the five major female characters, she is the only one who was raised to be a tool of patriarchy—and in that sense deserves pity.

While Adalind humorously chooses to endure the abject in these scenes of the ritual, her own body becomes abject because of her pregnancy. As she rubs a paste of dead Hexenbiest (and flowers) on her stomach, we are treated to the storied image of the naked witch performing magic (in this case, with a conveniently placed slatted chair-back preserving broadcast decorum). The moment slips into horror as a red arachnid shape appears on her pregnant belly (3.7). Not many episodes later, Diana's feet stretch out the skin of her mother's belly, and later in the episode, to Adalind's horror and pain, she can see the head clearly beneath the surface of the skin (3.11). This is an abject moment only slightly beyond the experience of many women.

Adalind's other most abject scenes relate to her second pregnancy. Hexenbiest Adalind has met Hexenbiest Juliette in battle and been bested. In order to create a potion to suppress the Hexenbiest in Juliette—a potion she will first test on herself—Adalind cuts up her own dead mother. This sequence is described in some detail in Chapter Eight; in it, Adalind and the kindly Rosalee together grind the evil dead mother's bones—a thoroughly wicked-witch-like activity except for its benevolent purpose: to help Juliette return to normality and to save Adalind and her unborn child from Juliette's wrath. When Adalind drinks the potion to test it, it is the second time she has performed an experiment on her body while pregnant. During her pregnancy with Diana, she performs the Contaminatio Ritualis, intensifying Diana's magic abilities; during her pregnancy with Kelly, she drinks the suppressing potion, presumably muting his Hexenbiest qualities and perhaps allowing his Grimm inheritance to flourish. Using her mother's witch's hat to strain the liquid to the clarity (but not the taste) of water, Adalind audibly gulps it down. When Rosalee asks how she feels, Adalind replies, "Like I just drank my mother" (4.20). As Kristeva says, the abject covers "three major categories of abomination: (1) food taboos; (2) corporeal alteration and its climax, death; (3) the feminine body and incest" (93). Adalind's ingestion of her mother seems to cover all the bases. Yet because of the actor's expressions and the hopeful goal (as well as the underlying playful distance that obtains in much of *Grimm*), the moment is humorous as well as horrific.

When Adalind drinks the suppressant, she asks all the "Scooby Gang" present (Monroe, Rosalee, Hank, Nick) to hold her down together, as the hag-spirit rises with seismic force. But the Crone within Adalind does not leave this time. It subsides into her, ready to come out when the need arises—as it later will. For the time being, she checks and sees that she cannot use her powers. The look on Coffee's face suggests both relief and regret as she says, with double meaning, "I guess I'm good" (4.20). This story does not in the end "eject the abject," as Creed says (14). Abjection and virtue are not mutually exclusive in *Grimm*.

Frau Pech: "I knew your mother well" Adalind: "Me too": Mothering in Context

This slightly absurdist, almost screwball exchange between Frau Pech and Adalind suggests that Adalind has nothing good to say about her mother. Adalind as a character in general and a mother in particular needs to be judged in the context of her own mother and the context of episodes that focus on mothering. In the last season, Adalind, reconciled with Juliette and giving her advice based on her mother Catherine's books, admits, "For the record—not a great mother" (6.9). Not only did Catherine neglect her child; she essentially sold her, endorsing the plan for Adalind to sleep with Hank to release her, Catherine, from debt. She trains Adalind to focus on appearance, saying, as she combs her daughter's hair before a mirror, that she herself uses this treatment for half an hour each day. When the camera moves, we see Adalind's face symmetrically covered in leeches, a chosen abjection that is not too far from the reality of some "beauty" treatments (1.17). When the weeping, beaten young woman returns later that night after Nick has taken her powers, Catherine slaps her. After Catherine's death, all her property is taken for unpaid taxes except the items in a storage unit. However, from this storage unit Adalind gets her inheritance: the venerable witch's hat and her mother's grimoire (though that term is never used in *Grimm*). Adalind's mother has given her knowledge if not a model of morality. When Rosalee talks about her own wild days, Adalind tells Rosalee that she instead became a "nerd student": "I guess I wanted to prove to my mother that I was nothing like her, so I became a lawyer" (5.12). Like many, Adalind both follows and reacts against her parent.

Adalind is also nothing like her mother in her treatment of her children. When she gives birth to her child with Nick, Adalind asks that he be named Kelly, after Nick's mother: In their brief time together, Kelly has modeled better mothering than Catherine ever did. Catherine neglects and emotionally abuses Adalind; Adalind fights for her children. Under Catherine's influence (and for love of Renard), Adalind attempts murder; Adalind teaches her own daughter not to murder (see Ch. 11). Instead of slaps, Adalind dispenses calm, loving, clear discipline: "It's really not a good idea to pick up a baby like that" (5.20); "You can't push people together—especially not a mommy and daddy" (5.21); "It's Kelly's turn to be with his daddy now, okay?" (6.4). Repeatedly, she tells Diana not to worry, that the adults will take care of things—in contrast to the mother who exploited her (e.g., 5.22, 6.5).

Contrast also elucidates Adalind's character in the context of episodes that focus on mothering. The fact that Adalind's character undergoes drastic moral improvement after motherhood could be seen as a sentimentally false depiction of the nature of motherhood making for automatic redemption (cf. the repudiated idea of being saved by the love of a good man, Ch. 7). But such sentimentality is avoided both through the abjection of motherhood and the context of episodes that problematize motherhood.

Most notably, Adalind gives birth during an episode titled "Mommy Dearest"—an episode many viewers recall as the Aswang episode (see Ch. 3). Some viewers will know that "Mommy Dearest" is the title of a book and film famously about child abuse. Those unfamiliar with the title need only pay attention to the "fairy tale" of this episode: The Aswang is a Filipino legend of a mother-monster (yes, the monstrous-feminine) that pierces the womb of pregnant women and then eats the newborn child (3.14). Furthermore, the Aswang mother demands, and normally gets, to eat the firstborn of her eldest son. The monstrous mother consumes the child, erasing separation (Kristeva 12–13, Creed 23–25). With this story taking the bulk of the episode's time, it is hard to understand how Adalind's childbirth could be seen as a simple celebration of the healing power of motherhood.

Adalind learns of her second pregnancy in another episode with an apropos title: "Bad Luck" (4.14). Adalind certainly does at first see it as bad luck that she has become pregnant with Nick's child while pretending to be Juliette. Once again, the main plot of the episode colors interpretation. In "Bad Luck," Wesen couples go to a fertility clinic to be connected to an illegal provider who sets up a grotesque and abject ritual, cutting off the foot of a rabbit-like Wesen (who then dies); the foot is to be placed under the bed of the mating couple to achieve fertility. Adalind may be a good mother, but pregnancy is not automatically unadulterated virtue. In this episode, to desire pregnancy at any cost is clearly shown to be wrong.

The fifth season heavily features Adalind as mother. Two back-to-back episodes early in the fifth season provide more thematic context that works against the false sweetening of motherhood: "Lost Boys," a riff on Peter Pan (5.3); and "Maiden Quest," based on medieval knight romance (5.4). After Adalind drinks her mother and suppresses her power, Nick promises no one will take Kelly, unlike Diana (4.20). When she has the baby, Nick hides her in a fortress-like home, and her isolation does recall that of the dismaying nineteenth-century ideal of the "womanly" woman in her separate sphere, the Angel in the House (based on Coventry Patmore's eponymous poem). However, this impression is undercut not only by Adalind's resuming her legal work but by these episodes that provide a context for mothering and reproductive issues. In "Lost Boys," a Rosalee-centric episode, Wesen children who have escaped from foster care trap a series of women to serve as mother in their woodland hideout—the latest of whom is Rosalee, selected for her kindness. One horror here is the children's situation. But there is another horror to consider: Children here enslave the woman as mother, a problem made more obvious (though it should not be) by the lack of genetic connection. Similarly, in "Maiden Quest," Emily, the beautiful young maiden on offer, does not wish to be gained in marriage by any of the competing knights. Instead, she kills them, one by one. Even the one with whom she already has a relationship is not exempt, though she tries to warn him from the quest. He makes it clear, however, that he sees her in terms of traditional marriage and property; he wants to put a ring on it, on her. He tells her, "Don't worry, babe. [...] You and me, we're gonna bring two great families together. And you and me are gonna make a big family, lots of kids. You just worry about how to raise them, okay?" "Babe" apparently does not want to be a baby-maker. She kills him and takes over her father's company instead. Having both of these episodes broadcast during the time that new-parent Nick and Adalind's romance heats up provides a clear counterpoint. Emily does not want to have children; Adalind does. As Ursula Le Guin says, there is more than one road to the city.

"Damn, you're good": Power in Knowledge, Rhetoric, Magic

Shortly after Adalind and baby Kelly come home with Nick from the hospital, she panics. Though she repeatedly tells Nick she does not expect anything from him, at the same time she voices her irrepressible fear that she cannot handle alone the challenges she will face, including the strange possibilities of a what a baby HexenGrimm might be. (She immediately gains a support group—though they are all from Nick's circle.)[15] However, even with her Hexenbiest spirit suppressed, Adalind has a great deal of power. Aside from her legal skills, she has extensive knowledge of arcana. Even more notable is her rhetorical skill, another power that is related to words and crosses the sort of gender barriers discussed by Kristeva and Creed—a skill not surprising in a lawyer. Like Rosalee, Adalind is a Wise Woman associated with books as well as lore, not a mysteriously vague female figure of ineffable force. Finally, in addition to her knowledge and rhetoric, Adalind resumes her magic power as well, when the moment is right for her.

After Adalind suppresses her magic powers and becomes more closely associated with other main characters, we more and more often see her as a Wise Woman. At the end of the fourth season, Nick consults her about spirit possession, which afflicts Sean Renard (4.21). In the fifth season, she helps him understand Fuilcré rituals for a case (5.9). In the sixth season, Renard thinks of her when he needs to ask about ghosts (6.2), and Juliette-Eve asks her about portal magic (6.10). By this point Adalind has access to her own magic again, but her role as Wise Woman (in distinction from that magic) has been made clear. In the finale, it is she who supervises the Force du Sang spell, with her face in woge and her hand atop Nick's and Monroe's—one of many shots that connect hand imagery with power.

Even more impressive is Adalind's rhetorical power. There are times when it alone allows her to succeed. In "Bad Luck," for example, while she is in town with Prince Viktor, she surprises Renard by secretly meeting him to ask him to side with her in her attempt to get Diana back. With a lawyer's care and a mother's emotion, she outlines the reasons for her hopes and fears, and ends by placing her hand on his in appeal. "Damn, you're good," he says, pulling himself back from untempered agreement. His statement combines the two sides of Adalind—the damned and the good—in its own bit of rhetorical play. In fact, on several occasions she uses her rhetorical skill on Renard (e.g., 3.20, 3.21).

Adalind's most memorable rhetorical feat, however, comes when she persuades Nick to help her with her unexpected pregnancy with their child (4.19). It takes place in a lengthy and beautifully blocked scene in the police captain's office, with Renard eerily present the whole time—an observer who initially prevents a violent reaction from Nick and then adds the peculiar level of understanding granted to the only other man who has had a child with Adalind. Adalind starts in a rhetorical hole: she is repeatedly slut-shamed in the episode, by Juliette, Renard, and Nick. She makes clear that she knows exactly who the father is, because she has not slept with anyone since Eric died except for the time she pretended to be Juliette with Nick. She challenges their assumptions about her motivation, saying that she was just trying to get her baby back. She challenges their masculinity, saying that Renard let his daughter go and "it's a room full of heroes." Then she pivots from challenge to persuasion: "Now I need [a hero]." She asks Nick to do it for Juliette, offering to show them how to suppress the Hexenbiest in her. She says that they will use the body of her dead mother. "Your mother killed her, remember?" she adds, layering in his family's complicity.[16] Then she tells the man that the baby is a boy (another likely appeal). Coffee as Adalind in one of her most physically beautiful versions pulls Nick's hand towards her, and Giuntoli as Nick snaps it back; then she firmly pulls it to her belly again, to feel the baby kick: "He's strong, like you." Adalind uses ethical, emotional, logical, and sensory appeals in a powerful display of rhetorical skill that is a turning point for the character's future.

There are many other scenes of Adalind's persuasive rhetoric. There is the postnatal scene when she says, "Don't hate me any more, Nick—for our son's sake" (5.1). She adds confirmation of her thoughtful good will when she tells him she wants to name the baby Kelly, after his mother, who helped raise Diana. (Nick later, in reporting the name to his friends, makes sure they know it was Adalind's idea [5.1].) It is an effectively shot scene, beautifully acted by Coffee and Giuntoli; it ends with one of the *Grimm* long-shots-down-the-hall-into-a-hospital-room, placing the family warmth in the context of the cold corridor of the outer world. Then there is the speech, discussed above, in which Adalind persuades Nick to sleep in the room with her and Kelly. There is her attempt to persuade Rosalee to give her a chance—which works only gradually, most notably after she makes Rosalee laugh at her wry comments (4.20).

Adalind's monologue at her mother's grave is diegetically addressed to her dead mother, expressing a combination of blame, love, and thanks. Its real audience seems to be the viewers who are about to watch one of the protagonists consume a parent's liquefied corpse. Given in the sunshine, with friends standing nearby as she addresses the raised coffin in the cemetery, it is another blend of humor, subtle ethics, and logical justification.

Her repeated fifth- and sixth-season refusal to interact conversationally with Renard is also an assertive rhetorical move. She will speak with him about their child and nothing else. When he asks her to secretly meet him at a coffee shop to discuss the possibility of getting Diana back, he tries to engage her in conversation, but she keeps resisting: "So this is Kelly." "What do you know about Diana?" "You look good." "So do you. Tell me about Diana" (5.14). At the close of the conversation, he says he does not want her to get hurt, and he places his hand on hers, acting the patriarchal protector. But then she places *her* hand atop his, saying, with implicit threat, that she does not want *him* hurt either. She is done with him and sees through patriarchal games. Her upper hand affirms her rhetorical power.

We first see Adalind's power, however, represented through her magic. When she suppresses that magic for the sake of her and her child's survival, it could be seen as a parallel to a real-world woman's suppressing her power to avoid intimidating a man. But the story is more complex; it does not stop there. Adalind's private conversations with Rosalee raise the issue of physiological or biological components to behavior. She tells Rosalee, "You don't understand what it's like being a Hexenbiest—what it does to you or the way it makes you think and feel—it's not good" (5.12).[17] There is an acknowledged physiological impact on psychology. Beyond the chemical treatment of the suppressant, which will wear off, Rosalee suggests, "You are so different now, maybe it [Hexenbiest power] would be different even if it came back" (5.12; see also 5.2). There is also the issue of behavior modification that results through simple kindness of the sort she receives from her new family of friends. Adalind's mixture of changed circumstances and her strong desire for family and love are presented as eventually sufficient. She regains power without turning to darkness.

Adalind regains power while Nick is out of the country, not protecting her. She intervenes when her friend Rosalee is attacked, and without willing it consciously, exerts magical power when she herself is attacked. This is thus not simply a motherhood matter; her magic does not return so she can protect her children. She is certainly happy to use her power for her children later. In fact, her magic makes her a better mother: when Diana magically tries to make her father and mother join romantically, Adalind is the first (presumably through her magical power) of the two to recognize what is happening and to pull out of the embrace; she then teaches Diana not to use magic that way (5.21). But Adalind just as often uses her magic for friends. To help save Juliette/Eve, she woges into her Crone face in front of Diana, saying "it's still me" (6.11). Prepared by the mother she trusts, Diana looks at her abject visage without repulsion. Adalind is then able to open one of her mother's magic books and learn more. But she also offers to magically cross through the mirror to save Juliette/Eve; she is modeling altruism, and Diana watches, silent and wide-eyed. We soon discover she has learned the lesson about the use of magic. The way Diana acts extends her mother's power: Diana opens the mirror on her own (that is another story). But Diana is a disciple, not a tool. For Adalind, power no longer has to be a zero sum game. She has learned to use power without denying it to others; instead, she helps it grow.

Conclusion in Complexity

In the series' first timeline conclusion, the ending that the writers deny, Adalind dies trying to save her children, axed with metaphoric heaviness in the heart, her last words asking Nick to save Kelly and Diana. In the revised world, Adalind lives on to model power and love. Rosalee uses her power for the larger community; Juliette-Eve uses her power as an assertion of self; Adalind uses her power for family and friends. That sentence, though an oversimplification, conveys something of their justifiably different emphases. Through the end, Adalind's character is enjoyably complex. In the penultimate episode, the series returns to the cabin in the woods where much of the magic began. Adalind is in the forest darkness with Nick and Renard, two men of power who once fought against her and now fight alongside her. They speak of the time they kept the magic key from her because of fear and mistrust. Adalind comments, "That was before I had a baby with you—or you," raising her eyebrows in an expression that is a complex melding of bemusement, whimsy, and satisfaction (6.12). In that moment, motherhood does not seem to make Adalind abject; it seems to be part of her power. Abjection itself seems not so troubling, after the long journey. And in the end, Adalind's mother's hat, the witch's hat, has been reclaimed; it sits, comfortably alongside Grimm weapons and potions, in the shiny new trailer full of secrets.

Ten

"I really didn't expect to live this long"
Trubel and the Combative Female

In the third season of *Grimm*, Greenwalt and Kouf added a new character, a young woman named Theresa Rubel, usually called Trubel.[1] At the end of this third season, Nick Burkhardt loses his powers. For the sake of the story, it was necessary to have another Grimm on hand to do his work of hunting those Wesen who are among "the bad ones" (1.1). The showrunners not surprisingly chose to include a younger person. They could easily have picked a male to do the job, but they instead selected a female, effectively played by neophyte actor Jacqueline Toboni. Nick becomes a mentor, almost a parent, to Trubel (pronounced "Trouble"). Although Trubel is not a regular, in her thirty-one episodes she plays a highly significant part in structuring the meaning of the series. Furthermore, in the larger television landscape, she claims significant territory as well. Focusing on the *Battlestar Galactica* character of Starbuck and her disappearance from the finale, Ewan Kirkland applies the concept of the "combative female" as a heroic, aggressive character who suffers what Sara Crosby calls the "snap" (162), being suddenly pulled back from her free expression of strength. Trubel is a combative female who does *not* suffer "the snap"; instead, she grows from a victimized outsider to a strong member of a community who has nonetheless chosen her own path and, at the series' end, helps to save the world by fighting alongside and guiding the man who once guided her.

Resisting Rape

Trubel's first scene is a scene of resisting rape. Patricia Pender reminds us that second-wave feminism focuses on "the fight against sexual violence"

(22), and the show-runners repeatedly face that issue through Trubel's early episodes.[2] For her introduction, she appears in the last four episodes of Season Three (with Nick losing his powers in the season's finale). Trubel's first scene is set on the classic dark, lonely, rain-wet road. We see a very young woman with short, dark hair determinedly walking with her head down, wearing a backpack from which dangles a small chess piece, a black knight in the form of a horse's head. Two men stop their truck, grab her, and drag her into the dark, down a leafy hillside, as she yells "No"; we see her knight fallen into the leaves; we see them *woge* into bestiality; she screams, they attack, and we cut to the credits (3.19). When, the next day, Nick, Hank, and Wu inspect the scene, Wu tells us, "Somebody had a really big knife and a really bad temper"—and we discover that the murder victims are the men, not the unknown young woman. Wu identifies them as having criminal records, including "Assault, B and E,—oh, here we go, rape—more than once." As Laura Mattoon D'Amore says, "the [contemporary] re/visioning of the fairy tale heroine intersects with an acute knowledge of rape culture" (386). It is not until later in the episode that we learn that the young woman was able to resist on her own because she is a Grimm—though she herself does not know what a Grimm is and had been told repeatedly that what she saw was madness.

Nick and Juliette take Trubel into their home in order to help her understand more about Wesen and Grimms, of whom she is one of a rare few (we only see five in the six-season series, and one of these is inactive). But Trubel, who has grown up in the foster care system, is accustomed to fending for herself, and almost immediately inserts herself into one of Nick and Hank's cases. Wesen are involved, and rape is involved again, too. A teenage girl is found dead, exsanguinated, and Trubel purposefully allows herself to be drawn into a shoplifting ring to uncover the Wesen killer (3.20). She pretends to be homeless (as she recently has been), and is brought into the group by a beautiful, well-dressed woman named Donna (whose very name means lady). Donna, however, does not run the shoplifting ring; it is a parodic representation of a patriarchal family, run by Ken, a Wesen of a sort that Nick, Hank, and Trubel discover is called a Lebensauger, a life-sucker. "Ken takes care of us," Donna tells Trubel. He rules over his four female thieves and requires them to acknowledge the power of what he calls "family"; we see them joining hands before a meal to give thanks to the family; we see the women sweeping the floor as Ken tells them what to say to the new girl. The dead girl whom Trubel is replacing came from a group home, where the house-mother tells Nick and Hank that she "was a sweet girl, but she never thought highly of herself. Not a rare thing in girls who have no family." The other girls in the group are terrorized by Ken. Once Trubel is taken in, she is not allowed to leave: "You're part of the family now," Ken tells her. And Ken explains her sexual duty: "New girls spend their first night with me"—a variant of the prima nocta story. Once again, however, Trubel resists the rape. As she battles Ken, she is dismayed to discover that Donna fights on his side. Representing the kind of woman who endorses such patriarchal practices, Donna, too, is revealed as a Lebensauger, a life-sucker. With two of them to battle, Trubel kills Donna; Nick and Hank show up in time for Nick to kill Ken, after Trubel's blows have weakened him.

In her third episode, dining with Nick, Juliette, and their close friends the Wesen couple Monroe and Rosalee, Trubel talks about her first experience seeing a Wesen. Described in Trubel's hesitant words, this event too seems to be attempted rape. Toboni's low-pitched voice, her changing pace, her irregular and naturalistic pauses make the moment intimate. Earlier, as they sit down to the dinner during which Trubel later tells her story, Rosalee compliments Trubel on how she is dealing with knowledge of the few Grimms and many Wesen. Trubel answers, in a very matter-of-fact tone, "Oh—I really didn't expect to live this long." The silent, wide-eyed response of the other four (on camera one by one) puts this comment into sad perspective. Soon Trubel tells of her first Wesen encounter, part of her foster care life. He was a handyman: "He was always really nice to me till—ah—one day he asked me to help him in the garage. And he grabbed me—[I] saw his face change—and he pushed me down on the floor. But I was so scared by what I saw that I just grabbed the first thing I could, which was a screwdriver. And really all I wanted to do was just push him away from me but—" and then she interrupts herself, pulling back from the memory. She reassures them that he did not die. But she adds, "I told everybody what I saw, and that was the first time they locked me up—said I was lying. Then when I said I wasn't, they said I had to be crazy, so…." (3.21). What she describes sounds very like a standard case of the sexual abuse of a young girl—a girl who is told that she is lying or crazy when she reports the abuse. The fantastic difference here, though, is that Trubel can fight back—though we might note that her household weapon is such that a normal girl could possibly use it too.

Trubel's experience with attempted rape may be one reason that she is never shown to have a sexual partner, but—though rape is about power, not sex—she is also not innocent regarding sexuality. In the fifth episode of Season Four, the characters learn that Nick may regain his powers by sleeping with Juliette in the magically transformed shape of Adalind, the witch who took those powers. Trubel is the one who voices a concern that many in the group presumably have: "It's about getting it done." In other words, it's about whether or not Nick can be sexually aroused to have intercourse with the form of a woman who tried to kill him. Later, in Season Five, after

Nick and Adalind have had a child together, Trubel converses with Adalind in a way that shows greater emotional understanding of the situation than the self-deceiving Adalind can contemplate (5.6). When Adalind tries to explain that she and Nick are not sleeping *with* each other, just *next* to each other, Toboni's disbelieving "uh-huh" and direct gaze weight the scene with wry amusement. In short, Trubel is far from inhabiting the Virgin/Whore dichotomy, in spite of having been a threatened innocent in the past. Her resistance to rape includes not being forced into distancing herself from the idea of sexuality. Had the series continued, with Trubel's life progressing, she might have been shown as sexually involved with someone.[3]

Physicality and Food

The combative Trubel, then, has resisted sexual violence in the past and continues to do so as we are getting to know her. She also conveys her strength in her overall physicality, well expressed by the physicality of actor Toboni—her style of walking, her arm movements, her abrupt gestures with the head.[4] Kirkland describes Starbuck as a "tomboy" (87), and that word could describe Trubel as well. He argues that "the tough heroine has become a required presence within science fiction action series" (83), and Trubel fills such a role within this fantasy series. As Greenwalt says, "We needed a really special actress—someone who was physical" ("Something Wesen"). Her signature move is a quick draw of the machete that she often wears in a back sheath (5.22, 6.13). Like Starbuck, she is shown boxing (4.3). During the time Nick is without his powers, she repeatedly saves him (4.3, 4.6), but she also saves him after he regains his powers, perhaps most notably at the end of the fourth season, when his beloved Juliette has become a deadly Hexenbiest whom he refuses to kill, but who is willing to kill him. Trubel, fond though she has become of Juliette, shoots her with a crossbow to save Nick. In a series that was Emmy-nominated for its fight scenes, we also see Trubel in many actively choreographed battle sequences, leaping onto and off cars, landing kicks in the air.[5] Though Nick and Hank at first try to protect her, they soon realize she is more protector than protected (3.21).

Her physicality is not restricted to battle, however; it is also expressed through eating. Susannah B. Mintz and Leah E. Mintz, discussing the widely admired series *Gilmore Girls* (2000–2007), contend that "although food tends to be abundant, characters are rarely shown eating it. […] [W]e see the food they plan to eat or the aftermath of their eating" (236). Though "rarely" seems too strong a term for the textual evidence in *Gilmore Girls*, Mintz and Mintz argue persuasively overall that gendered restrictions are implied. Erin Giannini expands the subject to ask that we consider how often women on any television series are seen actually eating, as opposed to preparing food or talking about food.[6] In contrast, Trubel, from her very first episode, enthusiastically, emphatically stuffs her face, again and again and again. In her second ever scene, we see her holding an almost empty fast-food bag of fries in the air, dropping the last crumbs into her mouth. In her second episode Nick and Juliette, discussing her surprise arrival, think briefly that she has disappeared—only to find that she is in another room feeding herself Chinese delivery food, dipping into the carton with her hand. When Nick and Juliette appear, Trubel says, "Sorry—it's been a while since I ate with other people" (3.20). In the dinner scene mentioned above with Nick, Juliette, Monroe, and Rosalee, Trubel has to be fetched to the table, and she asks, "Sorry, was everybody waiting for me?" (3.21). Many of Trubel's meals show her in the process of becoming civilized, integrated into a group, Enkidu to Nick's Gilgamesh. But even more emphatically, they show her as a physical being who is not self-conscious about weight, conventions, or appearance; she very simply rejoices in having something to eat. When she has food, she consumes it—like a hobbit, but with less delicacy. From one perspective, we could see Trubel's eating habits as childlike, displaying a healthy appetite that has not been restrained by civilization. On the other hand, some viewers might respond in a way that reflects Julia Kristeva's ideas from *Powers of Horror* on devouring orality (39–40). Certainly, one could connect the deadly strength of the Grimm with devouring power. But Trubel's eating is presented again and again with a cheerful tone of wholesomeness, a sense of release, with no guilt attached. Actor Jacqueline Toboni does say that "I think she was a child when she came on, and now she's finding her way" ("A Grimm New World"). But Trubel never outgrows the sheer physical pleasure of eating, and from my perspective, that makes her character the more admirable—the more free. Starbuck enjoys smoking and drinking, but Trubel will go for a lunch of two Italian subs (4.2).[7]

Clothing and Appearance

Trubel's physicality is also connected to her clothing and appearance. She seems more second-wave than third-wave in terms of clothing choices; but as is the case with her eating habits, her clothing choices, at least at first, can be seen as related to a simple need for survival, and the inability to reach much farther. Carla Kungl draws attention to "Starbuck's short hair and muscular body [as] giv[ing] her a notably masculine appearance" (cited in Kirkland 89). Trubel has short hair and a muscular body, though

I am not sure that would prompt me to call her body "masculine."[8] Kirkland also notes the "gray fatigues" of *BSG*'s "utilitarian" battleship, filled with people as desperate for survival as Trubel has been (89). In Trubel's second scene (3.19), the first shot is a close-up of her boot, with a sizable hole in it. The camera then reveals a cheap hotel room with classic noir window shades and bare lightbulb hanging down in the foreground, evoking loneliness. She eats fast food as if starving and looks through the wallet of one of the men who attacked her. She wears jeans, a medium gray cardigan over a light gray top, and blue woolen gloves to hide her fingerprints—no attempt at fashion. She removes the gloves to reveal blood on her hands; she removes the clothes to reveal scars on her back, as she walks towards the dingy shower. The bra that we see from behind is black and lacy—something decorative underneath the utilitarian surface. But in no way is the scene titillating; we are being shown a body that has had difficulty existing in this world, a body of scars covered in clothes of gray.

Later in the episode she steals a new pair of boots from a store. When a young female Wesen tries to steal the boots from Trubel, Trubel fights back and ends up killing her in self-defense. Again, her clothing is about survival, not playfulness or display.[9] In fact, her second episode, during which she goes undercover with the horridly patriarchal shoplifting crew, highlights by contrast. It involves having Trubel dress up in high fashion so that she can fit in at expensive shops. For the only time in the series, she wears a dress in a bright color—orange, no less—high heels in which she wobbles, and make-up applied by the other slave-girls of Ken's household.[10] "A good smile can be your best weapon," Ken tells her, and clearly appearance is a weapon in this context. Toboni puts an unnerving smile on Trubel's face. But Trubel will soon escape Ken with the weapon of her strength, freeing the two other girls, as well; and she will return to her chosen clothing. After she has been with Nick and Juliette a few weeks, Juliette offers to take her shopping "for new clothes, my treat?" Trubel responds, "I don't think that's a good idea. [...] 'cause I don't want to get used to this." Juliette replies, "'K. Let's go shopping anyway." We never learn whether or not that shopping trip took place, but Trubel seems to keep following her own apparel destiny—always wearing muted colors, never wearing sexually provocative designs; she seems to be camouflaging her special nature. She does wear stud earrings and favors a black leather jacket (3.21). And in the fifth season, when she has a real income, she sports a calf-length black coat that echoes those of Spike or Angel (5.11),[11]—attractive and gender-crossing, hinting at power.

One of the most significant elements of Trubel's appearance, however, is her similarity to Nick's family—specifically to Nick's mother Kelly, another Grimm. From the beginning, Trubel seems to reflect Nick in appearance,[12] with her short, dark hair, pale skin, and muscular but not over-developed physique; judging by the two of them, Grimms are typically shaped like well-built, average height humans, not comic-book superheroes.[13] In the last episode of the first season, "Woman in Black," we meet the presumed-dead Kelly for the first time. We view her black-clad legs and coat, her gender obscured; her identity is revealed only in the episode's last seconds. There is a similar scene for Trubel in the penultimate episode of the fourth season, just before Nick's mother is killed. Earlier in the season, Trubel has left Nick and Juliette's home to strike out on her own and help another young person who has just been introduced to the world of Wesen; in the interim Juliette has become a Hexenbiest. Juliette then decides to torch Aunt Marie's trailer. In a shot of the wreckage, we see a figure with black boots, black pants, and a black-gloved hand. Once again, we cannot identify the gender, much less the person, though it looks very like Nick's mom in "Woman in Black." Next we see enemies surveilling Nick's home, and the woman in black, her hood up, appears on Nick's porch, peering inside. "Is that Kelly Burkhardt?" asks one of the spies; but then they say it is "Just some kid." It is, instead, Trubel, whom we see in effect stepping into the clothes and in some ways the role of the mature Grimm, Kelly. Trubel's return is connected to the secret, womb-like trailer, now in ashes, in the destruction that marks transition, death and birth. By the end of the episode Kelly will be dead, and Trubel will be stepping into her shoes in more ways than one.

Open Affection and Emotional Intelligence

Despite her toughness, her combativeness, Trubel expresses her affection openly, particularly beginning with her second season—after she has been accepted into Nick's family, the small integrated community of men and women, Wesen, Kehrseite, and Grimms. In the sixth episode of the fourth season, when Juliette transforms bodily into Adalind, and only regains her own form after several uncertain hours, Trubel hugs her, saying, "I'm really glad you're you" (4.6). And when, in the next episode, Nick finally regains his powers, Trubel hugs Nick. In fact, she hugs Nick more often than anyone else (though Rosalee hugs more people overall). At one point in the fifth season, she wipes tears from her eyes after hugging him and asks, "Why do I always do this with you?" (5.6). She hugs Monroe and Rosalee as well (5.6) and later, the redeemed Adalind (6.13). She weeps for dead friends (Meisner, 5.22; Hank, 6.13). In these ways she is quite different from the combative Starbuck, who tends to hide emotions from others and herself, thus fitting into traditional stereotypes of masculinity and into what some, as Rory Dicker and Alison Piepmeier say, claim are qualities of second-wave feminism (14–15). Trubel, in her open emotions, fits comfortably into a third-wave feminist stance.

She also displays growing emotional intelligence. When she first enters the story, she is so emotionally blind that she attacks the kindly Monroe, with a fury of fists, feet, and blade (3.19). But by the fifth season, she probes Adalind about her feelings for Nick (5.6), and later confirms to Nick that Adalind genuinely loves him (5.20). Of course, her probing of Adalind's emotions comes while Trubel is using a monkey wrench on her motorcycle. Emotional intelligence and auto mechanics: Trubel has no problem stepping over traditional gender lines.

Shared Knowledge

Trubel also displays intelligence in the more standard sense that she learns a great deal in the course of her story and applies her knowledge effectively. Trubel fits into the Terrible Crone's Huntress aspect but also begins the work of the Wise Woman, studying lore and knowledge of the past (and sometimes the present or even the future). Rosalee has her medical tomes; the gender-liminal Monroe is a loremaster as well; even Nick becomes more and more of a scholar. When Trubel first arrives, she is almost feral, but she has her own book of drawings and commentary—the record of the Wesen she has thus far encountered and her journal of responses—the words "I WILL NOT BE BROKEN" writ large among them. When Nick and Hank take her to his trailer full of secrets, his trailer full of Grimm books, she, before entering, thinks this is yet another attempted rape. But when she realizes what he is showing her, she leaps to learn. Thereafter, when we see her not fighting or eating, she is often reading a Grimm book, studying the lore (3.21, 4.1). "I better learn as much as I can," she says (4.1). At first she knows as much as Jon Snow.[14] For example, Nick has to show her, by means of Monroe and Rosalee, that good Wesen exist; he has to explain to her that her condition is inherited (3.20). He is her mentor, in some ways her father. One of the other characters asks, "Are you his daughter?" (Rolek Porter, speaking in 3.21). She herself says to him, "You gave me my life" (4.7). As a good parent, he tries to help her learn.

But gradually she comes to know and learn more on her own. By Season Four, when they are visited by Josh Porter, a Grimm's son who is unable to perceive Wesen, Nick encourages Trubel to teach Josh by taking him to the trailer, a mark of great trust (4.7). By the fifth season, speaking to Nick about the Wesen insurgent group Black Claw, she is giving him information from her own expertise, her separate experience (5.6). Instead of Nick's handing knowledge down to Trubel, the two of them share knowledge with each other. Trubel later confers with Rosalee, Juliette/Eve, Adalind, and Diana as they analyze an ancient cloth that held an artifact that might save or damn the world (6.2). Kirkland points out that "Starbuck is not isolated in the manner whereby active women in films are frequently marked as 'exceptional' [...]. Instead, she is surrounded by other strong and developed female characters" such as President Laura Roslin (85). The same can be said of Trubel. In her intellectual growth, in particular, she is shown to be part of a community.

Community and Individuation

Another important part of Trubel's growth is that we have seen her individuate before joining not one but two communities: both the group of friends centered around Nick and also Hadrian's Wall, the hidden government organization founded to fight the Wesen insurgency. When Trubel arrives in the series, there could hardly be a more solitary character. She is locked alone in her perceptions, wondering if she is mad, knowing no other Grimms, attacked uncomprehendingly by Wesen. In her journal she writes, "How can you hate me so much? Who are you?" (3.19). The black chess knight she carries with her suggests the solitary fighter, the travelling paladin. (Have machete, will travel.)[15] It implies her abilities but also her loneliness. Nick brings her into a community of knowledge and good will (and really good dinners). Her initial loneliness makes it therefore all the more remarkable that she does not cling to her savior or become a mere extension of him. Repeatedly, the 21-year-old Trubel expresses the feeling that she needs to stand on her own. She tells Nick, "You know, I appreciate all you've done for me, but I can't keep living off you guys" (3.22). When Nick loses his powers at the end of Season Three, she stays longer. But when he regains them after Josh Porter, a potential Grimm, shows up needing help (4.7), she decides to return with Josh to Philadelphia to protect him. As Trubel and Josh leave, Nick is inspired to give them his Aunt Marie's car, which had pulled the trailer of Grimm books—a gesture of both continuity and separation, legacy and individuation. With her own car, Trubel is more independent; yet she will ride with the support of the Burkhardts, her distant relatives (though they do not yet know of the relationship). This image of family is crucially different from the patriarchal trap she has experienced with Ken and his female slaves. Trubel returns to Portland when Monroe and Rosalee contact her about Nick's difficulties after Juliette becomes a raging Hexenbiest. By then Hadrian's Wall has contacted Trubel and persuaded her to join them.

Ten—"I really didn't expect to live this long"   201

Trubel has already become fully accepted into Nick's group of friends; she is, for example, one of the half dozen or so who know of Nick and Monroe's trip to the German Schwarzwald to retrieve a treasure that has been sought and fought over for centuries (and a century of episodes— they arrive in the hundredth). Then she chooses to become part of a larger group, HW.[16] In the episode titled "Wesen Nacht" (in which Wesen insurgents break shop windows per Kristallnacht), Trubel explains that HW are "fighting this underground war [against] Wesen. Nobody knows how many there are or how big it is, but it's all over. Not just in this country, it's everywhere—like a revolution. I *had* to help" (5.6). She thus clearly identifies a purpose beyond herself as having guided her choice; her combativeness is no longer just self-protection. She later shows Nick and, eventually, some of the others the HW headquarters, which are utilitarian and spare; they are in an underground bunker of gray metal.[17] Trubel's own room is small and Spartan, a metal cell. In it we see no decorations, but a weapons cabinet with a display that evokes the weapons cabinet of Aunt Marie's trailer. Trubel has, essentially, become a soldier; she deploys when and where she is told. Monroe, Rosalee, Hank, and Wu are dubious about signing away choice, but the transformed Juliette, now reborn as the powerful but emotionally muted Hexenbiest Eve, has joined Trubel along with another generally positive character, Meisner, formerly a Resistance fighter.[18] HW is flawed in ways that many military organizations are flawed; we see Trubel observing and apparently enjoying supernatural torture of enemy fighters (whose mouths, eyes, and ears Eve temporarily magically seals, 5.9, 5.20). Toboni, as Trubel, brings her face up close to the damaged visages of her enemies, with no trace of empathy in her expression, but rather an eager curiosity. (Considering her Wesen-traumatized childhood, it is perhaps not surprising that she frequently seems cold in her dealings with Wesen she does not know personally.) We also see her responding to the death of enemies with a wartime soldier's nonchalance: "I'll update the database," she says cheerfully and repeatedly (5.19, 5.20). Trubel has no problem picking up body parts—a head here (4.22), a hand or two there (5.19)—to make use of in the larger fight.

The moral chiaroscuro of the character appears when she keeps secrets for HW from Nick's group. She knows where Adalind's missing daughter is being held but does not tell the distressed mother; she knows that the seemingly dead Juliette may be alive but does not tell Nick; indeed, Trubel does not let Nick know that she is herself alive and working for HW during weeks when he fears she is dead. The expression on Toboni's face when Adalind speaks to her about her daughter Diana shows Trubel's sympathy, but Trubel exerts the power of her choice in keeping certain knowledge secret (5.6). Her later choice to share knowledge about HW with Nick and others demonstrates her agency. There is both virtue and darkness in her devotion to HW. Her commitment places her in a group that works for a purpose beyond herself and that involves her in a power structure separate from Nick's group.

Trubel and the Larger Purpose

Having established herself as both devoted to and independent from the series' center, Nick,[19] she is able to correct him in the overall narrative's conclusion. An apocalyptically powerful being identified by some as Satan is attempting to enter from another dimension and conquer this world. To do so, he needs the artifact that a magical seven Grimm knights hid during the Crusades, that Nick and Monroe have retrieved from Germany with the advice and aid of others including Trubel. This artifact is capable of healing even to the point of reversing death, and seems to be a small segment of, as Trubel points out, a larger staff, possibly the staff of Moses (or possibly, as Rosalee and Juliette/Eve point out, other magic staffs of other cultures, 6.12). This artifact, appearing to be a humble piece of wood about seven or eight inches long, brings Nick back from death. Everyone bands together to protect Nick's magic stick.[20] Monroe reads a passage from the Grimm books that indicates that the power of blood can defeat an apocalyptic enemy. In order to fight off this Satanic adversary, also known as Zerstorer (the Destroyer), the friends cooperate in a spell that is almost impossible to carry out, because it requires the concurrent donation of blood from a Wesen, a Hexenbiest, and a Grimm.[21] Monroe, Adalind, and Nick join their blood, with Trubel guiding the knife hand that pierces them (the hand of the bastard Royal, Renard), and they successfully create a potion that represents the collaboration of formerly antagonistic groups. Not a few fans were disappointed to find that this concoction, while it damaged Zerstorer, did not stop him; it seemed that cross-cultural unity could not conquer all in the Grimm world.

Instead, characters in the series later explicitly tell us that "power of blood" refers to the power of family. The ghost of Nick's mother Kelly appears to tell him that he can win the fight because of "the strength of your blood, the blood of your Grimm ancestors" (6.13). This suggests a more hierarchical idea of power for the exceptional person, raising an issue of the sort that has troubled some students of other works, such as the Harry Potter series, as well.[22] However, Kelly's next statement works to broaden the application: she says "the strength we need—that we *all* need—comes from our family." She says this in the presence of the ghost of her sister Marie, who began the series and who raised Nick, and Marie notes that Trubel is a member of their family, too.

Trubel herself, however, provides an importantly different element to the finale's equation that balances this emphasis on family. In the final episode, every single adult close to Nick has been killed by Zerstorer, and Zerstorer is about to take Nick and Adalind's son Kelly and Adalind's daughter Diana. Zestorer restores Trubel to life in order to show Nick that he could restore all of Nick's loved ones, if Nick will voluntarily give Zertstorer the sacred artifact. Nick at this point is ready to give it to Zerstorer, but the reborn Trubel argues desperately against it, knowing that Nick would be giving Zerstorer ultimate power over humanity. "No, Nick—you can't give it to this lying sonofabitch devil," she tells him. Nick answers, "I want the people I love to live again," but Trubel tells him, "I understand what you want, but this'll be the end of humanity." In this finale, Nick and Trubel exchange traditional gender positions: Nick is the emotional one, willing to do anything for his family, while Trubel asks him to rationally extrapolate, to consider the larger consequences. Emphasizing the gender role reversal, her attitude is comparable to that of Juliette/Eve, who says in the antepenultimate episode that she sees beyond emotional satisfaction (6.11). Trubel's development as a character, moving from fighting for her own life to fighting for a larger purpose, has prepared her for this moment. Trubel and Nick then physically fight as she tries to prevent Nick from giving in to despair, giving in to the Destroyer.

The ghosts of Kelly and Marie actually come to support *Trubel*'s choice. Rather than telling him to put family above all, they tell him that family will give him the strength to fight for the larger cause—to fight for humanity, as Trubel insists they must. Over the course of the series, we have seen only four active Grimms: Marie, Kelly, Trubel, and Nick—three females, one male—and there is one male who chose not to employ his gifts, the old man Rolek Porter.[23] Now the battle against the Destroyer is fought onscreen by three women and one man. Fighting for all of humanity, Nick, Trubel, and the ghosts of family end up saving their own family among others, as the world resets after the battle. In addition to Nick, only Adalind's magical daughter Diana recalls this final fight, and she is the character who closes the book of the series at the end—a Grimm book in a newly restored trailer full of lore. But those in the audience share this privileged perspective and have seen how Trubel helped save the world.

Conclusion: Not Fade Away

Unlike Starbuck, whose combativeness ends in her disappearance,[24] Trubel is in the series' last scene for all the regular characters, the scene in which Nick expresses his love for them as a family.[25] Though she "really didn't expect to live this long," Trubel's combative, independent nature shows how family—in her case, Nick and all their friends—can help create the kind of separate strength that—no matter the gender—does not have to fall into line, does not have to be subsumed, in order to win the fight. In this fantasy of a redeemed world, a healthy world, we can grow in wisdom and power by embracing Trubel.

Eleven

"You haven't named her yet?"
Diana as Demon Child

Grimm includes many powerful, impressive female characters, yet its potentially most powerful fits into the archetype of the Demon Child.[1] Diana, who is conceived in the second season and born in the third, is the child of a Hexenbiest and a bastard prince who is also the child of a Hexenbiest. Even before birth, she is connected to images of death, and as a child she causes multiple deaths. Karen J. Renner, in *The "Evil Child" in Literature, Film and Popular Culture*, observes that "once the child [...] has committed a crime [...] she cannot be redeemed. Death, not rehabilitation, is the only option, and [...] fictional contrivances [...] allow us to witness the acting out of this belief with an entirely clear conscience" (21). Yet the regular adult characters in this series treat Diana with protective affection, and by the series' end, she is a champion for good. In traditional lore, demons are controlled by calling their true names.[2] The shaping of Diana's identity, like the choosing of her name, happens over time in the series. There are distinct stages to consider: first, conception and gestation; second, the infant; third, the toddler; fourth, the young girl; and last, the young woman. Gothic doubling between Diana and her mother underlines the fact that in this female child character, we see clearly written a theme of the series as a whole: the scary Other can be made evil by our fear of it, or can be made one of us, through determined love in community.

Diana's Conception and Gestation

Diana's conception is curious. As a young woman, Adalind has loved Renard, but after Nick takes Adalind's power, Adalind's mother and Renard kick Adalind out as useless, and Adalind plots revenge. She causes Nick's beloved Juliette to fall into a coma, from which only Renard's kiss can awaken her. But his kiss of Juliette triggers a magical sexual obsession between the two. In place of Juliette, Adalind offers herself, and she and Renard engage in tumultuous sex (2.13). Thus Diana is conceived in a fraught storm of emotions and a physical mix of once-witch, half-Zauberbiest, and Royal (which in this storyworld is physiologically distinguishable)—as Monroe later says, "a big, weird gene pool" (6.2).[3]

If Diana's conception is complicated, her gestation is ominous. It seems for a while to be entwined with the idea of her mother's lack of control—a peculiar horror for the manipulative Adalind. Having returned to Europe, Adalind contacts an ancient Hexenbiest, Frau Pech, who in turn contacts the queen of the Schwarzwald Roma in expectation that Adalind will sell the child. But Adalind declares her intention to trade the child for the return of her powers. (She may or may not plan to follow through on this plan.[4]) The magic required is difficult and deadly. Frau Pech threatens Adalind with death once she learns Adalind's intentions (2.21), and Adalind has no qualms about the Roma queen's murder of Frau Pech or about using her dead body to regain her powers. After participating in a grueling ritual, Adalind at first reluctantly uses the paste made from the body of Frau Pech. Standing before a full-length mirror, she rubs the paste onto her pregnant belly, and we see first the red paste then the shape of a red skull appearing on the skin of her womb (3.2). The mirror evokes the idea of doubling, both with the dead witch who has at one point assumed Adalind's shape, and the child to come.

Weeks later, we see her again stand before the mirror; this time, as she rubs in the paste, an arachnid image forms (3.7). This image is later made part of the series' opening credits for three seasons and thus is repeated in the minds of viewers again and again. As she rubs herself, Adalind slowly says the words "Mama—Mommy—Mother" (3.7). Betsy Dendy, writing on pregnancies in *Grimm*, says of Adalind that after the birth, "suddenly she wants the child" (9), but I would argue that the change in Adalind's attitude is more gradual. Coffee's portrayal of Adalind's facial expression in this arachnid scene evolves from pleasure and possibly affection to a muted horror that suggests alarm at the potential nature of her child. In this scene, it almost seems as though the child may be enthralling Adalind, in the magical sense of the word. Soon thereafter we see Adalind in a coffeeshop attending to some legal paperwork, and she expresses pleasure when her coffee cup moves without a touch; she and the unborn child are sharing magical power. Then the electric lights above explode, and her face expresses alarm at what seems to have been Diana's action without Adalind's intention.

As the pregnancy proceeds, there are echoes of *Rosemary's Baby* (1968). Once again standing before her body-length oval mirror and once again rubbing on Frau Pech paste, Adalind sees the child's feet almost emerge through her skin and shows distress (3.11). Later, as she lies in her satin sheets, the baby's face presses out, skull-shaped, and Adalind cries out and falls to the floor in pain. "Why does it hurt so much?" she asks (3.12). When agents for the royal family come to kidnap her, she and a Resistance fighter sent by Renard fight them off. A bearded agent pushes her belly and shortly after, a pen flies through the air into his eye, killing him. When Meisner, the Resistance fighter, thanks her for her help, Adalind says, "I'm not sure that was me" (3.13). Skulls, spiders, and stabbing: Diana is already deadly.

Diana's Infancy

At the moment of Diana's birth, when Adalind first sees the infant, Adalind regains her power: her face *woges* to that of the witch, with monstrous, Crone-like features (3.14). So Diana's powers feed her mother's; motherhood strengthens and changes Adalind. She affectionately cuddles the child and even asks Meisner (who has helped her give birth) if he has someone to love (3.15). Lest it seem that the series is offering an uncomplicated endorsement of the moral regenerative powers of motherhood, it should be remembered that the other plot of the episode is about a species of Wesen whose mothers demand to eat their child's first-born.[5] The unnamed infant Diana is not arachnid or skull-like, but she does sometimes exhibit glowing purple eyes and unnerving powers, causing Meisner to search for wood for the fire when she is cold (3.15), causing jewelry to float in the air, disturbing the instruments of a plane on which she and Adalind are flying, bending spoons, and cracking glass (3.17).

She is also surrounded by portents. As she is being born, across the world Monroe's father, after a confrontation with particularly fearsome creatures, tells him and Nick, "Your great-grandfather told us kids if [these creatures] ever came back, it meant something really bad was going to come next. [...] Something somewhere was going to happen that would change the world" (3.13). "I think it's coming!" shrieks Adalind, as she goes into labor. When she escapes the pursuing Royals, Nick's mother Kelly helps Diana and Adalind. Kelly tells Nick and Juliette, "This child has an extraordinary destiny. In the wrong hands, it can do great evil. But in the right hands, it can do great good. [...] How she is raised will make all the difference in who she becomes" (3.17). She also says, "the child can't belong to the Resistance or the Royals. She has to have a normal childhood—inasmuch as that's possible" (3.17). Monroe, for his part, refers to her as "the Chosen

One" (3.18). As for Renard's father King Frederick, he asserts, "That child must be raised within these [castle] walls. Otherwise, these walls will one day fall" (3.19).

In the midst of all these portents, the infant Diana is still repeatedly presented as a vulnerable, human child. Kathy Merlock Jackson argues that, in contrast to earlier monster children, by the latter part of the twentieth century, screen children "can be both good and bad, happy and troubled" (174). On the plane with Adalind and Kelly, Diana cries because her ears hurt, and Kelly teaches Adalind how to ease the baby's pain. Juliette and Adalind, even while detesting each other, change the baby's wet clothes after a storm to try to help keep her from getting sick. And Rosalee later reports that she has a "little fever," which is why, in perfectly natural fashion, the baby is crying. "It's not easy being a newborn," says Rosalee (3.18). The child seems particularly pitiable at the moment when we learn that, approximately ten days into her life (Adalind is unsure of the birthdate), she has no name. Juliette, alone with Adalind and the baby, asks, "You haven't named her yet?" and Adalind replies, "There were too many people trying to kill us" (3.17). From the beginning of Diana's life, there is a pull between violence and affection, between possession and protection. This uncertainty is reflected in the lack of name in a culture that usually names at birth.

Adalind finally names Diana in the very hour that her child is taken away. The naming itself expresses the Gothic doubling of the two characters, mother and child.[6] Adalind comes to the police station to testify regarding the death of her own mother, Catherine Schade—the one who had rejected her and who she learns was killed in a fight with Kelly Burkhardt. She tells Renard, "I've thought of a name—Diana. [...]." "Goddess of the hunt and the moon," he agrees (3.18). Thus explained, the name seems appropriate for the child of these two characters, but it is even more appropriate than is said aloud: One of the aspects of the moon-goddess Diana is Hecate, goddess of darkness and witches—a clear reflection of these parents (See Ch. 6). Furthermore, Adalind has chosen an almost perfect palindrome of her own name: the names Adalind and Diana, seeming quite dissimilar, have only one letter's difference. Their lives also reflect but, as is the way of reflection, are opposites as well: Adalind's mother Catherine used her then kicked her out,[7] but Adalind fights fiercely to regain her daughter when she is taken away. In another parallel/contrast, Kelly Burkhardt gave away her son to her sister in order to protect him. It is in the episode when Diana is taken from Adalind that Kelly flashes back to that time and tells Adalind, "Sometimes we have to sacrifice what we love most" (3.18). For a crucial period of her life (about as long as Harry Potter's parents raise him), it is Kelly who ends up secretly caring for Diana, hidden away, so that neither the Resistance nor the Royals can get the child—at least for a while.[8]

Diana as Toddler

In both real and diegetic time, Diana disappears for over a year, and when next she appears, she is a child in late toddler years, seeming about three, and continuing to present both the vulnerabilities of the normal child and the ominous qualities of the demon child. Renner, in *Evil Children in the Popular Imagination*, offers several subtypes, including feral children, possessed children, and gifted children (43), a category into which Diana fits. Renner argues that "the dangerous gifted child is sympathetic only for so long" (56), but I would argue that Diana eventually becomes more sympathetic. One of Diana's unnerving gifts is that she grows very quickly. When, after having Kelly killed, the Santa-Claus-faced King Frederick recovers Diana at the end of the fourth season, he says, inoculating the audience, "Is this really my grand-daughter? I can hardly believe it. Look how much she's grown in such a short time. She truly is special" (4.22). ("Oh, how I have longed to hold this child," he possessively and creepily adds.) Also unnerving are her powers: when the king attempts to build a castle of blocks with her, she knocks it down and then magically floats the blocks into a much more architecturally complex castle, her eyes glowing purple as she plays. Just before the king dies later in the same episode, Diana sees a skeletal reflection of his face in the window of the helicopter from which Meisner flings Frederick to his death. And when Meisner says, "Down with the king!" Diana smiles. The patriarchy has not successfully possessed this powerful little girl. Yet, powerful as she is, she is also shown in vulnerable moments. After Kelly's death, Juliette finds Diana sitting on the floor alone with a stuffed bunny. Later, not realizing that Kelly—the person she has come to know as her mother—is dead, the little girl quietly asks, "Where's my mommy?" (4.21).

During Diana's absence, Adalind has tried every means possible to get her daughter back, and that includes undoing Nick's powers as a Grimm by magically changing into the shape of Juliette and sleeping with him. This unprotected sex results in an unexpected pregnancy, and by the time Adalind sees Diana again, Adalind has another child, this one with Nick, a boy named Kelly for Nick's mother, who died trying to protect Diana. Even in her absence, Diana is frequently mentioned. For instance, in the first episode of the fifth season, Adalind says to Nick (with whom she has become reconciled because of their child), "The last time I was in this room it was with Diana" (5.1). In the third episode, Meisner tells Renard that Diana is "safe [...] with friends," meaning the Resistance (5.3). In the fifth episode, Adalind tells Trubel, "Losing [Diana] is the worst thing that ever happened to me" (5.5). Diana is never forgotten. By the thirteenth episode, Renard secretly tells Adalind that he knows a way to get Diana back, but it involves becoming indebted to Black Claw as they try to violently take over the world. At bloody cost, Black Claw operatives have stolen Diana from her safe house, and now offer her to Renard and Adalind in part to ensure that Renard will have a successful political career, gaining power for Black Claw, who plan eventually to use Diana's powers as well. Renner comments on the negative results that occur when organizations try to use the gifted child (*Evil Children*, 43); Black Claw and even HW (to whom she is "Asset X3," 5.18) operate in contrast to the loving family members who try to help the girl. It is after this interval away from loving care that Diana is most frightening and potentially demonic.

Diana as Young Girl

When Diana reappears, both her parents separately comment on her surprising growth ("Such a big girl now," says Renard, 5.17, and "So grown up!" says Adalind, 5.19). She now appears perhaps eight years old. In episodes airing in early 2016, she is played by Hannah R. Loyd, who was born in December of 2003. The anti–Black Claw organization Hadrian's Wall lists her as 4'4", 53 pounds, blonde, blue-eyed (5.18). But her powers are much more noteworthy than simply her growth. When Diana and Adalind are reunited, their joy is heart-wrenching. The vocal tones, facial expressions, and body language of both the adult and the child actor are intense. But when Diana is told that her mother will not be coming home immediately with her, she shakes the building and, without a touch, strips off a chunk of a metal wall, flinging it through the air to pierce a pillar. "I want her to come *now*," she says to her father, her eyes glowing (5.19). They manage to calm her, but Adalind is left looking slightly horrified, and visions of the *Twilight Zone*'s Billy Mumy character in "It's a Good Life" might haunt some viewers' minds. Later in the same episode, Diana calls to her mother telepathically and then seems to astrally project to the foot of Adalind's bed, saying insistently, "Where are you?" even though Adalind is directly in front of her. The child's power and blind desperation combine in this image, and the young actor effectively conveys the combination. Soon Diana calls out to Adalind again, and we, the audience, see Diana hovering outside the second-story window of Adalind and Nick's home before Adalind sees her. Those moments when the audience sees what the mother cannot are particularly uncanny. "Mommy, I'm waiting for you. I want you to come home now," says Diana, and Adalind grimaces in pain. At the same time Eve, who has become entwined with Adalind because of their having exchanged forms, sees Diana as well. Diana reacts angrily, exclaiming, "You're not my mommy!"—and pointing her finger, in close-up, directly at the screen, at us, the audience. Then Eve's doubling mirror cracks to form Diana's signature skull shape. Within this set of mirrored doubles, Diana seems to be taking charge. When Meisner asks if Eve thinks Diana is "reaching out to Adalind," Eve says, "More like demanding" (5.19).

There are more instances of Diana's power, but perhaps the most important to discuss are the two deaths she causes at this stage. Noticing that her parents do not love each other (Adalind has fallen in love with Nick), Diana twice manipulates them towards each other; each time they eventually realize and resist (5.20, 5.21). But Diana also recognizes something of the attraction between Renard and Rachel Wood, his political publicist, who has become his mistress. When Diana hears Conrad Bonaparte, the head of Black Claw, telling Rachel to become close to Diana (apparently with the idea of making Adalind superfluous), Diana astrally projects to Rachel's home. Standing at the foot of red-headed Rachel's red-sheeted bed, Diana, in her pale nightie with a pink ribbon across the chest, telekinetically strangles the operative with the sheets in which her father slept.[9] The little girl then blithely appears to Adalind, saying, "Mommy—I want to show you something!" We see Diana and a horrified Adalind standing at the foot of the bed where Rachel is suffocated (5.21). Adalind awakes in her own bed, so it is possible for her to consider this a dream; however, she later comes to know it is real. In the next episode, Bonaparte chokes Adalind to force her to tell him where Nick is. When Diana sees the marks on her mother's neck, Adalind tells her she does not have to worry about it, but in the last moments of the episode and the season, Diana guides her father's hand to stab Bonaparte, thus not only protecting her mother but also preventing Bonaparte from killing Nick.

While Diana's powers are frightening, her actions seem to be motivated by love of those that love her, and by a child's sense of justice. Despite her rapid growth, she would be approximately three years old in diegetic time, and we are occasionally reminded of her childlike cognition. When Meisner examines the safe house from which Diana was taken, we see, along with the dead bodies of her guardians, a childish drawing on a cork board above a child's desk—a very large head of a woman, possibly a picture of her absent mother. When, on election night, Renard tells her he may become mayor, she asks, "Is a mayor fun?" (5.20), her language formation indicating her youth. And when Rachel tries to manipulate Diana as the little girl starts to kill her, Diana says, "They're my mommy and daddy—not yours!"—a peculiarly childlike perspective (5.21).

The time spent with her unknown guardians after Kelly Burkhardt's death and before her reconnection with her parents seems to have reduced her connection to humanity. *TV Tropes* links the trope of the "Creepy Child" to that of "Emotionless Girls," and once Diana has reconnected with her parents, we can see her progress from emotionless to more empathetic. One motif can clarify this change: the ritual of putting the child to bed. The first time Renard puts her to bed, he kisses her forehead and says, "I love you"; she looks at him, then at the ceiling. "Good night," he adds, but she says nothing back (5.19). In the next episode, both Adalind and Renard put her to bed, saying "good night" and "I love you"; Diana smiles and looks towards them, though she does not speak (5.20). In the following episode, as they put her to bed, Adalind says, "We love you," and Diana responds aloud for the first time, saying, "Goodnight, Mommy. Goodnight, Daddy," with a smile (5.21). The writers clearly show her parents' care gradually changing the little girl (just as Adalind has changed through the series as well).

Diana is also recuperated through humor, as characters—including her mother—often are. In the early twentieth century, William Sydney Porter, better known as O. Henry, published a highly popular story called "The Ransom of Red Chief," in which a couple of thieves kidnap the ten-year-old child of a wealthy, powerful man only to find that the child is far too rambunctious to handle; the thieves end up paying the father two hundred and fifty dollars to take the child back (199–200). Many stories have been inspired by this one, perhaps most famously *Home Alone* (1990) (Heffley). In the sixth season of *Grimm*, Renard is briefly terrified to learn that one of his enemies has kidnapped Diana. But then he shrugs and eats one of Diana's cookies, realizing that the kidnapper is in more danger than Diana. In his hideout, we see the man woge into a frightening animal face that has absolutely no effect on Diana. When he refuses to send her home even when she points out that she has said, "please," and he follows up with a threatening gesture, she flicks her wrist and sends him scudding across the room. She proceeds to use him as a plaything, bouncing him gaily from wall to wall. We see him desperately calling Renard for help as Diana plays hide and seek with him. Explaining that he just has a few errands to do first, Renard eventually comes to pick her up, lifting his delighted daughter as she greets him and promising that she can have another "play date" with the man whenever she likes (6.7). They leave him sobbing on the floor. It is worth noting that in the original O. Henry story, the young boy is never depicted as malicious; he is highly imaginative and engages in play in a way that makes clear he does not really recognize the consequences. So, too, Diana. This is not the only instance of humor helping to ameliorate the character, but it is the clearest.

Eleven—"You haven't named her yet?"

All of the regular characters, especially Adalind, explain and model caring behavior for Diana. When, for example, Diana meets her half-brother Kelly for the first time, she happily declares, "He *likes* me." She asks to pick him up, and when Adalind says, "I don't know, sweetie," and turns her back for a moment, Diana cleverly attempts a workaround by not touching the baby but levitating him instead. When Adalind turns back to find her baby floating in mid-air, she does not scream or scold, but instead calmly takes Kelly into her arms and gently admonishes Diana (5.20). Diana's comment about Kelly's reaction to her suggests that she may be able to telepathically sense others' emotions; thus she probably knows that her parents actually do love her, a fact which would certainly help give them influence over her. Diana, as mentioned, also attempts to influence them: she uses her bride and groom dolls in sympathetic magic to push her parents together. After they resist and Adalind goes to check on Diana, Diana asks her mother to stay with her in bed. This child has been separated from her mother for far too long, and Adalind agrees with a smile. She takes the occasion to explain to Diana that pushing people together is not wise (5.21), and Diana does not try to work that magic again. When Adalind needs Diana to astrally project herself to give a message to Nick, the mother explains it to the little girl in terms of obligations and kindness: "His [Nick's] mommy helped raise you when you were a little girl, remember?" (5.22). And Diana's delivery of the message displays a child's processing of right and wrong: "Daddy's bad friend made Mommy tell him [...] where you live. She feels bad and she wants me to tell you she's sorry." Adalind, here and elsewhere, reinforces Diana's good behavior, saying, "You did such a good job. You are such a good girl" (5.22). When Kelly and Diana move with Adalind to Nick's place, Adalind teaches fairness, saying they need to take turns being with their daddies (6.4). Adalind is not the only one who addresses morality and behavioral norms with Diana. In a beautifully lit scene, Juliette/Eve (who has fallen ill at Adalind and Nick's place) wakes to find Diana observing her. Diana wants to know whether she is sad that Nick is no longer her boyfriend, and Juliette/Eve admits to some sadness. But asked if she wants him back, she says, still sitting in bed—someone integrated into this girl's home—that things are very different and "That would be wrong" (6.7). As for Renard, while he does allow Diana to make cookies for breakfast, he is repeatedly firm about bedtimes (e.g., 6.12) and the importance of men not hurting mommies (6.4).

One example demonstrates the pattern of emotional and moral modeling particularly well and also shows how Diana becomes a unifier of the community. Juliette/Eve has stepped through a mirror into another world in order to stop a skull-visaged monster who threatens them, and Nick has followed to try to save her. Diana witnesses all of the regular adult characters offer to go in after them (except for the pregnant Rosalee) and so she tries to help. While the adults think she is sleeping, she sneaks to the mirror and manages to open the portal, bringing Nick and Juliette/Eve back: "Mommy! I got Nick back for you," she says. She does not realize she has made it possible for the apocalyptic monster, Zerstorer, to come into this world elsewhere through another mirror. Earlier, Nick has said he had dreamed of Zerstorer; however, Diana has told them it was not a dream but "something that's not real yet" (6.9)—in short, a prophecy. Subsequently, the other adults learn that there is a prophecy that Zerstorer will claim a child-bride—apparently, Diana. We are reminded once again that Diana is a portentous person. But when she senses Zerstorer's pursuit of her, she breaks into tears and wailing. As Nick's partner Hank says, "All of us," all the adults, separately and together promise to protect the little girl who is so powerful in so many ways, yet still a vulnerable child. She witnesses that protection, and it will shape the woman she becomes. Sage Leslie-McCarthy contends that "since the late 1990s the portrayal of children in horror films has undergone a significant shift [...] towards a depiction of children as 'communicators' with the supernatural. [...] [I]n these films the very otherness of the children is a means of bringing about greater unity: families and communities eventually pull together through them" (2). Diana is indeed a communicator with the supernatural, though she does not completely fit the pattern Leslie-McCarthy analyses because she, Diana, is herself notably supernatural. Yet *Grimm* certainly shows the community unifying around her.

Diana as Young Woman

The depiction of Diana as an adult confirms that the regular characters' caring has helped to create a champion from someone who might have been demonic. The penultimate scene of the series, the last one with all the regulars, shows them embracing each other as family, with Zerstorer defeated. But the last character on screen in the series is the once seemingly demonic child who in the end was adopted by "all of us." In the final scene of the series, twenty years later (shades of *Harry Potter*), we see twenty-something Diana and her half-brother Kelly. They are in a futuristic version of the Airstream trailer in which Aunt Marie kept her books, herbs, and weapons. Kelly is writing in one of the large handwritten tomes that contain the Grimm lore, recording the story we have just witnessed and that he knows is true because "my father told me so" (6.13). But he is interrupted by Diana. Both her words and appearance express her confidence.

She is dressed in black skinny pants, a gray t-shirt, and a black and white jacket—colors perhaps symbolic of her mixture of qualities—and her long blonde hair is pulled back in an efficient ponytail that allows a glimpse of small earrings. The outfit is not sexualized, nor is it simply utilitarian. The two characters interact with sibling ease, and Diana notes that Monroe and Rosalee's children will be joining them. Telling Kelly "come on," "hurry up," and "let's go," Diana takes from the iconic Grimm weapons cabinet the staff they took from Zerstorer—and her little brother grabs it from her. But Diana smiles; she hardly needs it. She still exhibits her glowing eyes of power, and she follows him out after telekinetically closing the book in which he has been writing—the important one with the big G on its cover.

As Diana (Nicole Steinwedell) hurries her half-brother in this last scene, she tells him "Mom and Dad are waiting." So Adalind, the biological mother of both and the double of Diana, has moved through the series from deadly enemy to the heart of the fight for good, the center of the community. But the non-biological connections are at least as important. It seems likely that Adalind would be with Nick, and thus Diana is now referring to Nick as Dad—her father, though not by biology. Even the monstrous Zerstorer speaks to Nick of "your children"—both Kelly and Diana (6.13). Of course it is not impossible that "Dad" for both could be Diana's father Renard, who in the end stepped up for the children as well. In either case, one of the on-screen duo is accepting a non-biological parent.

Conclusion: Heroism of the Future

Twenty diegetic years earlier, and a few minutes earlier in this episode, it seemed that the apocalyptic Zerstorer would be defeated by a potion formed by the blood of Wesen, Hexenbiest, and Grimm—a symbol of reaching across divisions in a world with too many. Monroe, Adalind, and Nick—their hands held in place by Trubel and Renard—had bled together to try to save the world. Many fans were disappointed when this potion only slowed down the Satanic Zerstorer. Instead, he is stopped by Nick and three other Grimms—the ghost of his mother Kelly, the ghost of his Aunt Marie, and "Trubel, his third cousin on his mother's side"—and Diana is the only other person who can perceive these ghosts; she does indeed communicate with the spirit world. When the world is changed, she is Nick's witness. As the series directly states, Nick, Kelly, Marie, and Trubel represent the power of family, "the power of blood"; in the last moments, we even learn in that cheerful aside how Trubel is biologically connected. As much of this book argues, family is not the only matter: It seems significant that three out of four of this winning group are women. But it also seems worth noting that the last character on the screen is another woman, and she is not a biological member of Nick's family. Like her "waiting" mother, Diana is ready to fight. The character of Diana thus pulls together many threads of the series, both explicit and implicit. We do not even know the full extent of Diana's power in the world of twenty years hence, but clearly this individual who could have been demonic is now a force for good, operating within a loving community. And it is she who, with a gleam of her glowing, dangerous eyes, closes the book on *Grimm*.

Conclusion
Character and Auteurism

Early in 2021, as I was finishing the revision of this book, the *New York Review of Books* published an article on a renaissance in the study of character in literature. When my partner (the person who watches *Grimm* with me) pointed it out, I was delighted. Recognizing the difference in the study of literary characters and television characters, I nonetheless also recognized the overlap, and was pleased to learn of others who value this path of exploration. As the article's author, Evan Kindley, writes, "after decades of being persona non gratae, literary characters are finally getting scholarly attention again" (12). The assessment of scholarly attitude parallels the observations made in the introduction to this volume: Not enough has been done on the subject. While discussing an array of recent works, Kindley focuses on four books published in 2019–2020. Aaron Kunin asks that we connect to an older view of character and see "the power of character to generalize" (15), the ways they "associate a person with a group" (7), the ways "characters funnel whole societies of beings into shapes" (8). (Kunin also spends the first three pages of his book making a plaintive statement of the value of writing on something you actually care about, a view with which I could hardly agree more.) Marjorie Garber in some ways concurs; she notes that "a soccer mom is a Theophrastan character type" (323), referencing the student of Aristotle whose book of characters provided food for centuries of writers. She most heavily emphasizes, however, that the definition of character is "enigmatic and elusive" (12). The well-known scholar Peter Brooks defines by doing: In his *Balzac's Lives*, most of the chapters are constituted of "biographies" of individual characters who appear in multiple books of *The Human Comedy*, each "biography" adding evaluative commentary. (There is some similarity in the format of this book.) Brooks defends Balzac's sort of character from the charge of simply representing bourgeois ideology, arguing that "[t]he Balzacian character is on the contrary extraordinarily mobile, unfinished, known through actions that are hardly predictable" (8)—qualities that can in some degree be applied to characters in *Grimm*. Brooks also notes that "the television serial is nothing if not Balzacian" (5). Perhaps the most resonance for my work, however, comes in Amanda Anderson, Rita Felski, and Toril Moi's *Character: Three Inquiries in Literary Studies*. As they say in their introduction, "Our essays do not look at character in isolation from other formal, thematic, and social concerns" (1)—certainly a statement that applies to my examinations. And they assert, "Concern with character is a defining aspect of reader or *viewer* engagement with many forms of fiction" (1, emphasis added). Furthermore, as Felski says in the second essay, "the reality that radiates from fictional beings does not depend on the conventions of realism: some of the most vivid exemplars come from fantasy, science fiction, stories for children, Greek and Renaissance tragedy, and tales of divinities" (87)—or superheroes, witches, Wesen.

Another matter of scholarly debate impinges on the analyses of this book: the question of auteurism in television. Many, especially those who focus on cultural studies, emphatically repudiate the possibility of a television auteur. In the Blackwell Companions in Cultural Studies book *A Companion to Television*, the chapter "Television Production: Who Makes American TV?" serves to dismiss the idea of television artists, much less auteurs. Jane M. Shattuc writes that "[o]nce we jettison the belief in the Romanticized artistry of these works, we can get down to the business of mapping the constraints and understanding of [sic] the possibilities of innovation under the commercial imperative of television" (153). Shattuc illustrates her firmness of purpose by repeatedly mistaking television creators' names ("John Chase" rather than David Chase of *The Sopranos* [146], "Josh Whedon" rather than Joss Whedon of *Buffy the Vampire Slayer* [142]). In the more recent *A Portrait of the Author as Fanboy: The Construction of Authorship in Transmedia Franchises*, Anastasia Salter and Mel Stanfill declare that "what we have traditionally believed about the author is borderline mystical" (n.p.)—a tradition that goes back (as Shattuc recognizes) to the nineteenth-century Romantics. Salter and Stanfill add, "If authorship is a construct, the author is especially constructed in film and television, where a single author is inherently specious given the army of workers required to produce such texts" (n.p.). Comparably, Cynthia Chris, in Laurie Ouellette and Jonathan Gray's *Keywords for Media Studies*, says, "If critics and scholars *over*-valorize a few individuals' bodies of work, we may reproduce hierarchies of taste and power, and underestimate the diversity and vastness of any particular medium" (23). Gray himself has referred to authors in the age of online presence as "paratexts in their own right" (136), while suggesting that those such as the creator of *Buffy the Vampire Slayer* may not be dead, but "undead" (113). Farther over on the spectrum, Martha P. Nochimson, in 2019, published *Television Rewired: The Rise of the Auteur Series*, centering on what she calls "the David effect" (7)—the work of David Lynch (*Twin Peaks*), David Chase (*The Sopranos*), David Simon (*The Wire*), their avoidance of the formulaic and embrace of what she sees as modernism. Nochimson contributed to David Lavery's 1995 collection *Full of Secrets*. Lavery devoted most of his career (including over twenty books) to the study of creativity, especially in television; his last book was *Joss Whedon, a Creative Portrait*. A much narrower scope is claimed by Herbert Schwaab in the 2021 essay "Auteurism and Anonymity in Television," wherein Schwaab attempts to give names to many of the contributors to classic sitcoms, noting that "[t]elevision has always been, to a great extent, marked by the anonymity of its personnel" (n.p.).

I remember my indignation when, in the early years of my publishing on television (in the last century), I discovered that bibliography entries for TV shows did not include the writers. Did the shows write themselves? Why were the people behind the scenes not being recognized? They were *writers*, for heaven's sake—and I was an English major (by that point a professor, but always an English major). Nowadays, as readers of this volume presumably know, most documentation styles allow one to insert into the bibliography entry the name of the author and director—and, indeed, others whose contributions are being analyzed. On the first page of my book *Why Buffy Matters*, I wrote that Whedon "does not work alone" (1), and I proceeded to note some of the types of contributors (5–8), nonetheless arguing that Whedon's vision was central. If auteurism in television is taken to mean that only one person is seen as the creator (as for most of literature), then that hardly seems defensible; in fact, it is something of a "straw man" fallacy. Of course, to say that those who focus on television auteurs are disregarding market forces also implies a fallacious dissimilarity—as if novelists never felt market forces.

One of the purposes that I hope this study of television character will serve is to expand the idea of auteurism, to move beyond what has been the definition. I still believe that for a television show to be art, it needs to have a central vision; however, that vision does not have to be the vision of a single eye. Instead, it can come in collaboration. The very fact that showrunners David Greenwalt and Jim Kouf work as a team illustrates (I hope) that possibility. (And what about Gilbert and Sullivan? Or the Beatles? For that matter, David Lynch and Mark Frost?) The fact that Lynn Kouf is a producer and Brenna Kouf a writer gives an even heavier emphasis to collaboration. And, like Herbert Schwaab, I think we should dispel the anonymity for other creative partners. A focus on character can clarify the need for inclusivity. Surely most can recognize the contribution of the artistry of the actor to the television character (as I have tried to do in the preceding pages). And then what of the costumer? And the director of photography? And the production designer who gives the character a setting? The director who blocks the scene with the actor? And, most essentially, the writers who give them words and thus deeds? When rejection of auteurism means rejection of the idea that television can be art, even amidst market forces (as it does for commentators such as Shattuc), it fails to comprehend the many individuals who work not only for a paycheck but to create. As Anderson, Felski, and Moi say, one may question "an informing assumption of humans as fundamentally self-interested or always seeking to maximize their political advantage" (9). It's not all about the money, not all about power. And so what if motives aren't pure? As Monroe says, "Nothing in life is pure. It's not supposed to be" (4.10). I am not in favor of purity tests for art.

That's fortunate, because *Grimm* is certainly not pure. It has flaws and limitations, as I have pointed out, particularly in the introduction but elsewhere as well. Most of the main characters are middle class (not Balzacian there). The narrative symbolism regarding the police and minorities is a heavy weight for characters such as Hank, Wu, and Chavez to push against. The major women characters are all white, with only symbolic minority representation (Wexen, Hexenbiest, Grimm). There are no Latinx regulars. Thus some of the problems noted in the third-wave reassessment of feminism, especially in regard to the failure to consider intersecting problems of class and race/ethnicity, obtain here. But I would still contend that the series is doing good work. Hardly radical, most of the males still stretch traditional patterns of gender and/or sexuality, and the female characters do so more notably. As Garber says, "At a time when 'nonbinary,' 'gender neutral,' and 'trans' are all categories of increasing significance and vitality, the past and present gender-typing of character may seem hopelessly out of step. But we would have to be blinkered to suggest that it has disappeared, or indeed shows many signs of disappearance" (373). And Hank, Wu, Chavez, and others do make a difference as well.

Characters only make a difference when they are real to us. The characters of *Grimm* are vibrant beings in a lively context, not computer-generated figures made by checking off boxes. How did they get that way? I hope the preceding chapters have begun to give an answer to that question. But behind it all is the idea of creation in collaboration—writers, producers, actors, crew. There are power differences, there are money differences, there are differences in motive; but when the collaboration works, it is more than business: It is art. And long-term serial television can give us no artistic creation more indelible, more moving, more important, than its characters.

Appendix
Grimm *Episode List*

Title/Writer/Director/Original Air Date

Season One

1.1 Pilot/story by David Greenwalt, Jim Kouf, and Stephen Carpenter, teleplay by David Greenwalt and Jim Kouf/Marc Buckland/28 Oct. 2011
1.2 Bears Will Be Bears/David Greenwalt and Jim Kouf/Norberto Barba/ 4 Nov. 2011
1.3 Beeware/Cameron Litvack and Thania St. John/Darnell Martin/11 Nov. 2011
1.4 Lonelyhearts/Alan DiFiore and Dan E. Fesman/Michael Waxman/18 Nov. 2011
1.5 Danse Macabre/David Greenwalt and Jim Kouf/David Solomon/8 Dec. 2011
1.6 The Three Bad Wolves/Naren Shankar and Sarah Goldfinger,/Clark Mathis/9 Dec. 2011
1.7 Let Down Your Hair/Sarah Goldfinger and Naren Shankar/Holly Dale/ 16 Dec. 2011
1.8 Game Ogre/Cameron Litvack and Thania St. John/Terrence O'Hara/ 13 Jan. 2012
1.9 Of Mouse and Man/Alan DiFiore and Dan E. Fesman/Omar Madha/ 20 Jan. 2012
1.10 Organ Grinder/Akela Cooper and Spiro Skentzos/Clark Mathis/3 Feb. 2012
1.11 Tarantella/Alan DiFiore and Dan E. Fesman/Peter Werner/10 Feb. 2012
1.12 Last Grimm Standing/story by Cameron Litvack and Thania St. John, teleplay by Naren Shankar and Sarah Goldfinger/Michael Watkins/ 24 Feb. 2012

1.13 Three Coins in a Fuchsbau/David Greenwalt and Jim Kouf/Norberto Barba/2 Mar. 2012
1.14 Plumed Serpent/Alan DiFiore and Dan E. Fesman/Steven DePaul/9 Mar. 2012
1.15 Island of Dreams/Jim Kouf and David Greenwalt/Rob Bailey/30 Mar. 2012
1.16 The Thing with Feathers/Richard Hatem/Darnell Martin/6 Apr. 2012
1.17 Love Sick/Catherine Butterfield/David Solomon/13 Apr. 2012
1.18 Cat and Mouse/Jose Molina/Felix Alcala/20 Apr. 2012
1.19 Leave It to Beavers/Nevin Densham/Holly Dale/27 Apr. 2012
1.20 Happily Ever Aftermath/David Greenwalt and Jim Kouf/Terrence O'Hara/4 May 2012
1.21 Bigfeet/story by Alan DiFiore and Dan E. Fesman, teleplay by Richard Hatem/Omar Madha/11 May 2012
1.22 Woman in Black/David Greenwalt and Jim Kouf/Norberto Barba/18 May 2012

Season Two

2.1 Bad Teeth/Jim Kouf and David Greenwalt/Norberto Barba/13 Aug. 2012
2.2 The Kiss/Jim Kouf and David Greenwalt/Terrence O'Hara/20 Aug. 2012
2.3 Bad Moon Rising/Richard Hatem/David Solomon/27 Aug. 2012
2.4 Quill/David Simkins/David Straiton/3 Sep. 2012
2.5 The Good Shepherd/Dan E. Fesman/Steven DePaul/28 Sep. 2012
2.6 Over My Dead Body/Spiro Skentzos/Rob Bailey/5 Oct. 2012
2.7 The Bottle Imp/Alan DiFiore/Darnell Martin/12 Oct. 2012
2.8 The Other Side/William Bigelow/Eric Laneuville/19 Oct. 2012
2.9 La Llorona/Akela Cooper/Holly Dale/26 Oct. 2012
2.10 The Hour of Death/Sean Calder/Peter Werner/2 Nov. 2012
2.11 To Protect and Serve Man/Dan E. Fesman/Omar Madha/9 Nov. 2012
2.12 Season of the Hexenbiest/story by Jim Kouf, teleplay by Jim Kouf and David Greenwalt/Karen Gaviola/16 Nov. 2012
2.13 Face Off/Jim Kouf and David Greenwalt/Terrence O'Hara/8 Mar. 2013
2.14 Natural Born Wesen/Thomas Ian Griffith and Mary Page Keller/Michael Watkins/15 Mar. 2013
2.15 Mr. Sandman/Alan DiFiore/Norberto Barba/22 Mar. 2013
2.16 Nameless/Akela Cooper/Charles Haid/29 Mar. 2013
2.17 One Angry Fuchsbau/Richard Hatem/Terrence O'Hara/5 Apr. 2013
2.18 Volcanalis/Jim Kouf and David Greenwalt/David Grossman/26 Apr. 2013
2.19 Endangered/Spiro Skentzos/David Straiton/30 Apr. 2013

2.20 Kiss of the Muse/Sean Calder/Tawnia McKiernan/7 May 2013
2.21 The Waking Dead/Jim Kouf and David Greenwalt/Steven DePaul/14 May 2013
2.22 Goodnight, Sweet Grimm/Jim Kouf and David Greenwalt/Norberto Barba, 21 May 2013

Season Three

3.1 The Ungrateful Dead/Jim Kouf and David Greenwalt/Norberto Barba/25 Oct. 2013
3.2 PTZD/Jim Kouf and David Greenwalt/Eric Laneuville/1 Nov. 2013
3.3 A Dish Best Served Cold/Rob Wright/Karen Gaviola/8 Nov. 2013
3.4 One Night Stand/Sean Calder/Steven DePaul/15 Nov. 2013
3.5 El Cucuy/Michael Golamco/John Behring/29 Nov. 2013
3.6 Stories We Tell Our Young/Michael Duggan/Aaron Lipstadt/6 Dec. 2013
3.7 Cold Blooded/Thomas Ian Griffith/Terrence O'Hara/13 Dec. 2013
3.8 Twelve Days of Krampus/Dan E. Fesman/Tawnia McKiernan/13 Dec. 2013
3.9 Red Menace/Alan DiFiore/Allan Kroeker/3 Jan. 2014
3.10 Eyes of the Beholder/Thomas Ian Griffith/Peter Werner/10 Jan. 2014
3.11 The Good Soldier/Rob Wright/Rashaad Ernesto Green/17 Jan. 2014
3.12 The Wild Hunt/Jim Kouf and David Greenwalt/Rob Bailey/24 Jan, 2014
3.13 Revelation/Jim Kouf and David Greenwalt/Terrence O'Hara/28 Feb. 2014
3.14 Mommy Dearest/Brenna Kouf/Norberto Barba/7 Mar. 2014
3.15 Once We Were Gods/Alan DiFiore/Steven DePaul/14 Mar. 2014
3.16 The Show Must Go On/Marc Gaffen and Kyle McVey/Paul A. Kaufman/21 Mar. 2014
3.17 Synchronicity/story by Michael Duggan and Michael Golamco, teleplay by Michael Golamco/David Solomon/4 Apr. 2014
3.18 The Law of Sacrifice/story by Michael Duggan and Michael Golamco, teleplay by Michael Duggan/Terrence O'Hara/11 Apr. 2014
3.19 Nobody Knows the Trubel I've Seen/Jim Kouf and David Greenwalt/Norberto Barba/25 Apr. 2014
3.20 My Fair Wesen/story by Thomas Ian Griffith and Rob Wright, teleplay by Sean Calder/Clark Mathis/2 May 2014
3.21 The Inheritance/Dan E. Fesman/Eric Laneuville/9 May 2014
3.22 Blond Ambition/Jim Kouf and David Greenwalt/Norberto Barba, 16 May 2014

Season Four

- 4.1 Thanks for the Memories/David Greenwalt and Jim Kouf/Norberto Barba/24 Oct. 2014
- 4.2 Octopus Head/David Greenwalt and Jim Kouf/Terrence O'Hara/31 Oct. 2014
- 4.3 The Last Fight/Thomas Ian Griffith/Paul Kaufman/7 Nov. 2014
- 4.4 Dyin' on a Prayer/Sean Calder/Tawnia McKiernan/14 Nov. 2014
- 4.5 Cry Luison/Michael Golamco/Eric Laneuville/21 Nov. 2014
- 4.6 Highway of Tears/Alan DiFiore/John Behring/28 Nov. 2014
- 4.7 The Grimm Who Stole Christmas/Dan E. Fesman/John Gray/ 5 Dec. 2014
- 4.8 Chupacabra/Brenna Kouf/Aaron Lipstadt/12 Dec. 2014
- 4.9 Wesenrein/Thomas Ian Griffith/Hanelle Culpepper/16 Jan. 2015
- 4.10 Tribunal/David Greenwalt and Jim Kouf/Peter Werner/23 Jan. 2015
- 4.11 Death Do Us Part/Jeff Miller/Constantine Makris/30 Jan. 2015
- 4.12 Maréchaussée/David Greenwalt and Jim Kouf/Eric Laneuville/6 Feb. 2015
- 4.13 Trial by Fire/Sean Calder/Norberto Barba/13 Feb. 2015
- 4.14 Bad Luck/Thomas Ian Griffith/Terrence O'Hara/20 Mar. 2015
- 4.15 Double Date/Brenna Kouf/Karen Gaviola/27 Mar. 2015
- 4.16 Heartbreaker/Dan E. Fesman/Rob Bailey/3 Apr. 2015
- 4.17 Hibernaculum/Michael Golamco/John Behring/10 Apr. 2015
- 4.18 Mishipeshu/Alan DiFiore/Omar Madha/17 Apr. 2015
- 4.19 Iron Hans/David Greenwalt and Jim Kouf/Sebastián Silva/24 Apr. 2015
- 4.20 You Don't Know Jack/Sean Calder and Michael Golamco/Terrence O'Hara/1 May 2015
- 4.21 Headache/David Greenwalt and Jim Kouf/Jim Kouf/8 May 2015
- 4.22 Cry Havoc/Thomas Ian Griffith/Norberto Barba/15 May 2015

Season Five

- 5.1 The Grimm Identity/David Greenwalt and Jim Kouf/Eric Laneuville/30 Oct. 2015
- 5.2 Clear and Wesen Danger/Thomas Ian Griffith/Norberto Barba/6 Nov. 2015
- 5.3 Lost Boys/Sean Calder/Aaron Lipstadt/13 Nov. 2015
- 5.4 Maiden Quest/Brenna Kouf/Hanelle Culpepper/30 Nov. 2015
- 5.5 Rat King/Jeff Miller/David Solomon/4 Dec. 2015
- 5.6 Wesen Nacht/David Greenwalt and Jim Kouf/Darnell Martin/11 Dec. 2015

5.7   Eve of Destruction/Thomas Ian Griffith/John Behring/29 Jan. 2016
5.8   A Reptile Dysfunction/Michael Golamco/David Straiton/5 Feb. 2016
5.9   Star-Crossed/Sean Calder/Carlos Avila/12 Feb. 2016
5.10 Map of the Seven Knights/Jim Kouf/Aaron Lipstadt/19 Feb. 2016
5.11 Key Move/Thomas Ian Griffith/Eric Laneuville/4 Mar. 2016
5.12 Into the Schwarzwald/David Greenwalt and Jim Kouf/Norberto Barba/ 11 Mar. 2016
5.13 Silence of the Slams/Brenna Kouf/David Straiton/18 Mar. 2016
5.14 Lycanthropia/Jeff Miller/Lee Rose/25 Mar. 2016
5.15 Skin Deep/Michael Golamco/Karen Gaviola/1 Apr. 2016
5.16 The Believer/Jim Kouf and David Greenwalt/John Behring/8 Apr. 2016
5.17 Inugami/Kyle McVey/Sharat Raju/15 Apr. 2016
5.18 Good to the Bone/Martin Weiss/Peter Werner/22 Apr. 2016
5.19 The Taming of the Wu/Brenna Kouf/Terrence O'Hara/29 Apr. 2016
5.20 Bad Night/Sean Calder/Norberto Barba/13 May 2016
5.21 Beginning of the End Part One/David Greenwalt and Jim Kouf/David Greenwalt/20 May 2016
5.22 Beginning of the End Part Two/Thomas Ian Griffith/Norberto Barba/ 20 May 2016

Season Six

6.1   Fugitive/David Greenwalt and Jim Kouf/Aaron Lipstadt/6 Jan. 2017
6.2   Trust Me Knot/David Greenwalt and Jim Kouf/John Gray/13 Jan. 2017
6.3   Oh Captain, My Captain/Thomas Ian Griffith/David Giuntoli/ 20 Jan. 2017
6.4   El Cuegle/Brenna Kouf/Carlos Avila/27 Jan. 2017
6.5   The Seven Year Itch/Jeff Miller/Lee Rose/3 Feb. 2017
6.6   Breakfast in Bed/Kyle McVey/Julie Herlocker/10 Feb. 2017
6.7   Blind Love/Sean Calder/Aaron Lipstadt/17 Feb. 2017
6.8   The Son Also Rises/Todd Milliner and Nick Peet/Peter Werner/ 24 Feb. 2017
6.9   Tree People/Brenna Kouf/Jim Kouf/3 Mar. 2017
6.10 Blood Magic/Thomas Ian Griffith/Janice Cooke/10 Mar. 2017
6.11 Where the Wild Things Were/Brenna Kouf/Terrence O'Hara/ 17 Mar. 2017
6.12 Zerstörer Shrugged/story by David Greenwalt and Jim Kouf; teleplay by Brenna Kouf/Aaron Lipstadt/24 Mar. 2017
6.13 The End/David Greenwalt and Jim Kouf/David Greenwalt/31 Mar. 2017

Chapter Notes

Introduction

1. In sequence, the examples in this paragraph come from 1.19; 6.7; 2.8; 6.7; 4.15; 1.17; 5.19; 4.21; and, for the last example, 2.19 and *passim*. "Neander-Wu" is the term commonly used for Wu's transformed state. There is an appendix giving episode title, writer, director, and date, so episodes are identified by number (e.g., 4.2 for fourth season, second episode). Parts of this introduction were presented at the Popular Culture/American Culture in the South Conference, 12–16 October 2016, Nashville, Tennessee.

2. Newcomb generally focuses on various "character types" (245) as they operate within various formulas, but he does, even in 1974, identify character development through certain series such as the long-running Western *Gunsmoke* (73–74), the mystery *Ironside* (105, 248), and the comedy *All in the Family* (251). However, he identified a general lack of "continuity" of character "memory" as a problem in television up to the seventies (253).

3. Thanks to Tanya Cochran for recommending the work of Murray Smith and to Heather Porter for reminding me of the importance of Ien Ang.

4. As of this writing, a scholarly collection of essays on *Grimm* is forthcoming from McFarland. There have been few other scholarly analyses of the series, such as the articles by Nancy Taber, Angela Tenga, and Rachael Johnstone; the essays by Kristiana Willsey, Claudia Schwabe, Alissa Burger and Stephanie Mix, Matthew Lerberg, and Amanda Boyd.

5. Stephen Carpenter is also listed as a co-creator, someone who initiated the series concept, but he did not participate as a showrunner or writer, except that he is listed for the story, but not the teleplay, for the pilot.

6. David Bordwell (quoted in E. Bennett 13) says that "Hollywood movies are usually strategically ambiguous about politics," but whether the 86 hours that constitute *Grimm* (or similar lengths for other television series) are constructed with such strategy is another question. In any case, this book will focus mainly on the text.

7. Nick's son Kelly, child of Adalind and Nick, is allowed to enter when older, but he is an infant during the course of the series and therefore not analyzed as an important character. In the last scene, twenty years after the series' main events, he is in the trailer with Diana, child of Adalind Schade and Sean Renard and in effect adoptive child of Nick (see Ch. 11). Sean Renard's entry into the trailer is not by invitation. Adalind, who attempted to kill the trailer's first owner Marie in the pilot at the behest of Renard, is the one major character never seen in the trailer.

8. Tenga says that *Grimm* lore "flirts dangerously with notions of anthropological criminality," though she asserts that the series as a whole is ambivalent in terms of such stereotyping (38–39).

9. The British Union of Fascists, led by Sir Oswald Mosley, wore black shirts, though brown shirts are more widely associated with Nazis.

10. Monroe has earlier established the parallel between Wesen and closeted gays in reference to "coming out" (2.4), among other comments.

11. In terms of gender representation, it is worth noting that showrunner Jim Kouf's

professionally experienced wife Lynn Kouf is a co-executive producer for the series, and their daughter Brenna Kouf is a writer for ten of its episodes.

12. On the lack of representation of older women in recent fantasy/science fiction television, see, e.g., Eve Bennett 81.

13. On the increasing complexity of witch characters, see, e.g., Burger and Mix.

14. See, e.g., the Lacey and Knox edited special issue on television acting for *Critical Studies in Television*. Cf. Rawlins and Tait.

15. Huizinga applied the term *play* to all forms of drama on the stage (144), but I would posit that some dramas, including some television series, are more playful than others.

16. Contrast Pearson's statement that "characters can be judged good or great partly by how well they fit the needs of the story worlds they inhabit" ("Chain," 157).

Chapter One

1. An earlier version of this paper was presented at the Popular Culture/American Culture Association conference in San Diego, California, 11–15 April 2017.

2. Lynnette Porter argues more generally that 21st-century sidekicks are becoming "more powerful, if still secondary" (*Tarnished* 84).

3. Many scholars have written on the concept of liminality, perhaps most notably Victor Turner.

4. Joseph Campbell famously traced the hero's journey (or monomyth) through many cultures.

5. See Ch. 5 on Nick's hearing.

6. Whether intentional or not, the design of blue front and red brick side recalls Monroe's cool surface in opposition to the inner nature that shows when his eyes turn red. The pilot's production designer was Paul Eads.

7. See discussions about ethnicity/race in the introduction and Chapters Two–Four, Six.

8. On werewolves/wolves in *Grimm* and DC comics, see also Lerberg, focusing on Monroe mainly in the pilot.

9. While Nick cannot stop becoming a Grimm, he does make identity choices in terms of what a Grimm may be; see Ch. 5.

10. On the idea of choice and existential character development, see Richardson and Rabb and Koontz.

11. Series for which Thania St. John has written include *Lois and Clark* (1993–1997), *Buffy the Vampire Slayer* (1997–2003), *Roswell* (1999–2002), and *Eureka* (2006–2012).

12. Barney Fife was the humorous sidekick of the straight man lead of *The Andy Griffith Show* (1960–1968). This would be in one of Barney's expansive, as opposed to his anxious, moments.

13. Juliette knows of its existence, but she does not know of its significance while she is unaware of the Wesen world.

14. Tenga sees Wesen as immigrants/Othered.

15. On language, particularly changing function of speech, in *Buffy the Vampire Slayer*, see Adams and Wilcox, "'There Will Never.'"

16. For an analysis of Angelina emphasizing her female gendering, see Johnstone 54–56.

17. The cleaning up of the blood is made a trope in *Grimm*. Few television episodes show characters cleaning blood that has been spilled, but *Grimm* does so repeatedly—a seeming recognition of consequences. See Ch. 5.

18. A rare case of a hero who very successfully fits these characteristics is the Steven Moffatt- and Mark Gatiss-written version of Sherlock Holmes as performed by Benedict Cumberbatch. See, for example, Lynnette Porter's *Who Is Sherlock?* and Porter and Jennifer Wojton's *Sherlock and Digital Fandom*.

Chapter Two

1. An earlier version of this essay was presented at the Popular Culture/American Culture Association in the South conference, Wilmington, NC, 26–28 September 2019.

2. Thanks to Ananya Mukherjea for calling this to my attention. The 2010 Census also reports that Portland had an Asian American population of only 8.1 percent; Reggie Lee as Sergeant Drew Wu is the other person of color in the original six-member cast. Much more could be written on the use of Portland as the setting for the series.

3. See also the introduction; for

implications relating to particular characters, see especially chapters on Sergeant Wu, Captain Renard, and the Crones of Portland.

4. The Hummel figurines (shown in close-up) and needlepoint pillows stitched by the yellow-sweatered killer remind us that sentimentality need not be separate from violence, and of course they remind us of the age-old theme of appearance versus reality. They appear repeatedly in the series, e.g., 2.13, 6.12.

5. Thanks to Stephanie Graves for recommending Ratcliffe's work. For a historical tracing of "the social construction of race" (278), see Cheryl L. Harris's foundational article "Whiteness as Property."

6. In addition to "La Llorona" 2.9, see, for example, "The Good Soldier" 3.11, "El Cucuy" 3.5, "Chupacabra" 4.8, and "El Cuegle" 6.4, all of which have important and sympathetic Latinx characters. The latter three also also have creatures drawn from Latinx myths; interestingly, these characters have strongly sympathetic qualities as well as monstrous ones. "The Good Soldier" features a Latina "good soldier" who fights to correct the record after she endures a sexual assault that occurred on 11/11, Veteran's Day (though the holiday is never named). On Chavez, see Ch. 6.

7. Kenya Evelyn's article largely focuses on reporting on a study by the non-profit group Color of Change covering 26 crime genre series, broadcast 2017–2018 (just after *Grimm* ceased broadcasting). Color of Change noted that of 350 episodes, only six episodes discussed "possible solutions and reforms." Thanks to Ananya Mukherjea for recommending Evelyn's article.

8. The series raises questions in other and earlier places. See Ch. 4 on the confrontation between Nick and Renard after Nick extralegally kills someone who is *not* Wesen (3.3).

9. In fact, he sometimes expresses a wistful desire for their power (e.g., 3.2).

10. See, e.g., 1.9, 2.3, 2.14, 3.7, 5.6, 5.13, 5.17.

11. Nick says to Hank, "*I* am getting married once, not four times," thus leaving it ambiguous whether or not Hank might be married a fourth time in the future or has already been married four times.

12. See, e.g., 1.2, 1.10, 1.13, etc.

13. This is the third episode in a row in which male regulars are shown shirtless.

Former football player Hornsby is one of three male regulars who are repeatedly shown shirtless in the series, the other two being Roiz and Giuntoli—the other two who portray a relationship with Adalind. Though the spectacular physique of Roiz is most frequently on display, Hornsby is included in this presentation of male bodies to be gazed at.

14. In a Hank-centric episode, Hank's introduction to the world of Wesen comes because of his and Nick's interaction with one of Hank's old high school football buddies, whose child is Hank's goddaughter—both of whom are discovered to be Wesen. Thus Hank's introduction to the Wesen world comes about partly because of connections in his own life, not strictly through Nick—a way that Hank's character is strengthened through backstory.

15. For a noteworthy discussion of mass incarceration, see Michelle Alexander's *The New Jim Crow: Mass Incarceration in the Age of Colorblindness*.

16. According to the NAACP, in the U.S., "African Americans are incarcerated at more than 5 times the rate of whites." And according to Richard Delgado and Jean Stefancic, "the number of young black men in prison or jail is larger than the number attending college" (120).

17. Abdurraqib is speaking in a context of love between men but seems to allow for more than one kind of tenderness.

18. See Crenshaw, "Demarginalizing," on intersectionality.

19. *Pace* Murray Smith, I think the term "identify" conveys the meaning for the possibly momentary but very interesting effect for some viewers here. See Smith, Introduction, especially 1–3.

20. Had the series continued, the recurring character of Deputy Farris (Toni Trucks) might have been another love interest for Hank. The actors' visual exchanges and body language suggest a connection. Furthermore, in the Hank-centric episode "Mishipishu," which focuses on racism against Native Americans, the two characters engage in a ritual for which she is given a memento of the victim's mother and he, of the victim's father. With the series' cancellation, there was not the chance to develop a more positive romance for Hank. However, see also Chapter Three on Sgt. Wu and "Blind Love" (6.7) and its treatment of regular cast members played by persons of color.

21. The speech is from *Henry IV, Part I*, Act 1, Scene 3, ll. 28–34.

22. As of the 2016–2017 season (when *Grimm* ended), minorities constituted 21.5% of the leads in broadcast scripted drama (Hunt et al. 15). Thanks to Shauntae White and Kandace L. Harris for recommending the Hollywood Diversity Report.

Chapter Three

1. At a 2016 DragonCon panel, Lee added, "The head casting director for NBC said, 'We'll approve it if you name him after me,' and her name is Grace Wu" ("Grimm: Lowen"). Lee thus made sure to put on the record the fact that having an Asian American woman executive helped bring about the creation of an added role specifically for an Asian American character.

2. On racially troubling narrative symbolism in the series, see the introduction.

3. Zukimoto, declaring herself a fan of the series, noted of the cast that for the 2019 EWP awards, "they're all here." Lee stated, "they promote diversity and inclusion." These cast members are not producers, but the situation suggests a progressive atmosphere for the series.

4. See Laura Lammasniemi on the connection of the image of the innocent white female with early anti-trafficking movements. See also Susan Faludi on "the specter of the white maiden taken against her will" (212).

5. These characteristics are a combination of narrative, costume, casting, and more.

6. Over half a dozen appearances are made by African American Brenda Braxton, who plays herself, a veteran Portland NBC affiliate (KGW) reporter. See, e.g., 5.6.

7. Bogaert references the seminal 1954 work of Gordon Allport. Many have applied his work; in 2005 communications scholars Edward Schiappa, Peter B. Gregg, and Dean E. Hewes offered "The Parasocial Contact Hypothesis" specifically regarding television.

8. Kristopher Karl Woofter notes the contrast between Hank's desire for sex and Wu's for food (a more ambiguous desire).

9. The lower-class teens are also arrested, for self-confessed breaking and entering. On mass incarceration, see Ch. 2.

10. *Grimm* keeps returning to the Black Forest—as they frequently call it, the Schwarzwald.

11. Eve, though cisgendered, is less clear-cut sexually.

12. However, Asian females are often stereotyped as hypersexual (Mukherjea 70, Shimizu 2), in part in connection with historical legal immigration exclusions such as the Page Act of 1875.

13. The 1978 book title was spelled *Mommie Dearest*.

14. I am applying Philip Smith's comments on the Chinese American protagonist of Gene Luen Yang and Sonny Liew's comic *Shadow Hero*. Wu's powers at this point are not super.

15. On Wesen as reflecting the immigrant experience, see Tenga.

16. Thanks to Kristopher Karl Woofter for suggesting this possible reading.

17. Sam is one of a number of Wesen characters shown as resisting a negative history of behavior; cf. Hank's Coyotl friends (2.3) and most notably, Monroe.

18. The server is played by Tierra Valentine, perhaps the only actor ever to perform three separate roles in the series, starting with the pilot. In the final season, the producers brought back several players who had earlier been part of the series.

19. One of the quotes is inaccurate; for "the course of true love never did run true," the last word should have been "smooth" (*A Midsummer Night's Dream*, 1.1.134). One imagines that re-takes were few on the ground in the thirteen-episode last season.

20. I am revising this chapter weeks after the Atlanta spa killings of March 2021.

21. Lee stated that he was working on something with the Aswang episode's writer (Brenna Kouf) and the creator of *Grimm* (perhaps Jim Kouf).

Chapter Four

1. For a brief history of views on the Gothic and gender, see Brabon and Genz.

2. The gray gradually disappears.

3. The designer in charge was Steven Wolff.

4. For contemporary viewers, the names might evoke Donald Trump and Ted Cruz.

5. Rachel will receive her punishment when Diana kills her; see Ch. 11.

6. He gives another, more mysterious

ring as well, which looks like a wedding ring—for lost love?

7. On the failure of male protectiveness, see Ch. 5.

Chapter Five

1. In "Race, Reform, and Retrenchment," especially 1370, Crenshaw focuses on legitimation in terms of the status quo of race relations. My reaction did not focus specifically on race at that point of my viewing, but to the status quo in general, incorporating attitudes towards race/ethnicity, gender, age, class, aesthetics, and more.

2. On the significance of the ring, see Ch. 7 and 9.

3. There are two exceptions not chosen by Nick: on one occasion, during a physical fight, an enemy briefly goes in and out of the space (2.5); on another occasion, Captain Sean Renard sneaks in (2.12–2.13).

4. Cf. Claudia Schwabe on "one world fairy tale" and "third reality" (295–300).

5. The crash is fatal for his father and a family friend.

6. In only one episode is a boy Nick performed (3.17).

7. See Michael J. Diamond on self-definition by sexual potency (26).

8. On *Hamlet* allusions, see Ch. 4.

9. Because of a rare shoot-out (1.10), numbers are inexact.

10. Both Hank and Nick shoot at Soledad Marquesa, but Hank's shot appears to be the one that kills (1.13). If Marquesa is included, Nick's tally for Season One would be five.

11. The closest he comes is when threatened by Black Claw. The audience hears one of a Black Claw duo say, "He's mine"; soon, Nick kills both, saying, "Sorry—I'm in a hurry" (5.20). Nick's comment implies that there could have been other options, though later he tells Hank he had no choice (5.21). This killing happens shortly after Nick's son is taken and may therefore be, in part, deflected anger—a problematic kill even in Nick's context.

12. The episode is full of *The Hound of the Baskerville* references.

13. The only exception is a vague comparison in a comment by Kelly telling Nick he is "so like your father" (2.2).

14. See Ch. 1 regarding Nick's question "How do I stop it?"

15. See Linda Williams on "nick of time" versus "too late" scenarios in melodrama (69).

16. Peter Brooks' *The Melodramatic Imagination* opens with "This is a book about excess" (xiii).

17. Since Adalind has also shared blood-cookies with Hank and Wu, most of the regulars are in a blood-magic family.

18. See Ch. 2 of Bergson's *Laughter*.

19. Silas Weir Mitchell and Bree Turner comment on the effectiveness of Giuntoli's direction of this scene in a sixth-season DVD extra ("Directing").

20. This question in effect raises Crenshaw's concern about the dangers of legitimation ("Race, Reform").

Chapter Six

1. An earlier version of this paper was presented at the Popular Culture/American Culture in the South conference, New Orleans, 2–4 October 2014.

2. On Julia Kristeva, Barbara Creed, and Walker, see Ch. 9.

3. Hutton also mentions "environmentalism" and "humanitarianism," two elements not notably connected to *Grimm* Witches/Crones.

4. Except for the three characters noted below as stereotypical (Frau Pech, Stefania Vaduva Popescu, and Pilar) the characters in this chapter fit in the category of the Complete Female Character (as distinguished from the strong female character) as defined by Heather M. Porter. The defining characteristics are that the character (1) has a name and communicates, (2) has a backstory, (3) has traits and skills (4), has agency, (5) is flawed, and (6) has emotional resonance for the audience (26–27). Even the stereotypical characters discussed in this chapter have all but the last characteristic.

5. The name's gender ambiguity is also useful later when Nick and Adalind name their son Kelly.

6. In a careful examination of the characters, Burger and Mix argue that Juliette and (a little less successfully, in their view) Adalind "transcend a good/evil dichotomy"—the simplifying good witch/bad witch categorization (24).

7. I use the term *abjection* both in the sense defined by Julia Kristeva, referring to

bodily materials outside the body and thus in the wrong place, as *other* (see Ch. 9) and also in the traditional sense of being in a low or despised condition.

8. Walker connects the name Eve to Goddess worship (68).

9. Jakob Grimm also argued that in German culture (endemic to *Grimm*), females had more magic power than males (Hutton 72).

10. Her grandfather is the king of the House of Kronenberg of Austria, one of the Royal Seven Houses that know of the existence of Wesen and have operated shadow governments around the world for centuries.

11. Eve Bennett notes the focus on mother-child relationships as a rarity in such a context (189).

12. The use of mirrors in *Grimm* deserves further discussion, especially regarding Witches.

13. Starting with episode 4.4, there is another woman medical examiner, M.E. Bindra (Dana Millican), who appears in five episodes. The replacement is not explained diegetically or otherwise.

14. The Black Claw storyline was introduced in the fifth season, leading to the re-appearance of Zuri Ellis (see Ch. 2) rather than Farris in a relationship with Hank.

15. See, e.g., Hughey.

16. Newman won for Best Live Action Short Film for producing 2018's *Skin*.

Chapter Seven

1. An earlier version of this essay was presented at the eighth biennial *Slayage* Conference on the Whedonverses, University of North Alabama, 21–24 June 2018.

2. Greenwalt kept the title of consulting producer and directed the series' antepenultimate episode.

3. "Has she been smoking that hat again?" asks Hank (5.17).

4. *Angel*'s Eve gives up immortality for the sake of her lover and loses her place as liaison to the Senior Partners.

5. On Spike, see Ch. 1.

6. See Elisabeth Bronfen's *Over Her Dead Body* on the tradition of women sacrificed to give order to the world, especially 27–35.

7. Illyria has plotted her resurgence millions of years ago; like Fred in Pylea, she must escape from a cavern (the Deeper Well) to become free.

8. See Burger and Mix on issues of "ability and responsibility" shared by the Slayer and the Grimm (20).

9. Juliette states that she worked her way through veterinary school (1.17).

10. Another memorable moment of humor, mentioned in this book's first paragraph, comes after Juliette has become a Hexenbiest. Juliette forces Nick to turn his gun on Monroe and we hear the shot ring out as the episode ends. Only in the next episode do we see that Monroe has been saved—and Juliette releases an uncaring, playful "Whoop!" It comes at the same time the audience feels the release of tension, knowing Monroe is safe, so viewers can (if so minded) laugh in shared release (4.21). It also expresses some of Juliette's very real pleasure in her newfound, deadly power. It is a moment of jouissance.

11. When Nick opens the doors for her in the first season finale, she refuses to believe in the Wesen world, resisting entry.

12. Matthew Lerberg, focusing on the pilot, discusses the series' emphasis on story versus reality, e.g., the Big Bad Wolf versus Monroe.

13. Learning Nick and Juliette are unmarried, Trubel tells Juliette it is smart to be able to leave at will—a remark Juliette finds amusing (3.20).

14. Burger and Mix were writing before the end of the series. I argue that both Adalind and Juliette are complex figures. Indeed, Burger and Mix declare that both avoid the simple binary of good witch/bad witch (24).

15. Before she leaves their home, she defies him to kiss her in her woged state, fully embodied as the hag-witch (4.14).

16. When Renard dreams of her as a Crone, she has the typical gray hair (2.15).

17. On the weight of a television series ending, see Howard and Bianculli.

18. Tanya R. Cochran and I both privately noted this resemblance during the original broadcast run.

19. The "head tilt is immediately characteristic" (Calvert 187).

20. Juliette's hair starts to grow darker before the transformation.

21. On the militarization of female superheroes, see Nadkarni.

22. On Black Claw, see the introduction;

on the problematization of Hadrian's Wall, see Ch. 10.

23. "To break her," are Trubel's words.

24. On weaponized women, see Eve Bennett.

25. On The Initiative, see Ch. 10, note 17.

26. Visually attentive viewers might note that Juliette-Eve is speaking as the bluish white of her Hexenbiest skin advances up her neck: in the hell dimension, Wesen are in a permanently transformed state; her visit risks her humanity. The visual recollects Illyria's blue skin.

27. Compare Spike's assessment of Slayers in "Lies My Parents Told Me" (7.17).

28. See note 4, Ch. 6, on Heather M. Porter and the complete female character.

Chapter Eight

1. For a history of the gender stereotype of enmity between women, see Piper. On more recent instances of the stereotype, see Behm-Morawitz et al.

2. Creed identifies were-creatures as abject (10), but Rosalee's woge is not presented as loathsome. Reggie Lee (Wu) calls it "sexy," and Bitsie Tulloch calls it "the Pantene Pro-V morph" ("A Morphed Reality").

3. Lerberg and Perdigao emphasize the importance of stories/texts in *Grimm*.

4. Prince/Captain Sean Renard contacts the same Council member as Rosalee with similar information; Rosalee and Renard are both political animals, in very different ways.

5. Thanks to Richard Gess for identifying these allusions.

6. On reproductive politics, see Ch. 9. Rosalee is pregnant with triplets, but the series ends before her pregnancy is visible. The triplets, twenty years later, fight alongside Nick and Adalind's children.

7. One might argue that Rosalee's tones instance Kristeva's pre-symbolic communication (72), but these tones are usually aspects of words and never moments of horror. One should also recall Rosalee's books.

8. *Practical Magic* (1998) features a witch who operates a botanical shop and deeply desires to be normal. The film only briefly shows the shop. The character's relationships with her sister and other women are celebrated, but even more pervasive, from the character's childhood on, is a desire for (masked by fear of) romance.

Chapter Nine

1. Parts of this essay were presented in an earlier version at the Popular Culture/American Culture Association in the South conference, Wilmington, NC, 1–3 October 2015.

2. Adalind and Nick's relationship does not feature a screwball hero whose masculinity is challenged, and it does feature romantic comedy's greater emphasis on love than farce. See Gehring on the characteristics and distinctions.

3. On the significance of the engagement ring in *Grimm*, see the discussion in Ch. 7 and later in this chapter.

4. Claire Coffee did not expect to be a continuing character in the series (Benardello).

5. He gets the answer right on the first try, but adds, as back-up, the time in "Love Sick," to which Adalind replies, "*That* was not a kiss."

6. On female characters' eating on-screen, see Ch. 10. Adalind eats on-screen more often than anyone but Trubel, but only after she is a mother and more humanized.

7. Of course patriarchy is pervasive, but some are more patriarchal than others.

8. Betsy Dendy has written on endangered motherhood in *Grimm*.

9. On Frau Pech, Stefania, and stereotypes, see Ch. 6.

10. See also Kristeva 65–70 on Douglas.

11. Specifically, Kristeva refers to "carr[ying] the experience of the impossible to the point of scatology" (54).

12. Meanwhile, in another parallel, Nick too undergoes abjection: he has become, more or less, a zombie, 3.1, 3.2, after having been spat in the face by Baron Samedi.

13. Similar spells by Adalind, Juliette, and Nick do not involve an exchange of body shapes but instead replication: The subjects of the spells get to keep their own bodies.

14. In 3.13, she seems to be guided by Diana in killing a Verrat that has struck Adalind's pregnant belly, and in 3.15, after the baby is born and Adalind's powers are newly returned, she kills another Verrat that is attacking Meisner but says she had

meant only to make the attacker drop his gun.

15. On the absorption of the fantasy heroine into the male hero's family, see Wilcox, "Forced Glory."

16. Catherine dies in a fight with Kelly.

17. Compare Juliette's experience when becoming a Hexenbiest.

Chapter Ten

1. An earlier version of this essay was presented at the Popular Culture/American Culture Association in the South Conference, 4–6 October 2017, Savannah, Georgia.

2. On doubled incidents of sexual assault for Adalind and Nick, see Ch. 9.

3. Toboni, an out lesbian since high school, has also portrayed the recurring lesbian character Jo in the Netflix anthology series *Easy* (2016–2019) and was cast as a regular character, the lesbian Sarah Finley, in *The L-Word: Generation Q* (2020–). Perhaps if *Grimm* had continued, there might have been a lesbian relationship—something the series as it stands never explored.

4. See, for example, Toboni's motions for Trubel's initial interaction with Josh Porter in their first episode together, "The Inheritance" (3.21).

5. Toboni is the first focus in a DVD feature on fight choreography, "Double Take: Fighting a Hundjäger." *Grimm* was nominated for a Creative Arts Emmy of Outstanding Stunt Coordination in 2012 and 2014 (*Television Academy*). In "Double Take," stunt coordinator Matthew Taylor says, "We showed how badass Trubel is." Toboni has stage combat certification (Mason).

6. Giannini asked the question in a Facebook post and received a few suggestions of female eaters in a television series. For further discussion of the social significance of food, see Giannini's "'If I stop doing that job, they don't stop eating': *iZombie* and the Sociopolitical Dimensions of Food." *iZombie* protagonist Liv is one of those rare women we see eating on television, but she eats only brains.

7. Nick, in an unusually nurturing role for a superhero, is frequently shown supplying Trubel with food, even after she has left and returned as an adult working for HW (e.g., 5.6). Cf. Dunne.

8. However, see Jack Halberstam.

9. Costume Designer for 2012–2017 was Alexandra Welker.

10. In Nick's dream of a funeral for Juliette, Trubel wears a dark dress (5.1).

11. On the black leather coat as signifier, see, e.g., Abbott "From," pp. 338–39.

12. By Season Five she is seen wearing one of Nick's shirts when her own clothes are ruined, 5.6.

13. A brief shot of Trubel's criminal record for petty theft while on the run states that she is 5'8" and 132 pounds (4.1). Aunt Marie and Kelly Burkhardt also fit this physical pattern.

14. For those who do not know Jon Snow of *Game of Thrones*: He knows nothing.

15. The horse's head/chess knight image appears in the Richard Boone series *Have Gun, Will Travel* (1957–63), about a peripatetic, solitary, man-in-black cowboy ronin. Coincidentally, the actor who plays the apocalyptic enemy whom Trubel and Nick face in the series' final episodes is named Wil Traval.

16. While Trubel in some ways fits D'Amore's category of "vigilante feminism" (387), her association with these two groups differentiates her from that classification.

17. Cf. *Buffy the Vampire Slayer*'s Season Four story of The Initiative, which—like HW—operated in an underground bunker run by a secret government paramilitary organization which fought monsters. In the case of The Initiative, the underground cells held the monsters; for HW, the cells are reserved for the fighters, some of whom are themselves supernatural and arguably monstrous.

18. Meisner's Resistance fought the Royals, who were attempting to reassert world domination. On weaponized women, see Eve Bennett, especially Ch. 4; however, Trubel evinces significant agency, moving past victimhood and individuating from her mentor.

19. Her being a recurring character rather than a regular lends itself to the growth of this separation and independence, since in each season there are several episodes for which she does not appear. The writers use this by having her off pursuing her own interests—for instance, joining HW.

20. On the symbolism of Nick's stick, see Ch. 5.

21. Curiously ignoring Trubel's

presence at one point, the friends insist that they need Nick to donate as the Grimm. It is not clear why Trubel could not have donated her blood in terms of the diegesis; perhaps the reasons are purely extradiegetic—the writers wanted the hero to do the job.

22. See, for example, Mendelsohn.

23. Rolek tells Nick, "I couldn't do ... what you do" (3.21). Though he can see Wesen, he seems to have chosen not to fight them.

24. Not to mention the death of President Laura Roslin.

25. Neither she nor any of the regular actors/characters appear in the very last scene; it screens only adult versions of the formerly child characters Diana and Kelly.

Chapter Eleven

1. An earlier version of this essay was presented at the Popular Culture/American Culture in the South Conference, New Orleans, 3–5 October 2018.

2. In both her fiction and nonfiction, Ursula K. Le Guin provides illumination on naming. See, e.g., *The Language of the Night*, 46.

3. Monroe is referring to both Diana and her infant half-brother Kelly, son of Adalind and Nick.

4. Adalind may be planning to double-cross her partners and keep the child, or she may at this stage not care. Early in the pregnancy, she threatens not "to go to term"—possibly part of her bargaining strategy (2.18). On the other hand, a lack of care is indicated when she drinks wine while pregnant (2.22).

5. See Ch. 9 on motherhood and reproductive politics.

6. Truman Capote wrote about not just the Gothic in general but the "demon child" in particular in such doubling (Barron A17).

7. Adalind refers to "my mother, who threw me out of the house" (5.10).

8. Before Kelly takes Diana, the writers establish that Diana is fond of her; e.g., while Diana is crying and neither Adalind nor Rosalee can soothe her, when Kelly enters the room, the baby stops crying and looks to Kelly (2.17).

9. Diana's killing of her father's lover might be seen as Oedipal; Kathryn Bond Stockton, in discussing eerie children, asserts that "wanting to kill its rival lover [of the father], the Freudian child (the child penned by Freud) looks remarkably, threateningly, precocious" (291). However, the fact that Diana repeatedly tries to push her mother and father together argues against an Oedipal interpretation.

Works Cited

Abbott, Stacey. *Angel*. TV Milestones Series. Wayne State University Press, 2009.
_____. "From Madman in the Basement to Self-Sacrificing Champion: The Multiple Faces of Spike." *The Vampire Spike in Text and Fandom: Unsettling Oppositions in* Buffy the Vampire Slayer. Special issue of *European Journal of Cultural Studies*, vol. 8, no. 4, 2005, pp. 329–344.
Abbott, Stacey, and Lorna Jowett. *TV Horror: Investigating the Dark Side of the Small Screen*. I.B. Tauris, 2013, e-book.
Abdurraqib, Hanif. *A Little Devil in America: Notes in Praise of Black Performance*. Random House, 2021.
Abrams, Zara. "Countering Stereotypes about Asian Americans." *Monitor on Psychology*, vol. 50, no. 11, 1 Dec. 2019, American Psychological Association, https://www.apa.org/monitor/2019/12/countering-stereotypes. Accessed 6 July 2020.
Adams, Michael. *Slayer Slang: A Buffy the Vampire Slayer Lexicon*. Oxford University Press, 2003.
Alexander, Michelle. *The New Jim Crow: Mass Incarceration in the Age of Colorblindness*. The New Press, 2010.
Allport, Gordon. *The Nature of Prejudice*. Addison-Wesley, 1954.
American Anthropological Association. "AAA Statement on 'Race.'" American Anthropological Association, 1998. https://www.americananthro.org/ConnectwithAAA/Content/aspx?ItemNumber=2583. Accessed 3 July 2020.
"Amok Time." *Star Trek*, season 2, episode 1, written by Theodore Sturgeon, directed by Joseph Pevney, NBC, 15 Sept. 1967.
Amy-Chinn, Dee. "Queering the Bitch: Spike, Transgression and Erotic Empowerment." *The Vampire Spike in Text and Fandom: Unsettling Oppositions in* Buffy the Vampire Slayer. Special issue of *European Journal of Cultural Studies*, vol. 8, no. 4, 2005, pp. 313–328.
Amy-Chinn, Dee, and Milly Williamson, editors. *The Vampire Spike in Text and Fandom: Unsettling Oppositions in* Buffy the Vampire Slayer. Special issue of *European Journal of Cultural Studies*, vol. 8, no. 4, 2005.
Anderson, Amanda, Rita Felski, and Toril Moi. *Character: Three Inquiries in Literary Studies*. University of Chicago Press, 2019.
Andrievskikh, Natalia. "Food Symbolism, Sexuality, and Gender Identity in Fairy Tales and Modern Women's Bestsellers." *Studies in Popular Culture*, vol. 37, no. 1, 2014, pp. 137–50.
Ang, Ien. *Watching* Dallas*: Soap Opera and the Melodramatic Imagination*. Routledge, 1985.
Angel, created by Joss Whedon and David Greenwalt, Mutant Enemy, Fox, 1999–2004.
Arnaldo, Constancio. "'I'm Thankful for Manny': Manny Pacquiao, Pugilistic Nationalism, and the Filipino Body." *Global Asian American Popular Cultures*, edited by Davé, Nishime, and Oren. New York University Press, 2016, pp. 27–46.
The Asexuality Visibility & Education Network. "Definitions." AVEN, 2001–2020. https://www.asexuality.org/?q=general.html. Accessed 6 July 2020.
Barron, James. "In a Letter, Capote's Side of the Matter [on the short story 'Miriam']." *The New York Times* 14 May 2018, A17.

Works Cited

Battis, Jes. *Blood Relations: Chosen Families in* Buffy the Vampire Slayer *and* Angel. McFarland, 2005.

Behm-Morawitz, Elizabeth, Jennifer Lewallen, and Brandon Miller. "Real Mean Girls? Reality Television Viewing, Social Aggression, and Gender-Related Beliefs among Female Emerging Adults." *Psychology of Popular Media Culture*, vol. 5, no. 4, 2016, pp. 340–355. https://doi.org/10.1037/ppm0000074.

Bell, Derrick A., Jr. "Brown vs. Board of Education and the Interest-Convergence Dilemma." *Harvard Law Review*, vol. 93, no. 3, 1980, pp. 518–533.

Benardello, Karen. "Interview: Claire Coffee Talks Grimm Season Five." *Shock Ya*, 1 Nov. 2015, https://www.shockya.com/news/2015/11/01/interview-claire-coffee-talks-grimm-season-5/ .

Bennett, Eve. *Gender in Post-9/11 American Apocalyptic TV: Representations of Masculinity and Femininity at the End of the World*. Bloomsbury, 2019.

Bennett, Jessica. "No Need for a Hunt: Awash with Witches." *The New York Times*, 25 October 2019, pp. C15, C20.

Bergson, Henri. *Laughter, an Essay on the Meaning of the Comic*. Translated by Cloudesley Brereton and Fred Rothwell. Macmillan, 1911.

Blair, Karin. "Sex and *Star Trek*." *Science Fiction Studies*, vol. 10, 1983, pp. 292–297.

Bogaert, Anthony. *Understanding Asexuality*. Rowman & Littlefield, 2012.

Bogle, Donald. *Primetime Blues: African Americans on Network Television*. Farrar, Straus and Giroux, 2001.

_____. *Toms, Coons, Mulattoes, Mammies, and Bucks: An Interpretive History of Blacks in American Films, Updated and Expanded 5th Edition*. Bloomsbury, 2016.

Botting, Fred. "In Gothic Darkly: Heterotopia, History, Culture." *A Companion to the Gothic*, edited by David Punter. Blackwell, 2000, pp. 3–14.

Boyd, Amanda. "Bigfoot Meets the Wild Man: Monstrous Borders between Contemporary American and Early Modern European Culture." *Monsters and Borders in the Early Modern Imagination*, edited by Jana Byars and Hans Peter Broedel. Routledge, 2018 [2020], pp. 179–195.

Brabon, Benjamin A., and Stéphanie Genz. "Introduction: Postfeminist Gothic." *Postfeminist Gothic: Critical Interventions in Contemporary Culture*, edited by Brabon and Genz. Palgrave Macmillan, 2007, pp. 1–15.

Briede, Charles. "Grimm Interview with Stars, Bree Turner & Silas Weir Mitchell." *Fellowship of Fools*, 28 Jan. 2014, https://fellowshipoffools.com/2014/01/28/grimm-interview-with-stars-bree-turner-silas-weir-mitchell/. 14 July 2020.

Bronfen, Elisabeth. *Over Her Dead Body: Death, Femininity and the Aesthetic*. Routledge, 1992.

Brooks, Peter. *Balzac's Lives*. New York Review Books, 2020.

_____. *The Melodramatic Imagination: Balzac, Henry James, Melodrama, and the Mode of Excess*. Yale University Press, 1976.

Buchanan, Ron. "'Side by Side': The Role of the Sidekick." *Studies in Popular Culture*, vol. 26, no. 1, 2003, pp. 15–26.

Buffy the Vampire Slayer, created by Joss Whedon, Mutant Enemy, The WB, 1997–2001, UPN 2001–2003.

Burger, Alissa, and Stephanie Mix. "Something Wicked This Way Comes? Power, Anger, and Negotiating the Witch in *American Horror Story*, *Grimm*, and *Once Upon a Time*." *Buffy to Batgirl: Essays in Female Power, Evolving Femininity and Gender Roles in Science Fiction and Fantasy*, edited by Julie M. Still and Zara T. Wilkinson. McFarland, 2019, pp. 9–32.

Butt, Richard. "Melodrama and the Classic Television Serial." *Melodrama in Contemporary Film and Television*, edited by Michael Stewart. Palgrave Macmillan, 2014, pp. 27–41.

Byshop. "Is it just me, or is the TV show 'Grimm' kind of racist?" *Gamespot*, February 2014, www.gamespot.com.

Cairns, Bryan. "Cop Out." *Grimm: Below the Surface*, edited by Neil Edwards. Titan, 2014, pp. 140–145.

Calvert, Bronwen. "'The shell I'm in': Illyria and Monstrous Embodiment." *Joss Whedon: The Complete Companion: The TV Series, the Movies, The Comic Books and More*, edited by Mary Alice Money. Popmatters / Titan, 2012, pp. 181–190.

Campbell, Joseph. *The Hero with a Thousand Faces*, 2nd edition. Princeton University Press, 1968.
Cantrell, Tom, and Christopher Hogg. "Introduction." *Exploring Television Acting*, edited by Cantrell and Hogg. Methuen Drama, 2018, pp. 1–12.
Caputi, Jane. *Gossips, Gorgons, and Crones: The Fates of the Earth*. Bear, 1993.
Cashdan, Sheldon. *The Witch Must Die: The Hidden Meaning of Fairy Tales*. Basic Books, 1999.
Cavallaro, Dani. *The Gothic Vision: Three Centuries of Horror, Terror, and Fear*. Continuum, 2002.
Chavez, Yong. "Fil-Am Actor: Reggie Lee Joins Cast of 'NCIS: New Orleans.'" *Balitang America*, 23 Aug. 2018, https://balitangamerica.tv/fil-am-actor-reggie-lee-joins-cast-of-ncis-new-orleans/. Accessed 3 July 2020.
———. "'Grimm' Actor Reggie Lee Grateful to Kababayans for Successful 'Aswang' Episode." *Balitang America*, 14 Mar. 2014, https://www.youtube.com/watch?v=P73_RGQRomE. Accessed 8 July 2020.
"Chosen." *Buffy the Vampire Slayer: The Chosen Collection*, season 7, episode 22, Mutant Enemy, 2003, written by Joss Whedon, directed by Joss Whedon, Twentieth Century Fox, 2005.
Chris, Cynthia. "Author." *Keywords for Media Studies*, edited by Laurie Ouellette and Jonathan Gray. New York University Press, 2017, pp. 21–23.
"The Cloak & Swagger Affair: The Untold History of *The Man from U.N.C.L.E.*" *The Man from U.N.C.L.E.: The Complete Series*, Turner Entertainment and Warner Bros., 2014.
Coates, Ta-Nehisi. *Between the World and Me*. Spiegel & Grau, 2015.
Comeford, AmiJo. "Cordelia Chase as Failed Feminist Gesture." *Buffy Meets the Academy: Essays on the Episodes and Scripts as Texts*, edited by Kevin K. Durand. McFarland, 2009, pp. 150–160.
"Conviction." *Angel: Season Five on DVD*, season 5, episode 1, written and directed by Joss Whedon, Mutant Enemy, 2003, Twentieth Century Fox, 2004.
Conway, D. J. *Maiden, Mother, Crone: The Myth and Reality of the Triple Goddess*. Llewellyn, 1994.
"The Corbomite Maneuver." *Star Trek*, season 1, episode 10, written by Jerry Sohl, directed by Joseph Sargent, NBC, 10 Nov. 1966.
Covington, Jeannette. *Crime and Racial Constructions: Cultural Misinformation about African Americans in Media and Academia*. Lexington, Rowman & Littlefield, 2010.
Cranny-Francis, Anne. "Sexuality and Sex-Role Stereotyping in *Star Trek*." *Science Fiction Studies*, vol. 12, 1985, pp. 274–184.
Creed, Barbara. *The Monstrous-Feminine: Film, Feminism, Psychoanalysis*. Routledge, 1993.
"Creepy Child." *TV Tropes*. tvtropes.org. Accessed 28 Sep. 2018.
Crenshaw, Kimberl[é]. "Demarginalizing the Intersection of Race and Sex: A Black Feminist Critique of Antidiscrimination Doctrine, Feminist Theory and Antiracist Politics." *University of Chicago Legal Forum*, vol. 1989, no. 1, 1989, pp. 139–167.
Crenshaw, Kimberlé Williams. "Race, Reform, and Retrenchment: Transformation and Legitimation in Antidiscrimination Law." *Harvard Law Review*, vol. 101, no. 7, 1988, pp. 1331–1387.
Crosby, Sara. "The Cruellest Season: Female Heroes Snapped into Sacrificial Heroines." *Action Chicks: New Images of Tough Women in Popular Culture*, edited by Sherrie A. Inness. Palgrave Macmillan, 2004, pp. 153–78.
D'Amore, Laura Mattoon. "Vigilante Feminism: Revising Trauma, Abduction, and Assault in American Fairy-Tale Revisions." *Marvels & Tales*, vol. 31, no. 2, 2017, pp. 386–405. Project Muse muse.jhu.edu/article/680313.
Davé, Shilpa, Leilani Nishime, and Tasha Oren. "Introduction." *Global Asian American Popular Cultures*, edited by Davé, Nishime, and Oren. New York University Press, 2016, pp. 1–12.
Delgado, Richard, and Jean Stefancic. *Critical Race Theory: An Introduction*, third edition. New York University Press, 2017.
Dendy, Betsy. "'I Will Devour Your Babes': Endangered Motherhood in *Grimm*." PCAS/ACAS Conference, 2–4 October 2014, New Orleans.
Diamond, Michael J. "Masculinity and Its Discontents: Making Room for the 'Mother' Inside

the Male—An Essential Achievement for Healthy Male Gender Identity." *Heterosexual Masculinities: Contemporary Perspectives from Psychoanalytic Gender Theory.* Routledge, 2009, pp. 23–53.

Dicker, Rory, and Alison Piepmeier. Introduction. *Catching a Wave: Reclaiming Feminism for the 21st Century.* Northeastern University Press, 2003.

"Directing *Grimm*: Behind the Scenes with David Giuntoli." DVD feature, disk 1. *Grimm: Season Six,* Universal Pictures Home Entertainment, 2017.

Dolenga, Vicki. "Interview with Grimm's Bree Turner." *Three if by Space,* 20 May 2013, https://www.threeifbyspace.net/2013/05/interview-with-grimms-bree-turner/. 14 July 2020.

"Double Take: Fighting a Hundjäger." DVD feature, disk 5. *Grimm Season Three,* Universal Pictures Home Entertainment, 2014.

Douglas, Mary. *Purity and Danger: An Analysis of the Concepts of Pollution and Taboo.* Routledge, 1966.

Dunne, Sara Lewis. "The Brutality of Meat and the Abruptness of Seafood." *This Thing of Ours: Investigating* The Sopranos, ed. David Lavery, Columbia UP, 2002, pp. 215–226.

Eder, Jens, et al. *Characters in Fictional Worlds: Understanding Imaginary Beings in Literature, Film, and Other Media.* De Gruyter, 2010.

Evelyn, Kenya. "How TV Crime Shows Erase Racism and Normalize Police Misconduct." *The Guardian,* 25 Jan. 2020, www.theguardian.com/media/2020/jan/25/law-and-disorder-how-shows-cloud-the-public-view-of-criminal-justice. Accessed 30 Mar. 2020.

Fahy, Thomas. *The Writing Dead: Talking Terror with TV's Top Horror Writers.* University Press of Mississippi, 2015.

Faludi, Susan. *The Terror Dream: What 9/11 Revealed about America.* Atlantic Books, 2008.

"Fool for Love." *Buffy the Vampire Slayer: The Chosen Collection,* season 5, episode 7, Mutant Enemy, 2000, written by Doug Petrie, directed by Nick Marck, Twentieth Century Fox, 2005.

Fuller, Nikki. "'Touch me and die, vermin!': The Psychoanalysis of Illyria." *Joss Whedon: The Complete Companion: The TV Series, the Movies, The Comic Books and More,* edited by Mary Alice Money. Popmatters / Titan, 2012, pp. 199–205.

"Gag Reel." DVD feature, disk 5. *Grimm Season Five,* Universal Pictures Home Entertainment, 2016.

Garber, Marjorie. *Character: The History of a Cultural Obsession.* Farrar, Straus and Giroux, 2020.

Gehring, Wes D. *Romantic vs. Screwball Comedy: Charting the Differences.* Scarecrow, 2008.

Giannini, Erin. Facebook post. 20 Aug. 2017.

_____. "'If I stop doing that job, they don't stop eating': *iZombie* and the Sociopolitical Dimensions of Food." *Monstrum,* vol. 2, 2019, pp. 60–84.

Gilbert, Sandra M., and Susan Gubar. *The Madwoman in the Attic.* Yale UP, 1979.

"The Girl in Question." *Angel: Season Five on DVD,* season 5, episode 20, written by Stephen S. DeKnight and Drew Goddard, directed by David Greenwalt, Mutant Enemy, 2004, Twentieth Century Fox, 2004.

Gray, Jonathan. *Show Sold Separately: Promos, Spoilers, and Other Media Paratexts.* New York University Press, 2010.

"A Grimm Farewell." *Grimm: Season Six,* Universal Pictures Home Entertainment, 2017.

"Grimm: Lowen, Klaustreich, & Jagerbar, Oh My!" Panel at DragonCon, Atlanta, Georgia, USA, 4 September 2016.

Halberstam, Jack. *Female Masculinity: Twentieth Anniversary Edition with a New Preface.* Duke University Press, 2018.

Hamamoto, Darrell Y. *Monitored Peril: Asian Americans and the Politics of TV Representation.* University of Minnesota Press, 1994.

Harris, Cheryl L. "Whiteness as Property." *Critical Race Theory: The Key Writings That Formed the Movement,* edited by Kimberlé Crenshaw et al. The New Press, 1995, pp. 276–291.

Heffley, Lynne. "Red Chief Held Hostage to Its Adaptation." *Los Angeles Times,* 17 April 1993. articles.latimes.com. Accessed 1 Oct. 2018.

Henry, O. "The Ransom of Red Chief." *The Best Short Stories of O. Henry.* Modern Library, 1994, pp. 188–201.

"The Her Master's Voice Affair." *The Man from U.N.C.L.E.: The Complete Series,* season 3,

Works Cited

episode 1, written by Bernie Giler, directed by Barry Shear, 1966, Turner Entertainment and Warner Bros., 2014.

Hewett, Richard. "Performing Sherlock: A Study in Studio and Location Realism." *Exploring Television Acting*, edited by Tom Cantrell and Christopher Hogg. Methuen Drama, 2018, pp. 15–28.

Hills, Matt, and Rebecca Williams. "*Angel*'s Monstrous Mothers and Vampires with Souls: Investigating the Abject in Television Horror." *Reading* Angel: *The TV Spin-Off with a Soul*, edited by Stacey Abbott. I B. Tauris, 2005, pp. 203–217.

Hoeveler, Diane Long. *Gothic Feminism: The Professionalization of Gender from Charlotte Smith to the Brontës*. Pennsylvania State University Press, 1998.

"A Hole in the World." *Angel: Season Five on DVD*, season 5, episode 15, written and directed by Joss Whedon, Mutant Enemy, 2003, Twentieth Century Fox, 2004.

Hollander, Anne. *Seeing Through Clothes*. University of California Press, 1993.

Horner, Avril. "Transgression." *The Handbook to Gothic Literature*, edited by Marie Mulvey-Roberts, New York University Press, 1998, pp. 286–87.

Howard, Douglas L., and David Bianculli, editors. *Television Finales: From* Howdy Doody *to* Girls. Syracuse University Press, 2018.

Huddleston, Kathie. "Exclusive: Bree Turner on Why You Should Binge All 123 Grimm Episodes in One Weekend." *SyFy Wire*, 24 Feb. 2017, https://www.syfy.com/syfywire/exclusive-bree-turner-on-why-you-should-binge-all-123-grimm-episodes-in-one-weekend/. 14 July 2020.

Hughey, Matthew W. "Cinethetic Racism: White Redemption and Black Stereotypes in 'Magical Negro' Films." *Social Problems* vol. 56, no. 3, 2009, pp. 543–577. https://doi.org/10.1525/sp.2009.56.3.543.

Huizinga, Johann. *Homo Ludens: A Study of the Play Element in Culture*. Routledge and Kegan Paul, 1949. http://art.yale.edu. 15 September 2020.

Hunt, Darnell M. "Making Sense of Blackness on Television." *Channeling Blackness: Studies on Television and Race in America*, edited by Darnell M. Hunt. Oxford University Press, 2005, pp. 1–24.

Hunt, Darnell M., Ana-Christina Ramón, and Michael Tran. *The Hollywood Diversity Report 2019: Old Story, New Beginning*. University of California–Los Angeles Division of Social Sciences, 2019.

Hutton, Ronald. *The Witch: A History of Fear from Ancient Times to the Present*. Yale University Press, 2017.

"*Grimm*: Myths, Monsters & Legends." *Grimm: Season Two*. Universal Studios Home Entertainment, 2013.

"A *Grimm* New World." *Grimm Season Five*, Universal Pictures Home Entertainment, 2016.

"In the Dark." *Angel: Season One on DVD*, season 1, episode 3, written by Douglas Petrie, directed by Bruce Seth Green, Mutant Enemy, 1999, Twentieth Century Fox, 2002.

"Intervention." *Buffy the Vampire Slayer: The Chosen Collection*, season 5, episode 18, Mutant Enemy, 2001, written by Jane Espenson, directed by Michael Gershman, Twentieth Century Fox, 2005.

"Is There in Truth No Beauty?" *Star Trek*, season 3, episode 5, written by Jean Lisette Aroest and Arthur H. Singer, directed by Ralph Senensky, NBC, 18 Oct. 1968.

"It's a Good Life." *The Twilight Zone*, story by Jerome Bixby, teleplay by Rod Serling, directed by James Sheldon, CBS, 3 November 1961.

Jackson, Kathy Merlock. *Images of Children in American Film: A Sociocultural Analysis*. Scarecrow, 1986.

Johnstone, Rachael. "'Three days of the month I'm not much fun to be around either': Werewolves and the Gendered Body in *Buffy, True Blood*, and *Grimm*." *Supernatural Studies*, vol. 2, no. 1, 2015, pp. 47–61.

Jowett, Lorna. *Sex and the Slayer: A Gender Studies Primer for the* Buffy *Fan*. Wesleyan University Press, 2005.

Kade, Arthur. "Reggie Lee on the End of 'Grimm' (Full Interview)." *Behind the Velvet Rope TV*, 31 March 2017, https://www.youtube.com/watch?v=Kr4rZo5dFCY. Accessed 3 July 2020.

Kaveney, Roz. "A Sense of the Ending: Schrodinger's *Angel*." *Reading* Angel: *The TV Spin-Off with a Soul,* edited by Stacey Abbott. I.B. Tauris, 2005, pp. 57–72.
Kies, Bridget. "'A Friendship That Will Define You Both': *Star Trek* and the Devolution of American Masculinity." *Science Fiction Film and Television*, vol. 9, no. 3, 2016, pp. 417–438.
Kindley, Evan. "The People We Know Best." *New York Review of Books*, 25 March 2021, pp. 12–14.
Kirkland, Ewan. "Situating Starbuck: Combative Femininity, Figurative Masculinity, and the Snap." *The Woman Fantastic in Contemporary American Media Culture*, edited by Elyce Rae Helford et al. University Press of Mississippi, 2016, pp. 82–97.
Kitchens, Juliette C., editor. *At Home in the Whedonverse: Essays on Domestic Place, Space and Life.* McFarland, 2017.
Koontz, K. Dale. *Faith and Choice in the Works of Joss Whedon.* McFarland, 2008.
Kristeva, Julia. *Powers of Horror: An Essay on Abjection*, translated by Leon S. Roudiez. Columbia University Press, 1982.
Kunin, Aaron. *Character as Form.* Bloomsbury Academic, 2019.
La Ferla, Ruth. "Asleep No More." *The New York Times*, 3 Jan. 2020, pp. C17, C20. Print.
Lacey, Stephen, and Simone Knox, editors. *Acting on Television: Analytical Methods and Approaches.* Special issue of *Critical Studies in Television: The International Journal of Television Studies,* vol 13, no. 3, 2018.
Lamb, Patricia Frazer, and Diane L. Veith. "Romantic Myth, Transcendence, and *Star Trek* Zines." *Erotic Universe: Sexuality and Fantastic Literature*, edited by Donald Palumbo. Greenwood Press, 1986, pp. 235–255.
Lammasniemi, Laura. "'White Slavery': The Origins of the Anti-Trafficking Movement." *Open Democracy: Free Thinking for the World*, 16 Nov. 2017, https://www.opendemocracy.net/en/beyond-trafficking-and-slavery/white-slavery-origins-of-anti-trafficking-movement/. Accessed 28 July 2020.
Lavery, David. *Joss Whedon, a Creative Portrait: From* Buffy the Vampire Slayer *to Marvel's* The Avengers. I.B. Tauris, 2014.
Lavery, David, editor. *Full of Secrets: Critical Approaches to* Twin Peaks. Wayne State University Press, 1995.
Le Guin, Ursula K. *The Language of the Night: Essays on Fantasy and Science Fiction.* Rev. ed. HarperCollins, 1992.
Lerberg, Matthew. "Transforming the Big Bad Wolf: Redefining the Werewolf through *Grimm* and *Fables.*" *Werewolves, Wolves, and the Gothic*, edited by Robert McKay and John Miller. University of Wales Press, 2017, pp. 251–272.
Leslie-McCarthy, Sage. "'I See Dead People': Ghost-Seeing Children as Mediums and Mediators of Communication in Contemporary Horror Cinema." *Lost and Othered Children in Contemporary Cinema*, edited by Debbie Olson and Andrew Scahill. Lexington Books, 2012, pp. 1–18.
"Lineage." *Angel: Season Five on DVD*, season 5, episode 7, written by Drew Goddard, directed by Jefferson Kibbee, Mutant Enemy, 2003, Twentieth Century Fox, 2004.
Logan, Elliott. "How Do We Write about Performance in Serial Television?" *Series: International Journal of TV Serial Narratives*, vol. 1, 2015, pp. 27–38.
"Lovers Walk." *Buffy the Vampire Slayer: The Chosen Collection*, season 3, episode 8, Mutant Enemy, 1998, written by Dan Vebber, directed by David Semel, Twentieth Century Fox, 2005.
Mafe, Diana Adesola. *Where No Black Woman Has Gone Before: Subversive Portrayals in Speculative Film and TV.* University of Texas Press, 2018.
The Man from U.N.C.L.E., created by Sam Rolfe and Norman Felton, MGM Television, NBC, 1964–1968.
Mason, Aiden. "10 Things You Didn't Know About Jacqueline Toboni." *TVOM*, August 2019, www.tvovermind.com. Accessed 2 Mar. 2020.
Masson, Cynthia. "'It's a play on perspective': A Reading of Whedon's Illyria through Sartre's *Nausea.*" *The Literary* Angel: *Essays on Influences and Traditions Reflected in the Joss Whedon Series*, edited by AmiJo Comeford and Tamy Burnett. McFarland, 2010, pp. 159–172.
McClain, Katia. "Representations of the Roma in *Buffy* and *Angel.*" *Joss Whedon and Race:*

Critical Essays, edited by Mary Ellen Iatropoulos and Lowery A. Woodall III. McFarland, 2017, pp. 127–149.
Mendelsohn, Farah. "Crowning the King: Harry Potter and the Construction of Authority." *Journal of the Fantastic in the Arts,* vol. 12, no. 3, 2001, pp. 287–308.
Miles, Robert. "Introduction." *Female Gothic Writing,* edited by Miles. Special issue of *Women's Writing,* vol. 1, no. 2, 1994, pp. 131–42.
Milton, John. *Poetical Works,* edited by Douglas Bush. Oxford University Press, 1966.
Mintz, Susannah B., and Leah E. Mintz. "Pass the Pop-Tarts: The *Gilmore Girls*' Perpetual Hunger." *Screwball Television: Critical Perspectives on* Gilmore Girls, edited by David Scott Diffrient with David Lavery. Syracuse University Press, 2010, pp. 235–256.
Mittell, Jason. *Complex TV: The Poetics of Contemporary Television Storytelling.* New York University Press, 2015.
Moers, Ellen. *Literary Women.* Doubleday, 1976.
"A Morphed Reality: Behind the Scenes of *Grimm*." *Grimm: Season Four.* Universal Studios Home Entertainment, 2015.
Mukherjea, Ananya. "Somebody's Asian on TV: Sierra/Priya and the Politics of Representation." *Joss Whedon's* Dollhouse: *Confounding Purpose, Confusing Identity,* edited by Sherry Ginn, Alyson R. Buckman, and Heather M. Porter. Rowman & Littlefield, 2014, pp. 65–80.
NAACP. "Criminal Justice Fact Sheet." *NAACP.org.* https://www.naacp.org/criminal-justice-fact-sheet/ Accessed 19 November 2019.
Nadkarni, Samira. "'I was never the hero that you wanted me to be': Feminism and Resistance to Militarism in *Marvel's Jessica Jones.*" *Gender and the Superhero Narrative,* edited by Michael Goodrum, Tara Prescott, and Philip Smith. University Press of Mississippi, 2018, pp. 74–100.
Nelson, Jayne. "Royal Blood." *Grimm: Below the Surface,* edited by Neil Edwards. Titan, 2014, pp. 98–103.
_____. "The Wolf at the Door." *Grimm: Below the Surface,* edited by Neil Edwards. Titan Books, 2014, pp. 24–29.
Nepales, Janet R. "Reggie Lee on Grimm's Aswang Episode." 20 March 2014. *YouTube.* Youtube.com/watch?v=Qe_EYIYVh8I. Accessed 9 July 2020.
Newcomb, Horace. *TV: The Most Popular Art.* Anchor / Doubleday, 1974.
Nochimson, Martha P. *Television Rewired: The Rise of the Auteur Series.* University of Texas Press, 2019.
"Not Fade Away." *Angel: Season Five on DVD,* season 5, episode 22, written by Jeffrey Bell and Joss Whedon, directed by Jeffrey Bell, Mutant Enemy, 2004, Twentieth Century Fox, 2004.
"Once More, with Feeling." *Buffy the Vampire Slayer: The Chosen Collection,* season 6, episode 7, Mutant Enemy, 2001, written by Joss Whedon, directed by Joss Whedon, Twentieth Century Fox, 2005.
O'Reilly, Julie D. *Bewitched Again: Supernaturally Powerful Women on Television, 1996–2011.* McFarland, 2013.
Oyelowo, David. Interview by David Greene. *Morning Edition.* National Public Radio, 29 August 2019.
Peacock, Steven. "Borders and Boundaries in *Deadwood.*" *Genre and Performance: Film and Television,* edited by Christine Cornea. Manchester University Press, 2010, pp. 96–112.
Pearson, Roberta. "Chain of Events: Regimes of Evaluation and *Lost*'s Construction of the Televisual Character." *Reading 'Lost,'* edited by Roberta Pearson. I.B. Tauris, 2008, pp. 139–158.
_____. "The Multiple Determinants of Television Acting." *Genre and Performance: Film and Television,* edited by Christine Cornea. Manchester University Press, 2010, pp. 166–183.
Pender, Patricia. *I'm Buffy and You're History:* Buffy the Vampire Slayer *and Contemporary Feminism.* I.B. Tauris, 2016.
Penley, Constance. "Feminism, Psychoanalysis and the Study of Popular Culture." *Cultural Studies,* edited by Lawrence Grossberg, Cary Nelson, and Paula Treichler. Routledge, 1992, pp. 479–500.
Pentony, Samantha. "How Kristeva's Theory of Abjection Works in Relation to the Fairy Tale and Post Colonial Novel: Angela Carter's *The Bloody Chamber* and Keri Hulme's *The*

Bone People." *Deep South* vol. 2, no. 3, Spring 1996, https://www.otago.ac.nz/deepsouth/vol2no3/pentony.html.
Perdigao, Lisa K. "Grimm Grimoires: Disenchanting Fairy Tales in Contemporary Television." South Atlantic Modern Language Association Conference, Research Triangle Park, NC, 8–10 Nov. 2012.
Phillips, Jevon. "Q & A: 'Grimm's' [sic] Reggie Lee Rides a Wave of Emotion with Wu's Transformation." *Los Angeles Times*, 14 May 2016, https://www.latimes.com/entertainment/tv/la-et-st-grimm. Accessed 22 May 2020.
Piper, Alana Jayne. "'Woman's Special Enemy': Female Enmity in Criminal Discourse along the Long Nineteenth Century." *Journal of Social History*, vol. 49, no. 3, 2016, pp. 671–692.
Porter, Heather M. "In Search of the Complete Female Character in Marvel's Cinematic Universe." *Marvel's Black Widow from Spy to Superhero: Essays on an Avenger with a Very Specific Skill Set*, edited by Sherry Ginn. McFarland, 2017, pp. 22–37.
Porter, Lynnette. *Tarnished Heroes, Charming Villains, and Modern Monsters: Science Fiction in Shades of Gray on 21st Century Television*. McFarland, 2010.
Porter, Lynnette, and Jennifer Wojton, editors. *Sherlock and Digital Fandom: The Meeting of Creativity, Community and Advocacy*. McFarland, 2018.
Porter, Lynnette, editor. *Who Is Sherlock? Essays on Identity in Modern Holmes Adaptations*. McFarland, 2016.
Potvin, Jacqueline. "Pernicious Pregnancy and Redemptive Motherhood: Narratives of Reproductive Choice in Joss Whedon's *Angel*." *Slayage: The Journal of Whedon Studies*, vol. 14, no. 1, 2016, 33 par., https://www.whedonstudies.tv/uploads/2/6/2/8/26288593/potvin_slayage_14.1.pdf.
"Power Play." *Angel: Season Five on DVD*, season 5, episode 21, written by David Fury, directed by James A. Contner, Mutant Enemy, 2004, Twentieth Century Fox, 2004.
Purkiss, Diane. *The Witch in History: Early Modern and Twentieth-Century Representations*. Routledge, 1996.
"The Quadripartite Affair." *The Man from U.N.C.L.E.: The Complete Series*, season 1, episode 3, written by Alan Caillou, directed by Richard Donner, 1964, Turner Entertainment and Warner Bros., 2014.
Rambo, Elizabeth L. "Queen C in Boys' Town: Killing the Angel in Angel's House." *Slayage: The Online International Journal of Buffy Studies*, vol. 6, no. 3, 2007, 15 par., https://www.whedonstudies.tv/uploads/2/6/2/8/26288593/rambo_slayage_6.3.pdf.
Ratcliffe, Krista. *Rhetorical Listening: Identification, Gender, Whiteness*. Southern Illinois University Press, 2005.
Rawlins, Justin Owen, and R. Colin Tait, editors. *Recentering Television Performance*, special issue of *Journal of Film and Video*, vol. 68, no. 3–4, 2016.
Renner, Karen J. *Evil Children in the Popular Imagination*. Palgrave Macmillan, 2016.
———. Introduction. *The "Evil Child" in Literature, Film, and Popular Culture*, edited by Renner. Routledge, 2013, pp. 1–22.
Richardson, J. Michael, and J. Douglas Rabb. *The Existential Joss Whedon: Evil and Human Freedom in "Buffy the Vampire Slayer," "Angel," "Firefly," and "Serenity."* McFarland, 2007.
Rosemary's Baby. Directed by Roman Polanski, story by Ira Levin, screenplay by Roman Polanski, William Castle Productions, 1968.
Salter, Anastasia, and Mel Stanfill. *A Portrait of the Author as Fanboy: The Construction of Authorship in Transmedia Franchises*. University Press of Mississippi, 2020, e-book.
Scharrer, Erica. "The Man in the Box: Masculinity and Race in Popular Television." *Communicating Marginalized Masculinities: Identity Politics in TV, Film, and New Media*, edited by Jamie E. Moshin and Ronald L. Jackson. Taylor and Francis, 2015, pp. 159–173.
Schiappa, Edward, Peter B. Gregg, and Dean E. Hewes. "The Parasocial Contact Hypothesis." *Communication Monographs*, vol. 72, no. 1, 2005, pp. 92–115.
Schwaab, Herbert. "Auteurism and Anonymity in Television: On the Domestication and Dispersion of Television Authorship." *Constructions of Media Authorship: Investigating Aesthetic Practices from Early Modernity to the Digital Age*, edited by Christiane Heibach, Angela Krewani, and Irene Schutze. De Gruyter, 2021.
Schwabe, Claudia. "Getting Real with Fairy Tales: Magic Realism in *Grimm* and *Once Upon*

a Time." *Channeling Wonder: Fairy Tales on Television,* edited by Pauline Greenhill and Jill Terry Rudy. Wayne State University Press, 2014, pp. 294–315.

Selley, April. "'I Have Been, and Ever Shall Be, Your Friend': *Star Trek, The Deerslayer* and the American Romance." *Journal of Popular Culture,* vol. 20, no. 1, 1986, pp. 89–104.

Sempruch, Justyna. *Fantasies of Gender and the Witch in Feminist Theory and Literature.* Purdue University Press, 2008.

Shakespeare, William. *Hamlet. William Shakespeare: The Complete Works,* edited by Stephen Orgel and A. R. Brownmuller. Pelican/Penguin Books, 2002, pp. 1347–1391.

"The Shark Affair." The Man from U.N.C.L.E.: *The Complete Series,* season 1, episode 4, written by Alvin Sapinsley, directed by Marc Daniels, 1964, Turner Entertainment and Warner Bros., 2014.

Shattuc, Jane M. "Television Production: Who Makes American TV?" *A Companion to Television,* edited by Janet Wasko. Wiley-Blackwell, 2010, pp. 142–154.

"Shells." *Angel: Season Five on DVD,* season 5, episode 16, written and directed by Stephen S. DeKnight, Mutant Enemy, 2004, Twentieth Century Fox, 2004.

Shimizu, Celine Parrenas. *Straitjacket Sexualities: Unbinding Asian American Manhoods in the Movies.* Stanford University Press, 2012.

Smith, Murray. *Engaging Characters: Fiction, Emotion, and the Cinema.* Oxford University Press, 1995.

Smith, Philip. "Asian Stereotypes and American-Sino Relations in Marvel's Collective Man." *Academia Letters,* article 669. https://doi.org/10.20935/AL669.

"Something Wesen This Way Comes." *Grimm: Season Three,* Universal Pictures Home Entertainment, 2014.

Spicer, Arwen. "'Love's Bitch But Man Enough to Admit It': Spike's Hybridized Gender." *Slayage: The Online International Journal of* Buffy *Studies,* vol. 2, no. 3, 2002, www.whedonstudies.tv/uploads/2/6/2/8/26288593/spicer_slayage_2.3.pdf. Accessed 16 April 2020.

Star Trek, created by Gene Roddenberry, Desilu, 1966–1967, Paramount 1968–1969, NBC, 1966–1969.

Star Trek IV: The Voyage Home. Directed by Leonard Nimoy, written by Harve Bennett, Leonard Nimoy, et al., Paramount, 1986.

Stern, Lesley, and George Kouvaris. *Falling for You: Essays on Cinema and Performance.* Power, 1999.

Stewart, Michael. "Introduction: Film and TV Melodrama: An Overview." *Melodrama in Contemporary Film and Television,* edited by Michael Stewart. Palgrave Macmillan, 2014, pp. 1–21.

Stockton, Kathryn Bond. "Growing Sideways, or Versions of the Queer Child: The Ghost, the Homosexual, the Freudian, the Innocent, and the Interval of Animal." *Curiouser: On the Queerness of Children,* edited by Steven Bruhm and Natasha Hurley. University of Minnesota Press, 2004, pp. 277–315.

Stoddart, Helen. "Hero-Villain." *The Handbook to Gothic Literature,* edited by Marie Mulvey-Roberts, New York University Press, 1998, pp. 111–115.

Taber, Nancy. "Detectives and Bail Bonds 'Persons' as Fairy Tale Hero/ines: A Feminist Antimilitarist Analysis of *Grimm* and *Once Upon a Time.*" *Gender Forum: An Internet Journal for Gender Studies,* no. 44, 2013, pp. 13–27, genderforum.org/gender-and-fairy-tales-issue-44-2013/. Accessed 8 Apr. 2020.

Television Academy. www.emmys.com. Accessed 27 Mar. 2020.

Tenga, Angela. "Wandering Wesen: Immigration as Adaptation in *Grimm.*" *Supernatural Studies,* vol. 2, no. 1, 2015, pp. 34–46.

Thomas, Calvin. *Male Matters: Masculinity, Anxiety, and the Male Body on the Line.* University of Illinois Press, 1996.

Thompson, Robert J. *Television's Second Golden Age: From* Hill Street Blues *to* ER. Continuum, 1996.

"Through the Looking Glass." *Angel: Season Two on DVD,* season 2, episode 21, written and directed by Tim Minear, Mutant Enemy, 2001, Twentieth Century Fox, 2003.

Toles, George. "Don Draper and the Promises of Life." *Television Aesthetics and Style,* edited by Jason Jacobs and Steven Peacock. Bloomsbury, 2013, pp. 147–173.

Turnbull, Sue. "Performing *Veronica Mars*." *Investigating* Veronica Mars: *Essays on the Teen Detective Series*, edited by Rhonda V. Wilcox and Sue Turnbull. McFarland, 2011, pp. 35–48.
Turner, Victor. "Liminality and the Performative Genres." *Rite, Drama, Festival, Spectacle: Rehearsals Toward a Theory of Cultural Performance*, edited by John J. Macaloon. Institute for the Study of Human Issues, 1984.
Turnquist, Kristi. "Silas Weir Mitchell on Playing Monroe on 'Grimm,' and Filming in Portland." *The Oregonian*, 5 Mar. 2012, OregonLive.com. Accessed 30 Mar. 2017.
United States Census Bureau. *QuickFacts*. https://www.census.gov/quickfacts/fact/table/portlandcityoregon/PST045218. Accessed 30 Mar. 2020.
"Unlocking the Mystery: Inside the 100th Episode." *Grimm: Season Five*, Universal Studios, 2016.
U.S. Department of Health and Human Services. Office of Minority Health. "Profile: Asian Americans." https://minorityhealth.hhs.gov/omh. Accessed 26 June 2020.
"The Vulcan Affair [Pilot]." *The Man from U.N.C.L.E.: The Complete Series*, season 1, episode 1, written by Sam Rolfe, directed by Don Medford, 1964, Turner Entertainment and Warner Bros., 2014.
Walker, Barbara G. *The Crone: Woman of Age, Wisdom, and Power*. San Francisco: Harper & Row, 1985.
Wilcox, Rhonda V. "Forced Glory: Katniss Everdeen, Bella Swan, and Varieties of Virginity." *The Woman Fantastic in Contemporary American Media Culture*, edited by Elise Helford et al. University of Mississippi Press, 2016, pp. 193–208.
_____. "'There Will Never Be a "Very Special" *Buffy*': *Buffy* and the Monsters of Teen Life." *Journal of Popular Film and Television*, vol. 27, no. 2, 1999, pp. 16–23.
_____. *Why* Buffy *Matters: The Art of* Buffy the Vampire Slayer. I.B. Tauris, 2005.
Williams, Linda. "Melodrama Revised." *Refiguring American Film Genres: History and Theory*, edited by Nick Browne. University of California Press, 1998, pp. 42–88.
Willsey, Kristiana. "New Fairy Tales Are Old Again: *Grimm* and the Brothers Grimm." *Channeling Wonder: Fairy Tales on Television*, edited by Pauline Greenhill and Jill Terry Rudy. Wayne State University Press, 2014, pp. 210–228.
Wojton, Jennifer, and Lynnette Porter. "Towards an Ethos of Advocacy for Asexuality." *Sherlock and Digital Fandom: The Meeting of Creativity, Community, and Advocacy*, by Wojton and Porter. McFarland, 2018, pp. 124–153.
Worland, Rick. "The Cold War Mannerists: *The Man from U.N.C.L.E.* and TV Espionage in the 1960s." *The Journal of Popular Film and Television*, vol. 21, no. 4, 1994, pp. 150–160.
"The World of Grimm." *Grimm: Season One*. Universal Studios Home Entertainment, 2012.
"Wu's Views." *Grimm: Season Six*, Universal Pictures Home Entertainment, 2017.
Zarzosa, Agustín. *Refiguring Melodrama in Film and Television: Captive Affects, Elastic Sufferings, Vicarious Objects*. Lexington Books, 2013.
Zimmerly, Stephen M. *The Sidekick Comes of Age: How Young Adult Literature Is Shifting the Sidekick Paradigm*. Rowman & Littlefield, 2019.
Zipes, Jack. *The Invisible Fairy Tale: The Cultivated Social History of a Genre*. Princeton University Press, 2012.
Zukimoto, Cathy. "Reggie Lee EWP Visionary Awards 2019." *IdeateTV*, 19 April 2019, https://www.youtube.com/watch?v=GauDUIXoNks. Accessed 3 June 2020.

Index

Abbott, Stacey 23, 41, 146, 234*n*11
abduction 20, 24–27, 31, 35, 42, 46–47, 58, 81, 104–105, 107, 133, 160–161, 167, 208, 212; *see also* human trafficking
Abdurraqib, Hanif 53, 229*n*17
abjection 9, 14, 17, 59, 61, 78, 114–115, 118, 120, 121, 126, 148, 167, 169–175, 178–186, 190–191, 231–232*ch*6*n*7, 233*ch*8*n*2
abuse: child 67, 102, 128, 178, 186; domestic 102, 149; sexual 129, 172, 194, 206
Academy Award 136, 232*ch*6*n*16
Acker, Amy 137, 143
Acker, Jesse 107
acting 1, 10–13, 24, 39, 41, 47, 50, 51, 53, 54–55, 56, 59, 61, 70, 71, 72–73, 74, 89, 91, 98–99, 109, 111, 113, 116, 123, 126–129, 131–133, 136, 142, 150, 153–154, 159, 162, 164, 167, 173–177, 184, 189, 191, 194–195, 201, 206, 210, 212, 219–220, 228*n*14; *see also* body language; expression, facial; expression, vocal
Adams, Michael 228*n*15
Adams, Mr. (character) 58
addiction 16, 86, 118–119, 127, 139, 152–154, 161–162
African American 5, 12–13, 32, 40–55, 58, 73, 131–132, 140, 220, 229*n*16, 230*ch*3*n*6
age 2, 10–11, 51–52, 76, 95–96, 111, 121–136, 152, 170, 178, 182, 192, 200, 206, 209–210
agency 59, 69–70, 134, 137, 143, 145–147, 149, 150–151, 180, 182, 184, 197, 201, 206, 231*ch*6*n*4, 234*n*18; *see also* control
Aghdashloo, Shohreh 135
Ahluwalia, Karishma 58
Al (character) 101
Alexander, Michelle 229*n*15
Alias 148
Alicia (character) 8, 102
alien 21; *see also* Other
All in the Family 227*n*2
Allport, Gordon 230*n*7

altruism 27–32, 83, 92, 99, 150–151, 191, 201–204, 214
amnesia 34, 99, 109, 135, 143–144, 165
Amos (character) 8
Amy-Chinn, Dee 12, 23
Anderson, Amanda 218, 220
Andrevskikh, Natalia 157
The Andy Griffith Show 228*ch*1*n*12
Ang, Ien 1
Angel (character) 23, 126, 140, 142, 177, 197
Angel (TV series) 2, 9, 15, 23, 37, 41, 137–141, 143, 146–151, 232*n*4
The Angel in the House 17, 170, 187
Angelina *see* Lasser, Angelina
Angelo (character) 68–69
animal 3, 24, 30, 41, 53, 62, 68, 72, 95, 127, 143, 193, 212; *see also* wolf, spider
apocalypse 34, 36, 59, 76, 88, 92, 107, 118–120, 123, 138, 151, 179, 202, 214–215, 234*n*15
apothecary 3, 8, 15–16, 37–38, 45, 123, 127, 129, 152–168
appearance vs. reality 15, 54, 72, 123–125, 127–130, 133, 135–136, 145–146, 229*n*4; *see also* duality
archetype 8,, 15, 18, 35, 121–123, 126, 128, 152, 167, 205
Aristotle 217
Arivaca, Xavier 85
Arnaldo, Constancio 68
art: drawing 19, 51, 111, 157, 199, 211; painting 76–77
asexuality 13, 56–57, 65–71
Asexuality Visibility & Education Network (AVEN) 65
Asian American 5, 13, 56–74, 220, 228*ch*2*n*2, 230*ch*3*n*1; *see also* Filipino Chinese American; Taiwanese American
assassination 29, 36, 42, 79–80, 83, 85, 100–101, 117, 133, 155–156
assimilation 41, 44, 54

247

Index

Aswang 3, 61, 63–70, 186–187
atonement 44, 150
attractiveness 14, 15–16, 21, 36, 48, 75–77, 94–95, 100, 120, 123, 127, 129–133, 136, 139–140, 142, 147–148, 151, 152–153, 158, 160, 164–165, 169–170, 180, 183, 186, 189, 193, 196–197; *see also* body
auteurism 18, 217–220

Baba Yaga 124, 157
Bach, J.S. 20
badge 46, 101, 118
Bailey, George 119
Bailey, Rob 153
Ball, Lucille 142
Balzac, Honoré de 217–218, 220
baptism *see* water
Baribeau, Boyd, Det. 47
Baron Samedi 3, 45, 233n12
Baske, Doyle 109
Bastard *see* illegitimacy
Battis, Jes 138–139, 140–141
Battlestar Galactica see Starbuck
Beatles 20, 219
Beauvais, Garcelle 131
beer 26, 30–31, 97, 110, 165
Behm-Morawitz, Elizabeth 233ch8n1
Bell, Derrick 12, 43
Bell, Jeffrey 141
Bennett, Eve 2, 8, 123, 227n6, 228n12
Bergson, Henri 116
Beth (character) 58
Bianculli, David 232n17
Big Bad Wolf 3, 5, 24, 41, 43, 106, 232ch7n12
Bindra, M.E. 232ch6n13
birth 7, 15, 18, 67, 82, 89, 91, 100, 107, 121, 128, 139, 158, 181–182, 186–187, 198, 205–208
Black Claw (Schwarz Kralle) 6–8, 47, 54, 75, 84–92, 106–107, 114, 133, 159, 166, 175, 178, 199, 210–211, 231n11, 232ch6n14
Black Forest *see* Schwarzwald
Blackness 12, 40–55, 131–132; *see also* African American
Blade Runner 149
Blair, Karin 2 2
Blanche, Robert 66
blocking 10, 14, 23–29, 31, 36–38, 54, 60, 79–80, 84, 95–96, 110, 116, 123–125, 131, 143–145, 147, 150, 153, 171, 173, 176–177, 188–189, 213, 215, 220
blood 5–6, 26, 36, 38, 46, 48, 62, 68, 83, 87, 89–90, 102–103, 111, 113, 115, 117–118, 131, 134, 140, 148, 153, 155, 172–173, 180, 182–184, 188, 193, 197, 202, 210, 215, 228n17, 231n17, 235n21

Blutbad 4–7, 24–33, 39, 45–46, 71–72, 97, 103, 143, 156, 162, 167
body 10, 12–15, 17, 20, 22–24, 31–32, 35–36, 49, 56, 58, 60–61, 73, 78, 88–90, 95, 100–101, 111, 115, 123–125, 131, 133, 135–136, 137, 140–141, 145, 147–148, 150, 153, 159, 165, 167, 170, 172, 174, 181, 184–185, 189, 194, 196–198, 206–207, 209, 229n13; *see also* attractiveness; hair; strength, physical
body language 1, 13–14, 16, 18, 22, 25–26, 27, 30–31, 38, 49, 51, 53, 60–61, 70, 72–73, 89, 92–93, 95–96, 98–100, 102, 103, 108–109, 111–112, 116, 124, 131, 144, 146–148, 153–155, 158–159, 162, 164–167, 171–174, 176–179, 188–189, 193, 195, 198, 201, 206–207, 209–210, 212, 215, 229n20; *see also* expression, facial
Bogle, Donald 40, 47, 50
Bonaparte, Conrad 86, 89, 90–92, 178–180, 211
Bond, James 20
The Bone Collector 55
Bones 164
books 3–4, 16, 26, 31, 33–34, 36, 46, 63, 69, 72, 74, 80, 87, 96, 98, 118, 122, 124, 127–128, 131, 136, 147, 152, 154–157, 186, 188, 191, 199–200, 202–203, 214–216
Boone, Richard 234n15
Bordwell, David 227n6
Botting, Fred 76
Bowes-Lyon, Kenneth, Prince 83, 87, 102, 107, 113, 146, 182
Boyd, Amanda 227n4
Brabon, Benjamin A. 230ch4n1
Brahms, Johannes 35
bravery 13, 16, 26, 28, 31–32, 37, 47, 49, 57, 60–61, 70, 75, 84, 105–106, 126, 130, 152–156, 159–161, 164, 167
Braxton, Brenda 230ch3n6
breaking the fourth wall 211
British 20, 102, 131, 140, 227n9
British Union of Fascists 227n9
bromance 12, 29
Bronfen, Elisabeth 232n6
Brontë, Charlotte 88
Brooks, Peter 217–218
Brothers Grimm 2–3; *see also* Grimm, Jakob
Bruno, Danny 45
Buchanan, Ron 12, 42
Bud *see* Wurstner, Bud
buddy, African American 12, 40, 43
Buffy the Vampire Slayer 2, 19, 22–24, 37, 47, 138, 143, 218–219, 228ch1n11, 234n17; *see also* Summers, Buffy
Buffybot 24

Index

Bullock, Seth 10
Burger, Alissa 106, 125, 145, 147, 173, 227*n*4, 228*n*13, 231*ch*6*n*6, 232*ch*7*n*8
Burkhardt, Kelly (female) 3–4, 15, 82–83, 87–88, 91, 97, 111–113, 117, 121–125, 128, 130, 132–133, 148, 159, 174, 181, 186, 189, 197, 198, 202–203, 207–209, 212, 231*n*13, 234*ch*9*n*16, 235*n*8
Burkhardt, Kelly (male) 93, 99, 104, 119, 125, 175–176, 178, 185–191, 203, 213–215, 227*n*7, 235*n*25, 235*n*3
Burkhardt, Nicholas *passim*
Burkhardt, Reed 82, 97, 110, 231*ch*5*n*5
Burkle, Winifred 15, 137–143, 147–151, 232*ch*7*n*7
Burton, Kate 29, 123
business 3, 6, 16, 38, 68, 90, 127, 131, 152–158, 165–167, 170, 188, 201, 220, 233*ch*8*n*8
Butt, Richard 112
Byron, Lord 21; Byronic hero 76

Cabinet: weapons 3, 120, 143, 148, 201, 215; wigs 148
Caillech 122
Calvert, Bronwen 140–141, 148, 232*n*19
Calvert, Diyetta 162
Calvert, Frederick 16, 152–154, 162–164
Calvert, Gloria 129, 162
Calvert, Rosalee 1, 3–6, 15–16, 28, 32–41, 45, 50, 59, 64–65, 71–74, 82, 84, 97, 100–101, 105, 107, 109, 116–119, 123, 127–136, 139, 142–143, 145–168, 173–174, 178, 180, 185–191, 194–202, 208, 214, 215
camera work 2–3, 23, 25, 28–31, 37, 61, 63, 68, 71–72, 77, 80, 84, 88, 91, 94, 109–111, 114, 116, 123–125, 127–128, 131, 133, 142, 144, 150, 153, 171, 173, 176, 182–183, 186, 188–189, 194, 197–198
Campbell, Joseph 25, 27, 32, 37–38, 110, 124, 228*n*4
cannibal 62, 101, 187
Cantrell, Tom 10–12
capitalism 62; *see also* business
Capote, Truman 235*n*6
Caputi, Jane 9, 121
Carpenter, Stephen 227*n*5
Carroll, Leo G. 20
Carroll, Lewis 63
Cashdan, Sheldon 121
casting 5, 15, 29, 40–41, 55–56, 58, 137, 152, 228*ch*2*n*2, 230*ch*3*n*1, 234*n*4
cat 4, 60, 66, 71, 142, 155, 181; *see also* Samson
Census, U. S. 41, 57
Cervantes, Miguel de 20
character: study of in literature 18, 217–218, 220; in television scholarship 1–2, 217, 219–220, 227*n*2, 228*n*14, 228*n*15
Charmed 122
Chase, Cordelia 138–139
Chavez, Special Agent Katrina 15, 58, 84, 123, 132–134, 220
Chen, Camille 5, 63,
chiasmus of character 16, 174–175, 177
child 4, 7, 9, 11, 17–18, 24–28, 31, 40, 42, 44, 46, 48, 57, 76, 82–84, 86–88, 90–93, 96, 98–102, 104, 107–108, 112–113, 115, 119–120, 123–124, 135–136, 138, 144, 146–147, 151, 160–161, 170, 173–175, 178–179, 181, 183, 186, 188–189–191, 195, 205–216, 229*n*14
child abuse *see* abuse, child
Chilling Adventures of Sabrina 122
Chris, Cynthia 218
El Chupacabra 3, 64, 229*n*6
cisgender 8, 12, 19, 65, 230
Citizen, Robyn 50
class 13–14, 51, 53, 62, 76, 85, 100, 220; *see also* status
cleaning 38, 97, 115, 182, 228*n*17
cliffhanger 124
clocks 25–26, 31, 33, 38–40, 165–167
clothing *see* costume
Coates, Ta-Nehisi 43, 52
Cochran, Tanya R. vi, 227*n*3, 232*n*18
coffee 29, 49, 90, 97, 190, 206
Coffee, Claire 8, 10, 16–17, 126, 135, 171, 173–181, 184, 189–190, 206, 233*ch*9*n*4
Coins of Zakynthos 86, 112, 133
color of change 229*n*7
combative female 17, 192–204
comedy, physical 59, 116, 170, 212; *see also* farce; humor; wit
Comeford, AmiJo 138–139
comic book 15, 140, 160, 198, 228*n*8, 230*n*14
Comic-Con 148
coming out 8, 38–39, 65–66, 227*n*10
communion 73–74, 84, 163–164, 196; *see also* eating
community 13, 18, 33, 50, 73–74, 84, 92, 100, 105–106, 112, 127, 135, 147, 151, 152, 154, 156, 158–164, 191, 192, 196, 198, 200–204, 205, 213–216; leaders 16, 127, 162–163, 167; *see also* family
Complete Female Character 151, 231*ch*6*n*4
computers 42, 62, 66, 126, 220
contact hypothesis 58; parasocial 230*n*7
Contaminatio Ritualis 183, 185
control 6, 13, 38, 48–50, 54, 56–74, 81, 85–89, 106, 108, 115, 119–120, 126, 131, 141, 178, 205–206; *see also* agency
Conway, D.J. 9, 121

cooking and food preparation 26, 29, 38–39, 50, 62, 68, 71, 73, 97, 124–125, 154, 157, 165, 175–177, 213; *see also* eating
costume 7, 10–12, 15, 17, 21, 24–25, 36, 49–50, 58, 60–61, 77–79, 83, 89–90, 100, 111, 116, 125, 127–128, 131, 135, 148, 150–151, 160, 162, 170–171, 174–177, 180, 182–183, 193, 196–198, 211, 215, 220, 229n4, 230ch3n5, 234n9
Covington, Jeannette 4, 41
Coyotl 229n14, 230n17
Cranny-Francis, Anne 12, 22
Crawford, Joan 67
credits, series 29, 32, 40, 70, 86, 137, 193, 206
Creed, Barbara 9, 121, 171, 182, 185, 187–188, 233
Crenshaw, Kimberlé 4, 7, 94, 229n18, 231ch5n1
Crone 9–11, 15; 121–136, 139, 147, 152–153, 156–157, 169, 173, 182, 185, 199; *see also* Huntress; Maiden/Mother/Crone; Wise Woman; Witch
Crone face 9, 15, 121, 123, 125, 131, 145, 147, 171, 191, 207; *see also* woge
Crone theory 9–11, 121–123
Crosby, Sara 17, 192
cross, burning 5–6, 33, 146
Cruz, Dallas 85, 230ch4n4
Cruz, Ted 230ch4n4
El Cucuy 136, 229n6
Cumberbatch, Benedict 228n18

Damas, Bertila 136
D'Amore, Laura Mattoon 193, 234n16
damsel in distress 15, 137, 139–140, 150
Danes, Clare 10
Dante 27
Darla (character) 138–139
Davé, Shilpa 66, 68
Davis, Miles 91
Deadwood 10
death 3, 6–7, 9, 18, 24, 30–31, 36–38, 40, 42, 44–47, 62, 75, 79–80, 82–83, 88–92, 95–96, 99, 105–108, 112–113, 116–119, 121–130, 132–133, 138–139, 146, 148–150, 153, 155, 162, 172–175, 180, 183–186, 193, 198, 201–203, 205–209, 211–212, 235n24; sacrificial 24, 36–38, 133, 135, 140
decapitation 101–103, 112–113, 115, 133, 148
deception 4–5, 71, 65, 80, 104, 113, 135, 146, 156, 181, 195
The Decline and Fall of the Roman Empire 33
Dedlock, Lady Honoria 112
Delgado, Richard 4, 229n16
demographics 41, 57–58

Demon child 11, 18, 128, 205–216, 235n6
Dendy, Betsy 206, 233ch9n8
Denisof, Alexis 78, 138
depth of field (characters) 57–59, 162
detection 40, 42–43, 52, 62–63, 79, 83–84, 95, 105, 132–134
dialogue 10, 13, 20, 24, 28–29, 36–37, 56, 60–61, 71, 91, 97, 108–109, 112–113, 115–116, 145, 150–151, 158, 161, 165–166, 170, 172, 176–177, 180, 183, 189, 212, 215
Diamond, Michael J. 101, 231ch4n7
Diana *see* Renard, Diana Schade
diaspora 68; *see also* immigration
Dickens, Charles 88, 112, 149
Dicker, Rory 199
Dietrich, Felix, Uncle 4, 36, 117
dimension, alternate 92, 119, 139–140, 150–151, 202, 213–214, 233n26
Dionysus 34
director 11, 37, 56, 84, 142, 150, 153, 165, 219–220, 231n19
director of photography 11, 220; *see also* camera work
diversity 5, 9–10, 40–41, 57–59, 84, 103, 133, 135, 198, 202
Dixie Chicks [The Chicks] 140
Dixon, Andrew 85
doctor, medical 44, 55, 64, 104, 123–124, 131–133, 153–157, 162, 171; *see also* healer; veterinarian
domestic abuse *see* abuse, domestic
Donna [O'Hara] (character) 193–194
Door *see* threshold
doubling 18, 25, 27–28, 38, 54, 81–82, 96, 130, 162, 165, 169–171, 173–175, 177–178, 181, 205–206, 208, 211, 215, 234n2; *see also* foils
Douglas, Mary 183, 233n10
DragonCon 19, 56, 143, 230ch3n1
Draper, Don 10
dream 49, 68, 72, 74, 86, 108, 149, 211, 214, 232n16, 234n10
drinking 26, 29, 30, 38, 46–47, 64, 71, 73–74, 84, 91, 97, 162–163, 169, 185, 187, 196, 235n4; *see also* beer; coffee; wine
drugs 16, 26, 62, 127, 138–139, 152–154, 161–162, 167; *see also* addiction
Drusilla (character) 23
duality 32, 35, 75, 78–81, 96, 103, 125, 127; *see also* moral variety/complexity; woge

Eads, Paul 228n6; *see also* production design
Earp, Wyatt 10
Easy 234n3
eating 1, 5, 17, 26, 29–30, 48–49, 58–59, 63, 66, 68–69, 73–74, 101, 124, 126, 142, 154,

Index 251

162–166, 175–177, 185, 187, 193–197, 199, 212, 233*ch*9*n*6, 234*n*6; *see also* cooking and food preparation
Eder, Jens 2
editing 80, 113–114, 117, 124–125, 127–128, 165, 171, 189, 193–194, 207; *see also* camera work
Eisbieber 6; *see also* Wurstner, Bud
ekphrasis 10
Ellis, Jared 51–53
Ellis, Tyler Zuri 50–53
eloquence 1, 12, 19–24, 33–35, 56–57, 61–63, 68; *see also* dialogue; expression, vocal; language
embodiment *see* body
Emmy (television Academy) 195, 234*n*5
emotion 5, 11–12, 14–24, 36–38, 61, 69–70, 73, 81, 87, 89, 91, 98–100, 106–114, 126–127, 133, 136, 137–138, 141, 146–147, 150, 153, 162, 167, 169–187, 189, 191, 195, 198–199, 201, 205, 212
environmentalism 62, 231*ch*6*n*3
epigraph 7, 49, 149, 172; *see also* writing
Espinosa, Valentina 44, 101
Estella (character) 149
E.T. the Extraterrestrial 129
ethnicity 4–8, 10, 15, 21, 26, 32, 57, 63, 67, 96, 123, 132–136, 159, 220; *see also* African American; Asian American; British; Filipino Chinese American; German; Hispanic; immigration; Iranian American; Jewishness; Latinx characters; Mexican American; race; Taiwanese
Eureka 228*n*11
Eve (*Angel* character) 232*n*4
Eve (Biblical) 138, 232*ch*6*n*8
Eve (*Grimm* character) 8, 16, 84, 90, 92, 99, 104, 113–114, 123, 126–128, 137–138, 148–150, 161, 201, 211, 230*n*11; *see also* Juliette/Eve; Silverton, Juliette
Evelyn, Kenya 46, 229*n*7
Evers-Swindell, Nico 83
Everyman 5, 19, 47, 58–59
existentialism 141, 228*n*10
exoticization 67
The Expanse 135
expression, facial 1, 20, 22–23, 25–26, 29, 36–39, 49, 51, 53, 63, 70–71, 73, 87–89, 91, 109, 111, 113–114, 116, 125, 131, 142, 144, 148, 150, 153–154, 159, 164–165, 170–171, 173–178, 184–185, 191, 194, 197–198, 201, 206, 210, 212, 215–16, 229*n*20
expression, vocal 1, 10, 16, 20, 23, 27, 30, 35, 53, 57, 89, 111, 124–125, 131–132, 135, 142, 144, 148, 153, 155, 158, 164–167, 173, 175, 177, 179, 183, 185, 193–194, 207, 210
extrajudicial *see* extralegality

extralegality 5, 7, 13, 43–47, 73–74, 79–81, 84, 101, 105–106, 134–135, 229*n*8
extratextuality 21, 37, 209, 234–235*n*21

Fairey, Shepard 85
fairy tales 2–3, 9, 24–26, 62–63, 68, 110, 117, 121, 143–144, 147, 157, 179–180, 182, 187, 193, 231*ch*5*n*4
Faludi, Susan 230*ch*3*n*4
family 2, 4, 7, 13, 16–18, 28, 34, 37, 52–53, 67–68, 73–74, 83, 88–89, 92–93, 102, 111, 115, 119, 129, 131, 136, 138, 147, 151, 152, 155, 157, 162–165, 167, 169, 176–177, 188–191, 193–194, 197–198, 200–204, 207, 210, 213–216, 219, 231*n*17, 234*ch*9*n*15
fan fiction 22
farce 45, 70, 170, 175, 212, 233*ch*9*n*2; *see also* humor
Farris, Deputy Sheriff Janelle 123, 132, 134, 229*n*20, 232*ch*6*n*14
The Fast and the Furious 56
father 13, 21, 29, 32. 39, 48, 52–53, 55, 62, 67, 75–76, 81–82, 85, 88, 90–93, 100, 102–105, 107, 110, 113, 124–125, 128–129, 134–135, 155, 162–163, 176, 178, 188–189, 190, 199, 203, 207–208, 210–212, 214–215, 229*n*14, 229*n*20, 231*n*5; *see also* mother; parents; paternalism; patriarchy
Feinstein, Rachel 122
Felski, Rita 218, 220
Felton, Norman 20
feminism 122, 125, 143, 156; second-wave 17, 192, 196, 199; third-wave 196, 199, 220; vigilante 234*n*16
Fences 55
Fife, Barney 30, 228*ch*1*n*12
Filipino 3, 68, 187; Filipino American 5, 13, 56–58, 63, 67; Filipino Chinese American 63, 220
foils 14, 75, 81–82, 103–104, 130, 135–136, 170–177, 181, 186; *see also* doubling
Fonda, Henry 10
food *see* cooking and food preparation; eating
foreshadowing 18, 50, 171–172; *see also* prophecy/portents
forest 27–28, 33, 63–64, 72, 97, 110, 116–117, 134–135, 147, 187, 191, 193, 201, 206, 230*n*10
Frain, James 78
Fran, Nurse 58
Franco, Sgt. 66, 69, 90
Frank, Anne 7
Fred *see* Burkle, Winifred
Frederick, King 90, 181, 208–209
Freed-Golden, Bryar 129
Freud, Sigmund 171, 235*n*9

Index

friends 3, 5–6, 11–12, 16–17, 24–39, 40, 42–48, 55, 57, 69–73, 76, 84–85, 87, 89–92, 97, 99, 101, 103, 105, 107, 109–110, 115–117, 127, 133, 143, 146, 151, 152–153, 158–165, 167–168, 170, 172, 175, 177, 181, 184, 189–191, 194, 198, 200–204, 210, 213, 230n17, 231ch5n5, 235n21
Frost, Mark 219
Frost, Robert 34
Fuchsbau 4, 5, 33, 45, 103, 116, 156, 167
Fuller, Nikki Faith 140–141
Furamusu, Beth 58
furniture 3, 27, 31, 38, 42, 49–50, 60, 87, 89, 91, 99, 103, 108, 111, 120, 142–144, 145, 147–148, 173–174, 176–178, 187, 201, 211–213, 215

Game of Thrones 122, 199, 234n14
gaming 52, 62–63, 66
Garber, Marjorie 217, 220
Gatiss, Mark 228n18
Gaudot, Mia 86
gay see homosexuality
gaze 116, 131, 165, 171, 173, 195, 229n13
Gelumcaedus 100
gender liminality 8, 9, 12–13, 19–24, 38–39, 53, 55, 141, 157, 197–199, 203
Genio Innocuo 4
genre 16, 170–171, 229n7; see also detection; horror; police procedural; romantic comedy; screwball comedy
gentleness 36, 53, 66, 70–71, 87, 102, 164, 213
Genz, Stéphanie 230ch4n1
German 2–3, 6, 34, 78, 116–117, 135, 201–202, 232ch6n9; see also immigration; Schwarzwald
Gertrude 81; see also Shakespeare, William
ghost 34, 44, 49, 88, 90–91, 101, 113, 119, 140, 173, 184, 188, 202, 203, 215
Giannini, Erin 196, 234n6
Gilbert, Sandra M. 14, 76
Gilbert and Sullivan 219
Gilda (Darner, character) 102
Gilgamesh and Enkidu 196
Gilmore Girls 195
Giuntoli, David 7, 14, 30, 94, 98, 109, 113, 116, 120, 175–176, 189, 225, 229n13
goddess 121–125, 128, 134, 208, 232ch6n8; see also Diana; Hecate; Maiden/Mother/Crone
Gothic hero-villain 14, 75–93
graduate school 5, 33, 139
Grausen 160–161
Graves, Stephanie vi, 229n5
Gray, Jonathan 218
gray-asexual 65, 68–69

Grayer, Dalpre 52
Green, Keiko 58
Greenwalt, David 2–3, 5, 9, 15, 19, 35, 41, 47, 77, 94, 137–138, 142, 148, 153, 192, 195, 219, 232n2
Griffin, Hank 1, 4–5, 8–9, 13, 19, 28, 31–32, 36–37, 40–55, 56, 58–66, 69–74, 77, 79–80, 83–85, 94, 96–98, 100–101, 104–109, 115–118, 127, 129, 132–134, 144, 149, 154–155, 158, 160–164, 167, 170, 172, 177, 179, 181, 185–186, 193–195, 198–199, 201, 214, 220, 229n11, 14, 20, 231n10, 232ch6n14, 232ch7n3
Grimm (type of being) 2–3, 5, 7–8, 26, 29, 42, 53, 64, 76, 80, 84, 95–96, 101, 105, 107–113, 117, 120, 124–125. 127, 153, 155, 159, 161, 171, 177–178, 193, 209, 228n9
Grimm, Jakob 128, 232ch6n9; see also Brothers Grimm
Grimm episodes (and note the Appendix: Grimm Episode List): "Bad Luck" 58, 99, 145, 147, 187–188, 232n15; "Bad Moon Rising" 42, 50, 229n10, 230n17; "Bad Night" 86, 177–178, 186, 199, 201, 211–213, 231n11; "Bears Will Be Bears" 3, 28, 36, 48, 62, 79, 132; "Beeware" 66, 77, 79, 172; "Beginning of the End Part One" 36, 47, 58, 86–87, 108, 141, 166, 179, 186, 191, 211–213, 231n11; "Bigfeet" 25, 33, 58, 60, 78, 108, 142; "Blind Love" 28, 67, 150, 167, 212–213, 227n1, 229n20; "Blond Ambition" 60, 74, 114, 143, 159, 162, 200; "Blood Magic" 34, 44, 118, 162, 166, 188; "Cat and Mouse" 4–5, 32, 76–78, 80, 98, 100–101, 159, 172; "Chupacabra" 54, 65, 107–108, 229n6; "Cold Blooded" 100, 109, 184, 206, 229n10; "Cry Havoc" 9, 46, 58, 73, 78, 102, 126, 128, 174, 201, 209; "Danse Macabre" 32, 35, 61, 78–79, 97, 132; "A Dish Best Served Cold" 36, 42, 84, 143, 180, 229n8; "The End" 29, 34, 92–93, 195, 198, 202, 214–215; "Eyes of the Beholder" 34, 43, 50–54, 107, 161; "Face Off" 35, 78, 97, 100, 116, 181, 206, 229n4, 231ch5n3; "Game Ogre" 36, 44, 80, 107; "Good Night, Sweet Grimm" 60, 78, 82–83, 100–101, 120, 159, 166, 184, 235n4; "The Good Soldier" 4, 162, 166, 184, 207, 229n6; "Good to the Bone" 88, 178, 210; "The Grimm Identity" 69, 74, 83–84, 107, 133, 140, 189, 209, 234n10; "Happily Ever Aftermath" 32, 35, 97–98; "Hibernaculum" 58, 61, 147, 167; "Highway of Tears" 5–6, 33, 57, 82, 134, 146, 164, 174, 195, 198; "The Hour of Death" 33, 58, 60, 103; "The Inheritance" 87, 189, 194–197, 199, 234n4, 235n23;

"Into the Schwarzwald" 42, 85, 161, 186, 190; "Inugami" 8, 65, 67, 85, 99, 210, 229*n*10, 232*n*3; "Iron Hans" 26, 38, 107, 147, 159, 182, 189; "Island of Dreams" 40, 49, 59, 76, 142, 153–154, 172, 179; "Last Grimm Standing" 31–32, 76, 79, 83, 98, 144; "Leave It to Beavers" 1, 39, 97, 101; "Let Down Your Hair" 31, 42, 60, 78; "Lonelyhearts" 33, 38, 78, 80; "Lost Boys" 171, 174, 176, 187, 210; "Love Sick" 1, 48, 59, 77, 79–80, 83, 98, 129, 157, 160, 172, 179–180, 182, 186, 232*ch7n*9; "Lycanthropia" 61, 72, 85–86, 190; "Maiden Quest" 8, 176, 187; "Mishipishu" 147, 178, 229*n*20; "Mommy Dearest" 56, 67, 91, 186–187, 207; "My Fair Wesen" 15, 64, 103–104, 127, 164, 189, 193, 196, 199, 232*ch7n*13; "Nameless" 5, 59, 62–63, 65, 143, 164; "Natural Born Wesen" 35, 58, 97, 115, 162–163, 229*n*10; "Nobody Knows the Trubel I've Seen" 45, 60, 62, 97, 100, 161, 192–193, 197, 199–200, 208; "Oh Captain, My Captain" 88, 92, 116, 119, 175; "One Angry Fuchsbau" 35–36, 45, 97, 143, 157, 235*n*8; "Over My Dead Body" 36–37, 46, 86, 100–101, 107, 156, 165; "Pilot" 2–3, 5, 10, 24–28, 32, 35, 40–44, 48, 60, 75–77, 81, 89, 95–96, 98, 101, 106–111, 115–116, 123, 126, 167, 171, 173–174, 179, 182, 227*n*5, 228*n*8, 230*n*18, 232*ch7n*12; "Quill" 59, 83, 101, 157, 164, 166–167, 227*n*10; "Stories We Tell Our Young" 98, 143, 163; "Synchronicity" 83, 91, 125, 144–145, 207–208, 231*ch5n*6; "The Taming of the Wu" 45, 72, 91, 99, 105, 116, 178, 201, 210–212, 237*n*1; "The Thing with Feathers" 4, 32, 49, 59, 66, 77, 97, 179; "The Three Bad Wolves" 30–31, 33, 38, 79, 115; "Three Coins in a Fuchsbau" 6, 48, 78, 81, 86, 88, 107, 133, 231*n*10; "Tribunal" 6, 33, 36, 46, 61, 73–74, 84, 101, 107–108, 116, 147, 161, 167; "The Ungrateful Dead" 34, 60, 83, 143, 158, 160, 183–184, 233*n*12; "Volcanalis" 78, 80, 97–98, 110, 183; "Wesen Nacht" 6, 33, 57, 60, 98, 103–104, 115, 160, 162, 177, 195, 198–199, 201, 229*n*10, 230*ch3n*6; "You Don't Know Jack" 9, 60, 89, 148, 169, 185, 187, 189
Grimoire 186
Guadalajara 136
Gubar, Susan 14, 76
guide 18, 27–29, 124, 163
gun 1, 20, 24–25, 31, 35–36, 40–41, 43–44, 46, 60, 62, 64, 70, 78, 80, 82, 90, 95–97, 100, 111, 130, 140, 142, 154–155, 164, 231*n*9, 231*n*10, 232*ch7n*10, 234*ch9n*14

Gunn, Charles 138, 140
Gunsmoke 227*n*2

Hadrian's Wall 8, 17, 84, 89, 90, 103–104, 106, 126, 133–124, 148–149, 150, 200–202, 210, 233*n*22, 234*n*7
hair 21, 23, 60, 77, 94, 120, 123, 125, 129–130, 137, 147–148, 150, 170–171, 173, 177, 180, 186, 188, 193, 196, 196, 198, 210–211, 215, 230*ch4n*2, 232*n*16, 232*n*20; *see also* cabinet, wigs
Hamamoto, Darrell 13, 57–58, 66
Hamlet 21, 46, 81, 139; *see also* Shakespeare, William
Hamm, Jon 10
hand imagery 38, 49, 53, 60, 73, 77, 92, 111, 118, 144–145, 154, 155, 158, 170, 178, 183, 188–190, 196, 198, 201, 202, 211
Hanged Man 89
Hannah, Darryl 149
Hansel and Gretel 124
Hap *see* Lasser, Hap
Hargrove, Dean 20–21
Harmon, Ian 155–156, 164
Harper, M.E. 9, 15, 123, 132–34
Harris, Cheryl L. 4, 229*n*5
Harris, Kandace L. vi, 230*n*22
Harry Potter books 202, 214
hat, witch's 130, 137–138, 146, 149, 151, 185–186, 188, 191, 232*n*3; *see also* symbolism, hat, witch's
The Hate U Give 55
Have Gun, Will Travel 234*n*15
Hawk, Julie vi
healer 9, 16, 59, 118, 121, 152–159, 161–162, 167–168; *see also* apothecary; Crone; doctor, medical; Wise Woman
hearing 3, 14, 25, 95, 108–109, 119; *see also* sound
Hecate 122, 128, 208
Henrietta (character) 15, 82, 89, 123, 129, 131–132, 134, 136, 148
hero, Campbellian: difficult return 38; journey 27, 37, 228*ch1n*4; reluctance 27, 31, 110; *see also* Campbell, Joseph
hero-sidekick *see* liminal hero-sidekick
hero-villain *see* Gothic hero-villain
heterosexuality 8, 13–15, 39, 65, 67, 69, 76, 94, 98–99, 138–145, 153
Hewett, Richard 10
Hexenbiest 8, 17, 50, 76, 78, 82, 87–88, 96, 99, 102, 104, 108, 113, 120–132, 135–136, 142, 145–151, 159–160, 169, 174, 177–178, 182–185, 188–190, 195, 198, 200–202, 206–206, 215, 220, 233*n*26, 234*n*17; *see also* Witch
Hills, Matt 140

Hispanic 123, 133; *see also* Latinx characters; Mexican American
Hitchcock, Alfred 91
Hitler, Adolf 6–7, 86
Hoeveler, Diane Long 81, 88
Hogg, Christopher 10–12,
Hollander, Anne 21
Holly (character) 71
Hollywood Diversity Report see *UCLA Hollywood Diversity Report*
Holmes, Sherlock 228*n*18
Home Alone 212
Homeland 10
homosexuality 8–9, 13, 38–39, 62, 69–70
Hornsby, Russell 5, 12–13, 40, 47, 49–51, 53–55, 71, 229*n*13
horror 14, 41, 61, 70, 72, 89, 126, 131, 146–147, 154, 169–172, 175, 182–185, 187, 196, 206, 214, 233*n*7
horror rom-com see romantic comedy
hospital scene 29, 31, 36, 44, 68–69, 70, 107, 111, 116, 124, 130, 171, 189
Hotspur, *Henry IV, Part I* 55; *see also* Shakespeare, William
Howard, Doug 232*n*17
Howell, Robin 24–25
Huizinga, Johan 11, 228*n*15
human trafficking 58, 139, 187, 197, 200, 230*ch*3*n*4
Hummel figurines 43, 229*n*4
humor 5, 7, 14, 16–17, 25, 27, 29–31, 34–35, 45, 48, 56–59, 61–62, 66, 70–71, 83, 88, 90, 97, 114–120, 124, 126–127, 132, 135, 139, 142, 155, 161–162, 167, 169–170, 172, 175–176, 182–185, 189–190, 212, 228*n*12, 232*ch*7*n*10; *see also* comedy, physical; farce; wit
Hundjäger 234*n*5
Hunt, Darnell M. 48, 57, 230*n*22
hunting 3, 24, 30, 36, 41, 61, 72, 79–80, 100, 104, 108, 120, 128, 192, 208,
Huntress 9, 15, 122–128, 133–136, 199; *see also* Crone
Hutton, Ronald 9, 121–122, 127–128, 156–157, 231*ch*6*n*3, 232*n*9
hybrid 12, 19–24, 32–33
hypermasculinity 14, 105

I Spy 40
illegitimacy 7, 14, 75–76, 78, 83, 103, 147, 169, 202, 205
Illyria (character) 15, 137–141, 147–151, 232*n*17, 233*n*26
immigration 6, 68, 228*n*14, 230*n*12; *see also* diaspora
individuation 16–17, 112, 192, 200–204
Inferno 27

The Initiative 149, 233*n*25
innocence 18, 27, 32, 44, 52, 69, 82, 94–95, 100, 110, 194–195, 230*ch*3*n*4
intellect, intelligence 5, 12, 19–24, 33–35, 39, 54, 57, 59, 61–65, 75, 85, 95, 105, 117, 120, 130, 134, 137–139, 142, 154, 156, 170, 198–200
interest convergence 12–13, 43–44, 51
intermarriage 4–6, 33, 46, 84, 129, 146, 152, 167; *see also* marriage
intersectionality 2, 12–13, 15, 53, 123, 133–134, 220
Iranian American 135
Ireland, Jill 20
Ironside 227*n*2
It's a Wonderful Life 119
iZombie 234*n*6

Jack the Ripper 42, 88–89, 132
Jackson, Kathy Merlock 208
Jagerbar 29
Japanese American 67
Jasmine (*Angel* character) 139–140
Jewishness 6–7, 21, 33, 67
Johnstone, Rachael 227*n*4, 228*n*16
journey, hero's see hero, Campbellian
Jowett, Lorna 2, 41
Joy (character) 51, 53
Juliet 126, 142, 144–145, 177
Juliette see Silverton, Juliette
Juliette/Eve 15, 71, 73, 118, 123, 127–128, 132–133, 136–139, 141, 147, 149–151, 161, 170, 177, 188, 191, 199–200, 202–203, 208, 213–214, 233*n*26; *see also* Eve; Silverton, Juliette
Jung, Carl 145

Kali 122, 125, 134
Kaveney, Roz 140, 148
Keary, Daniel 108
Kehrseite 6–7, 54, 133, 135, 198; kehrseiteschlichkennen 143
Ken (character) 193–194, 197, 200
Kendall, Harmony 24, 139
Kenneth see Bowes-Lyon, Kenneth, Prince
Kessler, Marie, Aunt 2–4, 7, 15–16, 24, 26, 28–29, 31, 36, 43, 63, 69, 75–77, 79–80, 95–98, 110–112, 117, 119, 121–126, 133, 136, 143–144, 147, 151–152, 157, 161, 167, 171–172, 174, 180, 198, 200–203, 214–215, 227*n*7, 234*n*13
Key 34, 74, 77, 80–81, 92, 102, 111, 116–118, 129, 149–150, 167–168, 172, 181, 191, 201–202
Kies, Bridget 21–22
killing: attitudes towards 82, 106–108;

Index 255

statistics for Nick 106–108; *see also* death; guns
Kim-Bryan, Stephanie 58
Kindley, Evan 217
King, Martin Luther, Jr. 40
Kirk, Capt. James T. 21–22, 37
Kirkland, Ewan 17, 192, 195–196, 200
Kitchens, Juliette 142
Klaustreich 4
Knotts, Don 30
knowledge: cultural 3, 5, 12, 17, 19–24, 33–35, 78, 82, 135; magical 3–4, 15, 63, 82, 84, 124, 127–129, 131, 135, 142, 147, 152, 154, 156–157, 169, 188, 199–200; scientific 126–127, 129, 131, 143, 152, 156–158; *see also* lore
Knox (character) 139
Knox, Simone 228
Königschlange 46
Kouf, Brenna 219, 228n11, 230n21
Kouf, Jim 3, 7, 9, 35, 77, 94, 111–112, 118, 142, 148, 153, 162, 164, 192, 227n11, 228n11
Kouf, Lynn 219, 228n11
Kouvaris, George 10
Krampus 3
Kristallnacht 6–7, 33, 177, 201
Kristeva, Julia 9, 114, 121, 169, 171, 182–185, 187–188, 196, 231ch6n2, 233n7, 233n10
Kronenberg, House of 232ch6n10
Ku Klux Klan 6, 33, 46
Kungl, Carla 196
Kunin, Aaron 217
Kuryakin, Illya 12, 19–21, 23–24, 36, 39

The L-Word: Generation Q 234n3
labor 8, 37–38, 44, 58–59, 61–62, 79, 86–87, 95, 98, 132–134, 136, 138, 142–143, 151–154, 163, 165–166, 175–176, 192, 210, 234n6
Lacey, Stephen 228n14
Lagadec, Christian 83
Lamb, Patricia Frazer 22
Lammasniemi, Laura 230ch3n4
language 1–2, 5, 10–11, 14, 19–23, 34–35, 61–62, 66, 80, 97–98, 112, 119, 141, 145, 150, 166, 177, 189–190, 211, 228ch1n15; foreign language 6, 34, 68, 78, 117, 135, 157; *see also* dialogue
Lascelles, Elizabeth 15, 78, 81–82, 123, 129–131, 174
Lasser, Angelina 10, 31, 36–38, 46, 136, 164–165, 228n16
Lasser, Hap 30, 33, 115
Laszlo, Victor 164
Latinx characters 44, 58, 64, 67, 84, 123, 132–136, 220, 229n6; *see also* Hispanic; Mexican American

Latinx myths 229n6; *see also* El Chucapabra; El Cucuy; La Llorona
Lavery, David 11, 219
law 8, 15, 32, 42–47, 64, 73, 78, 81, 103, 105–106, 123, 132–135, 140, 156, 163, 170, 176, 182
lawyer 8, 17, 32, 45, 126, 169–170, 175, 178, 186–188, 206
Leal, Sharon 50–51, 53, 136
Lebensauger 193–194
Lee, Reggie 5, 13, 56–62, 68, 70, 72, 74, 228n2, 230ch3n1, 233ch8n2
legitimation 7, 231ch5n1, 231n20
Le Guin, Ursula 188, 235n2
Leighton, Anne 85
Lerberg, Matthew 227n4, 228n8, 232ch7n12
lesbian 234n3; *see also* homosexuality
Leslie-McCarthy, Sage 214
Li, Suzanne 58
librarian 4, 124
Lichelle, Sapphire 58
Liew, Sonny 230n14
lighting 12, 25, 28, 43, 49, 61, 72, 89, 98, 102, 109–110, 117, 124, 144, 146, 150, 153, 173, 182, 190–191, 197, 213
liminal hero-sidekick 12, 19–39
liminality 14, 19–39, 64, 134–135, 160, 220, 228ch1n3; *see also* gender liminality
Lincoln Rhyme: The Hunt for the Bone Collector 55
The Lion, the Witch, and the Wardrobe 3
Lipslums, Trinket 62
Lipstadt, Aaron 150
La Llorona 44, 101, 135, 229n6
Lockley, Kate, Det. 138
Logan, Elliot 10
Lois and Clark 228n11
Lombard, Louise 131
lore 3, 15–16, 96, 124–125, 128–129, 152, 156–158, 188, 199, 203, 205, 214, 227n8
lover 4, 15, 23–24, 46, 97, 113, 125–126, 142, 155, 232n4, 235n9
Loyd, Hannah R. 8, 18, 128, 210
Lynch, David 68, 89, 219

Mad Men 10
Mafe, Diana Adesole 42, 50
"Magical Negro" 135
Maiden/Mother/Crone 9, 15, 121–122
make-up 77, 177
Malcolm X 47
Malleus Maleficarum 130
The Man from U.N.C.L.E. 12, 19–20–21, 23–24, 36, 39
Marie, Aunt *see* Kessler, Aunt Marie
Marquesa, Soledad 231n10

marriage 4, 13, 16–17, 21, 32, 39, 40, 48, 51, 71, 104, 127, 138, 142, 144–145, 149, 151–152, 158, 162–168, 173, 178–179, 187, 229n11; *see also* intermarriage; romance
Marshall, Jenna 5, 63
Marsters, James 23, 39
Marvin, Richard 72
masculinity 8–9, 12–14, 20–22, 32, 57, 66, 71, 76, 95, 97–106, 109–115, 141, 157–158, 189, 196, 198; *see also* hypermasculinity
mass incarceration 51–53, 62, 229n15, 229n16
Masson, Cynthea 140–141
Masters, Kate, Det. 47, 58
Mastrantonio, Mary Elizabeth 125, 159
Mathison, Carrie 10
matriarchy 121–122, 124, 182
mayor 13, 76, 84–86, 88, 90, 92, 178, 211
McCallum, David 20–21, 39
McDonald-Lewis, Mary 135
McKiernan, Tawnia 142
Meisner, Martin 8, 76, 83–84, 87, 89–92, 149, 198, 201, 207, 209, 211, 233n14, 234n18
melodrama 109–110, 117, 120, 231n15; family 111–112; male 9, 11, 14, 94–95, 109–114, 116, 119–120
medical practitioner *see* doctor, medical; healer; veterinarian
memory 1, 26, 28, 38, 52, 70, 89, 143–144, 148–149, 194, 203, 227n2; *see also* amnesia
Mendelsohn, Farah 235n22
mental health 13, 17, 44–45, 50, 57, 59, 61–65, 70, 72, 95, 127, 139, 142, 147, 167, 193–194, 200
mentor 18, 97, 102–103, 109, 131, 139, 192, 199, 234n18
Mexican American 67, 123, 135–136; *see also* Latinx characters
A Midsummer Night's Dream 230n19; *see also* Shakespeare, William
Millican, Dana 232ch6n13
A Million Little Things 120
Minear, Tim 146
minority *see* ethnicity; race
Mintz, Leah E. 195
Mintz, Susannah B. 195
mirror 36, 73, 89, 129, 188, 191, 206–207, 211, 213–214, 232ch6n12
mise-en-scène 10, 12, 25, 27–29, 31, 33, 38, 42, 49, 89, 91, 102, 144–145, 151, 155, 162, 164–165, 171, 177, 182–183, 197, 206–207, 209, 211, 213; *see also* production design; set decoration; setting
Mitchell, Silas Weir 5, 7, 12, 19, 24, 26–27, 29, 34–36, 38–39, 63, 152, 158, 164, 231n19,

Mittell, Jason 1–2
Mix, Stephanie 106, 125, 145, 147, 173, 227n4, 228n13, 231ch6n6, 232ch7n8
mixed race *see* race
Moers, Ellen 14, 76, 81
Moffatt, Steven 228n18
Moi, Toril 218, 220
Mommie Dearest 230n13; *see also* Grimm episode "Mommy Dearest"
Monroe (character) 1, 3, 4–9, 12, 16, 19–39, 40–41, 43–46, 50, 60–61, 63–65, 71–74, 78, 82, 84–85, 96–102, 105–110, 112, 115–119, 127–129, 133, 136, 137, 142–146, 149–151, 152–167, 173–174, 177–178, 180, 185, 188, 194, 196, 198–202, 206–207, 215, 220, 227n10, 228n6, 228n8, 230n17, 232ch7n10, 232ch7n12, 235n3
monster 1, 23, 26, 40, 43, 46, 57, 59, 61, 68–69, 75, 78, 96, 111, 182, 187, 208, 213–215, 229n6, 234n17
morality: moral variety/complexity 4, 9–10, 15–16, 26, 29, 32, 41, 96, 110, 121–123, 130–131, 133, 136, 139, 148, 150–151, 153, 161–162, 167–168, 180, 185–187, 190–191, 201–202, 205, 207–208, 211–213; morally gray 14, 16–17, 28, 76, 93, 128, 130, 146, 189, 201–202, 205
Morgan, Lilah 138
Moses 202
mother 2, 16–17, 46, 67–68, 72, 81–82, 93, 97, 102, 110–113, 119, 124–126, 128–131, 140, 144, 147–148, 169–170, 172–174, 178, 182, 184–188, 205–216, 229n20; *see also* Maiden/Mother/Crone
Mukherjea, Ananya vi, 58, 68, 228ch2n2, 229n7, 230n12
Mumy, Billy 210
Murcielago 32
Murray, Margaret 122
music 2, 5, 12, 20–24, 29–30, 32–35, 41–43, 49, 67–68, 72, 91, 108, 115–117, 134, 163, 165, 171, 180–181, 183; *see also* sound
My Darling Clementine 10
Myers, Dr. 58

NAACP 229n16
Nadalind 170
Nadine (character) 48, 50
Nadkarni, Samira 232n21
name significance 18, 47, 84, 85, 90, 92, 114, 126, 131–132, 137–138, 149, 169, 172, 178, 186, 189, 193, 205, 208, 218, 230ch4n4
narrative, long-term serial 2, 4–11, 41, 58–59, 63, 138–140, 144–145, 170–178, 218; *see also* symbolism, narrative
Native American 134, 229n20

Nazis 6–7, 33, 46, 201, 227*n*9; *see also* Hitler, Adolf
N.C.I.S. 39
Neander-Wu 1, 72, 227*n*1
Nebojsa, Josef 4
Needham, Rodney 121
Newcomb, Horace 1, 227*n*2
Newman, Jaime Ray 37, 136, 232*ch6n*16
Nichols, Nichelle 60
Nimoy, Leonard 21–22, 39
Nishime, Leilani 66, 68
Nochimson, Martha P. 219
noir 87, 171, 197
nonbinary 8, 220
Nuages, Hugues 165–166

O. Henry 212
objectification 24, 83, 165
Oblinger, John 107
Ojibwe 134
Olyphant, Timothy 10
Ophelia 139; *see also* Shakespeare, William
O'Reilly, Julie 16, 160
Oren, Tasha 66, 68
Orson, Peter, Lt. 158
Other 12, 14, 18, 19–39, 43, 76, 78, 97, 157, 167, 205
Ouellette, Laurie 218
The Ox-bow Incident 84
Oyelowo, David 40, 55

Panassié, Hugues 165
Paradise Lost 7
parallels *see* doubling; foils
parents 7, 16, 26, 33, 52–53, 58, 85, 88, 91, 93, 103, 108, 111, 124, 127, 139–141, 152, 154–156, 167, 178, 188, 205, 208–213; *see also* father; mother
partners 1, 4–5, 19–20, 28, 31–32, 38–39, 40–48, 56, 70, 87, 94–98, 100, 107, 114, 116, 142, 144, 146, 153–154, 161, 164, 167, 170, 179, 214, 232*n*4, 235*n*4
paternalism 14, 64, 103–107, 119–120; *see also* patriarchy
pathos 14, 109–114
Patmore, Coventry 187
patriarchy 8–9, 13–14, 17–19, 50, 75–93, 102, 104, 115, 118–120, 121, 124, 128, 130, 169, 178–182, 190, 193–194, 197, 209
Peacock, Steven 10
Pearson, Roberta 2, 228*n*16
Peasants' War, German, 1525 33
Pech, Frau 123, 135, 183–185, 206–207, 231*ch6n*4
Pender, Patricia 192–193
Penley, Constance 22
Pentony, Samantha 182

performance, definition and study of 10–12
Peter Pan 187
Pharmakides 127, 131, 156
pheromones 35, 38, 45, 157
physicality *see* body; body language
Pica 59; *see also* mental health
Piepmeier, Alison 199
Pilar (character) 123, 135–136, 231*ch6n*4
Pip (character) 149; *see also* Dickens, Charles
Piper, Alana Jayne 233*ch8n*1
Pip's Donuts 159
playfulness 11, 21, 34–35, 48, 69, 185, 197, 212; *see also* Huizinga, Johann
poetry 7, 23, 34, 166
police 2, 5, 7–8, 12–13, 25, 28, 40, 42–47, 50–53, 57, 62, 65–66, 75, 79, 81, 83, 95, 101, 105–106, 120, 121, 132–135, 153–154; procedural 8, 41, 46, 59, 95, 106
politician 13, 16, 76, 85–86, 90, 117, 152, 155, 158, 160–163, 175, 178, 210, 230*ch4n*4
Popescu, Queen Stefania Vaduva 123, 135, 183–184, 206, 233*ch9n*9
popularity 12, 19–23, 37, 39, 56, 79, 122, 152, 212
Porter, Heather M. vi, 227*n*3, 231*ch6n*4
Porter, Josh 4, 200, 234*n*3
Porter, Lynnette 65, 228*n*2
Porter, Rolek 4, 199
Porter, William Sidney *see* O. Henry
Portland, Oregon 2, 24, 41, 59, 64, 68, 76–77, 81–82, 85–87, 98, 106, 113, 117–118, 121, 123, 127, 131, 136, 150, 153, 155, 163, 174, 178, 180, 200, 228*ch2n*2, 230*ch3n*6
possession: magical 42, 83, 88–89, 132, 134, 188; ownership 83, 105, 117, 208–209
potion 3, 15, 48–49, 58–59, 71, 96, 115–116, 126–127, 129–130, 146–147, 154, 156, 159, 170, 180, 185, 191, 202, 215
Potter, Harry 97, 208; *see also* Harry Potter books
power 3–4, 7, 9–10, 12–18, 21–22, 25–26, 28, 31, 35, 40–54, 56–57, 59–60, 68, 71–74, 75–93, 95–106, 113–120, 122–123, 125–135, 137–151, 152–153, 155–157, 160–161, 163–164, 167–168, 169–171, 173–174, 177–191, 192–198, 200–204, 205–216, 217–218, 220, 228*ch1n*2, 229*n*9
Practical Magic 233*ch8n*8
pragmatism 16, 84–86, 152, 158, 160–161, 166
predator 25, 125
pregnancy 17, 48, 67, 69, 71, 87, 100, 128, 132, 135, 139, 145–146, 160, 166, 169, 173–174, 181–185, 187, 189, 206–207, 209, 214, 233*n*6, 235*n*4
prince: Eric *see* Renard, Eric; Kenneth

Index

see Bowes-Lyon, Prince Kenneth; Sean *see* Renard, Capt. Sean; Viktor *see* von Konigsburg, Viktor
princess 17–18, 35, 129, 179
producer 36, 41, 56, 58, 67–68, 220; *see also* Greenwalt, David; Kouf, Jim; Kouf, Lynn
production design 24, 36, 78, 147, 165, 168, 197, 201, 206, 210, 220, 228*ch*1*n*6; *see also* mise-en-scène; set decoration; setting
profiling 4, 32, 41, 96, 170
prophecy/portents 18, 34, 101, 207–208, 214
protectiveness, male 14, 91, 101–107, 119, 140, 190, 195; failure of 14, 104–106, 190, 195
Pru (character) 149
Puckler, Damien 83
purity 6, 33, 167, 183, 220
Purkiss, Diane 9
Pylea 139–140, 232*ch*7*n*7

Queen of the Schwarzwald Roma *see* Popescu, Queen Stefania Vaduva
queer reading 66–67, 141, 151; *see also* homosexuality; lesbian
quest 8, 35, 82, 111–112, 116, 160, 187

race 2, 4–8, 10–13, 15, 21, 26, 28, 31–33, 37, 40–55, 56–74, 76, 78, 84–86, 90, 96, 110, 123, 132–136, 146, 152, 156, 159, 162, 167, 175, 182, 220, 229*n*5; *see also* ethnicity; symbolism, narrative
Rachel (*Angel* character) 23
Rambo, Elizabeth 9, 138
Randy (character) 71
"The Ransom of Red Chief" 212
rape 17, 37, 45, 127, 162, 192–195, 199; parallels 17, 114, 139, 169–170, 173–174, 183
Ratcliffe, Krista 43
rationality 18, 21, 101, 114, 119, 189–190, 203
Raven, Marian 20–21
Reamer, Adam *see* production design
Reapers of the Grimms 31, 43, 79, 95, 101, 111, 112
rebirth 4, 37–38, 88–89, 119, 138, 149–150, 198, 201, 203
Red Riding Hood 3, 24–25, 95
Reinhardt, Django 165
religion 76, 117–118, 121–122, 134, 182–183
Renard, Diana Schade 4, 8, 15, 18, 67, 76, 83, 87–93, 97, 109, 119, 123, 128, 130, 144, 150, 173–174, 178, 181–191, 200–201, 203, 205–216, 227*n*7, 230*ch*4*n*5, 233*n*14, 235*n*25
Renard, Prince Eric 45, 78, 81–84, 87, 89, 179–181, 189

Renard, Capt. Sean 4, 7, 8–9, 13–14, 17, 18, 35, 48, 60, 62, 65, 73, 75–93, 97, 99–100, 102–103, 105, 107–109, 115–116, 118, 123, 128–132, 143, 146–147, 163, 165, 169, 172, 174–175, 178–182, 186, 188–191, 202, 205–213, 215, 227*n*7, 231*ch*5*n*3, 233*ch*8*n*4
Renner, Karen J. 18, 205, 209, 210
reporter 32, 58, 155, 230*ch*3*n*6
Resistance 32, 75, 83, 89, 155, 164, 181, 201, 207, 209–210
Réveillon Riots, 1789 33
Revolutionaries, left-wing 6–7, 47, 54, 76, 84, 103, 106–107, 148, 200–201; *see also* Black Claw (Schwarz Kralle)
Reynolds, Donna 58
Rheinigen 30, 35
rhetorical skill 17, 188–191; *see also* language
Richards, J. August 138
Rimsky Korsakoff 34
ring 16–17, 48, 90, 95, 119, 143–145, 147, 170, 178–179, 187, 230–231*ch*4*n*6; *see also* symbolism, ring
ritual 32, 76, 145, 163, 183–188, 206, 212, 229*n*20
Rochester, Edward 88
Rodgers and Hammerstein 165
Rodriguez, Elizabeth 133
Roiz, Sasha 7, 13–14, 75, 77–78, 88, 91, 179, 229*n*13
Roma 123, 135, 165, 183, 206
romance 13–16, 22–23, 30, 41, 50–51, 53–55, 57, 65, 68–71, 86–88, 98, 120, 126, 138–145, 150–151, 154–155, 159–160, 162–168, 179, 190, 205, 211; *see also* romantic comedy; screwball comedy
romantic comedy 16, 170–178, 182; *see also* romance; screwball comedy
Romeo 142, 144–145, 177
Romeo and Juliet 142, 144–145, 177; *see also* Shakespeare, William
Romulus and Remus 33
Rosemary's Baby 206
Roslin, Laura 200, 235*n*24
Roswell 228*n*11
Royals 75–93, 117–118, 130, 133, 135, 148, 169, 174, 181, 183, 207, 209; seven royal families 76–77, 117, 155, 232*ch*6*n*10
Rubel, Theresa *see* Trubel
Rumpelstiltskin 62–63

Sabrina the Teenage Witch 122
Sachs, Sharon 9, 132
St. John, Thania 30, 228*n*11
Salter, Anastasia 218
Samson 60, 66, 105, 146

Index 259

sarcasm 1, 50, 61–62, 64, 70, 85, 140, 156, 162, 172, 189; *see also* wit
Satan *see* Zerstorer
Schade, Adalind 1, 8, 10–11, 15–18, 20, 34, 40, 46, 48–50, 58, 65–67, 71, 73–74, 76–79, 82, 86–89, 91–92, 96–99, 104–106, 108, 114–115, 123, 126–132, 135, 139, 142, 144–147, 149–150, 152, 154–155, 159–161, 164, 169–191, 194–195, 198–203, 205–213, 215, 227n7, 229n13, 231n17, 232ch7n14, 233ch8n6
Schade, Catherine 77, 123, 129, 130–133, 135, 146, 159, 169–170, 172–173, 179–180, 186–187, 189–191, 205, 208, 234ch9n16, 235n7
Scharrer, Erica 67
Scheherazade 34
Schrödinger's cat 119
Schwaab, Herbert 219
Schwabe, Claudia 35, 227n4, 231ch5n4
Schwarzwald 63, 116–117, 123, 135, 201, 206, 230n10
science 15–16, 43, 126–127, 137–140, 142, 152, 156–158, 167
science fiction 123, 195, 218, 228n12
Scooby Gang 62, 71, 73, 143, 185
screwball comedy 16, 170, 174–175, 185, 188, 233ch9n2
"Season of the Witch" (song) 49
Sebastian (character) 83
Secundum Naturae Ordinem Wesen *see* Wesenrein
self-sacrifice 24, 36–38, 160, 167, 170
Selley, April 22
Selma 40
Sempruch, Justyna 9, 122, 156–157
sensation scenes 14, 109–114
set decoration 33, 38, 43, 147, 155, 165, 168, 197, 201, 206–207, 211, 213, 229n4; *see also* mise-en-scène; production design; setting
setting 7, 24, 27, 31, 34, 68, 72, 76, 80, 89, 98–101, 113–114, 117, 129–131, 133, 142, 148, 151, 170, 176, 178, 180–181, 183, 187, 193, 197, 201, 220; Austria 78; cabin in the woods 81, 89, 191; Manila 68; Monroe's 24–26, 31, 38, 92, 228n6; police station 38, 77, 90; Renard's 77, 89; Rosalee's Spice Shop 117, 130, 152, 156–157, 161, 166, 168; *see also* German; mise-en-scène; production design; set decoration; trailer
Sex Pistols 23
sexual abuse *see* abuse, sexual
sexual ambiguity 9, 13, 57, 65–71, 74, 230n11
sexual orientation 8, 13, 38–39, 57, 65–71, 74; *see also* asexuality; heterosexuality; homosexuality; lesbian
sexuality 2, 8, 13, 16, 20, 22, 24, 30, 35, 38, 40, 47–54, 57, 77–78, 85–89, 98–99, 105, 131–132, 138–139, 143, 146–147, 153, 155, 158–159, 164, 166, 170–182, 189, 194–195, 197, 211, 215
Shadow Hero 230n14
Shah, Pritesh 5
Shakespeare, William 46, 55, 71, 126, 141–142; *see also* Gertrude; *Hamlet*; *Henry IV, Part I*; Hotspur; Juliet; *A Midsummer Night's Dream*; Ophelia; Romeo; *Romeo and Juliet*; *Twelfth Night*
Shatner, William 21
Shattuc, Jane M. 218, 220
Shimizu, Celine Parrenas 13, 58, 65, 67, 230n12
Showrunner 2, 7, 9, 41, 94, 112, 118, 137, 141, 148, 157, 162, 164, 227n5; *see also* Greenwalt, David; Kouf, Jim
sidekick 12, 19, 40–43, 228ch1n2; *see also* liminal hero-sidekick
Siegbarste 31, 80
Siegevolk 38
sight 3, 14, 17, 91, 95–97, 101, 105, 117, 126, 215
Silverton, Juliette 1, 4, 8, 15, 16–17, 34–35, 38–39, 64–65, 71, 73–74, 77–78, 82, 84, 87, 89, 97–101, 109, 111–118, 120, 123–124, 126–128, 130–133, 135–136, 137–151, 152, 158, 160–161, 163–165, 169–181, 185–189, 191, 193–198, 200–204, 205–209, 213–214, 228n13, 231ch6n6, 232ch7n9, 232ch7n10, 232ch7n13, 232ch7n14, 234n10
Skentzos, Spiro 165
skull 18, 117, 206–207, 209, 211, 213
slavery, sexual *see* human trafficking
Sleeping Beauty 77, 142, 180
smell 25, 27, 30, 34
Smith, Murray 2, 229n19
Smith, Philip 68, 230n14
Smulson, Ryan 103
snake 46, 130
Snow White 129
soldier 14, 16–17, 57, 106, 137, 148–149, 201, 229n6
Solo, Napoleon 20
Soong, Sophie 58
Sophia or Sapientia 121; *see also* Wise Woman
Sorkin, Aaron 79
sound 61, 68, 70, 89–90, 108, 111, 113, 117, 124, 144, 164–167, 170, 173, 179, 183, 185, 193; 207, *see also* expression, vocal; music
Spanish 135

Index

spell 35, 48, 50, 71, 78, 87, 126, 142, 155, 172–174, 179–181, 184, 188, 202, 233n13
Spice Shop *see* setting, Rosalee's Spice Shop
Spicer, Arwen 23
spider 18, 143, 128, 184, 206–207
Spike 12, 19, 22–24, 36–39, 126, 140–141, 148, 197, 233n27
Spinnetod 143
Spock 12, 19, 21–24, 35–39
sports 97, 109–110
staff 118–120, 202, 215
Stanfill, Mel 218
Star Trek 19, 21, 60, 66; *see also* Spock; Sulu, Hikaru
Starbuck (*Battlestar Galactica* character) 39, 192, 195–196, 198, 200, 203
Stark, Oleg 80
status 2, 13–14, 48, 51, 53, 56, 59–61, 76–78, 81, 88, 153, 155; *see also* class
status quo 31–33, 37, 94–95, 120, 231ch5n1
Stefancic, Jean 4
Steinwedell, Nicole 215
stereotype 12–13, 15–16, 38, 40, 43, 55, 57, 65–67, 70, 124, 135–136, 152, 157, 198
Stern, Lesley 10
Steward, Weston 133
Stewart, Jimmy 119
Stewart, Michael 110, 113
stick, Nick's 116–120, 149–150, 202; *see also* symbolism, phallic; symbolism, stick, Nick's
Stockton, Kathryn Bond 235n9
strength, physical 3, 12, 17, 19–23, 32, 35–36, 71, 82, 95, 148, 151
stunts *see* Taylor, Matthew
Sulu, Hikaru 66
Summers, Buffy 22, 24, 37, 97, 126, 142, 177
Summers, Dawn 23
Summerson, Esther 112; *see also* Dickens, Charles
superhero 9, 14–15, 95, 100, 105–106, 108, 151, 160, 198, 232n21, 234n7
"Sweet Dreams" (song) 108, 115
symbolism 2, 7–14, 31–32, 37, 39, 41, 43, 49–50, 63, 119, 157, 169, 182, 188, 191, 200; hat, witch's 138, 146; narrative 4–10, 55, 56, 139, 220; phallic 14, 116–120, 146, 149–150, 157, 215; racial 4–8, 53–54, 84–86, 96, 182; ring 16–17, 90, 143–145, 147, 179; setting 77, 161, 166, 168, 228n6; stick, Nick's 14, 116–120, 149–150; trailer 80, 96, 111–112, 147, 191, 198

Taber, Nancy 8, 32, 102, 227n4
Tagalog 68
Taiwanese 63
Takeda, Scott 58
Talamonti, Tony 161
Taylor, Matthew 234n5
telekinesis 211, 213, 215–216
telepathy 210, 213
Tenga, Angela 3, 6, 135, 237n4, 228n14, 230n15
Terrible Crone *see* Crone
terrorists, right-wing 6–7, 146; *see also* Wesenrein
Terry, Michael Grant 103
testing 27–29, 64–65, 90, 131, 141, 144, 151, 175, 181, 183, 185, 220
Teutoburg Forest Battle 33
themes 2, 11, 18, 39, 55, 74, 76, 95, 120, 123, 136, 138, 151, 152–153, 167, 170, 191, 203–204, 205, 215–216
Theophrastus 217
Thomas, Calvin 98, 114
Thompson, Robert 1
threshold 3, 25–28, 39, 49, 109, 111, 119, 143, 188, 214
Toboni, Jacqueline 8, 18, 128, 192, 194–197, 201, 234n3
Toles, George 10
Tolkien, J.R.R. 117, 119
Tomas, Dana 13, 67–71
Tomas, Lani 68–70
Tomas, Sam 67–70, 230n17
torture 35, 89–90, 103, 106, 201
trailer, Aunt Marie's 3–4, 15, 26, 31, 34, 46, 63–64, 69, 72, 74, 80, 82, 96, 102, 111–112, 120, 124–126, 128, 143, 147, 152, 157, 191, 198–201, 203, 214, 227n7; *see also* symbolism, trailer
transgression 12, 16, 21, 40, 95, 152, 158–159, 167
Traval, Wil 234n15
Trubel (character) 4, 8, 15, 17–18, 45, 64, 84, 90, 92, 97–98, 102–106, 109, 113, 115, 117, 119, 123, 126–128, 133, 139, 142, 148–149, 151, 161, 164, 177, 192–204, 210, 215, 232ch7n13, 233n23, 233ch9n6, 234n4, 234n7, 234n10, 234n13, 234ch10n15, 234ch10n16, 234n18, 234–235n21
Trucks, Toni 134, 229n20
Trump, Billie 85, 234ch4n4
Trump, Donald 230ch4n4
trust 5, 14, 27–31, 44, 75, 78, 82, 85–93, 102, 111, 130, 133, 143, 162–163, 168, 176–178, 181, 191, 199
Tuck, Jessica 129
Tulloch, Bitsie (aka Elizabeth) 8, 16, 126, 137, 142–143, 148, 150, 174, 233ch8n2
Turnbull, Sue 10
Turner, Bree 8, 16, 56, 127, 152–154, 158, 160, 162–166, 168, 231n19

Index 261

Turner, Ike 35
Turner, Tina 35
Turner, Victor 27, 64, 228ch1n3
Twelfth Night 141; *see also* Shakespeare, William
Twelve Angry Men 45, 116
Twilight Zone, "It's a Good Life" 210
Twin Peaks 11, 219

UCLA Hollywood Diversity Report 57
Uhura 60
Uncle Felix *see* Dietrich, Felix, Uncle
Uncle Tom 12, 47

Valentine, Tierra 230n18
vampire 19, 22–24, 37, 39, 126, 140, 148, 171–172
Vaughn, Robert 20–21
vegetarian 5, 26–27, 29, 35, 41, 165, 159; *see also* eating
Veith, Diana L. 22
verbal expression *see* eloquence
Verrat 80, 233n14
veterinarian 8, 16, 26, 100, 126, 138, 142–143, 148, 232ch7n9
villain 9, 12, 32, 37–38, 43, 50, 64, 71, 82, 114, 134, 137, 159; *see also* Gothic hero-villain
violence 4, 7, 12, 14, 25, 29–31, 36–38, 40, 43–47, 57, 61, 70, 73, 80, 85, 95–96, 103–108, 112–114, 120, 124, 126, 129, 137, 149–150, 153–155, 159–161, 167, 171, 173, 176, 184, 186–187, 189, 192–195, 197–199, 207–211, 229n4
Virgil 27
virgin 9, 121–122, 169; *see also* Maiden/Mother/Crone; Virgin/Whore
Virgin/Whore 16, 136, 195
visual composition 11–12, 25, 42, 49, 68, 70, 77, 89, 91, 95–96; 109–110, 116, 123–125, 142, 144, 147, 177, 182–183, 188, 198, 213; *see also* blocking; camera work; hospital scene
voice, vocalizations *see* expression, vocal
Volkswagen 24, 27, 31, 36
von Konigsburg, Prince Viktor 78, 82–83, 173–174, 181, 188
Vu, Cathy 58
Vulcan 21–22
vulnerability 14, 59, 105–106, 110, 114–115, 150, 153, 173, 176, 208–209, 214

Walker, Barbara 9, 115, 121–122, 124–125, 139, 156, 169, 182–183, 232ch6n8
Wallace, Dee 129
Waltz, Edgar 80

warrior 15, 103, 125, 139, 141; *see also* hunting; Huntress; soldier
Washington, Denzel 55
water 27–28, 49, 88–89, 104, 115, 134, 177, 185
Waverly, Mr. 20
Way Down East 114
wealth 14, 61, 72, 76–77, 82, 100, 102, 123, 130, 212; *see also* class; status
weapon 3, 96–97, 120, 143, 147–148, 174, 191, 194, 195, 196–197, 214–215; *see also* cabinet, weapons
Weaponized Female 8, 149
Wells, Andrew 24
werewolf 19, 129; *see also* Blutbad; wolf
Werner, Peter 84
Wesen, definition of 3–5
Wesen Council 6, 143, 152, 160–161, 163, 233ch8n4
Wesenrein 6, 33, 74, 107, 164, 167; *see also* terrorists, right-wing
Whedon, Joss 2, 9, 35, 138, 141, 218, 219
"When You Are Old" 34, 166
White, Shauntae vi, 230n22
whiteness 7, 13, 28, 31, 40–41, 43–44, 47, 49–51, 53–55, 58, 61–62, 72–73, 94, 107, 120, 220, 229n5, 233n26
Wilcox, Rhonda V. 228n15, 234ch9n15
Williams, Linda 14, 95, 110–111, 114, 120, 231n15
Williams, Rebecca 140
Williamson, Milly 23
Willow (Rosenberg, *Buffy the Vampire Slayer* character) 23, 39
Willsey, Kristiana 227n4
window *see* threshold
wine 26, 30, 34, 49–50, 71, 84, 97, 162, 235n4
Wise Woman 3, 9, 15–16, 121–132, 134–136, 139, 147, 152–158, 160–164, 167–168, 188–191, 199–200; *see also* Crone; healer
wit 5, 13, 22–23, 54, 56–57, 60–62, 66, 70, 74, 132, 140, 153, 156; *see also* comedy, physical; humor
witch 8–9, 10, 15–17, 18, 49, 75, 96, 121–132, 135–136, 137–151, 154, 156; 169–191, 194, 206–208, 228n13, 231ch6n6, 232ch7n14, 232ch7n15, 233ch8n8; *see also* Crone; hat, witch's; Hexenbiest
witch hunts 122, 128, 130, 163
woge 24–25, 46, 72–73, 125–126, 129, 131–132, 145, 147, 153, 159, 163–165, 169, 171–173, 178, 181, 188, 191, 193, 207, 212, 232ch7n15, 233ch8n2
Wojton, Jennifer 65, 228n18
wolf 3–6, 19, 24, 26–30, 33, 40–43, 71, 96, 106, 122, 127, 129, 138–140, 143, 166, 232ch7n12; *see also* Blutbad

Wolff, Stephen 230*ch*4*n*3
Wolfram & Hart 138–140
wolfsangle 6
Wood, Rachel 85–87, 91, 99, 211, 230*ch*4*n*5
Woofter, Kristopher Karl vi, 230*n*8, 230*n*16
Worland, Rick 12, 20–21
wounds 31, 73, 87–91, 117–118, 149, 155, 177
The Wrath of Khan 37
writing 3–4, 11, 26, 30, 34, 37, 56, 61, 63–64, 67, 71, 74, 96, 98, 124–125, 138, 157, 163, 165, 191, 199–200, 212, 214, 219–220, 227*n*1, 228*n*11, 230*n*21, 234*n*19, 235*n*21; *see also* dialogue; narrative, long-term serial; symbolism, narrative
Wu, Drew 1, 4–5, 8–9, 13, 44–45, 56–74, 84, 97, 100, 102, 107–109, 115–118, 127, 133, 149, 154–155, 163, 193, 201, 220, 227*n*1, 228*n*2, , 228–229*n*3, 230*n*1, 231*n*17, 233*ch*8*n*2
Wu, Grace 230*ch*3*n*1

Wurstner, Bud 45, 101, 103, 107, 109–110, 143, 163
Wyndam-Price, Wesley 138, 141

Xander (Harris, *Buffy the Vampire Slayer* character) 47

Yang, Gene Luen 230*n*14
Yeats, William Butler 34, 166

Zarzosa, Agustin 110, 114
Zauberbiest 6–7, 14, 47, 78, 81, 84, 86, 206
Zerstorer (character) 34, 92, 118–120, 202–203, 214–215
Zimmerly, Stephen M. 12, 42
Zipes, Jack 122
zither 165, 180
zombie 34, 45, 59, 81, 84, 100, 115, 143, 157, 159, 233*n*12, 234*n*6
Zukimoto, Cathy 57, 230*ch*3*n*3

www.ingramcontent.com/pod-product-compliance
Lightning Source LLC
Chambersburg PA
CBHW032035300426
44117CB00009B/1063